Marketing Strategy

Planning and Implementation

The Irwin Series in Marketing
Gilbert A. Churchill, Jr., Consulting Editor
University of Wisconsin, Madison

Marketing Strategy

Planning and Implementation

Orville C. Walker, Jr.
James D. Watkins Professor of Marketing
University of Minnesota

Harper W. Boyd, Jr.
Donaghey Distinguished Professor of Marketing
University of Arkansas—Little Rock

Jean-Claude Larréché
Alfred H. Heineken Professor of Marketing
European Institute of Business Administration
INSEAD

IRWIN

Chicago • Bogotá • Boston • Buenos Aires • Caracas
London • Madrid • Mexico City • Sydney • Toronto

Irwin Book Team

Senior sponsoring editor: *Stephen M. Patterson*
Editorial assistant: *Andrea Hlavacek*
Senior marketing manager: *Jim Lewis*
Production supervisor: *Dina L. Treadaway*
Assistant manager, graphics: *Charlene R. Breeden*
Project editor: *Waivah Clement*
Designer: *Matthew Baldwin*
Compositor: *Weimer Graphics, Inc.*
Typeface: *10/12 Bembo*
Printer: *R. R. Donnelley & Sons Company*

Times Mirror
Higher Education Group

Library of Congress Cataloging-in-Publication Data

Walker, Orville C.
    Marketing strategy : planning and implementation / Orville C.
Walker, Harper W. Boyd, Jr., Jean-Claude Larréché.—2nd ed.
        p.   cm.—(Irwin series in marketing)
    Includes bibliographical references and index.
    ISBN 0-256-13692-0   ISBN 0-256-0692-9 (International Student's Ed.)
    1. Marketing—Management.   I. Boyd, Harper W.   II. Larréché, Jean
-Claude.   III. Title.   IV. Series.
    HF5415. 13.W249   1995
    658.8'02—dc20   95–22508

Preface

At the top of many executives' "things-to-do" list for the 1990s is the objective of making their organizations more market-oriented, more attuned to customer needs and competitive threats, and quicker to respond to changing market conditions. The question is, How can that goal be achieved? Recent studies conclude that the activities essential for achieving a market orientation are too important and pervasive to be left solely to marketers. Employees in every functional area must be trained and motivated to pay attention to and direct their efforts toward satisfying customer needs and desires. A director of the Marketing Science Institute recently reinforced this broad view of the importance and scope of marketing activities by predicting that marketing as a stand-alone function will become extremely rare in the typical organization of the future. Instead, marketing—in the sense of doing what is necessary to serve and satisfy customers—will become everybody's business, at least within those organizations that survive and prosper in an increasingly competitive climate.[1]

But even when the day-to-day responsibility for marketing activities is diffused across employees in every part of the organization, someone still has to plan, coordinate, and control those activities for each product or service the firm offers the market. Someone must devise a marketing strategy aimed at providing value to customers and gaining an advantage over competitors, and someone must ensure that the various functional activities necessary to implement that strategy are effectively carried out. That "someone" might be a traditional product or marketing manager, a vice president of marketing, a general manager of a business unit, or even a team of managers drawn from a variety of functional areas. Regardless of who bears the responsibility, that process of formulating and managing the marketing strategy for a given market entry is the central focus of this book.

It is also important to recognize, however, that marketing strategies are not formulated or implemented in a vacuum. Most organizations have corporate and business-level strategies that establish guidelines concerning objectives to be attained, directions for future growth,

---

[1] Frederick E. Webster, Jr., "It's 1990—Do You Know Where Your Marketing Is?" MSI White Paper (Cambridge, Mass.: *Marketing Science Institute*, April 14, 1989).

and how the organization will compete and seek to gain a sustainable advantage in the marketplace. These guidelines impose constraints on the range of marketing strategies a marketing manager can pursue within the larger strategic context of his or her organization. But on the other hand, marketing managers are also uniquely positioned to provide information and insights for the development of corporate and business strategies because they straddle the boundary between the external environment and the inner workings of the firm. Thus as organizations strive to become more customer-oriented and face ever more hostile and rapidly changing competitive environments, the marketer's role in strategy formulation is likely to increase.

Similarly, while marketing managers play a crucial role in translating the firm's broad objectives into strategic marketing programs designed to win customer acceptance and competitive advantage in specific markets, they do not implement those programs by themselves. Effective execution requires cooperative and coordinated efforts across many functional areas. Thus the range of viable marketing strategies available to a manager is constrained by the resources and functional competencies available within his or her organization. And the successful implementation of a chosen strategy depends on the marketer's ability to win the cooperation and support of people in other functional areas.

WHY WE WROTE THIS BOOK

As the discussion so far suggests, the process of formulating and implementing marketing strategy is intimately linked with strategic decisions made at higher organizational levels and with the operational decisions and actions taken in a variety of functional departments. It is these internal linkages—together with their direct links to the external market and competitive environment—that make the management of strategic marketing programs such a challenging and interesting endeavor.

Unfortunately, most of the existing marketing management and strategy textbooks do not provide a very complete picture of the complexities involved in managing marketing strategies. Some examine strategic decisions that are made at the corporate or business level but devote relatively little attention to how those decisions might best be translated into strategic marketing programs for individual products or services. Others tend to treat marketing management as a stand-alone business function. While they do a good job of describing the concepts, analytical tools, and planning techniques that are useful for formulating marketing strategies, they pay only scant attention to the web of internal strategic and operational relationships that surround that formulation process. Consequently, our major motivation for writing this book was a desire to provide a broader, more complete, and realistic view of marketing's strategic and operational roles and relationships within today's organizations.

A focus on the strategic planning process

As a basis for understanding the strategic role of marketing, one must first understand *how* strategies are formulated: the planning processes and the analytical tools and techniques managers might use when developing strategies. Thus this book is structured around the analytical and decision-making processes involved in formulating, implementing, and controlling a strategic marketing program for a given product-market entry. It includes discussions of customer, competitor, and environmental analysis; market segmentation and targeting; competitive positioning; implementation; and control. Because we assume that the reader is already familiar with many of the concepts and analytical tools relevant to these topics, however, we go beyond a simple review of definitions and procedures to examine strategic implications. In our discussion of positioning decisions in Chapter 7, for instance, we not only review the techniques a manager might use to analyze a product's competitive position in the marketplace, we also discuss various positioning strategies and the conditions under which each is likely to be most appropriate.

A unique concern for strategic and interfunctional relationships

This book differs from other marketing management and strategy texts in that it examines in detail how marketing interacts with other levels of strategy and with other functional departments within an organization. Specifically, it includes an examination of three sets of relationships that are given little or no attention in other texts.

1. *The relationships between corporate, business-level, and marketing strategies.* As mentioned, managers responsible for developing and implementing marketing strategies for specific products and target markets are also uniquely qualified to provide insights and information needed to formulate competitive strategies at the business and corporate levels of the organization. And as organizations strive to become more customer-oriented, the marketing manager's role in strategic planning is likely to increase. At the same time, those higher-level strategic decisions often impose guidelines and constraints on the marketing manager's freedom of action in designing marketing strategies and programs for individual products or services.

   This book examines this complex set of relationships between the different levels of strategy in several ways. First, Chapter 1 presents a general discussion of the hierarchy of strategies found in most multiproduct organizations, their interrelationships, and the marketer's role in helping to formulate strategies at different organizational levels. Chapter 3 provides a more specific and unique discussion of business-level competitive strategies and their implications for marketing strategies and actions appropriate for individual products or services within the business unit. Finally, each of the chapters discussing alternative strategic marketing programs appropriate for specific market conditions (Chapters 8–11) examines how those programs should fit the firm's higher-level strategies.

2. *Relationships between the content of marketing strategies and the strategic environment.* Most texts talk in general terms about how the marketing strategy for a given product or service should fit the characteristics of the market and competitive environment. But they usually do not provide much detail concerning the specific kinds of strategic marketing programs that are best suited to different environmental contexts. Nor do they discuss the specific tactical decisions and actions necessary to effectively carry out each strategy.

   In contrast, this book provides an entire section of four chapters that discuss the marketing strategies and tactics best suited to specific environmental situations. Those situations are defined both in terms of market characteristics as defined by the stage in the product life cycle and by the product's relative competitive position. Thus Chapter 8 discusses marketing strategies for new market entries. Chapter 9 examines strategies for growth markets, both share-maintenance strategies for market leaders and growth strategies for low-share followers. Strategies for mature and declining markets are described in Chapter 10. Finally, global marketing strategies are detailed in Chapter 11.

3. *Relationships between marketing and other functional areas.* A marketing manager's ability to effectively implement a strategic marketing program depends in large measure on the cooperation and competence of other functional areas within the organization. Consequently, we devote substantial attention to the interfunctional implications of specific marketing strategies. Each of the marketing strategies appropriate for the particular circumstances described in Chapters 8 through 11 is also examined in terms of the requirements it imposes on other functional departments such as product and process R&D, production, quality control, logistics, and finance. In addition, Chapter 12 provides an overview of the functional competencies required to effectively implement different competitive and marketing strategies. It also discusses organizational mechanisms appropriate for coordinating efforts and resolving conflicts across functional areas.

THE TARGET AUDIENCE FOR THIS BOOK

Most MBA programs offer at least one course on marketing strategy. While they carry many different names—such as "Marketing Policy," "Strategic Marketing," or "Advanced Marketing Management"—they are usually positioned as capstone courses whose primary purpose is to help students integrate what they have learned about the analytical tools and the four Ps of marketing within a broader framework of competitive strategy. Such courses are often required of all marketing majors toward the end of their academic programs. And similar capstone courses are usually either required or offered as electives in many of the better undergraduate marketing programs as well. We designed this book primarily to serve the needs of students in these kinds of courses.

FEATURES APPROPRIATE FOR A CAPSTONE MARKETING STRATEGY COURSE

We think this book's organization structure and its unique content make it particularly well suited for use in integrative capstone courses at either the graduate or advanced undergraduate level. Some particularly relevant features include the following:

- Because the book is organized around the analytical and decision-making processes involved in formulating and implementing marketing strategies, it provides the opportunity for students to review and integrate many of the concepts and techniques they encountered in earlier courses. But rather than simply rehash basic definitions and descriptions, this text emphasizes the strategic implications of such topics as market segmentation, competitor analysis, target market selection, and positioning.

- The book also provides a sound review of the tactical elements—the four Ps—of marketing. But rather than forcing students to wade through yet another set of chapters on product, pricing, promotion, and distribution decisions, each of these program elements is discussed within the context of a variety of alternative marketing strategies, the objectives they are designed to accomplish, and the situations where their use is most appropriate.

- This book pays a great deal of attention to the role of marketing managers in the formulation and implementation of higher-level strategies within the firm and to the influences and constraints those higher-level strategies subsequently impose on the range of marketing actions appropriate for individual products or services. This helps students more fully understand and appreciate the linkages and interactions among an organization's corporate, business, and marketing strategies.

- We also provide unusually extensive discussions of the various functional competencies and resources required by different types of marketing strategies and the kinds of interfunctional coordination necessary to implement those strategies effectively. Thus this book provides a good framework for reviewing and integrating the material that students have been exposed to in courses in other functional areas as well as in previous marketing courses.

- The ultimate objective of any capstone course is to prepare students to make a smooth transition from their academic program into the business world. All of the features described above should help prepare students to better understand and deal with the kinds of activities and decisions they will soon face on the job. But in addition, we have attempted to write the book in a way that reflects both the excitement and the practical realities of marketing management as it happens in a variety of real world settings. The book incorporates hundreds of up-to-date examples that demonstrate marketing strategies and practices as they are applied to industrial as well as consumer products, services as well as goods, not-for-profit organizations as well as business firms, and foreign as well as domestic markets. And to further enhance student interest and understanding, every chapter begins with a minicase example that introduces and illustrates the major concepts or strategies discussed in that chapter. These introductory examples are referred to at appropriate places throughout each chapter to further help the student see the relationships among concepts and their relevance to real problems.

MAJOR CHANGES IN THIS REVISION

This revision incorporates some new features and changes in emphasis from the first edition. These changes were based on information obtained from both users and nonusers of the first edition, academic associates and industry friends, and our own experiences both in the classroom and in the real world. We think they reflect some of the important developments occurring in the rapidly changing global marketplace.

- We have substantially increased our coverage of global marketing. In addition to devoting a chapter to this subject, we have integrated detailed examinations of global marketing, actions, programs, and examples throughout every other chapter.

- We have increased our examination of the ethical issues present in many marketing decisions.

- We have included more material on the development and marketing of services. We discuss strategic marketing actions and programs appropriate for service firms, and we examine the important role of customer service as a basis for gaining and sustaining a competitive advantage.

- Finally, as described in more detail below, we have added an international computer simulation program that exposes students to marketing program and resource allocation issues across five countries.

FEATURES APPROPRIATE FOR DIFFERENT TEACHING APPROACHES

Capstone courses dealing with marketing strategy not only parade under a variety of different titles, they are also taught in a variety of different ways. Consequently, this book and its package of supporting materials were designed to fit a variety of teaching approaches. While we have tried to avoid excessive repetition and thereby keep the book relatively short and succinct, instructors who prefer a lecture-discussion approach will find ample material for either a quarter or semester course. For those who prefer case-oriented instruction, the book provides a solid foundation of concepts, techniques, and examples to prepare students for effective case analysis and discussion.

A unique feature of the book is its inclusion of a computerized international simulation case, developed by Jean-Claude Larréché, who also developed the highly regarded SAMAR, MARKSTRAT, and INDUSTRAT simulations. His latest program has been developed to integrate a number of critically important strategic issues involved in deciding how to allocate marketing resources across a portfolio consisting of both countries and product categories.

The GAMAR case provides an exciting and realistic way to expose students to the dynamics of resource allocation problems in a global setting. Students can manage a firm over a period of time, analyze situations, make decisions, receive rapid feedback, and adjust their strategies and tactics. GAMAR is a highly flexible teaching instrument because it can be used either as a team project with various degrees of complexity or as an integrated part of the course requiring a limited number of class sessions. The teaching note in the instructor's manual suggests a variety of ways it can be integrated with material in various parts of the text and with different course structures, including those for executive programs.

We also note the following with respect to the book's adaptability to various teaching approaches:

- For those instructors wanting a second—and somewhat simpler—resource allocation case we have included Jean-Claude Larréché's SAMAR case (from the first edition) along with detailed teaching notes in the instructor's manual.

- While no cases other than the GAMAR and SAMAR simulations are included in the text, the instructor's manual includes detailed information about how to locate both domestic and global cases relevant to a variety of marketing topics.

- A set of discussion questions on each chapter is also included in the instructor's manual. These questions are designed to provide a vehicle for meaningful student exercises or class discussions. Rather than simple review questions that ask students to regurgitate material found in the chapter, these questions are more application-oriented and often take the form of minicases that reflect actual company problems.

- The instructor's manual also includes a list of additional readings from a variety of up-to-date sources that illustrate or expand upon major topics in each chapter of the text.

ACKNOWLEDGMENTS

A book like this is never solely the work of the authors. Many people aided this enterprise, and we gratefully acknowledge their contributions.

First, we thank our faculty colleagues in our respective schools for their wise counsel and advice. We are also grateful to our friends in industry. Our conversations with them over the years, both informally and within various executive programs, have contributed much to our understanding of how marketing strategy works in the real world.

We have tried to be customer-oriented in preparing a revision that meets the needs of both instructors and students. We are, therefore, most grateful to our many undergraduate, graduate, and executive program students for their constructive criticism of the first edition and useful suggestions for making the revision a better book. We also appreciate the help of the following colleagues who provided detailed and constructive suggestions for the revision: Sally Boyles-Hyslop, California State Poly University; Greg Carpenter, Northwestern University; Faye McIntyre, University of Mississippi; Elaine Notarantonio, Bryant College; and Steven Thrasher, Pacific Lutheran.

We owe a debt of gratitude to Gil Churchill, professor at the University of Wisconsin-Madison and consulting editor for Irwin's marketing series, for his help with this revision. And we acknowledge with thanks the different tasks performed by Roberta Moore in preparing this manuscript.

We also thank the staff at Richard D. Irwin, Inc., for their ability to convert a rough manuscript into an attractive and readable book. We would especially like to thank our editor, Steve Patterson, for guidance both before and during the manuscript preparation, editorial assistant Andrea Hlavacek, for manuscript support coordination, and project editor Waivah Clement for her help in finalizing the project.

Finally we salute our wives for their patience and support throughout the many months during which we focused on this revision. Orville Walker thanks Linda, Harper Boyd thanks Virginia, and Jean-Claude Larréché thanks Denyse.

Orville C. Walker, Jr.
Harper W. Boyd
Jean-Claude Larréché

Contents in Brief

Contents

3 Business strategies and their marketing implications   64

SECTION TWO
OPPORTUNITY ANALYSIS

SECTION THREE

FORMULATING MARKETING STRATEGIES

SECTION   4

IMPLEMENTATION AND CONTROL

Marketing Strategy

Planning and Implementation

INTRODUCTION TO STRATEGY

The Strategic Role of Marketing

COMPAQ SHIFTS STRATEGIES[1]

From the beginning Compaq built its reputation, and a $3 billion personal computer business, on superior technology. Its competitive strategy was to match industry leader IBM's prices but to offer more innovative PCs for the money. That strategy worked like a charm for nearly a decade, but then the market environment changed.

Changing customer demands and competitor actions lead to a shift in strategy

The earliest buyers of personal computers were either large organizations with professional information managers or technically sophisticated consumers. But as the industry matured, later buyers were more price conscious, more interested in buying equipment that was easy to use, and more concerned with receiving good post-purchase training and service. By the late 1980s a number of firms—most notably Dell Computer—were appealing to this new breed of customer by offering not only mail-order delivery at very low prices but also impressive service and support programs as well.

For a time Compaq stuck with its traditional competitive strategy and marketing program. It continued to invest heavily in technical R & D, distributed its products only through specialty computer dealers, devoted little attention to customer problems or complaints, and tied its prices to those of IBM. But as one Compaq executive points out, "When IBM lost touch with the . . . realities of the marketplace, we walked off the cliff with them." By

---

[1]This case example is based on material found in Peter H. Lewis, "Weary of Price Cuts, Companies Try to Sell Value," *New York Times*, December 6, 1992, p. 9F; David Kirkpatrick, "The Revolution at Compaq Computer," *Fortune*, December 14, 1992, pp. 80–88; "Stuck! How Companies Cope When They Can't Raise Prices," *Business Week*, November 15, 1993, pp. 146–55; and David Kirkpatrick, "Why Compaq Is Mad at Intel," *Fortune*, October 31, 1994, pp. 171–78.

1991 the firm's market share, revenues, and earnings had all begun to plunge and it had little choice but to shift strategic direction.

New corporate and competitive strategies

The day after announcing Compaq's first-ever quarterly loss, the firm's board of directors replaced the CEO. The incoming president established an aggressive new corporate goal: to become the market share leader of the worldwide personal computer industry by the late 1990s while regaining historical levels of profitability and returns to shareholders. To achieve those objectives he charted three paths of future corporate growth: (1) win an increased share of the domestic PC market—particularly among individual consumers—by developing more user-friendly machines and more customer services at lower prices; (2) use the new low-price, high-value product offerings to expand Compaq's presence in global markets; and (3) use the firm's technical R & D competencies to develop new product lines aimed at business markets, such as servers used to manage information on computer networks.

Compaq's new growth objectives required major changes in how the firm competed with other PC manufacturers around the world. They switched from competing primarily on technical superiority and a constant parade of new products to a competitive strategy appealing to larger but less sophisticated market segments by developing simpler and easy-to-use product lines, offering excellent customer support, and charging dramatically lower prices.

Of course, Compaq had to revamp many of its internal policies and proce-dures in order to effectively implement its new price-oriented competitive strategy and still reach its profit and shareholder value objectives. For openers, the firm re-negotiated contracts with many of its suppliers and for the first time asked them to submit competitive bids. As a result, the cost of the components used in its PCs dropped nearly 30 percent. Similarly, the firm sought ways to make more efficient use of the capital invested in its plants and equipment. By adding second and third shifts at its three plants, for instance, it doubled the output of PCs from its existing factory space and reduced unit costs by more than half.

The new competitive strategy also forced Compaq's executives to consider reorganizing the firm. Because its strategy focused on several distinct markets—businesses, institutions, and individual consumers in many different countries—some felt that separate divisions or business units should be formed to coordinate the firm's efforts in each of those markets. At the time of this writing, however, no final decision had yet been made.

New strategic marketing programs

Compaq's new competitive strategy required adjustments in its strategic marketing programs as well. First, in order to appeal to more broadly defined and price-sensitive consumer markets the firm had to expand its product offerings. It added several new computer lines, including the low-priced ProLinea desktop PCs and Contura notebooks, and the user-friendly Presario line of preprogrammed PCs. Of course, the firm continued to develop technically sophisticated new products such as the Concerto notebook with pen-writing capability, but at a slower pace than in the past. Indeed, the firm reduced its engineering staff by 20 percent and shifted some of its R & D efforts to developing the firm's new lines of printers and servers.

To increase awareness of Compaq's revamped policies and products among its new target customers, the firm expanded its advertising budget by 60 percent in 1992 to $90 million. It also changed the content of its ads. Where they used to emphasize computer terminology, they became more reader-friendly and stressed customer benefits such as exactly why a Compaq notebook is easy to use on an airplane.

To make Compaq computers easier for potential customers to find, and to improve the availability of service and customer support. the company more than doubled its worldwide retail outlets to over 9,000. It added office supply discounters like Office Depot to its distribution channel to supplement the traditional computer stores, and it was considering selling computers through the mail and over the phone.

The bottom line

As of this writing Compaq's new competitive and marketing strategies were performing well. Even though average prices and profit margins per unit were much lower under the new strategies, the firm's total revenues skyrocketed 64 percent in the first year after the changes were made, and total profits nearly doubled. By 1994 the firm had become the domestic share leader with nearly 14 percent of PC sales in the U.S. market and was closing in on its ultimate goal of replacing IBM as the worldwide market share leader.

Inevitably, the firm's future success will depend on how well it continues to adapt to the ongoing changes in technology, competition, and customer desires that characterize the computer industry.

It will also depend on the company's ability to maintain productive alliances with its major suppliers, retailers, and corporate customers in order to hold down costs and improve customer service. Unfortunately, Compaq's new low-price strategy in the consumer market has strained some of those relationships—particularly its long-standing relationship with Intel, the firm's primary supplier of microprocessor chips.

Under its previous strategy Compaq acted as Intel's close technical partner. The company spent more on engineering than most of its rivals and was always among the first to bring out new models with the latest Intel chip. But its new strategy motivated the firm to court Intel's rivals, the makers of copycat chips, in hopes of fostering the development of a commodity market for microprocessors. That would enable Compaq to spread its purchases over several competing suppliers and thereby attain lower component costs. Of course, it would also cut into Intel's margins, which are as much as five times higher for its newest state-of-the-art chips than for its older "commodity" chips. Therefore, Intel fought back with an extensive advertising campaign (including the "Intel Inside" campaign extolling the superiority of the firm's Pentium chip) to promote the advantages of PCs—including those offered by Compaq's competitors—carrying the company's most advanced microprocessor. Intel also threatened to integrate forward and start producing its own competing line of PCs. Thus, Compaq's new strategy has not only influenced its own sales and profit performance in the global PC market, it may also shake up established alliances and even change the competitive structure of the industry.

CORPORATION, BUSINESS, AND MARKETING STRATEGIES: DIFFERENT ISSUES AT DIFFERENT ORGANIZATIONAL LEVELS

The recent experiences of Compaq in the PC industry illustrate some important points about strategy that will recur as themes throughout this book. First, most firms, particularly larger corporations with multiple divisions or business units, pursue a hierarchy of interdependent strategies. Each strategy is formulated at different levels in the organization and deals with different sets of issues. For example, Compaq's goal of capturing market share leadership in the PC industry and its decision to seek future growth primarily by increasing its penetration of global consumer markets and developing new products for corporate networks reflect its new **corporate strategy**. This level of strategy provides direction on the company's mission, the kinds of businesses it should be in, and its growth policies.

On the other hand, attempts to differentiate Compaq's offerings from those of IBM and other competitors by providing greater customer value via lower prices, improved customer services, and the development of more user-friendly products reflect the firm's **business-level strategy** in the consumer market. This level of strategy primarily addresses the way a business will compete within its industry.

Finally, interrelated functional decisions about how to divide the market into customer segments, which segments to target, what products and service enhancements to offer each segment, what promotional appeals and media to employ, and what prices to charge all reflect the **marketing strategies** for each of Compaq's various product-market entries. Each marketing strategy provides a plan for pursuing the company's objectives within a specific market segment.

Because the different levels of strategy are all closely interrelated, individual marketing strategies and programs are not created in a vacuum. Instead, the marketing objectives and strategy for a particular product-market entry should be consistent with the direction and resources provided by the firm's corporate and business-level strategies. Thus, a marketing manager's freedom of action is constrained by strategic decisions made at higher levels within the firm. For instance, the manager responsible for the firm's Prolinea line of PCs has little freedom to increase prices without higher approval because such a move would be inconsistent with the competitive strategy of providing superior value to price-sensitive customers.

On the other hand, a major part of the marketing manager's job is to monitor and analyze the needs and wants of customers and potential customers and to identify emerging opportunities and threats posed by competitors and trends in the external environment. Marketers thus often play a major role in providing input to and influencing the development of corporation and business-level strategies. For instance, when the need for new corporate and competitive strategies at Compaq became obvious due to declining sales and profits, decisions about the content of those new strategies were strongly influenced by customer and competitor information and analyses provided by the firm's sales and marketing personnel. Indeed, the new CEO appointed to lead the firm back to financial health rose through the firm's marketing ranks.

Regardless of who is involved in formulating the various levels of strategy or how appropriate those strategies are for addressing the market and competitive circumstances faced by a firm, they will not lead to successful outcomes unless they are implemented effectively. As Compaq's experience exemplifies, sound implementation requires a clear vision, specific goals, and solid support from top management. And the organization's structure, policies, and processes must also be designed to enable and encourage employees at all levels to take the actions necessary to make the strategy work.

The next section of this chapter takes a closer look at the nature of and the interrelationships among corporate, business, and marketing strategies. We then examine some of the alternative processes that different firms have used to formulate such strategies over the years and the important role that marketing managers often play in the strategic planning process. Finally, we summarize the various processes and decisions involved in formulating and implementing marketing strategies for a particular product-market entry. Those processes provide a framework for organizing the remaining chapters in this book.

Strategy: a definition

Although strategy first became a popular business buzzword during the 1960s, it continues to be the subject of widely differing definitions and interpretations. The following definition, however, captures the essence of the term as it is most commonly used.

> A **strategy** is a fundamental pattern of present and planned objectives, resource deployments, and interactions of an organization with markets, competitors, and other environmental factors.[2]

As this definition suggests, a good strategy should specify (1) *what* is to be accomplished, (2) *where* (on which industries or product-markets it will focus), and (3) *how* (which resources and activities will be allocated to each product-market to meet environmental opportunities and threats and to gain a competitive advantage).

The components of strategy

More specifically, there are five components or sets of issues within a well-developed strategy.

1. *Scope.*   The scope of an organization refers to the breadth of its strategic domain: the number and types of industries, product lines, and market segments it competes in or plans to enter. Decisions about an organization's strategic scope should reflect management's view of the firm's mission or strategic intent. This common thread among its various activities and product-markets defines the essential nature of what its business is and what it should be in the future.

2. *Goals and objectives.*   Strategies should also specify desired levels or accomplishment on one of more dimensions of performance—such as volume growth, profit contribution, or

---

[2]For a summary of the definitions offered by a number of other authors, see Roger A. Kerin, Vijay Mahajan, and P. Rajan Varadarajan, *Contemporary Perspectives on Strategic Market Planning* (Boston: Allyn and Bacon, 1990), pp. 8–9. Our definition differs from some others, however, in that we view the setting of objectives as an integral part of strategy formulation, whereas they see objective setting as a separate process. Because a firm's objectives are influenced and constrained by many of the same environmental and competitive factors as the other elements of strategy, it seems logical to treat both the setting of objectives and the allocation of resources aimed at reaching those objectives as two parts of the same strategic planning process.

return on investment—over specified periods for each of the firm's businesses and product-markets and for the organization as a whole.

3. *Resource deployments.*   Every organization has limited financial and human resources. Thus, a strategy should specify how such resources are to be obtained and allocated across businesses, product-markets, functional departments or management teams, and activities within each business or product-market.

4. *Identification of a sustainable competitive advantage.*   Perhaps the most important part of any strategy is a specification of how the organization will compete in each business and product-market within its domain. How can it position itself to develop and sustain a differential advantage over current and potential competitors? To answer such questions, managers must examine the market opportunities in each business and product-market and the company's distinctive competencies or strengths relative to its competitors.

5. *Synergy.*   Synergy exists when the firm's businesses, product-markets, resource deployments, and competencies complement and reinforce one another. Synergy enables the total performance of the related businesses to be greater than it would otherwise be: The whole becomes greater than the sum of its parts. Consequently, strategies should be designed to exploit potential sources of synergy across the firm's businesses and product-markets as a means of improving the organization's overall efficiency and effectiveness.

The hierarchy of strategies

Explicitly or implicitly, these five basic dimensions are part of all strategies. However, rather than a single comprehensive strategy, most organizations pursue a hierarchy of interrelated strategies, each formulated at a different level of the firm.[3] The three major levels of strategy in most large, multiproduct organizations are (1) corporate strategy, (2) business-level strategy, and (3) functional strategies focused on particular product-market entries. These three types of strategy are diagrammed in Exhibit 1–1.

While our primary focus is on the development of marketing strategies and programs for individual product-market entries, Exhibit 1–1 shows that other functional departments, such as R&D and production, may also have strategies and plans. Thus, the organization's success in a given product-market depends on the effective coordination of strategies and activities across functions. Throughout this book, then, we will pay attention to the interfunctional implications of marketing strategies, the potential conflicts across functional areas, and the mechanisms that firms use to resolve those conflicts.

Strategies at all three levels contain the five components just outlined, but because each strategy serves a different purpose within the organization, each emphasizes different sets of issues. Exhibit 1–2 summarizes the specific focus and issues dealt with at each level of strategy, and they are discussed in the next sections.

---

[3] The recognition of a hierarchy of strategies within a single firm is a relatively recent, but increasingly common, concept in both the strategic management and marketing literatures. See, for example, Frederick E. Webster, Jr., "The Changing Role of Marketing in the Corporation," *Journal of Marketing* 56, October 1992, pp. 1–17.

EXHIBIT 1–1

The Hierarchy of Strategies

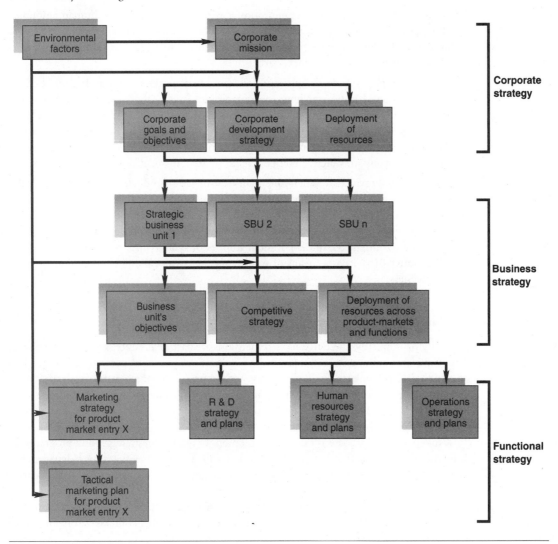

Corporate strategy

At the corporate level managers must coordinate the activities of multiple business units and (in the case of conglomerates) even separate legal business entities. Thus, decisions about the organization's scope and appropriate resource deployments across its various divisions or businesses are the primary focus of corporate strategy. The essential questions to be answered at this level are, What business(es) are we in? What business(es) should we be in? and What

EXHIBIT 1–2

Key Components of Corporate, Business, and Marketing Strategies

Strategy components	Corporate strategy	Business strategy	Marketing strategy

Scope	• Corporate domain — "Which businesses should we be in?"
	
	 • Corporate development strategy
	  Conglomerate diversification (expansion into unrelated businesses)
	  Vertical integration
	  Acquisition and divestiture policies
		• Business domain — "Which product-markets should we be in within this business or industry?"
		 • Business development strategy
		  Concentric diversification (new products for existing customers or new customers for existing products)
			• Target market definition
			 • Product-line depth and breadth
			 • Branding policies
			 • Product-market development plan
			 • Line extension and product elimination plans

Goals and objectives	• Overall corporate objectives aggregated across businesses
	  Revenue growth
	  Profitability
	  ROI (return on investment)
	  Earnings per share
	  Contributions to other stakeholders
		• Constrained by corporate goals
		 • Objectives aggregated across product-market entries in the business unit
		  Sales growth
		  New product or market growth
		  Profitability
		  ROI
		  Cash flow
		  Strengthening bases of competitive advantage
			• Constrained by corporate and business goals
			 • Objectives for a specific product-market entry
			  Sales
			  Market share
			  Contribution margin
			  Customer satisfaction

Allocation of resources	• Allocation among businesses in the corporate portfolio • Allocation across functions shared by multiple businesses (corporate R&D, MIS)	• Allocation among product-market entries in the business unit • Allocation across functional departments within the business unit	• Allocation across components of the marketing plan (elements of the marketing mix) for a specific product-market entry
Sources of competitive advantage	• Primarily through superior corporate financial or human resources; more corporate R&D; better organizational processes or synergies relative to competitors across all industries in which the firm operates	• Primarily through competitive strategy; business unit's competencies relative to competitors in its industry	• Primarily through effective product positioning; superiority on one or more components of the marketing mix relative to competitors within a specific product-market
Sources of synergy	• Shared resources, technologies, or functional competencies across businesses within the firm	• Shared resources (including favorable customer image) or functional competencies across product-markets within an industry	• Shared marketing resources, competencies, or activities across product-market entries

portion of our total resources should we devote to each of those businesses to achieve the organization's overall goals and objectives? For instance, the highest managerial levels at Compaq made the decisions to provide the resources necessary to pursue market share leadership in both domestic and global PC markets and to invest in developing new businesses focused on printers, servers, and other peripheral equipment.

Attempts to develop and maintain distinctive competencies at the corporate level tend to focus on generating superior financial, capital, and human resources; designing effective organizational structures and processes; and seeking synergy among the firm's various businesses. Synergy can become a major competitive advantage in firms where related businesses reinforce one another by sharing corporate staff, R&D, financial resources, production technologies, distribution channels, or marketing programs.

Business-level strategy

The question of how a business unit will compete within its industry is the critical focus of business-level strategy. Thus, a major issue addressed in a business strategy is how to achieve and sustain a competitive advantage. What distinctive competencies can give the business unit a competitive advantage? And which of those competencies best match the needs and wants of the customers in the business's target segment(s)? For example, a business with low-cost sources of supply and efficient, modern plants might adopt a "low cost" competitive strategy, while one with a strong marketing department and a competent salesforce might compete by offering superior customer service.[4]

Since different customer segments may want different benefits from the same category of products, a business unit may not have the competencies needed to compete effectively in all market segments. Therefore, another important issue that a business-level strategy must deal with is that of appropriate scope: how many and which market segments to compete in, and the breadth of product offerings and marketing programs needed to appeal to these segments.

Finally, synergy should be sought across product-markets and across functional departments within the business. Thus, Compaq uses some of the same salespeople and distribution channels that handle its PCs to also sell its new printers.

Marketing strategy

The primary purpose of a marketing strategy is to effectively allocate and coordinate marketing resources and activities to accomplish the firm's objectives within a specific product-market. Therefore, decisions about the scope of a marketing strategy involve specifying the target market segment or segments to be pursued and the breadth of the product line to be offered. Next, firms seek a competitive advantage and synergy through a well-integrated program of marketing mix elements (primarily the "Four Ps" of product, price, promotion, and place or distribution channels) tailored to the needs and wants of customers in the target segments. For example, user-friendly features, low prices, extensive

---

[4]C. K. Prahalad and Gary Hamel, "The Core Competence of the Corporation," *Harvard Business Review* 68, May–June 1990, pp. 79–91.

distribution, and heavy media advertising aimed at buyers seeking PCs for household use are all elements of Compaq's new marketing strategy in the domestic consumer market.

STRATEGIC PLANNING SYSTEMS

Compaq is an example of a company with well-developed, integrated strategies at all three levels. Unfortunately, such is not the case with all companies. Part of the reason is the wide variations across firms in the extensiveness of strategic planning and the procedures followed in formulating strategies.

The value of formal planning systems

At one extreme, some companies—particularly smaller, entrepreneurial firms—employ few, if any, formal strategic planning procedures. Of course, this does not necessarily mean that they have no strategy. The owner or top executive may have had a clear strategic vision in the beginning. And he or she may give some sporadic thought to strategic issues as the firm and its industry evolve over time. Nevertheless, evidence suggests that such piecemeal, informal approaches to strategic planning are not as effective as more formal systems for formulating strategy. For example, one review of 15 studies comparing firms with formal planning systems to firms without such systems found that the formal planners outperformed the informal planners in two-thirds of the cases examined.[5]

The obvious question, of course, is whether such research findings are still valid in today's more volatile economy. Do firms that engage in formal strategic planning continue to outperform those that don't, even in the face of the rapidly changing market and competitive conditions? Most experts would answer the question with a resounding "Yes!" Even though strategic plans may have to be revised or adapted more frequently than in the past, most organizations still benefit from the process of developing them.[6]

For one thing, a formal planning process forces managers to take time from daily activities to consider strategic issues that might otherwise be overlooked. It also helps structure and operationalize the otherwise daunting task of responding to a dynamic environment and strategically managing a complex organization with limited resources. Thus, research suggests that formal planning is even more useful under conditions of major change in the firm or its environment, when uncertainty is high, and when complex decisions must be reached.[7]

Finally, a formal plan can help prevent firms from making too many erratic changes in response to short-lived environmental disruptions, which only confuses both employees and customers. As one author suggests, a formal plan is like the rudder on a ship. The plan may be disrupted by changing conditions, just as a ship's rudder may not be very useful during heavy

---

[5]J. Scott Armstrong, "The Value of Formal Planning for Strategic Decisions: Review of Empirical Research," *Strategic Management Journal* 3 (1982), pp. 197–212.

[6]Hal Goetsch, "Are Marketing Plans Passé?" *Marketing News*, December 5, 1994, pp. 4–5.

[7]J. Scott Armstrong, "The Value of Formal Planning for Strategic Decisions."

seas. Yet a plan, like a rudder, is essential for providing direction and holding the firm on course when the storm is over.

Evolution of planning systems

Even among firms that do employ formal planning systems, there are great differences in who participates, the procedures followed, and the content of the strategic plans ultimately produced. In spite of this diversity, some attempts have been made to categorize broad types of planning systems. In one of the best-known studies, Gluck, Kaufman, and Walleck of the McKinsey consulting firm examined the planning procedures followed by 120 firms in seven different countries.[8] They identified four types of planning systems: financial planning, long-range planning, strategic planning, and strategic management.

Gluck and his colleagues argue that these four systems reflect an evolutionary process; each type appeared at a different time during the 20th century and each subsequent system added to, rather than replaced, earlier systems. They also found that planning systems within individual companies tend to develop along a similar evolutionary path, with new start-ups concentrating on financial planning but then moving toward strategic management as they grow and the strategic issues they face become more complex. As we shall see, though, many firms have not yet developed the most sophisticated types of planning systems. Major characteristics of each type are summarized in Exhibit 1–3 and are discussed below.

Financial planning systems

This type of system planning consists mainly of an annual budgeting process that focuses on forecasting revenue, costs, and capital requirements. Annual budgets are then set for the firm's various businesses and departments, and careful attention is paid to deviations from those budgets to find explanations and determine whether remedial actions are required.

The assumption underlying financial planning systems is that the past will repeat itself, that the market and competitive environment a business will face next year will be largely the same as this year. Thus, detailed strategies are seldom formalized, although implicit strategies often are reflected in the resource allocation decisions made by top management when they approve or adjust budgets for their various businesses. As a result, the planning process, such as it is, under this kind of system is highly centralized at the top levels of corporate management.

Financial planning systems were first widely adopted by firms during the first half of the 20th century. Yet over half the businesses Gluck and colleagues surveyed in the early 1980s, including some very successful firms, still followed this kind of "meeting-the-numbers" approach.

Long-range planning systems

Relative to financial planning and its emphasis on annual budgets, long-range planning systems cover longer time frames (5 or 10 years) and are more future-oriented. Focusing

---

[8]Frederick W. Gluck, Stephen P. Kaufman, and A. Steven Walleck, "The Four Phases of Strategic Management," *Journal of Business Strategy* 3 (1982), pp. 9–21.

EXHIBIT 1–3

Characteristics of Alternative Planning Systems

	Type of planning system			
Characteristic	**Financial planning**	**Long-range planning**	**Strategic planning**	**Strategic management**
Management emphasis	Control budget deviations	Anticipate growth and manage complexity	Creative response to changing environment by changing strategic thrust and capabilities	Cope with strategic surprises and fast-developing opportunities or threats
Major assumptions	The past repeats	Past trends will continue	New trends and discontinuities are predictable	Planning cycles are inadequate to deal with rapid changes
Direction of strategic decision making	Top-down	Bottom-up	Mixed (leaning toward top-down)	Mixed (leaning toward bottom-up)
Planning time frame	Periodic	Periodic	Periodic	Real time
Underlying value system	Meet the budget	Predict the future	Think strategically	Create the future
Time period when first developed	Early 1900s	1950s	1960s	Mid-1970s

SOURCE: Adapted from material found in F. Gluck, S. Kaufman, and A. Walleck. "The Four Phases of Strategic Management," *Journal of Business Strategy*, Winter 1982, pp. 9–21; D. Aaker, *Strategic Market Management*, 2nd ed. (New York: John Wiley & Sons, 1988), p. 10; and R. Kerin, V. Mahajan, and P. Varadarajan, *Contemporary Perspectives on Strategic Market Planning* (Boston: Allyn and Bacon, 1990), p. 18.

on anticipating growth and managing increasing complexity, they attempt to project future sales, costs, technological changes, and the like. Any gaps between projected sales and profits and the organization's goals are analyzed to determine what operational changes—such as a new plant or a larger salesforce—might be necessary to achieve long-term objectives.

A major assumption underlying long-range planning systems is that past trends can be extrapolated into the future. Unfortunately, this means that little consideration is given to anticipating new opportunities or initiating new directions. Resources tend to be allocated across businesses and product-markets already in the firm's portfolio.

Because many of the projections and forecasts that serve as the foundation for long-range planning are produced by the managers of individual businesses within the firm, such systems tend to be relatively decentralized. While top management makes major resource allocation decisions and monitors the short-term performance of each business, objectives are often set from the bottom up, with each business bearing the responsibility for determining its own goals and strategies.

In spite of its shortcomings, most planning systems in use during the 1980s did not go much beyond this kind of planning by extrapolation according to Gluck and his colleagues. Indeed, observation suggests that such long-range planning systems are still in use at some firms.

Strategic planning systems

Increasingly rapid and disruptive changes in the market environment—such as the energy crisis, high inflation, and increased foreign competition—helped precipitate the development of strategic planning during the 1960s and early 1970s. Because such changes caused discontinuities and shifts in past trends, simply extrapolating such trends into the future was no longer an adequate basis for planning in many industries.

Consequently, strategic planning systems attempt to achieve a more in-depth understanding of the firm's market environment, particularly its customers and competitors. The objective is to anticipate changes and shifts that might have strategic implications. Thus, strategic planning is more dynamic than earlier systems. It focuses on identifying possible opportunities or threats in the environment, evaluating alternative responses, and, when necessary, changing the strategic direction and capabilities of the firm. Current business units and their strengths and weaknesses are not assumed as given; they can change according to market conditions. Thus, a firm's various businesses are not all expected to perform in the same way, and each may pursue its own competitive strategy and objectives.

Like earlier systems, though, strategic planning is a periodic, usually annual, process. Most organizations employing such systems update their strategic plans in the spring or summer. Then, during the fall, those plans provide a foundation for developing annual operating plans and budgets for the individual businesses and products within the firm.

While marketing and business-unit managers often have some input into annual strategic planning processes, top corporate executives usually make final decisions concerning strategic directions and the allocation of company resources. Corporate management hands down strategy and budget guidelines to the business units at the beginning of the planning process, and it reviews and approves each unit's final plan and budget. Thus, while most strategic planning systems involve elements of both bottom-up and top-down planning, corporate management tends to play the dominant role.

One advantage of annual strategic planning is that it forces managers to address strategic issues at scheduled times. Without such a formal process, managers might become absorbed in day-to-day problems and lose sight of the bigger strategic picture. On the other hand, competitive threats and market opportunities can arise so quickly in today's global economy that rigidly tying managers to an annual planning process can severely reduce a firm's flexibility and lead to disastrous outcomes.

Strategic management systems

By the mid-70s some firms, particularly diversified manufacturing companies in dynamic industries such as electronics, recognized that an annual formal strategic planning cycle was inadequate to respond in a timely way to rapid changes occurring in their global environments. Consequently, they developed strategic management systems that supplement the formal planning process with procedures and structures designed to enable the organization to be more responsive to fast-developing opportunities and threats.[9]

---

[9]Some authors refer to the kind of responsive, real-time strategic decision making envisioned by strategic management systems as *adaptive planning*. For more detailed discussions of the rationale for and procedures involved

EXHIBIT 1-4

Guidelines for Market-Driven Strategic Management

1. Create customer focus throughout the business.	9. Measure and manage customer expectations.
2. Listen to the customer.	10. Build customer relationships and loyalty.
3. Define and nurture your distinctive competence.	11. Define the business as a service business.
4. Define marketing as market intelligence.	12. Commit to continuous improvement and innovation.
5. Target customers precisely.	13. Manage culture along with strategy and structure.
6. Manage for profitability, not sales volume.	
7. Make customer value the guiding star.	14. Grow with partners and alliances.
8. Let the customer define quality.	15. Destroy marketing bureaucracy.

SOURCE: Frederick E. Webster, Jr., "Executing the New Marketing Concept," *Marketing Management* 3, no. 1 (1994), p. 10.

Firms pursuing this new form of strategic management have developed a variety of new procedures and structures to improve the responsiveness of their decision making, including more detailed environmental scanning; continuous, real-time information systems; seeking frequent feedback from and coordinating plans with cutting-edge customers and major suppliers; decentralization of strategic decisions; encouragement of entrepreneurial thinking among lower-level managers; and the use of interfunctional management teams to analyze issues and initiate strategic actions outside the formal planning process.[10] For instance, Compaq formed a multifunctional management team to assess market conditions and develop its new line of low-priced PCs. The firm has also formed close relationships with retail chains such as Office Depot to expand distribution and (with the possible exception of Intel) worked closely with suppliers to improve quality and reduce the cost of components for its new machines. These and other actions recommended to make organizations' strategic planning efforts more market-driven and flexible are summarized in Exhibit 1-4.

Because strategic management systems emphasize staying in close and constant touch with the environment and decentralized decision processes, lower-level managers tend to play a more crucial role in formulating strategy. Of course, top management is still responsible for defining the organization's basic strategic thrust and has the final authority to approve or reject new strategic initiatives emanating from the lower ranks. Thus, strategic management systems also involve elements of both bottom-up and top-down planning. However, lower-level managers tend to be more active and influential participants in such systems than in firms that rely on more formal, periodic strategic planning.

---

in such systems, see George S. Day, *Market-Driven Strategy: Processes for Creating Value* (New York: The Free Press, 1990), chs. 3 and 4; and Frederick E. Webster, Jr., *Market-Driven Management: Using the New Marketing Concept to Create a Customer-Oriented Company* (New York: John Wiley & Sons, 1994).

[10] Frederick E. Webster, Jr., "Executing the New Marketing Concept," *Marketing Management* 3, no. 1 (1994), pp. 9–16.

Characteristics of effective planning systems

As planning systems have evolved over the years, each new type has added features to, rather than replaced, earlier systems. But the fact that the newer systems represent attempts to improve upon and overcome the weaknesses of earlier ones should not be interpreted as meaning that the newest planning approach—strategic management—is the most appropriate and effective for all organizations. Research suggests that any type of planning system can be effective if tailored to the firm's environment, the nature of its businesses, and the organizational context.[11] Thus, for a firm engaged in commodity businesses that competes primarily on price in relatively predictable market and competitive environments, a financial or long-range planning system might be adequate. For example, Cargill—one of the nation's largest dealers in agricultural products like wheat and soybeans—reaches many of its strategic decisions through long-range planning based on projections of future grain production and global demand.

Regardless of the type of system used, firms effective at strategic planning have three things in common.[12] First, there is little resistance to the planning process within the firm. Managers strongly believe that planning is essential for the organization's continued success. Consequently, they are active, willing participants in the planning process; and they are committed to successfully implementing the strategies that are developed.

A second and closely related characteristic is strong support from top management. Clearly, other employees are more likely to take planning seriously when top executives are strongly committed to the planning process and its outcomes. This is particularly true for decentralized strategic management systems. When lower-level managers are given more responsibility for making strategic decisions, they should also be given commensurate authority and support, including resources for environmental scanning, market analysis, and other systems needed to provide adequate information for planning and effective implementation of the plans that are developed.

Finally, effective planning systems strike a balance between creativity and control. That is, they encompass elements of both top-down and bottom-up planning. Top management must formulate a clear strategic vision for the firm, guard against the various business and product-market strategies straying too far from that vision, and make sure that strategies at different levels are coordinated with one another. At the same time, lower-level managers must be encouraged to stay in close touch with the market environment, identify emerging threats and opportunities, and initiate strategic responses when necessary.

While all four types of planning systems are in use today, many analysts argue that most companies will need to move toward the more adaptive strategic management–type systems to remain competitive. Increasingly dramatic and rapid environmental changes, brought about by advancing technology, fragmenting markets, global competition, and the like, will

---

[11]Balaji Chakravarthy, "On Tailoring a Strategic Planning System to Its Context: Some Empirical Evidence," *Strategic Management Journal*, November–December 1987, pp. 517–34.

[12]V. Ramanujam, N. Venkatraman, and John C. Camillus, "Multi-Objective Assessment of the Effectiveness of Strategic Planning: A Discriminant Analysis Approach," *Academy of Management Journal*, June 1986, pp. 347–72.

require firms to become more market-oriented and more strategically responsive.[13] But the changing business environment not only necessitates changes in how companies formulate and implement their strategies, it is also likely to affect the role that marketing and marketing managers play in those processes.

THE ROLE OF MARKETING IN FORMULATING AND IMPLEMENTING STRATEGIES

Marketing managers bear the primary responsibility for formulating and implementing strategic marketing plans for individual product-market entries. As mentioned earlier, though, their freedom of action in designing such plans is often constrained by their firm's corporate and business-level strategies. The marketing manager for Heinz ketchup, for instance, probably could not gain approval for an aggressive promotional campaign aimed at increasing Heinz's already commanding share of its market. Such a marketing strategy would be inconsistent with a corporate growth strategy that allocates the bulk of the firm's marketing resources to newer, more rapidly growing product categories (such as pet foods and the Weight Watchers' line of entrees) and with a business strategy dedicated to competing in basic food categories by maintaining the lowest-cost position in the industry.[14]

On the other hand, the essence of strategic planning at all levels is identifying threats to avoid the opportunities to pursue. The primary strategic responsibility of any manager is to look outward continuously to keep the firm or business in step with changes in the environment. Because they occupy positions at the boundary between the firm and its customers, distributors, and competitors, marketing managers are usually most familiar with conditions and trends in the market environment. Consequently, they not only are responsible for developing strategic plans for their own product-market entries but also are often primary participants and contributors to the planning process at the business and corporate level as well. As an example, see the wide-ranging influence of marketing managers on strategic planning within SBUs at General Electric, as outlined in Exhibit 1–5. GE's marketing managers have primary responsibility for, or are among the key participants in, formulating nearly all aspects of an SBU's business strategy, as well as planning and implementing many functional program elements within the business unit.

Factors that mediate marketing's role in strategic planning

Unfortunately, marketing managers do not always play so extensive a strategic role as they do at General Electric. This is because not all firms are as market-oriented as GE. Not surprisingly, marketers tend to have a greater influence on strategy at all levels in organizations that embrace a market-oriented philosophy of business.

---

[13]For a more detailed discussion of this argument, see George S. Day, *Market-Driven Strategy*, ch. 1; and Frederick E. Webster, Jr., *Market-Driven Management*.

[14]Bill Saporito, "Heinz Pushes to Be the Low-Cost Producer," *Fortune*, June 24, 1985, pp. 44–54; and Andrew E. Serwer, "How to Escape a Price War," *Fortune*, June 13, 1994, pp. 84–85.

EXHIBIT 1–5

Influence and Participation in Strategic Planning by Marketing Managers at General Electric

Strategic planning activity	Marketing's role
Determination of SBU's objectives and scope	Key participant along with SBU's general manager
Environmental assessment (customers; economic, political, regulatory trends)	Primary contributor and a major beneficiary of the results
Competitive assessment (actual and potential competitors)	Primary contributor, working with other functional managers and staff planners
Situation assessment (input to portfolio analysis; industry and market attractiveness; firm and product position)	Primary contributor, working with staff planners and general manager
Objectives and goals	Key participant with other functional managers, including responsibility for measuring several performance indicators
Strategies	Major contributor to determination of SBU's competitive strategy; responsible for marketing strategy and for coordinating plans with other functional strategies
Key program elements	**Marketing's role**
Product-market development	Leadership role
Product quality	Leading responsibility for quality
Distribution	Primary responsibility
Technology	Varies according to the importance of technology to the product or service
Human resources	Responsible for functional area
Business development*	Key supporting role with strategic planning and manufacturing responsible for implementation
Manufacturing facilities	Typically, only limited involvement

*Decisions to expand, improve, or contract the business.

SOURCE: Adapted from a speech presented by Stephen G. Harrell (then of the General Electric Company) at the American Marketing Association Educator's Conference, Chicago, August 5, 1980. Mr. Harrell is currently a Partner in Megamark Partners, a consulting firm specializing in marketing and new product development.

Market-oriented management

Market-oriented organizations tend to operate according to the business philosophy known as the marketing concept. As originally stated by General Electric four decades ago, the **marketing concept** holds that the planning and coordination of all company activities around the primary goal of satisfying customer needs is the most effective means to attain and sustain a competitive advantage and achieve company objectives over time.

Thus, market-oriented firms are characterized by a consistent focus by personnel in all departments and at all levels on customers' needs and competitive circumstances in the market environment. They are also willing and able to quickly adapt products and functional programs to fit changes in that environment. Such firms pay a great deal of attention to customer research *before* products are designed and produced. They embrace the concept of market segmentation by adapting product offerings and marketing programs to the special needs of different target markets. Finally, their organizational structures and procedures reflect a market orientation. Marketing managers or product teams play an active role in planning strategies, developing products, and coordinating activities across functional departments to ensure that they are all consistent with the desires of target customers. Thus, the market-oriented firm keeps its businesses focused on well-defined market segments and continually seeks to enhance its competitive advantages.[15]

Does being market-oriented pay off? Recent evidence suggests that it does, at least in a highly developed economy like the United States. Several studies involving a total of more than 400 business units in a variety of industries indicate that a market orientation has a significant positive effect on various dimensions of performance, including return on assets, sales growth, and new product success.[16]

Nevertheless, many companies around the world are not particularly market-oriented. Among the reasons why firms are not always in close touch with their market environments are these:

- Competitive conditions may enable a company to be successful in the short run without being particularly sensitive to customer desires.

- Different levels of economic development across industries or countries may favor different business philosophies.

- Firms can suffer from strategic inertia—the automatic continuation of strategies successful in the past, even though current market conditions are changing.

Competitive factors affecting a firm's market orientation

The competitive conditions some firms face enable them to be successful in the short term without paying much attention to their customers, suppliers, distributors, or other organizations in their market environment. Early entrants into newly emerging industries—particularly industries based on new technologies—are especially likely to be internally focused and not very market-oriented. This is because there are likely to be relatively few strong competitors during the formative years of a new industry; customer demand for the new product is likely to grow rapidly and outstrip available supply; and production problems and resource constraints tend to represent more immediate threats to the survival of such new businesses.

---

[15] Ajay K. Kohli and Bernard J. Jaworski, "Market Orientation: The Construct, Research Propositions, and Managerial Implications," *Journal of Marketing* 54, April 1990, pp. 1–18.

[16] John C. Narver and Stanley F. Slater, "The Effect of a Market Orientation on Business Profitability," *Journal of Marketing* 54, October 1990, pp. 20–35.; Stanley F. Slater and John C. Narver, *Market Orientation, Performance, and the Moderating Influence of Competitive Environment*, Report No. 92-118 (Cambridge, Mass.: The Marketing Science Institute, 1992); and Bernard J. Jaworski and Ajay K. Kohli, *Market Orientation: Antecedents and Consequences*, Report No. 92-104 (Cambridge, Mass.: The Marketing Science Institute, 1992).

EXHIBIT 1–6

Differences between Production-Oriented and Market-Oriented Firms

Business activity or function	Production orientation	Marketing orientation
Product offering	Company sells what it can make; primary focus on functional performance and cost	Company makes what it can sell; primary focus on customers' needs and market opportunities
Product line	Narrow	Broad
Pricing	Based on production and distribution costs	Based on perceived benefits provided
Research	Technical research; focus on product improvement and cost cutting in the production process	Market research; focus on identifying new opportunities and applying new technology to satisfy customer needs
Packaging	Protection for the product; minimize costs	Designed for customer convenience: a promotional tool
Credit	A necessary evil; minimize bad debt losses	A customer service; a tool to attract customers
Promotion	Emphasis on product features, quality, and price	Emphasis on product benefits and ability to satisfy customers' needs or solve problems

Businesses facing such market and competitive conditions are often **product-oriented** or **production-oriented**. They focus most of their attention and resources on such functions as product and process engineering, production, and finance in order to acquire and manage the resources necessary to keep pace with growing demand. The business is primarily concerned with producing more of what it wants to make, and marketing generally plays a secondary role in formulating and implementing strategy. Indeed, such firms commonly rely on financial or long-range planning systems and base their strategies on extrapolations of the current situation. Some other functional differences between production-oriented and market-oriented firms are summarized in Exhibit 1–6.

As industries grow, they become more competitive. New entrants are attracted and existing producers attempt to differentiate themselves through improved products and more efficient production processes. As a result, industry capacity often grows faster than demand and the environment shifts from a seller's market to a buyer's market. Firms often respond to such changes with aggressive promotional activities—such as hiring more salespeople, increasing their advertising budgets, or offering frequent price promotions—to maintain market share and hold down unit costs.

Unfortunately, this kind of **sales-oriented** response to increasing competition still focuses on selling what the firm wants to make rather than on customer needs. Worse, competitors can easily match such aggressive sales tactics. In other words, simply spending more on selling efforts usually does not create a sustainable competitive advantage.

As industries mature, sales volume levels off and technological differences among brands tend to disappear as manufacturers copy the best features of each other's products. Consequently, a firm must seek new market segments or steal share from competitors by offering lower prices, superior services, or intangible benefits other firms cannot match. At this stage, managers can most readily appreciate the benefits of a market orientation, and marketers are often given a bigger role in developing competitive strategies.[17] It is not surprising, then, that many of America's most market-oriented firms—and those working hardest to become market-oriented—are well-established competitors in relatively mature industries.

The influence of different stages of development across industries and global markets

The previous discussion suggests that the degree of adoption of a market orientation varies not only across firms but across entire industries. Industries that are in earlier stages of their life cycles, or that benefit from barriers to entry or other factors reducing the intensity of competition, are likely to have relatively fewer market-oriented firms. For instance, due in part to government regulations that restricted competition, many service industries—including banks, airlines, physicians, lawyers, accountants, and insurance companies—were slow to adopt the marketing concept. But with the trend toward deregulation during the past decade and the increasingly intense global competition in such industries, many service organizations are working much harder to understand and satisfy their customers.[18]

Given that entire economies are in different stages of development around the world, the popularity and even the appropriateness of different business philosophies may also vary across countries. A production orientation was the dominant business philosophy in the United States, for instance, during the period of industrialization that occurred from the mid-1800s through World War I.[19] Similarly, a primary focus on developing product and production technology may still be appropriate in developing nations that are in the midst of industrialization.

International differences in business philosophies can cause some problems for the globalization of a firm's strategic marketing programs, but it can create some opportunities as well, especially for alliances or joint ventures. Consider, for example, General Electric's joint venture with the Mexican appliance manufacturer Organization Mabe. The arrangement benefits GE by providing direct access to Mexico's rapidly growing market for household appliances and its low-cost supply of labor. But it also benefits Mabe—and the Mexican

---

[17] Slater and Narver, *Market Orientation, Performance, and the Moderating Influence of Competitive Environment*; and John P. Workman, Jr., "When Marketing Should Follow Instead of Lead," *Marketing Management* 2, no. 2 (1993), pp. 8–19.

[18] For example, see "Banks Discover the Consumer," *Fortune*, February 12, 1990, pp. 96–104. For a more general discussion, see Valarie A. Zeithaml, A. Parasuraman, and Leonard L. Berry, "Problems and Strategies in Services Marketing," *Journal of Marketing* 49, Spring 1985, pp. 33–46.

[19] E. Jerome McCarthy and William D. Perreault, Jr., *Basic Marketing: A Global-Managerial Approach*, 11th ed. (Burr Ridge, Ill.: Irwin, 1993), ch. 2.

economy—by giving the firm access to cutting-edge R&D and production technology and the capital necessary to take advantage of its newfound know-how.[20]

Strategic inertia

In some cases a firm that achieved success by being in tune with its environment loses touch with its market because managers become reluctant to tamper with strategies and marketing programs that worked in the past. They begin to believe there is one best way to satisfy their customers. Such strategic inertia is dangerous for the simple reason that customers' needs and competitive offerings change over time. Staying successful requires constant analysis of and adjustments to changes in what customers want and competitors offer. Thus, in environments where such changes happen frequently, the strategic planning process needs to be ongoing and adaptive, and marketers need to provide detailed information about what is happening with their customers and competitors.

The future role of marketing

Strategic inertia will be even more dangerous in many industries in the future because of increasing magnitudes and rates of change resulting from some of the following:

- Mature markets fragment into smaller segments with unique needs and preferences.
- Previously self-contained national markets are transformed into linked global markets.
- Technological, demographic, and lifestyle changes create new market opportunities.
- Competitive advantages become harder to sustain as product life cycles shorten and global competitors contest more markets.
- Overcapacity intensifies competitive pressures by giving customers greater bargaining power.
- New information technologies enable closer links between customers and their suppliers and improve customers' ability to evaluate the performance of alternative suppliers.

In light of such changes, it is apparent that firms in most, if not all, industries will have to be market-oriented, tightly focused on customer needs and desires, and highly adaptive to succeed and prosper in the future. This suggests, in turn, that the effective performance of marketing activities—particularly those associated with tracking, analyzing, and satisfying customers' needs—will become even more critical for the successful formulation and implementation of strategies at all organizational levels.

It is important to note, however, that such marketing activities may not always be carried out by marketing managers located in separate functional departments. As more firms embrace the use of multifunctional teams or network structures, the boundaries between

---

[20] "GE's brave New World," *Business Week,* November 8, 1993, pp. 64–70.

functions are likely to blur and the performance of marketing tasks will become everybody's business. Similarly, as organizations become more focused and specialized in developing unique core competencies, they will rely more heavily on suppliers, distributors, dealers, and other partners to perform activities—including marketing and sales tasks—that fall outside those areas of competence. All of this suggests that the ability to create, manage, and sustain exchange relationships with customers, vendors, distributors, and others will become a key strategic competence for firms in the future—and that is what marketing is all about.[21]

THE PROCESS OF FORMULATING AND IMPLEMENTING MARKETING STRATEGY

This book's primary focus is on the development and implementation of marketing strategies for individual product-market entries. Exhibit 1–7 briefly diagrams the activities involved in this process, and it also serves as the organizational framework for the rest of this book.

Interrelationships among different levels of strategy

Before we can discuss the development of a marketing strategy for a specific product, however, we must first examine corporate and business-level strategies in more detail. As we have seen, marketers often play a major role in formulating such strategies, and that role is likely to expand in the future. At the same time, strategic decisions at the corporate and SBU level often influence or constrain the range of options a marketing manager can realistically consider when designing a marketing strategy for his or her product. After all, the marketing program for an individual product must be consistent with the strategic direction, competitive thrust, and resource allocations decided on at higher management levels. Therefore, Chapters 2 and 3 examine the components of corporate and business-level strategies and their implications for the design and implementation of marketing strategies at the product-market level.

Market opportunity analysis

A major factor in the success or failure of a strategy at any level is whether it fits the realities of the firm's external environment. Thus, in developing a marketing strategy for a product, the marketing manager must first monitor and analyze the opportunities and threats posed by factors outside the organization.

Environmental, industry, and competitor analysis

To understand potential opportunities and threats over the long term, marketers must first attempt to identify and predict the impact of broad trends in the economic and social environment. In some situations a firm might even try to influence the direction of such trends.

---

[21] Frederick E. Webster, Jr., "The Changing Role of Marketing in the Corporation," *Journal of Marketing* 56, October 1992, pp. 1–17.

EXHIBIT 1-7

The Process of Formulating and Implementing Marketing Strategy

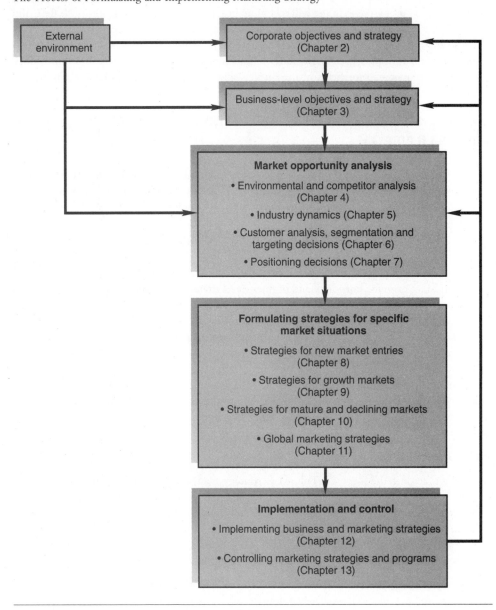

Chapter 4 discusses a number of macroenvironmental factors that marketing managers should pay attention to, along with some methods for monitoring, analyzing, and perhaps influencing the impact of those factors on the future performance of their product-market entries.

One of the most critical aspects of the external environment for marketers to keep tabs on is the competition. What are the strengths and weaknesses of existing and potential competitors relative to those of the firm? How might the firm gain a sustainable competitive advantage in a given product-market? How might those competitors react to changes in the environment and to the firm's marketing actions in the future? Chapter 4 presents some methods for attempting to answer such questions.

Of course, the competitive environment of an industry is not static but can change dramatically over time. For example, the aggressive pricing of the clone manufacturers and the threat of potential new entrants such as Intel motivated Compaq to revamp its product line, slash its costs and prices, change its distribution and customer service policies, and increase its advertising budget to strengthen its competitive position in the global PC market. Chapter 5 explores the competitive dynamics of an industry, particularly emphasizing how competition and customers' buying patterns are likely to change as the industry or product-market moves through various life-cycle stages.

Customer analysis: segmentation, targeting, and positioning

The primary purpose of any marketing strategy is to facilitate and encourage exchange transactions with potential customers. One of a marketing manager's major responsibilities, then, is to analyze the motivations and behaviors of present and potential customers. Of course, it is unlikely that every potential customer will have the same needs, seek the same product benefits, or be influenced in the same way by the same marketing program. Thus, marketing managers must also determine whether there are multiple market segments that will respond differently to their products and marketing programs and how to best define, identify, and appeal to those segments. Chapter 6, therefore, examines dimensions and techniques that can be used to analyze customers and to define and identify market segments in both consumer and organizational markets.

But not every segment of a market is likely to be equally attractive to a firm. Some may be too small to be profitable, and others may desire benefits the firm cannot provide as efficiently or effectively as some competitors. Compaq, for instance, does not feel it has the technical capabilities or reputation necessary to compete effectively for buyers of engineering work stations or other sophisticated segments of the computer market. Therefore, after examining customer needs and competitive strengths and weaknesses, a marketing manager must decide which market segment or segments to target and how to position the product in the target segment relative to competitive offerings. Chapter 6 examines some considerations in selecting target segments, and Chapter 7 discusses various methods for choosing a competitive position for the product within those markets.

Formulating strategies for specific market situations

The strategic marketing program for a particular product-market entry should reflect market demand and the competitive situation within the target market. As demand and competitive conditions change over time, the marketing strategy should also be adjusted. During the

1970s, for instance, American Express's successful "Do you know me?" promotional campaign was aimed at building primary demand by emphasizing the convenience and prestige of carrying a credit card. But as competing bankcards proliferated, American Express switched to a "Membership has its privileges" campaign designed to differentiate the green card from its competitors by promoting superior customer service.

Because demand and competitive conditions change as product-markets grow and mature, the third section of this book discusses a variety of different marketing strategies appropriate for different stages in a market's life cycle. Chapter 8 examines some marketing strategies for introducing new products or services to the market. Chapter 9 discusses strategies appropriate for building or maintaining a product's share of a growing market in the face of increasing competition. And Chapter 10 considers the strategies a marketing manager might adopt in mature or declining product-markets. Finally, many companies try to grow by pursuing target markets in other countries. However, cultural and political differences across nations often require different strategic approaches for marketing success. Chapter 11, therefore, discusses global marketing strategies.

Implementation and control

A final critical determinant of a strategy's success is the firm's ability to implement it effectively. And this, in turn, depends on whether the strategy is consistent with the firm's resources, organizational structure, coordination and control systems, and the skills and experience of company personnel. In other words, managers must design a strategy that fits existing company resources, competencies, and procedures—or try to construct new structures and systems to fit the chosen strategy.[22] Therefore, Chapter 12 discusses the structural variables, planning and coordination processes, and personnel and corporate culture characteristics related to the successful implementation of different marketing strategies.

Finally, the marketing manager must determine whether the marketing program is achieving its objectives and adjust the strategy when performance is disappointing. This evaluation and control process provides feedback to managers and serves as the basis for a subsequent market opportunity analysis. Chapter 13 examines ways to evaluate marketing performance and develop contingency plans for when things go wrong.

SUMMARY

This chapter argues that a strategy should specify *what* is to be accomplished, *where* it is to be accomplished (which industries and product-markets to focus on), and *how* (the resources and activities to be allocated to each product-market to meet environmental opportunities and threats and gain a competitive advantage). Consequently, a well-developed strategy contains five components: (1) scope, or the desired breadth of the organization's strategic domain, (2) goals and objectives, (3) resource deployments, indicating how financial and

---

[22]N. Venkatraman and John C. Camillus, "Exploring the Concept of 'Fit' in Strategic Management," *Academy of Management Review* 9 (1984), pp. 513–25.

human resources are to be distributed across businesses, product-markets, and/or functional departments and activities, (4) identification of a source of sustainable competitive advantage, and (5) specification of potential sources of synergy across businesses and/or functional departments.

Most firms—especially those with multiple businesses or divisions—have not a single comprehensive strategy but rather a hierarchy of corporate strategy, business-level strategies, and functional strategies focused on individual product-market entries. A marketing manager's strategy for a specific product-market entry is constrained by the strategic decisions made at the corporate and business-unit levels. On the other hand, marketing managers often play a crucial role in providing necessary information and analyses to the strategic planning process at higher levels of the organization.

The extent of the marketer's role in strategic planning is mediated by the type of planning system the firm uses. As firms grow and mature, their planning systems tend to evolve from the simplest kind of financial planning to long-range and strategic planning. And in some cases, firms ultimately embrace the most adaptive, ongoing type of strategic market management planning system. As this evolution occurs, the role of marketing managers in the strategic planning process tends to increase in importance.

The marketer's role in formulating and implementing strategy is also influenced by the market orientation of the firm and its top managers. Some firms are not very market-oriented because competitive conditions may enable the firm to be successful without being particularly sensitive to customer desires; the firm may be committed to past policies that are no longer appropriate in view of changing conditions in the market; or market and competitive concerns may be outweighed by short-term financial imperatives. However, a clearer focus on customer needs and competitive responses is likely to become more crucial for the future strategic success of most firms because of the increasing rate and magnitude of changes occurring in the domestic and global market environments. And this suggests that marketers will play an even more important strategic role in the years to come.

Corporate Strategy Decisions

BAUSCH & LOMB: KEEPING AN EYE OUT FOR GROWTH[1]

When Daniel Gill became CEO of Bausch & Lomb in 1981, the company was adrift. Most of its sales came from products built on aging technologies—such as hard contact lenses—many of which held market shares of less than 5 percent. Gill immediately set more aggressive performance and growth objectives for the firm. And after researching the firm's competencies and its reputation in the marketplace, he redefined the corporate mission as providing top-quality products for "every human organ above the neck." Gill then started divesting businesses and product lines that were either inconsistent with the new mission or unlikely to reach the new performance targets. Over his first five years as CEO he shed operations that had generated half the company's sales. But he knew the downsizing alone would not guarantee the firm's future. He says, "I had been raised in a culture that said you make money by making wise investments."

Gill focused those investments on core businesses where Bausch & Lomb had technical or marketing strengths that could be used to achieve market share leadership and substantial global volume growth: businesses like soft contact lenses, lens care products, and Ray Ban sunglasses. Proceeds from the divestitures were used to triple capital spending aimed at modernizing production facilities and improving product quality and market coverage in those core businesses. For example, contact lenses and solutions grew into a general eye care business. New over-the-counter preparations and lenses were developed by the firm's internal R & D group, while prescription eye drugs were added through acquisitions.

---

[1]This case example is based on material found in Myron Magnet, "Let's Go for Growth," *Fortune*, March 7, 1994, pp. 60–72.

The firm also diversified into some new but related product categories. For instance, the company acquired the maker of the Interplak electric toothbrush. And when market research showed that many buyers of Bausch & Lomb's Sensitive Eyes eye drops also had sensitive skin, the company developed a skin lotion and cream business. Those new products benefited not only from Bausch & Lomb's established brand name and reputation but also from sharing the same salesforce and distribution channels the firm used to market its eye care products.

Finally, the company's revitalized product lines were introduced into entirely new markets as Gill strengthened and expanded Bausch & Lomb's global market presence. In a joint venture with Beijing Optical, for example, he built factories in China in 1987, and Bausch & Lomb taught thousands of local opticians how to fit contact lenses. To sell them, the company established China's first contact lens shops in major department stores. In an economy with relatively few goods for consumers to buy, the Chinese made Bausch & Lomb's subsidiary profitable within two years.

With a total investment of under $20 million, Bausch & Lomb created and now dominates the Chinese contact lens market. And the market expansion phase of the firm's growth strategy, which includes the penetration of other underdeveloped markets such as India and Poland, has raised overseas sales from 25 percent of total revenues to more than 50 percent while boosting operating profit margins from 8 percent to around 20 percent.

Indeed, all of the various avenues by which Bausch & Lomb has pursued growth seem to have led to success. In the decade from 1984 to 1994 the firm's sales jumped from $400 million to nearly $2 billion. The market value of the company's stock grew even more impressively, increasing from less than $400 million to nearly $3 billion.

STRATEGIC DECISIONS AT THE CORPORATE LEVEL

The corporate strategy crafted over the years by Daniel Gill and his top lieutenants provides a clear sense of direction and useful guidance for all of Bausch & Lomb's managers because it speaks to all five dimensions of strategy that we discussed in Chapter 1. First, it defines the overall scope and mission of the company by targeting health and beauty products that address eye, ear, mouth, and skin problems as areas for future growth and development. It also sets challenging volume, market share, and profit objectives for the company and its various businesses.

One aspect of Bausch & Lomb's corporate strategy that has changed over the years is the planned direction for future growth and development: the means by which the firm aims to achieve and sustain an overall competitive advantage and that guide its allocation of resources. During the 1980s the firm emphasized growth via the internal development of line extensions and new products targeted at existing customers, such as disposable contact lens and skin lotions. The firm also grew by diversifying into related businesses through the acquisition of smaller firms, such as manufacturers of prescription eye drugs, the Interplak toothbrush, and other dental products.

More recently, the firm's growth strategy has placed greater emphasis on building the volume and profitability of its established brands through more efficient production and aggressive marketing programs—particularly programs aimed at expanding global markets for Bausch & Lomb products. This change in growth strategy has also necessitated changes in the allocation of resources across different functional activities within the firm. For instance, more funds have been allocated to marketing activities aimed at building distribution and primary demand in developing countries like China and India. Finally, the firm has sought possible synergies by using a common brand name, salesforce, and distribution channels for marketing many of its eye and skin care products in the domestic market.

Another thing that should be obvious from reading the Bausch & Lomb example is that a clearly defined corporate strategy can definitely influence and constrain the decisions that a firm's marketing managers make when designing marketing strategies and programs for individual products. For instance, the marketing manager for soft contact lenses has benefited in recent years from the corporate decision to shift more financial and marketing resources to the development of global markets for that product line. On the other hand, the implementation of the company's global expansion strategy has dictated some new marketing actions, such as the development of retail contact lens shops in Chinese department stores.

In view of the influence of corporate-level decisions on the development and implementation of strategic programs for individual product-market entries, then, the remaining sections of this chapter discuss the five dimensions of a well-defined corporate strategy in more detail. As a guide, Exhibit 2–1 summarizes some of the crucial questions about each of these strategy components.

CORPORATE SCOPE: DEFINING THE FIRM'S MISSION AND INTENT

A well-thought-out mission statement guides an organization's managers as to which market opportunities to pursue and which fall outside the firm's strategic domain. A clearly stated mission can help instill a shared sense of direction, relevance, and achievement among employees and a positive image of the firm among customers, investors, and other stakeholders.

To provide a useful sense of direction, a corporate mission statement must clearly define the organization's strategic scope. It should answer such fundamental questions as What is our business? Who are our customers? What kinds of value can we provide to these customers? and What should our business be in the future? For example, a few years ago PepsiCo, the manufacturer of Pepsi-Cola, broadened its mission to focus on "marketing superior quality food and beverage products for households and consumers dining out." That clearly defined mission guided the firm's managers toward the acquisition of several related companies, such as Frito-Lay, Pizza Hut, and Taco Bell, and the divestiture of operations that no longer fit the firm's primary thrust.[2]

---

[2]"Pepsi's Marketing Magic: Nobody Does It Better," *Business Week*, February 10, 1986, pp. 52–57. Also see Patricia Sellers, "Pepsi Keeps on Going after No. 1," *Fortune*, March 11, 1991, pp. 62–70.

EXHIBIT 2–1

Corporate Strategy Components and Issues

Strategy component	Key issues
Scope, mission, and intent	• What business(es) should the firm be in?
	• What customer needs, market segments, and/or technologies should be focused on?
	• What is the firm's enduring strategic purpose or intent?
Objectives	• What performance dimensions should the firm's business units and employees focus on?
	• What is the target level of performance to be achieved on each dimension?
	• What is the time frame in which each target should be attained?
Development strategy	• How can the firm achieve a desired level of growth over time?
	• Can the desired growth be attained by expanding the firm's current businesses?
	• Will the company have to diversify into new businesses or product-markets to achieve its future growth objectives?
Resource allocation	• How should the firm's limited financial resources be allocated across its businesses to produce the highest returns?
	• Of the alternative strategies that each business might pursue, which will produce the greatest returns for the dollars invested?
Sources of synergy	• What competencies, knowledge, and customer-based intangibles (e.g., brand recognition, reputation) might be developed and shared across the firm's businesses?
	• What operational resources, facilities, or functions (e.g., plants, R & D, salesforce, etc.) might the firm's businesses share to increase their efficiency?

Factors that influence the corporate mission

Like any other component of strategy, an organization's mission should fit its internal characteristics, resources, and competencies and its external opportunities and threats. Thus, while defining the firm's mission is usually a first step in developing corporate strategy, it should be intertwined with analyses of the organization's strengths and weaknesses and of its environment.

Social values and ethical principles.   A firm's mission statement should reflect internal characteristics such as the historical accomplishments, top management preferences, and shared values, myths, and symbols that, taken together, make up the company's culture. An increasing number of organizations are developing mission statements that also attempt to define the social and ethical boundaries of their strategic domain. The annual reports of firms like Borden and 3M, for example, often include sections on social responsibility that outline the ethical principles the firms try to follow in dealings with customers, suppliers, and employees and the firms' policies concerning such social issues as charitable contributions and environmental protection. Indeed, by 1990 more than 90 percent of the Fortune 1,000 companies had developed formal codes of ethical conduct, up from 75 percent in 1985.[3]

Internal resources and competencies.   The mission should also be compatible with the firm's more tangible internal characteristics: its resources, distinctive competencies, and possible synergies across its various businesses. Thus, after PepsiCo redefined its mission it divested its Wilson Sporting Goods and North American Van Lines divisions because the firm's marketing and product development skills did not provide much of a competitive advantage in the moving or sporting goods industries.

Opportunities and threats.   Finally, a firm's mission statement should take into account opportunities and threats in the external environment. It should guide the organization toward product-markets where customer needs and competitive conditions offer attractive growth possibilities; at the same time, it should steer the company away from industries where stagnant demand, strong competitors, or emerging new technologies might make it difficult for the firm to establish a competitive advantage and achieve corporate objectives. In this sense a mission statement represents both a response to environmental conditions and an attempt to control them by spelling out which markets and competitors a firm should avoid confronting in the future. Thus, Gill's new mission for Bausch & Lomb steered the firm away from some of its traditional businesses (such as scientific instruments) where technical advances and strong global competitors had reduced the firm's chances for growth, share leadership, or profitability.

Dimensions for defining the corporate mission

A number of dimensions can be used to define an organization's strategic scope or mission. Some firms specify their domain in physical terms, focusing on products or services the company will produce or technologies it will use. Such mission statements, however, can lead to confusion and slow reaction times if technologies or customer demands change. For example, in a classic article Leavitt argues that Penn Central Railroad's view of its mission as being "the railroad business" helped cause the firm's failure. Penn Central did not respond to major changes in transportation technology, such as the rapid growth of air travel and the increased efficiency of long-haul trucking. Nor did it react to changes in customer preferences, such as a growing willingness to pay higher prices for the speed and convenience of air travel. Leavitt argues that it is better to define a firm's mission in terms of what customer needs are to be satisfied and the functions that must be performed to do so.[4] Products and technologies change over time, but basic customer needs tend to endure. Thus, if Penn

---

[3]Betsy Weisendanger, "Doing the Right Thing," *Sales & Marketing Management*, January 1991, pp. 82–83. Also see Lynn Sharp Paine, "Managing for Organizational Integrity," *Harvard Business Review*, March–April 1994, pp. 106–17.

[4]Theodore Leavitt, "Marketing Myopia," *Harvard Business Review*, July–August 1960, pp. 45–56.

EXHIBIT 2-2

Characteristics of Effective Corporate Mission Statements

	Broad	Specific
Functional Based on customer needs	Transportation business	Long-distance transportation for large-volume producers of low-value, low-density products
Physical Based on existing products or technology	Railroad business	Long-haul, coal-carrying railroad

SOURCE: Reprinted by permission from p. 43 of *Strategy Formulation: Analytical Concepts* by C. W. Hofer and D. Schendel. Copyright © 1978 by West Publishing Company. All rights reserved.

Central had defined its mission as satisfying its customers' transportation needs rather than simply being a railroad, it might have been more willing to expand its domain to incorporate newer technologies.

One problem with Leavitt's advice, though, is that a mission statement focusing only on basic customer needs can be too broad to provide clear guidance and can fail to take into account the firm's specific competencies. If Penn Central had defined itself as a transportation company, should it have diversified into the trucking business? Started an airline? Considered manufacturing cars? As the upper-right quadrant of Exhibit 2–2 suggests, the most useful mission statements focus on *both* the customer need to be satisfied and how the firm will attempt to satisfy that need. They are specific as to the customer groups and the kinds of products or technologies on which the firm will concentrate its efforts.[5] Thus, instead of thinking of itself as being in the railroad business or as satisfying the transportation needs of all potential customers, Burlington Northern's mission is to provide long-distance transportation for large-volume producers of low-value, low-density products, such as coal and grain.

Strategic intent or vision: a motivational view of corporate mission

Recently some writers have argued that mission statements stated in terms of specific customer needs, target markets, technologies, and/or products (such as Burlington Northern's) may also have some shortcomings as a foundation for a corporate strategy.[6] For one thing, it can be hard to get company employees fired up over something as mundane as

---

[5]Derek Abell, *Defining the Business: The Starting Point of Strategic Planning* (Englewood Cliffs, N.J.: Prentice Hall, 1980), ch. 3.

[6]For a more detailed discussion of strategic intent and its implications for formulating corporate strategy, see Gary Hamel and C. K. Prahalad, "Strategic Intent," *Harvard Business Review* (May–June 1989), pp. 63–76; James C. Collins and James I. Porras, "Making Impossible Dreams Come True," *Stanford Business School Magazine*, July 1989,

"providing long-distance transportation," no matter how necessary or desirable the task. Also, while such specific mission statements may accurately reflect the market situation and the firm's strengths and weaknesses at present, they may prove too rigid as things change. Employees may overlook some new market opportunities or new ways of building on the company's strengths or overcoming its weaknesses because the firm's stated mission doesn't explicitly recognize those approaches.

These authors suggest that a firm's basic scope and focus might be more effectively defined by a more general but personally motivating statement of **strategic intent** or **vision**. Consider, for instance, the difference between Burlington Northern's mission statement and the rallying cry that expresses the strategic intent of one Japanese auto manufacturer: "Beat Benz!" The first accurately describes the scope of BN's business, but it fails to inspire. "Beat Benz," on the other hand, not only expresses the firm's ultimate goal of taking over world leadership in the manufacture of luxury cars, it appeals to every employee's competitive instinct and desire for accomplishment. This is the essence of a good statement of strategic intent or vision. It provides a motivational perspective on the corporate purpose by setting an enduring goal worthy of employee commitment, usually couched in terms of unseating the best, or remaining the best, worldwide.

While an effective statement of strategic intent is clear about the organization's long-term ends, it should be flexible as to means. It must leave room for employee improvisation. Indeed, strategic intent usually implies a sizable stretch for an organization. Whereas the traditional approach to strategic planning seeks a good fit between existing resources and current opportunities, strategic intent creates an extreme misfit between the firm's resources and future ambitions. Current capabilities and resources will not suffice. Instead, top management challenges the organization's employees to make the most of limited resources, to be more inventive, and to develop new capabilities. To increase the probability that such challenges will be met, the firm must first provide its employees with the necessary skills (usually via increased training) and then give them substantial freedom to initiate new procedures or programs aimed at moving the organization toward its goal. Such decentralization of decision making can increase both the amount of worker participation and the creativity brought to the process of defining the corporation's strategy.[7]

The risk inherent in this approach, however, is similar to that which arises when a firm defines its mission in terms of satisfying a generic customer need. Although the ultimate objective is clear, there may be many ways to pursue it. And some of those ways may be inconsistent or compete with one another. Even a clear strategic vision, in other words, may not provide a sufficiently specific direction to focus employee efforts.

One possible solution to this dilemma is for management to combine a statement of strategic intent with a more traditional mission statement: one to stimulate employee commitment and the other to focus efforts on a more clearly defined domain of product-

---

pp. 14–19; and Gary Hamel and C. K. Prahalad, *Competing for the Future* (Cambridge, Mass.: Harvard Business School Press, 1994).

[7]Shawn Tully, "Why to Go for Stretch Targets," *Fortune*, November 14, 1994, pp. 145–58.

markets. While PepsiCo employees are urged to "beat Coke," for instance, they also understand that their competitive efforts should be focused on "marketing superior quality food and beverage products for households and consumers dining out." Thus, when Coke entered the entertainment business a number of years ago via the acquisition of Columbia Pictures and other investments, PepsiCo did not follow because entertainment did not fit the firm's mission.

Management can also convert a broad statement of strategic intent into a more specific mechanism for focusing the organization's efforts by breaking it down into a sequential series of shorter-term objectives or challenges that must be accomplished for the intent to be realized. In attempting to become the worldwide market share leader in the PC industry, for instance, Compaq's CEO first set a goal of becoming number one in the U.S. market by 1996. Once that is accomplished, the firm will seek share leadership in Europe (an objective it has already achieved in Great Britain). Later the firm will set its sights on the number one position in the Pacific Rim and other parts of the world.

While a firm's strategic intent should remain constant over time, its shorter-term objectives may change in response to changing market and competitive circumstances and the firm's own changing competencies and resources as it moves toward its ultimate goal. Also, those shorter-term goals should be both challenging and specific about the ends to be accomplished but flexible as to the means employees might use to achieve them. Finally, such goals should also carry specific time frames. Note, for instance, that Compaq specified 1996 as the deadline for achieving share leadership in the domestic market. As we shall see in the next section, the points just discussed all illustrate characteristics of useful corporate objectives.

CORPORATE OBJECTIVES

Confucius said, "For one who has no objective, nothing is relevant." Formal objectives provide decision criteria that guide an organization's business units and employees toward specific dimensions and levels of performance. Those same objectives provide the benchmarks for evaluating subsequent outcomes. One factor that shaped Gill's decision to divest some of Bausch & Lomb's traditional businesses, for instance, was the difficulty of achieving his ambitious revenue growth and return on equity objectives in mature markets where the firm had no advantage relative to its competitors. In the decade after he redefined the firm's mission, however, sales revenues quintupled and the market value of the company's stock increased more than six times.

To be useful as decision criteria and evaluative benchmarks, corporate objectives must be both specific and measurable. Therefore, each objective should contain four components:

- A *performance dimension* or attribute sought.
- A *measure* or *index* for evaluating progress.
- A *target* or *hurdle level* to be achieved.
- A *time frame* within which the target is to be accomplished.

Enhancing shareholder value: the ultimate objective

In recent years a growing number of executives of publicly held corporations have concluded that the organization's ultimate objective should be to increase its shareholders' economic returns as measured by dividends plus appreciation in the company's stock price.[8] To do so management must balance the interests of various corporate constituencies, including employees, customers, suppliers, debtholders, and stockholders. The firm's continued existence depends on a financial relationship with each of these parties. Employees want competitive wages. Customers want high quality at a competitive price. Suppliers and debtholders have financial claims that must be satisfied with cash when they fall due. And shareholders, as residual claimants, look for cash dividends and the prospect of future dividends reflected in the stock's market price.

If a company does not satisfy its constituents' financial claims, it ceases to be viable. Thus, a going concern must strive to enhance its ability to generate cash from the operation of its businesses and to obtain any additional funds needed from debt or equity financing.

The firm's ability to attain debt financing (its ability to borrow) depends in turn on projections of how much cash it can generate in the future. Similarly, the market value of its shares, and therefore its ability to attain equity financing, depends on investors' expectations of the firm's future cash-generating abilities. People willingly invest in a firm only when they expect a better return on their funds than they could get from other sources without exposing themselves to any greater risks. Thus, management's primary objective should be to pursue capital investments, acquisitions, and business strategies that will produce future cash flows sufficient to return positive value to shareholders. Failure to do so will not only depress the firm's stock price and inhibit the firm's ability to finance future operations and growth, it may also make the organization more vulnerable to a takeover by outsiders who promise to increase its value to shareholders.

Given this rationale, many firms set explicit objectives targeted at increasing shareholder value. These are usually stated in terms of a target return on shareholder equity, increase in the stock price, or earnings per share. Recently, though, some executives have begun expressing such corporate objectives in terms of "economic value added" or "market value added" (MVA). A firm's MVA is calculated by combining its debt and the market value of its stock, then subtracting the capital that has been invested in the company. The result, if positive, shows how much wealth the company has created.[9]

Unfortunately, such broad shareholder-value objectives do not always provide adequate guidance for a firm's lower-level managers or benchmarks for evaluating performance. For one thing, standard accounting measures, such as earnings per share or return on investment, are not always reliably linked to the true value of a company's stock.[10] And as we shall see later in this chapter, tools are available to evaluate the future impact of alternative strategic actions

---

[8]Alfred Rappaport, *Creating Shareholder Value: The New Standard for Business Performance* (New York: The Free Press, 1986), ch. 1; and Shawn Tully, "America's Best Wealth Creators," *Fortune*, November 28, 1994, pp. 143–62.

[9]Shawn Tully, "America's Best Wealth Creators," p. 143.

[10]Bradley T. Gale and Donald J. Swire, "The Tricky Business of Measuring Wealth," *Planning Review*, March–April, 1988, pp. 14–17, 47.

EXHIBIT 2–3

Schlitz: An Example of Increasing Stock Price at the Expense of Competitive Position

> In the early 1970s Schlitz Brewing made the mistake of boosting its share price at the expense of its competitive position. The firm shortened its brewing process by 50 percent, reduced labor cost, and switched to less costly ingredients. As a result, it became the lowest-cost producer in the industry, its profits soared, and its stock price rose to a high of $69 by 1974. Unfortunately, however, Schlitz's aggressive cost-cutting campaign also degraded the quality of its beer. By 1976, the firm was receiving constant customer and dealer complaints and its market share was slipping badly. In 1978, a new management team attempted to get product quality back on track, but by then consumers had such a low opinion of Schlitz beer that the company could not recover. By 1981, Schlitz's market share position had slipped from number two all the way to number seven, and its share price had dropped to a mere $5.

SOURCE: George S. Day and Liam Fahey, "Putting Strategy into Shareholder Value Analysis," *Harvard Business Review*, March–April 1990, pp. 156–62.

on shareholder value; but those valuation methods have inherent pitfalls and can be difficult to apply at lower levels of strategy such as trying to choose the best marketing strategy for a particular product-market entry.[11]

Finally, there is a danger that a narrow focus on short-term financial, shareholder-value objectives may lead managers to pay too little attention to actions necessary to provide value to the firm's customers and sustain a competitive advantage. In the long term, customer value and shareholder value converge; a firm can continue to provide attractive returns to shareholders only so long as it satisfies and retains its customers. But some managers may overlook this in the face of pressures to achieve aggressive short-term financial objectives, as illustrated by the experience of Schlitz Brewing discussed in Exhibit 2–3.

Most organizations pursue multiple objectives

Given the limitations of a single objective focused on enhancing shareholder value, most companies establish multiple objectives to guide and evaluate their managers' performance. Some of those objectives—such as increasing market share, improving product quality, or reducing operating expenses—relate to specific actions that directly influence the firm's ability to generate future cash flows and greater shareholder value.[12] Others may aim at making specific contributions to the firm's various constituencies, such as improving the skill levels of the workforce or contributing to community charities. Exhibit 2–4 lists some

---

[11]Patrick Barwise, Paul R. Marsh, and Robin Wensley, "Must Finance and Strategy Clash?" *Harvard Business Review* (September–October 1989), pp. 85–90; and George S. Day and Liam Fahey, "Putting Strategy into Shareholder Value Analysis," *Harvard Business Review*, March–April 1990, pp. 156–62.

[12]Alfred Rappaport, "Linking Competitive Strategy and Shareholder Value Analysis," *Journal of Business Strategy*, Spring 1987, pp. 58–67.

EXHIBIT 2–4

Common Performance Criteria and Measures That Specify Corporate, Business-Unit, and Marketing Objectives

Performance criteria	Possible measures or indexes
• Growth	$ sales Unit sales Percent change in sales
• Competitive strength	Market share Brand awareness Brand preference
• Innovativeness	$ sales from new products Percentage of sales from product-market entries introduced within past five years Percentage cost savings from new processes
• Profitability	$ profits Profit as percentage of sales Contribution margin* Return on investment (ROI) Return on net assets (RONA) Return on equity (ROE)
• Utilization of resources	Percent capacity utilization Fixed assets as percentage of sales
• Contribution to owners	Earnings per share Price/earnings ratio
• Contribution to customers	Price relative to competitors Product quality Customer satisfaction
• Contribution to employees	Wage rates, benefits Personnel development, promotions Employment stability, turnover
• Contribution to society	$ contributions to charities or community institutions Growth in employment

*Business-unit managers and marketing managers responsible for a product-market entry often have little control over costs associated with corporate overhead, such as the costs of corporate staff or R & D. It can be difficult to allocate those costs to specific strategic business units (SBUs) or products. Consequently, profit objectives at the SBU and product-market level are often stated as a desired *contribution margin* (the gross profit prior to allocating such overhead costs).

common performance dimensions and measures used in specifying such corporate, as well as business-unit and marketing, objectives.

Many firms have more than one objective, as the results of a study of the stated objectives of 82 large corporations clearly demonstrate. While the largest percentage of respondents (89 percent) had explicit profitability objectives, 82 percent reported growth objectives, 66 percent had specific market share goals, more than 60 percent mentioned social responsibility, employee welfare, and customer service objectives, and 54 percent of the companies had

R & D/new product development goals.[13] These percentages add up to much more than 100 percent, showing that most firms had several objectives.

In addition, while the most commonly reported corporate objective involved some aspect of profitability or return on investment, more than three-quarters of the respondents also had a growth or market share objective. Many firms thus face potential conflicts in trying to fulfill their objectives: the level of investment and expenditure required to aggressively pursue long-term growth may reduce short-term profitability.[14] Similar trade-offs can occur between social responsibility or employee welfare goals and short-term profit objectives. One way to reconcile such potentially conflicting goals is to rank them in a hierarchy, establishing priorities for action. Another approach is to state one of the conflicting goals as a constraint or hurdle. Thus, a firm might attempt to maximize growth subject to the constraint that ROI remain above a specified minimum level each year.

Business-unit and product-market objectives

Once broad corporate objectives have been set, they must be broken down into a consistent set of subobjectives for each of the businesses and product-markets in which the firm competes. In some cases, every business unit is expected to match the corporate objective. The 3M Company, for instance, expects each business division to meet the corporate goal of producing 30 percent of its sales volume from products introduced within the past four years as a means of stimulating innovation and growth. More commonly, however, the businesses and product-markets are assigned objectives that reflect differences in their competitive positions or the maturity of their markets. A business unit with large market shares in a number of mature product-markets, for example, might be given a lower sales growth objective but a higher profit goal than a unit with a weaker competitive position or more rapidly growing markets.

CORPORATE DEVELOPMENT STRATEGY

Often, the projected combined future sales and profits of a corporation's business units and product-markets fall short of the firm's long-run growth and profitability objectives. There is a gap between what the firm expects to become if it continues on its present course and what it would like to become. This is not surprising because some high-growth markets are likely to mature over time, and some high-profit, mature businesses may decline to insignificance as they get older. Thus, to answer the critical question Where is future growth coming from? management must choose a specific strategy to guide future corporate development.

Essentially, a firm can go in two major directions in seeking future growth: **expansion** of its current businesses and activities or **diversification** into new businesses through either internal business development or acquisition. Exhibit 2–5 outlines some specific options a firm might pursue in seeking growth via each of these directions.

---

[13]Y. K. Shetty, "New Look at Corporate Goals," *California Management Review*, Winter 1979, pp. 71–79.

[14] Gordon Donaldson, *Managing Corporate Wealth* (New York: Praeger, 1984).

EXHIBIT 2–5
Alternative Corporate Growth Strategies

	Current products	New products

Current markets	**Market penetration strategies**
	• Increase market share
	
	• Increase product usage
	  Increase frequency of use
	  Increase quantity used
	  New applications
		Product development strategies
		
		• Product improvements
		
		• Product-line extensions
		
		• New products for same market

New markets	**Market development strategies**
	• Expand markets for existing products
	  Geographic expansion
	  Target new segments
		Diversification strategies
		• Vertical integration
		  Forward integration
		  Backward integration
		
		• Diversification into related businesses (concentric diversification)
		
		• Diversification into unrelated businesses (conglomerate diversification)

Expansion

Market penetration.   One way current businesses expand is by increasing their share of existing markets. This typically involves making product or service improvements, cutting costs and prices, or outspending competitors on such things as advertising and consumer or trade promotions. For example, Compaq is pursuing a combination of such actions in its attempt to improve customer value and wrest the leading market share position in the U.S. PC market away from IBM.

A second approach to improving a business's penetration of existing markets encourages current customers to use more of the product, use it more often, or use it in new ways. Packages of Kellogg's Cracklin' Oat Bran cereal, for instance, include recipes such as bran muffins that use the cereal as an ingredient and a coupon good for 50 cents off the purchase of another box.

Product development.   Another way for businesses to grow is to develop product-line extensions or new product offerings aimed at existing customers. For example, Arm & Hammer successfully introduced a laundry detergent, an oven cleaner, and a carpet cleaner. Each capitalized on baking soda's image as an effective deodorizer and on a high level of recognition of the Arm & Hammer brand.

Market development.   Perhaps the growth strategy with the greatest potential for most companies is the development of new markets for their existing products or services, particularly through expansion into global markets. As we have seen, for example, much of Bausch & Lomb's recent and expected future growth centers on developing markets such as China and Poland. Similarly, General Electric has announced a growth strategy that will shift the firm's strategic center of gravity from the industrialized West to Asia and Latin America. GE expects much of its growth over the 1990s to come from three developing nations— India, China, and Mexico. The company predicts that revenues from those markets will double to $25 billion by the year 2000 and will account for about one-quarter of GE's total sales.[15]

Diversification

Firms also seek growth by diversifying their operations. This is typically riskier than the various expansion strategies because it involves learning new operations and dealing with unfamiliar customer groups. Nevertheless, the majority of Fortune 500 companies are diversified to one degree or another.

Vertical integration.   Vertical integration is one way for corporations to diversify their operations. **Forward integration** occurs when a firm moves downstream in terms of the product flow, as when a manufacturer integrates by acquiring a wholesaler or retail outlet. **Backward integration** occurs when a firm moves upstream by acquiring a supplier.

Integration gives a firm access to scarce or volatile sources of supply or tighter control over the marketing, distribution, and servicing of its products. But it increases the risks inherent in committing substantial resources to a single industry. Also, the investment necessary for firms to vertically integrate often offsets the additional profitability generated by those integrated operations, resulting in little improvement in return on investment.[16]

Related diversification.   Related (or concentric) diversification occurs when a firm internally develops or acquires another business that does not have products or customers in common with its current businesses but that might contribute to internal synergy through the sharing of production facilities, brand names, R & D know-how, or marketing and

---

[15]"GE's Brave New World," *Business Week*, November 8, 1993, pp. 64–70.

[16]Robert D. Buzzell, "Is Vertical Integration Profitable?" *Harvard Business Review*, January–February 1983, pp. 92–102; also see Robert D. Buzzell and Bradley T. Gale, *The PIMS Principles: Linking Strategy to Performance* (New York: The Free Press, 1987), ch. 8.

distribution skills. Thus, P & G decided to enter the packaged cookie business a few years ago to take advantage of the popularity of its Duncan Hines brand and its massive promotional resources.

Unrelated diversification.   The motivations for unrelated (or conglomerate) diversification are primarily financial rather than operational. By definition, an unrelated diversification involves two businesses that do not have any commonalities in terms of products, customers, production facilities, or functional areas of expertise. Such diversification is most likely to occur when a disproportionate number of a firm's current businesses face decline due to decreasing demand, increased competition, or product obsolescence; the firm must seek new avenues to provide future growth. Other more fortunate firms may move into unrelated businesses because they have more cash than they need to expand their current businesses or because they wish to discourage takeover attempts.

Unrelated diversification is the riskiest growth strategy. Consequently, one might expect conglomerate firms to have inferior financial performance compared to less diversified organizations. Indeed, most empirical studies conducted to date support the notion that related diversification is more conducive to capital productivity and other dimensions of performance.[17] However, some studies have reported contrary findings and suggest that the financial performance of diversified firms may be moderated by the particular industries they choose to diversify into. This suggests that a firm's future success is determined as much by the accuracy of management's analysis of the attractiveness of potential products and markets—and of the firm's competitive advantages in those markets—as it is by the specific growth strategy adopted.[18]

ALLOCATING CORPORATE RESOURCES

Diversified organizations have several potential advantages over more narrowly focused firms. They have a broader range of areas in which they can knowledgeably invest, and their growth and profitability rates may be more stable because they can offset declines in one business with gains in another. To exploit the advantages of diversification, though, corporate managers must make intelligent decisions about how to allocate financial and human resources across the firm's various businesses and product-markets. Two sets of analytical tools have proven especially useful in making such decisions: **portfolio models** and **value-based planning**.

Portfolio models

One of the most significant developments in strategic management during the 1970s and 1980s was the development and widespread adoption of portfolio models to help managers

---

[17] For example, see P. Rajan Varadarajan, "Product Diversity and Firm Performance: An Empirical Investigation," *Journal of Marketing* 50, January 1986, pp. 43–57.

[18] For a more detailed review of the evidence concerning the effects of diversification on firm performance, see Roger A. Kerin, Vijay Mahajan, and P. Rajan Varadarajan, *Contemporary Perspectives on Strategic Market Planning* (Boston: Allyn and Bacon, 1990), ch. 6.

allocate corporate resources across multiple businesses. These models enable managers to classify and review their current and prospective SBUs by viewing them as a portfolio of investment opportunities and then evaluating each business's competitive strength and the attractiveness of the markets it serves.

The Boston Consulting Group's (BCG) growth-share matrix

One of the first, and best known, portfolio models is the growth-share matrix developed by the Boston Consulting Group (BCG). It analyzes the impact of investing resources in different business units on the corporation's future earnings and cash flows. Each business is positioned within a matrix, as shown in Exhibit 2–6. The vertical axis indicates the industry's growth rate, and the horizontal axis shows the business unit's market share relative to its largest competitor.

The growth-share matrix assumes that a firm must generate sufficient cash from businesses with strong competitive positions in mature markets to fund the investments necessary to build the market shares of other businesses in more rapidly growing industries that represent attractive future opportunities. Thus, the **market growth rate** shown on the vertical axis is a proxy measure for the maturity and attractiveness of an industry. This model views businesses in relatively rapidly growing industries as more attractive investment opportunities for future growth and profitability. In Exhibit 2–6 an annual market growth rate of 10 percent is the

EXHIBIT 2–6

BCG's Market Growth Relative Share Matrix

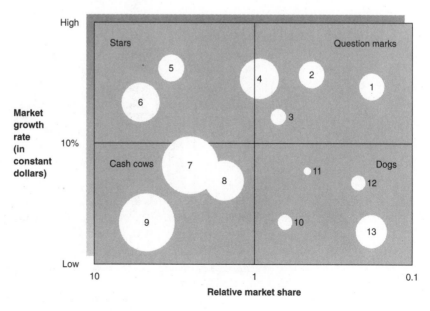

Source: Adapted from Barry Hedley, "Strategy and the Business Portfolio," *Long Range Planning* 10 (February 1977).

cutoff level between fast- and slow-growing industries. This dividing line can vary, however, depending on a corporation's objectives and available opportunities.

Similarly, a business's **relative market share** is a proxy for its competitive strength within its industry. It is computed by dividing the business's absolute market share in dollars or units by that of the leading competitor in the industry. Thus, in Exhibit 2–6 a business unit is in a strong competitive position if its share is equal to, or larger than, that of the next leading competitor (i.e., a relative share of 1.0 or larger). But it is competitively weak if the leading competitor holds a larger share of the market. Finally, in the exhibit, the size of the circle representing each business unit is proportional to that unit's sales volume. Thus, businesses 7 and 9 are the largest-volume businesses in this hypothetical company, while business 11 is the smallest.

Resource allocation and strategy implications

Each of the four cells in the growth-share matrix represents a different type of business with different strategy and resource requirements. The implications of each are discussed here and summarized graphically in Exhibit 2–7.

- *Question marks.* Businesses in high-growth industries with low relative market shares (those in the upper-right quadrant of Exhibit 2–7) are called *question marks* or *problem children.* Such businesses require large amounts of cash, not only for expansion to keep up with the rapidly growing market but also for marketing activities (or reduced margins) to build market share and catch the industry leader. If management can successfully increase the share of a question mark business, it becomes a star. But

E X H I B I T   2 – 7
Cash Flows across Businesses in the BCG Portfolio Model

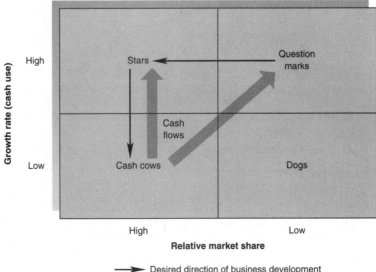

→ Desired direction of business development

if they fail, it eventually turns into a dog as the industry matures and the market growth rate slows. When this happens it can be difficult for the firm to recoup its past investments in the business. The strategic implication, then, is that management must be careful in selecting which question marks to invest in for future growth. Without sufficient resources and a competitive advantage it can exploit to successfully overtake the market leader, the firm is best advised to divest or harvest the business before its resources are drained.

- *Stars.* A *star* is the market leader in a high-growth industry. Stars are critical to the continued future success of the firm. As their industries mature, they move into the bottom-left quadrant and become cash cows. Paradoxically, while stars are critically important, they often are net users rather than suppliers of cash in the short run (as indicated by the possibility of a negative cash flow shown in Exhibit 2–7). This is because the firm must continue to invest in such businesses to keep up with rapid market growth and to support the R & D and marketing activities necessary to stave off competitors' attacks and maintain a leading market share. Indeed, share maintenance is crucial for star businesses to become cash cows rather than dogs as their industries mature.

- *Cash cows.* Businesses with a high relative share of low-growth markets are called *cash cows* because they are the primary generators of profits and cash in a corporation. Such businesses do not require much additional capital investment. Their markets are stable, and their share leadership position usually means they enjoy economies of scale and relatively high profit margins. Consequently, the corporation can use the cash from these businesses to support its question marks and stars (as shown in Exhibit 2–7). However, this does not mean the firm should necessarily maximize the business's short-term cash flow by cutting R & D and marketing expenditures to the bone—particularly not in industries where the business might continue to generate substantial future sales. When firms attempt to harvest too much cash from such businesses, they risk suffering a premature decline from cash cow to dog status, thus losing profits in the long term.

- *Dogs.* Low-share businesses in low-growth markets are called *dogs* because although they may throw off some cash, they typically generate low profits or losses. Divestiture is one option for such businesses, although it can be difficult to find an interested buyer. Another common strategy is to harvest dog businesses. This involves maximizing short-term cash flow by paring investments and expenditures until the business is gradually phased out. In some cases, though, an argument can be made for continuing to invest in a dog. Such a strategy may make sense, for instance, if the business can be focused on one or a few product-markets where it has some competitive strengths and additional profitable growth can be found.

Limitations of the growth-share matrix

Because the growth-share matrix uses only two variables as a basis for categorizing and analyzing a firm's businesses, it is relatively easy to understand. But while this simplicity helps explain its popularity, it also means that the model has limitations:

- *Market growth rate is an inadequate descriptor of overall industry attractiveness.* For one thing, market growth is not always directly related to profitability or cash flow. Some high-growth industries have never been very profitable because low entry barriers and capital intensity has enabled supply to grow even faster, resulting in intense price competition. Also, rapid growth in one year is no guarantee that growth will continue in the following year.

- *Relative market share is inadequate as a description of overall competitive strength.* It is based on the assumption that an experience curve resulting from a combination of scale economies and other efficiencies gained through learning and technological improvements over time leads to continuing reductions in unit costs as a business's relative market share increases. But a large market share within an industry does not always give a business a significant cost advantage—especially when the product is a low-value-added item, when different products within the business require different production or marketing activities, where different competitors have different capacity and utilization rates, or where some competitors are more vertically integrated or have lower-cost suppliers than others.[19]

  Also, market share is more properly viewed as an outcome of past efforts to formulate and implement effective business-level and marketing strategies rather than as an indicator of enduring competitive strength.[20] If the external environment changes, or the SBU's managers change their strategy, the business's relative market share can shift dramatically.

- *The outcomes of a growth-share analysis are highly sensitive to variations in how "growth" and "share" are measured.* Using information from 15 business units within a single firm, one study explored how their positions within a growth-share matrix would vary when different measures of growth and market share were used. The study used four measures of share and four of growth (both past and forecasted future growth). Only 3 of the 15 businesses ended up in the same quadrant of the matrix no matter what measures were used.[21]

  Another measurement problem has to do with how the industry and the SBU's "served market" (that is, the target market segments being pursued) should be defined. For example, Coke Classic holds about a 20 percent share of the U.S. soft drink market but less than 8 percent of the market for all liquid beverages. Given that consumers substitute other beverages, such as coffee, bottled water, and fruit juice, for soft drinks to varying degrees, which is the most appropriate market definition to use?

- *While the matrix specifies appropriate investment strategies for each business, it provides little guidance on how best to implement those strategies.* While the model suggests that a firm

---

[19]David B. Montgomery and George S. Day, "Experience Curves: Evidence, Empirical Issues and Applications," in *Strategic Marketing and Strategic Management*, eds. David Gardner and Howard Thomas (New York: John Wiley and Sons, 1984), pp. 213–38.

[20]Robert Jacobson argues that market share and profitability are joint outcomes from successful strategies and, further, that management skills likely have the greatest impact on profitability. See "Distinguishing among Competing Theories of the Market Share Effect," *Journal of Marketing* 52, October 1988, pp. 68–80.

[21]Yoram Wind, Vijay Mahajan, and Donald J. Swire, "An Empirical Comparison of Standardized Portfolio Models," *Journal of Marketing* 47, Spring 1983, pp. 89–99.

should invest cash in its question mark businesses, for instance, it does not consider whether there are any potential sources of competitive advantage that the business can exploit to successfully increase its share. Simply providing a business with more money does not guarantee that it will be able to improve its position within the matrix.

- *The model implicitly assumes that all business units are independent of one another except for the flow of cash.* If this assumption is not accurate, the model can suggest some inappropriate resource allocation decisions. For instance, if other SBUs depend on a dog business as a source of supply—or if they share functional activities, such as a common plant or salesforce, with that business—harvesting the dog might increase the costs or reduce the effectiveness of the other SBUs.

Alternative portfolio models

In view of these limitations, a number of firms have attempted to improve the basic portfolio model. Such improvements have focused primarily on developing more detailed, multifactor measures of industry attractiveness and a business's competitive strength and on making the analysis more future-oriented.

Multifactor portfolio models, typically referred to as *industry attractiveness–business position matrices* or *directional policy matrices*, rely on factors other than just market growth to judge the future attractiveness of different industries. Similarly, they use multiple variables in addition to relative market share to judge the competitive strength and position of each of their businesses.

Exhibit 2–8 shows some of the factors that managers might use to evaluate industry attractiveness and a business's competitive position. Corporate managers must first select factors most appropriate for their firm and weight them according to their relative importance. They then rate each business and its industry on the two sets of factors. Next they combine the weighted evaluations into summary measures used to place each business within one of the nine boxes in the matrix shown in Exhibit 2–8. Businesses falling into boxes numbered 1 (where both industry attractiveness and the business's ability to compete are relatively high) are good candidates for further investment for future growth. Businesses in the 2 boxes should receive only selective investment with an objective of maintaining current position. Finally, businesses in the 3 boxes are candidates for harvesting or divestiture.

These multifactor models are richer and more detailed than the simple growth-share model and consequently provide more strategic guidance concerning the appropriate allocation of resources across businesses. They are also more useful for evaluating potential new product-markets. However, the multifactor measures in these models can be subjective and ambiguous, especially when managers must evaluate different industries on the same set of factors. Also, the conclusions drawn from these models still depend on the way industries and product-markets are defined.[22]

Some firms also use portfolio analysis to evaluate how they should allocate resources across the different technologies (as opposed to particular businesses or products) in their asset base. A **technology portfolio matrix** typically categorizes different technologies according to

---

[22]For a more detailed discussion of the uses and limitations of multifactor portfolio models, see Kerin, Mahajan, and Varadarajan, *Contemporary Perspectives on Strategic Marketing Planning*, ch. 3.

EXHIBIT 2–8

The Industry Attractiveness–Business Position Matrix

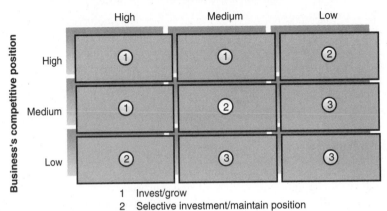

1 Invest/grow
2 Selective investment/maintain position
3 Harvest/divest

Variables that might be used to evaluate:

Business's competitive position		Industry attractiveness	
Size	Distribution	Size	Profitability
Growth	Technology	Growth	Technological
Relative share	Marketing skills	Competitive intensity	sophistication
Customer loyalty	Patents	Price levels	Government regulations
Margins			

whether the firm is, or will be, an industry leader or follower in the development of the technology, the amount of development needed to commercialize the technology, and the likely market potential for products based on the technology.[23] This form of portfolio analysis is particularly useful for high-tech firms or business units that have more potential new technologies and/or applications in the early stages of development than they have the resources to fully commercialize.

Value-based planning

As mentioned, one limitation of portfolio analysis is that it specifies how firms should allocate financial resources across their businesses without considering the competitive strategies those businesses are, or should be, pursuing. Portfolio analysis provides little

[23]Noel Capon and Rashi Glazer, "Marketing and Technology: A Strategic Coalignment," *Journal of Marketing* 51, July 1987, pp. 1–14.

guidance, for instance, in deciding which of two question mark businesses—each in attractive markets but following different strategies—is worthy of the greatest investment or in choosing which of several alternative competitive strategies a particular business unit should pursue.

Worse, because indicators of past market attractiveness and competitive strength do not always accurately predict the future financial returns a strategic investment will produce, relying on portfolio analysis as a tool for allocating resources across businesses or strategic marketing programs can lead to suboptimal outcomes. In one experiment involving managers from six different countries, for instance, 86 percent of those managers who used a portfolio matrix as a decision-making tool made suboptimal investments in a situation where future profits from two alternative strategic investments were negatively related to market growth and the firm's relative market share. In contrast, only 15 percent of those managers who based their decision on net present value analysis, or other profit-based calculations, made suboptimal decisions in the same situation.[24]

Value-based planning is a resource allocation tool that attempts to overcome the shortcomings and unanswered questions inherent in portfolio analysis by assessing the shareholder value a given strategy is likely to create. Thus, value-based planning provides a basis for comparing the economic returns to be gained from investing in different businesses pursuing different strategies or from alternative strategies that might be adopted by a given business unit.

A number of value-based planning methods are currently in use, but all share three basic features.[25] First, they assess the economic value a strategy is likely to produce by examining the cash flows it will generate rather than relying on distorted accounting measures such as return on investment.[26] Second, they estimate the shareholder value that a strategy will produce by discounting its forecasted cash flows by the business's risk-adjusted cost of capital. Finally, they evaluate strategies based on the likelihood that the investment required by a strategy will deliver returns greater than the cost of capital. The amount of return a strategy or operating program generates in excess of the cost of capital involved is commonly referred to as its **economic value added** or EVA.[27] This approach to evaluating alternative strategies is particularly appropriate for use in allocating resources across business units because most capital investments are made at the business unit level, and different business units typically face different risks and therefore have different costs of capital.

---

[24]J. Scott Armstrong and Roderick J. Brodie, "Effects of Portfolio Planning Methods on Decision-Making: Experimental Results," *International Journal of Research in Marketing* 11, 1994, pp. 73–84.

[25]Two of the most commonly used approaches to value-based planning are the market-to-book ratio model and the discounted cash flow model. The market-to-book ratio model is described in William W. Alberts and James M. McTaggart, "Value-Based Strategic Investment Planning," *Interfaces* 14, January–February 1984, pp. 138–51. The discounted cash flow model, which is the approach focused on in this chapter, is detailed in Alfred Rappaport, *Creating Shareholder Value: The New Standard for Business Performance*.

[26]For a detailed discussion of the shortcomings of accounting data for evaluating the value created by a strategy, see Alfred Rappaport, *Creating Shareholder Value: The New Standard for Business Performance*, ch. 2.

[27]Shawn Tully, "The Real Key to Creating Wealth," *Fortune*, September 30, 1993, pp. 38–50; and Tully, "America's Best Wealth Creators."

Discounted cash flow model

Perhaps the best known and most widely used approach to value-based planning is the discounted cash flow model proposed by Alfred Rappaport and the Alcar Group, Inc. In this model, as Exhibit 2–9 indicates, shareholder value created by a strategy is determined by the cash flow it generates, the business's cost of capital (which is used to discount future cash flows back to their present value), and the market value of the debt assigned to the business. The future cash flows generated by the strategy are, in turn, affected by six factors or "value drivers." They are the rate of sales growth the strategy will produce, the operating profit margin, the income tax rate, investment in working capital, fixed capital investment required by the strategy, and the duration of value growth.

The first five value drivers are self-explanatory, but the sixth requires some elaboration. The duration of value growth represents management's estimate of the number of years over which the strategy can be expected to produce rates of return that exceed the cost of capital. This estimate, in turn, is tied to two other management judgments. First the manager must decide on the length of the planning period (typically three to five years); he or she must then estimate the residual value the strategy will continue to produce after the planning period is

EXHIBIT 2–9

Factors Affecting the Creation of Shareholder Value

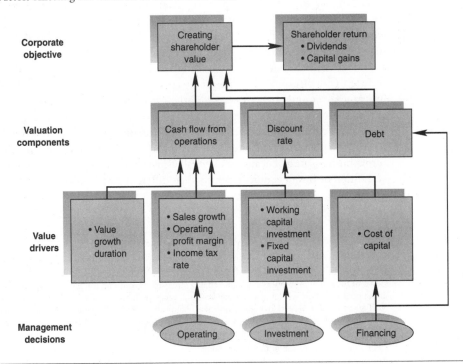

SOURCE: Reprinted with the permission of The Free Press, an imprint of Simon & Schuster Inc., from *CREATING SHARE-HOLDER VALUE* by Alfred Rappaport. Copyright © 1986 by Alfred Rappaport.

over. Such decisions are tricky, for they involve predictions of what will happen in the relatively distant future. Unfortunately, managers must wrestle with several such thorny estimation problems when implementing value-based planning. A detailed discussion of the procedure involved and the kinds of forecasts and predictions a manager must make in using discounted cash flow analysis to evaluate a business strategy appears in this chapter's appendix.

Some limitations of value-based planning[28]

Value-based planning is not a substitute for strategic planning; it is only one tool for evaluating strategy alternatives identified and developed through managers' judgments. It does so by relying on forecasts of many kinds to put a financial value on the hopes, fears, and expectations managers associate with each alternative. Projections of cash inflows rest on forecasts of sales volume, product mix, unit prices, and competitors' actions. Expected cash outflows depend on projections of various cost elements, working capital, and investment requirements.

While good forecasts are notoriously difficult to make, they are critical to the validity of value-based planning. Once someone attaches numbers to judgments about what is likely to happen, people tend to endow those numbers with the concreteness of hard facts. Therefore, the numbers derived from value-based planning can sometimes take on a life of their own, and managers can lose sight of the assumptions underlying them.

Consequently, inaccurate forecasts can create problems in implementing value-based planning. For one thing, there are natural human tendencies to overvalue the financial projections associated with some strategy alternatives and to undervalue others. For instance, managers are likely to overestimate the future returns from a currently successful strategy. Evidence of past success tends to carry more weight than qualitative assessments of future threats. Managers may pay too little attention to how competitive behavior, prices, and returns might change if, for example, the industry were suddenly beset by a slowdown in market growth and the appearance of excess capacity.

On the other hand, some kinds of strategy alternatives are consistently undervalued. Particularly worrisome from a marketing viewpoint is the tendency to underestimate the value of keeping current customers. Putting a figure on the damage to a firm's competitive advantage from *not* making a strategic investment necessary to maintain the status quo is harder than documenting potential cost savings or profit improvements that an investment might generate. For example, a few years ago Cone Drive Operations, a small manufacturer of heavy-duty gears, faced a number of related problems. Profits were declining, inventory costs were climbing, and customers were unhappy because deliveries were often late. Cone's management thought that a $2 million computer-integrated manufacturing system might help solve these problems; but a discounted cash flow analysis indicated the system would be an unwise investment. Because the company had only $26 million in sales, it was hard to justify the $2 million investment in terms of cost savings. However, the financial analysis underestimated

---

[28] This section summarizes points made in more detail in George S. Day and Liam Fahey, "Putting Strategy into Shareholder Value Analysis." Also see Alfred Rappaport, "CFOs and Strategists: Forging a Common Framework," *Harvard Business Review*, May–June 1992, pp. 84–91.

intangibles like improved product quality, faster order processing, and improved customer satisfaction. Management decided to install the new system anyway, and new business and nonlabor savings paid back the investment in just one year. More important, Cone retained nearly all of its old customers, many of whom had been seriously considering switching to other suppliers.

Finally, another kind of problem involved in implementing value-based planning occurs when management fails to consider all the appropriate strategy alternatives. Since it is only an analytical tool, value-based planning can evaluate alternatives, but it cannot create them. The best strategy will never emerge from the evaluation process if management fails to identify it.

To realize its full benefits, management must link value-based planning to sound strategic analysis that is rigorous enough to avoid the problems associated with undervaluing certain strategies, overvaluing others, and failing to consider all the options. As Day and Fahey argue:

> Managers must fully consider the competitive context of cash flows and ensure that cash flow projections are directly tied to competitive analysis projections. They must question whether the cash outflows contribute to competitive advantage and to what extent cash inflows are dependent on those advantages. Specifically, they should broaden the range of strategy alternatives, challenge the inherent soundness of each alternative, and test the sensitivity of each alternative to changes in cash inflows and outflows.[29]

In spite of its limitations, when value-based planning is used correctly as an integral part of the broader strategic planning process it can be a useful tool for evaluating, and deciding how to allocate resources among, alternative strategies. An example of a successful application of value-based planning at the Coca-Cola Company is discussed in Exhibit 2–10.

EXHIBIT 2–10

A Strategic Application of Value-Based Planning at the Coca-Cola Company

The Coca-Cola Company uses value-based planning to help make decisions both about what businesses to acquire or divest and about the relative attractiveness of alternative strategies within each of its businesses. An example of the usefulness of the approach is provided by Coke's recent experience within its soda fountain business. The firm had long considered this business to be very profitable because there were no bottles or cans to fill, transport, or store. But a discounted cash flow analysis revealed that the business was actually destroying shareholder value. Over time, the business had become quite capital intensive. As a result, the business's return on capital was only 12.6 percent, while its cost of capital was estimated to be 16 percent.

The main culprit turned out to be the expensive, five-gallon, stainless steel containers used to transport the Coke syrup to retail outlets. Therefore, the business changed its distribution and packaging policies. It adopted cheaper, disposable bag-in-a-box containers and sent larger 50-gallon drums to its bigger customers. By thus reducing its investment in containers, the business's return on capital rose to 17 percent. At the same time, by increasing its financial leverage, Coke reduced its cost of capital to 14 percent. Thus, the soda fountain business was turned into a strong contributor to shareholder value.

SOURCE: Bernard C. Reimann, "Managing for the Shareholders: An Overview of Value-Based Planning," *Planning Review*, January–February 1988, pp. 10–22.

---

[29]George S. Day and Liam Fahey, "Putting Strategy into Shareholder Value Analysis," pp. 160–61.

SOURCES OF SYNERGY

A final strategic concern at the corporate level is to increase synergy across the firm's various businesses and product-markets. As mentioned, synergy exists when two or more businesses or product-markets, and their resources and competencies, complement and reinforce one another so that the total performance of the related businesses is greater than it would be otherwise.

Some potential synergies at the corporate level are knowledge-based. The performance of one business can be enhanced by the transfer of competencies, knowledge, or customer-related intangibles—such as brand-name recognition and reputation—from other units within the firm. For instance, the technical knowledge concerning image processing and the quality reputation that Canon developed in the camera business helped ease the firm's entry into the office copier business.

In part, such knowledge-based synergies are a function of the corporation's scope and mission—or how its managers answer the question, What businesses should we be in? When a firm's portfolio of businesses and product-markets reflects a common mission based on well-defined customer needs, market segments, or technologies, the company is more likely to develop core competencies, customer knowledge, and strong brand franchises that can be shared across businesses. However, the firm's organization structure and allocation of resources may also enhance knowledge-based synergy. A centralized corporate R & D department, for example, is often more efficient and effective at discovering new technologies with potential applications across multiple businesses than if each business unit bore the burden of funding its own R & D efforts. Similarly, some experts argue that strong corporate-level coordination and support is necessary to maximize the strength of a firm's brand franchise, and to glean full benefit from accumulated market knowledge, when the firm is competing in global markets.[30]

A second potential source of corporate synergy is inherent in sharing operational resources, facilities, and functions across business units. For instance, two or more businesses might produce products in a common plant or use a single salesforce to contact common customers. When such sharing helps increase economies of scale or experience-curve effects, it can improve the efficiency of each of the businesses involved. However, the sharing of operational facilities and functions may not produce positive synergies for all business units. Such sharing can limit a business's flexibility and reduce its ability to adapt quickly to changing market conditions and opportunities. Thus, a business whose competitive strategy is focused on new-product development and the pursuit of rapidly changing markets may be hindered more than helped when it is forced to share operating resources with other units[31] For instance, when Frito-Lay attempted to enter the packaged cookie market with its Grandma's line of soft cookies, the company relied on its 10,000 salty-snack route salespeople to distribute the new line to grocery stores. The firm thought its huge and well-established snack salesforce would

---

[30] Gary Hamel and C. K. Prahalad, "Strategic Intent," p. 74.

[31] Robert W. Ruekert and Orville C. Walker, Jr., *Shared Marketing Programs and the Performance of Different Business Strategies*, Report #91-100 (Cambridge, Mass.: The Marketing Science Institute, 1991).

give its cookies a competitive advantage in gaining shelf space and retailer support. But because those salespeople were paid a commission on their total sales revenue, they were reluctant to take time from their salty-snack products to push the new cookies. The resulting lack of a strong sales effort contributed to Grandma's failure to achieve a sustainable market share.

As we shall see in the next chapter, the type of competitive strategy a business unit chooses to pursue can have a number of implications for corporate-level decisions concerning organizational structure and resource allocation as well as for the marketing strategies and programs employed within the business.

SUMMARY

Decisions about the organization's scope or mission, its overall goals and objectives, avenues for future growth, resource deployments, and potential sources of synergy across business units are the primary components of corporate strategy.

A mission statement provides guidance to an organization's managers about which market opportunities to pursue and which fall outside the firm's strategic domain. Similarly, a statement of strategic intent establishes a long-term direction for the firm and motivates employee effort; but it is flexible in giving employees substantial freedom to decide what means are best for achieving the firm's purpose.

Formal objectives guide a firm's businesses and employees toward specific dimensions and levels of performance by establishing benchmarks against which performance can be compared and evaluated. Increasing shareholder value is the ultimate objective for publicly held companies. But difficulties in determining whether specific actions will create such value lead most firms to set specific objectives for performance outcomes such as sales volume, market share, and return on investment.

The corporate development strategy addresses the question of where the firm's future growth will come from. A company might seek growth either by expanding its current businesses or by diversifying into new businesses.

A firm should allocate its resources across its various businesses to reflect both the relative competitive strength of each business and variations in the attractiveness and growth potential of the markets they serve. Portfolio models help managers make these allocation decisions. Value-based planning is another useful resource allocation tool. It attempts to evaluate potential investments in a firm's businesses, and in the alternative strategies each business might pursue, on the basis of how much value those investments will produce for the firm's shareholders over time.

Finally, corporate synergy can be gained by developing competencies, knowledge, and customer-based intangibles, such as brand-name recognition and reputation, that can be shared across multiple businesses within the company. Similarly, synergy might be sought through the sharing of operational resources and functions, such as a common plant or salesforce, across businesses. Caution is necessary, however, because sharing operational facilities and activities can reduce a business's flexibility and hinder its ability to respond quickly to changing market conditions.

APPENDIX: VALUE-BASED PLANNING PROCEDURES

This appendix briefly details the procedure involved in using a discounted cash flow analysis to evaluate a particular business strategy. The steps in this procedure are outlined in Exhibit A–1. Those interested in a more detailed discussion of the procedure and its rationale may wish to consult one of the books on the subject.[32]

The process begins with a forecast of the annual operating cash flows the strategy will produce over the course of the planning period. These consist of cash inflows [(sales) × (operating profit margin) × (1 − income tax rate)], plus depreciation, minus cash outflows [(incremental fixed capital investment) + (incremental working capital)]. Next the analyst must calculate a risk-adjusted cost of capital for the business, weighted to reflect the proportion of debt and equity capital. In step 3, the forecasted annual cash flows are discounted back to the initial time period and summed to arrive at their present value. Step 4 requires the analyst to estimate the residual value of the strategy at the end of the planning period, which is then discounted back to its present value. Next the total present value of the strategy is calculated by adding the present values of future cash flows and the residual value and subtracting the market value of debt assigned to the business, if any. The sixth step involves estimation of the business's initial or prestrategy shareholder value, which is the current value of the business assuming no additional value will be created by any prospective investments or strategy changes. Finally, the shareholder value creation potential of the strategy can be calculated by subtracting the prestrategy value of the business estimated in step 6 from the total present value determined in step 5.

A simple illustration of discounted cash flow analysis applied to the evaluation of a business strategy is shown in Exhibit A–2. In this example, provided by Bernard Reimann,[33] the following assumptions are made:

- Sales growth remains constant at 10 percent per year.
- Gross margins and selling, general, and administrative expenses remain constant at 25 percent and 10 percent, respectively.
- Asset turnover remains constant.
- The risk-adjusted cost of capital (discount rate) is 15 percent.
- Aftertax earnings in the initial period are equivalent to cash flow because no incremental investment exists.
- The business unit has no assignable debt.

Note that the strategy examined in Exhibit A–2 is estimated to have a total present value (that is, the present value of annual cash flows during the five-year planning period plus its residual value) of $56.98 million. Its prestrategy value—assumed to be the cash flow in the current year divided by the discount rate—is $50 million. Thus, the strategy has the potential

---

[32]For example, see Alfred Rappaport, *Creating Shareholder Value: The New Standard for Business Performance.*

[33]Bernard C. Reimann, "Stock Price and Business Success: What Is the Relationship?" *Journal of Business Strategy* Spring 1987, pp. 38–49.

EXHIBIT A–1

Procedure for Conducting a Discounted Cash Flow Analysis of a Proposed Business Strategy

	Step	Elaboration

Step 1:	Forecast annual operating cash flows for the strategy during the planning period.	A_i = net after-tax cash flow in year i
		   = cash inflow
		      [(sales) × (operating profit margin) ×
		      (1 − income tax rate)]
		   − depreciation
		   + cash outflow
		      [(incremental fixed capital investment) +
		      (incremental working capital investment)]

Step 2:	Calculate a risk-adjusted cost of capital for the business.	Cost of capital should be weighted to reflect the proportion of debt and equity capital.

Step 3:	Discount the forecasted cash flows back to their present value (PV_a).	$$PV_a = \sum_{i=1}^{i} \frac{Ai}{(1+R)^i}$$ where
		   t = planning period in years
		   Ai = net after-tax cash flow in year i
		   R = risk-adjusted cost of capital

Step 4:	Estimate the residual value at the end of the planning period and discount it back to the present (PV_b).	Residual value $(PV_b) = \dfrac{\text{Perpetuity cash flow}}{\text{Cost of capital}}$
Step 5:	Compute the total present value of the strategy by summing the present values of future cash flows and the residual value.	Total present value = $PV_a + PV_b$
Step 6:	Calculate the prestrategy shareholder value of the business.	Prestrategy value = $\dfrac{\text{Current cash flow before new investment}}{\text{Cost of capital}}$ − Market value of assignable debt
Step 7:	Compute the strategy's value creation potential.	Strategy's value creation potential = Total present value − Prestrategy value

for creating an additional $6.98 million in shareholder value if adopted. The strategy is therefore worth the investment from a shareholder value point of view, assuming other strategy alternatives available to the business unit wouldn't create even more value.

Estimation problems

This rather bland examination of the steps involved in a discounted cash flow analysis downplays some difficult judgment calls and produces hard numbers that may carry an unwarranted aura of precision. Three variables are especially difficult for managers to

EXHIBIT A-2

An Example of the Use of Discounted Cash Flow Analysis to Evaluate a Business-Unit Strategy

	Current values 1995	Income statement projections					Residual value 2000+
		1996	1997	1998	1999	2000	
Sales*	$100.00	110.00	121.00	133.10	146.41	161.05	161.05
Gross margin (= 25%)	25.00	27.50	30.25	33.28	36.60	40.26	40.26
S. & G. A. (= 10%)	10.00	11.00	12.10	13.31	14.64	16.11	15.11
Profit before tax	$ 15.00	16.50	18.15	19.97	21.96	24.16	24.16
Income tax	7.50	8.25	9.08	9.98	10.98	12.08	12.08
Net profit	$ 7.50	8.25	9.08	9.98	10.98	12.08	12.08

Statement of financial position (year-end)

	Current values 1995	1996	1997	1998	1999	2000	Residual value 2000+
Net working capital	10.00	11.00	12.10	13.31	14.64	16.11	16.11
Depreciable assets	30.00	33.00	36.30	39.93	43.92	48.32	48.32
Assets employed	$ 40.00	44.00	48.40	53.24	58.56	64.42	64.42
Return on assets	18.8 %	18.8 %	18.8 %	18.8 %	18.8 %	18.8 %	18.8 %

Cash flow statement

	Current values 1995	1996	1997	1998	1999	2000	Residual value 2000+
Net earnings	7.50	8.25	9.08	9.98	10.98	12.08	12.08
Depreciation	7.00	3.00	3.30	3.63	3.99	4.39	4.39
Capital expenditures		6.00	6.60	7.26	7.99	8.78	4.39
Increase in working capital		1.00	1.10	1.21	1.33	1.46	0.00
Cash flow		$ 4.25	4.68	5.14	5.66	6.22	12.08
PV factor (at 15% discount)		0.87	0.76	0.66	0.57	0.50	3.31†
Present value of cash flow		3.70	3.53	3.38	3.23	3.09	40.04
Total present value	$ 56.98	(Annual cash flows + residual value)					
Current (preplan) value	50.00	(Year 0 net operating earnings/discount rate)					
Net present value	$ 6.98	= Shareholder value contribution					

*Sales growth: 10%

†"Perpetuity" assumption: PV factor/discount rate = 50/.15

Source: Adapted from Bernard C. Reimann, "Stock Price and Business Success: What Is the Relationship?" *Journal of Business Strategy*, Summer 1987, p. 44.

estimate and may be subject to dubious assumptions: the cost of capital, the residual value of the strategy, and the prestrategy or initial value of the business.[34]

The cost of capital

The rate used for discounting the cash flow stream of a strategy should be the weighted average costs of debt and equity capital. This rate may differ considerably across businesses within the same corporation because of differences in their risk exposure and amount of debt needed to finance their assets.

The cost of debt capital is relatively easy to estimate. It is the rate the parent company would have to pay for new debt given its capital structure. To determine the cost of equity capital, however, the analyst must estimate three components that reflect the minimum return expected by shareholders: (1) a "real" interest rate, or their compensation for making a risk-free investment, (2) further compensation for expected inflation, and (3) a risk premium to offset the possibility that actual results will fall short of expectations. The risk premium is the most difficult to estimate. In theory, it should be correlated with stock price movements. But this is not practical with business units because they have no publicly traded stock. Therefore, analysts have to resort to indirect estimation methods such as examining the stock price movements of surrogate publicly traded firms. Because good surrogates are hard to find, risk is often gauged judgmentally by looking at the variability of the business's past earnings, the size of differences between its projected and actual earnings, and the susceptibility of its future earnings to environmental changes.

Residual value

The question of how much residual value will be created after the planning period is crucial because the residual is often the largest portion of the total present value of a strategy. For instance, a study of 620 businesses found that more than 30 percent were net cash users during an entire five-year planning period. On the other hand, the study also confirmed the propensity of American managers for near-term results, as more than half the businesses had positive cash flows during the planning period at the expense of a reduction in total shareholder value.[35]

The amount of residual value depends on the length of the planning period the analyst has chosen, the strategy being considered, and assumptions about the competitive situation that will exist at the end of the planning period. The planning period should be long enough to enable the strategy to be implemented and to observe its results in the market. But if the strategy involves building a business's position by increasing its investment in R & D and launching new products, for instance, even a relatively long planning period may encompass

---

[34]The following discussion summarizes material found in George S. Day, *Market-Driven Strategy: Processes for Creating Value* (New York: The Free Press, 1990), Chap. 13.

[35]Robert D. Buzzell and Bradley T. Gale, *The PIMS Principles: Linking Strategy to Performance.*

nothing but negative or negligible cash flows. Virtually all the value generated by such a strategy is likely to come from exploiting the business's enhanced market share position after the planning period ends. On the other hand, a harvest strategy might generate significant cash flows over a short planning period at the expense of an eroded residual value at the end of the period.

No matter what the length of a planning period, most managers agree that beyond the end of it the future is too murky to forecast. So how can they generate an estimate of a strategy's residual value? Perhaps the most popular method—and the one employed in the example in Exhibit A–2—is the **perpetuity approach**. Its rationale is the assumption that any business able to generate returns greater than the cost of capital will attract competition. Eventually, the entry of competitors will drive profits down to the minimum acceptable level—a level equal to the cost of capital. Thus, by the end of the planning period, the business will be earning only the cost of capital on an average new investment. Once the rate of return has fallen to this level, period-to-period differences in cash flows do not alter the value of the business. Thus, these future cash flows can be treated as though they were a perpetuity, or an infinite stream of identical cash flows. Because the present value of any financial perpetuity is the annual cash flow divided by the cost of capital, it follows that:

$$\text{Residual value} = \frac{\text{Perpetuity cash flow}}{\text{Cost of capital}}$$

One reason for the popularity of the perpetuity method is its simplifying assumption that any cash flows from investments made after the planning period can be ignored because they will not change the value of the business. However, the method also assumes that the annual cash flows will be maintained at the same level they reached at the end of the planning period. This assumption is worrisome because it ignores differences across businesses in the sustainability of size or access advantages that are the basis for superior performance.

Prestrategy value

A business's prestrategy value is the benchmark for determining whether proposed strategies will further enhance shareholder value over what would otherwise be produced. Once again, the perpetuity approach is a popular method for estimating a business's prestrategy value. It assumes that if the business were to stay with its current strategy, no additional value would be created through prospective new investments. This assumption allows the annual cash flows of the current strategy to be treated as a financial perpetuity, in which case the prestrategy value of the business is the cash flow from the most recent period divided by the cost of capital.

While the perpetuity assumption is convenient and makes estimation of prestrategy value more tractable, it does not fit well with reality. Even if a business does not change its current strategy, it is still likely to adjust to changes in the market and competitive situation by making investments necessary to maintain its position as the market evolves. Some of these investments, such as adding plant capacity to keep up with growing demand, may further increase shareholder value. Consequently, a more realistic alternative to the perpetuity approach for estimating prestrategy value might be to forecast the financial outcomes of the current strategy after taking into account likely adjustments for anticipated trends in market demand and competitive actions. Unfortunately, introducing strategic and environmental considerations into the baseline forecast of value creation opens up even more possibilities for subjectivity and bias.

Business Strategies and Their Marketing Implications

BUSINESS STRATEGIES AND MARKETING PROGRAMS AT 3M[1]

The Minnesota Mining and Manufacturing Company, better known as 3M, began manufacturing sandpaper nearly a century ago. Today it is the leader in over 100 technical areas from fluorochemistry to optical recording. The firm makes more than 60,000 different products that generated $14 billion in global sales and a 20 percent return on investment in 1993. Recent trends in the firm's sales, earnings, and R & D expenditures are shown in Exhibit 3–1.

As you might expect of a firm with so many products, 3M is organized into a large number of strategic business units (SBUs). The company contains 47 such SBUs organized into three sectors: the Industrial and Consumer Sector, making such things as industrial tapes, abrasives, adhesives, and consumer products like

Post-it brand repositionable notes and Scotch brand Magic Transparent Tape; the Information, Imaging, and Electronic Sector, concerned with the areas of commercial graphics, audiovisuals, magnetic media, and imaging systems; and the Life Sciences Sector, consisting of such diverse businesses as pharmaceuticals, medical equipment, and reflective highway materials, all designed to enhance health and safety.

While 3M has acquired many smaller firms over the years, its growth strategy has focused primarily on internal new product development, emphasizing both improved products for existing customers and new products for new markets. Indeed, one of the formal objectives assigned to every business unit is to obtain at least 30 percent of annual sales from products

[1]Material for this example was drawn from The 3M Company *1993 Annual Report* (St. Paul, Minn.: The 3M Company, 1994); and Shawn Tully, "Why to Go for Stretch Targets," *Fortune*, November 14, 1994, pp. 145–58.

introduced within the last four years. The company supports its growth strategy with an R & D budget of more than $1 billion, nearly 7½ percent of total revenues.

3M also pursues growth by aggressively developing foreign markets for its many products. Indeed, a fourth organizational sector is responsible for coordinating the firm's marketing efforts across countries, and, as Exhibit 3–1 indicates, revenue obtained from global markets accounts for half the firm's income.

Differences in customer needs, technologies, and product life-cycle stages across industries, however, lead 3M's various business units to pursue their growth objectives in different ways. The Industrial Tape group, for example, operates in an industry where both the product technologies and the customer segments are relatively mature and stable. Growth in this group results from extending the scope of adhesive technology (for example, attaching weather stripping to auto doors), product improvements and line extensions targeted at existing customers, and expansion into global markets.

In contrast, the firm's Medical Products unit develops new medical applications for emerging technologies developed in 3M's many R & D labs. The unit sells a broad range of innovative medical devices, such as blood gas monitors and an electric bone stapler. Most of the unit's growth, therefore, comes from developing totally new products aimed at new markets.

The competitive strategies of 3M's various business units also differ. For instance, the Industrial Tape unit is primarily concerned with maintaining its commanding market share in existing markets while preserving or even improving its profitability. Its competitive strategy is to differentiate itself from competitors on the basis of product quality and excellent customer service.

On the other hand, the Medical Products unit's strategy is to avoid head-to-head competitive battles by being the technological leader in the industry and introducing a constant stream of unique products. To be successful, though, the unit must devote substantial resources to R & D and to the stimulation of primary demand. Thus, its main objective is volume growth, and it must sometimes sacrifice short-run profitability to fund the product development and marketing efforts needed to accomplish that goal.

These differences in competitive strategy, in turn, influence the strategic marketing programs within the various business units. For instance, the firm spends little on advertising or sales promotion for its mature industrial tape products. However, it does maintain a large, well-trained technical salesforce that provides valuable problem-solving assistance and other services to customers and gives informed feedback to the firm's R & D personnel about potential new applications and product improvements.

In contrast, the pioneering nature of many of the Medical Products Group's products and services calls for more extensive promotion programs to develop customer awareness and stimulate primary demand. Consequently, the unit devotes a relatively large portion of its revenues to advertising in technical journals aimed at physicians and other medical professionals. It also supports a well-trained salesforce, but those salespeople spend much of their time demonstrating new products and prospecting for new accounts in addition to servicing existing customers. Finally, the unit conducts substantial marketing research to test new product concepts and forecast their demand potential.

EXHIBIT 3-1

Recent Trends in 3M's Sales, Earnings, and R & D Expenditures

	Net sales ($)			Net income ($)			R&D ($)	
	Total	United States	Int'l	Total	Dividends	Retained earnings	Total	Percent of sales
1993	$14,020	50%	50%	$1,260	57%	43%	$1,030	7.3%
1992	13,883	50	50	1,230	57	43	1,007	7.3
1991	13,340	51	49	1,150	59	41	914	6.8
1990	13,021	51	49	1,308	49	51	865	6.6
1989	11,990	54	46	1,244	46	54	784	6.5
1988	11,323	55	45	1,154	42	58	721	6.4

NOTE: All dollars are in millions.

THE CONCEPT OF STRATEGIC FIT

The situation at 3M again illustrates that firms with multiple businesses usually have a hierarchy of strategies extending from the corporate level down to the individual product-market entry. As we saw in the last chapter, corporate strategy addresses such issues as the firm's mission and scope and the directions it will pursue for future growth. Thus, 3M's corporate growth strategy focuses primarily on developing new products and new applications for emerging technologies.

The major strategic question addressed at the business-unit level is How should we compete in this business? For instance, 3M's Industrial Tape unit attempts to maintain its commanding market share and high profitability by differentiating itself on the basis of high quality and good customer service. On the other hand, the Medical Products unit seeks high growth via aggressive new product and market development.

Finally, the strategic marketing program for each product-market entry within a business unit attempts to allocate marketing resources and activities in a manner appropriate for accomplishing the business unit's objectives. Thus, most of the strategic marketing programs within 3M's Medical Products SBU involve relatively large expenditures for marketing research and introductory advertising and promotion campaigns aimed at achieving sales growth.

One key reason for 3M's continuing success is that all three levels of strategy within the company have usually been characterized by good internal and external consistency, or **strategic fit**. 3M's managers have done a good job of monitoring and adapting their strategies to the market opportunities, technological advances, and competitive threats in the company's external environment. The firm's marketing and sales managers play critical roles both in developing market-oriented strategies for individual products and in influencing and helping to formulate corporate and business-level strategies that are responsive to environmental conditions. At the same time, those strategies are usually internally compatible. Each strategy fits with those at other levels as well as with the unique competitive strengths and competencies of the relevant business unit and the company as a whole.[2]

These interdependencies among strategies—particularly those at the business and product-market levels—are the major focus of the rest of this chapter. First we briefly examine the strategic decisions that must be made at the business level, paying particular attention to a number of generic competitive strategies a business unit might choose to pursue and the environmental circumstances in which each type is most appropriate. We then examine the implications those strategies have for the marketing activities and programs that are most appropriate for businesses pursuing each type.

STRATEGIC DECISIONS AT THE BUSINESS-UNIT LEVEL

When a firm is involved in multiple businesses, it is typically organized in separate components responsible for each business. While these organizational components go by many different names, they are most commonly called **strategic business units** or **SBUs.** Managers of each unit must decide what objectives and strategies to pursue within their specific business, subject to the approval of corporate management.

The first step in developing business-level strategies, then, is for the firm to decide how to divide itself into SBUs. The managers of each business unit then must make recommendations about the SBU's objectives and scope, how resources should be allocated across its product-market entries and functional departments, and which competitive strategy to pursue to build a sustainable advantage in its product-markets.

Defining strategic business units

Ideally, a strategic business unit should be designed to incorporate a unique set of products aimed at a homogeneous set of markets. It should also have responsibility for its own performance and control over the resources that affect that performance.

As Exhibit 3–2 indicates, there is a rationale for each of these desired business-unit characteristics. But as might be expected, firms do not always meet all of these ideals when designing their SBUs. There are usually trade-offs between having many small homogeneous business units versus fewer, but larger and more diverse, SBUs that top management can more easily supervise.

---

[2]For a more detailed discussion of the concept of strategic fit and the role of various external and internal variables in influencing the effectiveness of a firm's strategies, see N. Venkatraman and James Camillus, "The Concept of 'Fit' in Strategic Management," *Academy of Management Review* 9, 1984, pp. 513–25.

EXHIBIT 3-2
Characteristics of the Ideal Strategic Business Unit

Characteristic	Rationale
• Serves a homogeneous set of markets with a limited number of related technologies	Minimizing the diversity of a business unit's product-market entries enables the unit's manager to do a better job of formulating and implementing a coherent and internally consistent business strategy.
• Serves a unique set of product-markets	No other SBU within the firm should compete for the same set of customers with similar products. This enables the firm to avoid duplication of effort and helps maximize economies of scale within its SBUs.
• Has control over the factors necessary for successful performance, such as R & D, production, marketing, and distribution	This is not to say that an SBU should never share resources, such as a manufacturing plant or a salesforce, with one or more business units; but the SBU should have authority to determine how its share of the joint resource will be used to effectively carry out its strategy.
• Has responsibility for its own profitability	Because top management cannot keep an eye on every decision and action taken by all its SBUs, the success of an SBU and its managers must be judged by monitoring its performance over time. Thus, the SBU's managers should have control over the factors that affect performance and then be held accountable for the outcomes.

The crucial question, then, is, What criteria should be used to cluster product-markets into a business unit? The three dimensions suggested earlier as criteria for defining the scope and mission of the entire corporation can also serve as the basis for defining individual SBUs:

- *Technical compatibility*, particularly with respect to product technologies and operational requirements, such as the use of similar production facilities and engineering skills.
- Similarity in the *customer needs* to be satisfied or the product benefits sought by customers in the target markets.
- Similarity in the *personal characteristics* or behavior patterns of customers in the target markets.

In practice, it is often not possible to meet all three criteria. Instead, the choice is often between technical/operational compatibility and customer homogeneity. Management commonly defines SBUs on the basis of technical and operational interdependence, clustering product-market entries that require similar technologies, production facilities, and employee skills to minimize the coordination problems involved in administering the unit. In some firms, however, the marketing synergies gained from coordinating technically different products aimed at the same customer need or market segment outweigh operational considerations. In these firms, managers group product-market entries into SBUs based on similarities across customers or distribution systems. For instance, 3M's Medical Products unit includes a wide range of products involving very different technologies and production processes. They are grouped within the same business unit, though, because they all address health needs, they are marketed to physicians and other health professionals, and they can be sold through a common salesforce and distribution system.

Business-unit objectives

Companies break down corporate objectives into subobjectives for each SBU. In most cases, those subobjectives vary across SBUs according to the attractiveness of their industries, the strength of their competitive positions within those industries, and resource allocation decisions by corporate management. For example, managers may assign an SBU in a rapidly growing industry relatively high volume and share-growth objectives but lower ROI objectives than an SBU with a large share in a mature industry.

A similar process of breaking down overall SBU objectives into a set of subobjectives should occur for each product-market entry within the unit. Those subobjectives obviously must reflect the SBU's overall objectives; but once again they may vary across product-market entries according to the attractiveness and growth potential of individual market segments and the competitive strengths of the company's product in each market. For example, when 3M's consumer products group first introduced its Scotch-Brite Never Rust soap pads—a new form of scouring pad that will never rust or splinter because it is made from recycled plastic beverage bottles—its objective was to capture a major share of the $100 million soap pad market from well-entrenched competitive brands like SOS and Brillo. 3M wanted to maximize Never Rust's volume growth and market share even if the new line did not break even for several years. Consequently, the firm's top managers approved a major investment in a new plant and a substantial introductory advertising budget. At the same time, though, the consumer group maintained high profitability goals for its other established products—like Scotch brand Magic Transparent Tape and Post-it brand notes—to provide the cash required for Never Rust's introduction and preserve the group's overall profit level.[3]

Allocating resources within the business unit

Once an SBU's objectives and budget have been approved at the corporate level, its managers must decide how the available resources should be allocated across the unit's various product-market entries. Because this allocation process is quite similar to allocating corporate resources across SBUs, many firms use similar economic value, value-based planning, or

---

[3] Tully, "Why to Go for Stretch Targets," p. 150.

portfolio analysis tools for both.[4] Of course, at the SBU level managers must determine the attractiveness of individual target markets, the competitive position of their products within those markets, and the cash flows each product entry will likely generate rather than analyzing industry attractiveness and the overall competitive strengths of the firm.

Unfortunately, value-based planning is not as useful a tool for evaluating alternative resource allocations across product-market entries as it is for evaluating allocations across SBUs. This is because the product-market entries within a business unit often share the benefits of common investments and the costs of functional activities, as when multiple products are produced in the same plant or sold by the same salesforce. The difficulty of deciding what portion of such common investments and shared costs should be assigned to specific products increases the difficulty of applying a discounted cash flow analysis at the product-market level.

The business unit's competitive strategy

The essential question to be answered in formulating a business strategy is, How will the business unit compete to gain a sustainable competitive advantage within its industry? Achieving a competitive advantage requires a business unit to make two choices:

- What is the SBU's *competitive domain or scope*? What market segments should it target, and what customer needs will the unit attempt to satisfy? This decision provides guidelines for the desired breadth and complexity of the unit's product line and a foundation for the formulation of marketing strategies for each product-market entry.
- How will the business unit *distinguish itself from competitors* in its target market(s)? What distinctive competencies can it rely on to achieve a unique position relative to its competitors?

Even though a business unit may contain a number of different product-market entries, most analysts argue that the unit should pursue the same overall source of competitive advantage in all of them. In this way the SBU can take full advantage of its particular strengths and downplay its weaknesses. As Porter argues in his book on competitive advantage,

> If a [business] is to attain a competitive advantage, it must make a choice about the type of competitive advantage it seeks to attain and the scope within which it will attain it. Being "all things to all people" is a recipe for strategic mediocrity and below-average performance, because it often means that a [business] has no competitive advantage at all.[5]

Porter argues that a business might seek a competitive advantage on two broad dimensions: It can try to be the low-cost producer within its target markets, or it can differentiate itself from the competition through its product offerings or marketing programs. It might

---

[4]Phillipe Haspeslagh, "Portfolio Planning: Uses and Limits," *Harvard Business Review* (January–February 1982), pp. 59–73; and Shawn Tully, "The Real Key to Creating Wealth," *Fortune*, September 30, 1993, pp. 38–50.

[5]Michael E. Porter, *Competitive Advantage: Creating and Sustaining Superior Performance* (New York: The Free Press, 1985), p. 12.

EXHIBIT 3–3

Porter's Four Business Strategies

Source of competitive advantage

	Low cost	Differentiation
Broad target	Cost leadership	Differentiation
Narrow target	Cost focus	Differentiation focus

(Competitive scope)

SOURCE: Adapted with permission of The Free Press, an imprint of Simon & Schuster Inc., from *Competitive Advantage: Creating and Sustaining Superior Performance* by Michael E. Porter. Copyright © 1985 by Michael E. Porter.

achieve differentiation, for example, by offering a higher-quality or more technically advanced product, more extensive promotion, broader distribution, or better customer service. Indeed, some businesses attempt to differentiate their various product offerings on multiple dimensions by developing an entire set of competencies.

For instance, Compaq attempts to market PCs that offer lower prices, superior customer service, and more user-friendly features than competing machines. This multidimensional approach to developing a differentiated competitive strategy is sometimes labeled with the buzzwords "total quality management".[6]

Also, a business unit's strategic scope might be defined either broadly or narrowly. That is, it might pursue a wide range of market segments within its industry or focus on only one or a few target segments. As Exhibit 3–3 indicates, then, Porter suggests that there are four basic or "generic" competitive strategies that a business unit might adopt: (1) **cost leadership** across a broad range of product market entries, (2) cost leadership focusing on a narrow group of target segments, (3) **differentiation** across a wide variety of segments, or (4) more narrowly focused differentiation.

---

[6]Frank Rose, "Now Quality Means Service Too," *Fortune*, April 22, 1991, pp. 97–111; and Rahul Jacob, "Beyond Quality and Value," *Fortune*, Special Issue, Autumn–Winter 1993, pp. 8–11.

EXHIBIT 3-4

Summary Definitions of Miles and Snow's Four Business Strategies

Prospector
- Operates within a broad product-market domain that undergoes periodic redefinition.
- Values being a "first mover" in new product and market areas, even if not all of these efforts prove to be highly profitable.
- Responds rapidly to early signals concerning areas of opportunity, and these responses often lead to new rounds of competitive actions.
- Competes primarily by stimulating and meeting new market opportunities, but may not maintain strength over time in all markets it enters.

Defender
- Attempts to locate and maintain a secure position in relatively stable product or service areas.
- Offers relatively limited range of products or services compared to competitors.
- Tries to protect its domain by offering lower prices, higher quality, or better service than competitors.
- Usually not at the forefront of technological/new product development in its industry; tends to ignore industry changes not directly related to its area of operation.

Analyzer
- An intermediate type; makes fewer and slower product-market changes than prospectors but is less committed to stability and efficiency than defenders.
- Attempts to maintain a stable, limited line of products or services, but carefully follows a selected set of promising new developments in its industry.
- Seldom a first mover, but often a second or third entrant in product-markets related to its existing market base — often with a lower cost or higher-quality product or service offering.

Reactor
- Lacks any well-defined competitive strategy.
- Does not have as consistent a product-market orientation as its competitors.
- Not as willing to assume the risks of new product or market development as its competitors.
- Not as aggressive in marketing established products as some competitors.
- Responds primarily when it is forced to by environmental pressures.

SOURCE: Adapted from R. E. Miles and C. C. Snow, *Organizational Strategy, Structure, and Process* (New York: McGraw-Hill, 1978).

Of course, there are other dimensions besides low cost, high quality, or superior service on which a business unit may try to gain a competitive advantage. For example, Miles and Snow have identified another set of business strategies based on a business's intended rate of product-market development (new product development, penetration of new markets, and so on).[7] They classify business units into four strategic types: **prospectors, analyzers, defenders,** and **reactors**. Exhibit 3–4 describes each of these business strategies briefly. As indicated, businesses pursuing a prospector strategy focus on growth through the development of new products and markets. 3M's Medical Products business unit provides a good

---

[7]Robert E. Miles and Charles C. Snow, *Organizational Strategy, Structure, and Process* (New York: McGraw-Hill, 1978).

EXHIBIT 3–5

Combined Typology of Business-Unit Competitive Strategies

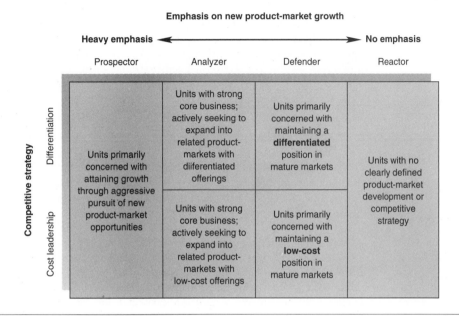

example of this. Defender businesses concentrate on maintaining their positions in established product-markets while paying less attention to new-product development, as is the case with 3M's Industrial Tape business unit. The analyzer strategy falls in between these two. An analyzer business attempts to maintain a strong position in its core product-market(s) but also seeks to expand into new, but usually closely related, product-markets. Finally, reactors are businesses with no clearly defined strategy.

Even though both the Porter and the Miles and Snow typologies have received popular acceptance and research support, neither is complete by itself. For example, a defender business unit might pursue either of Porter's sources of competitive advantage—a low-cost position or differentiation—to protect its market position. Thus, we have combined the two typologies in Exhibit 3–5 to provide a more comprehensive overview of possible business strategies. The exhibit classifies business strategies on two primary dimensions: the unit's desired rate of product-market development and the unit's intended method of competing in its established product-markets.[8]

Of course, each strategy in Exhibit 3–5 could be further subdivided according to whether a business applies the strategy across a broadly defined product-market domain or concentrates on a narrowly defined segment where it hopes to avoid direct confrontation with major competitors (in other words, the focus strategy of Porter). While this is a useful distinction to make, it is more relevant to a discussion of the business's choice of a target-market strategy (as examined in Chapter 6) than to its competitive strategy. Most businesses compete in a consistent way (at least in terms of basic dimensions) across all of their product-markets, whether their domain is broad or narrow.

Note too that Exhibit 3–5 describes only six different business strategies rather than the eight that one might expect. One reason for this is that we view reactor and prospector businesses as two homogeneous categories.

Evidence suggests that a substantial number of business fall into the reactor category. One study, for instance, found that 50 out of 232 businesses examined could be classified as reactors.[9] However, these businesses do not have well-defined or consistent approaches either to new product or market development or to ways of competing in their existing product-markets. As a manager of Sheldahl, Inc.—a firm that designs and manufactures flexible circuit boards and other components for the electronics and defense industries—complained in a discussion with one of the authors,

> Our division is a reactor in the sense that we are constantly changing directions and getting into new areas in response to actions taken by our competitors or special requests from large customers. We are like a job-shop; we take on new projects without ever asking whether there will be a viable future market for what we are doing. Consequently, neither our volume growth nor our profitability has been as good as it should have been in recent years.

The first action managers should take to improve the performance of reactors is to develop and implement a clearly defined and coherent competitive strategy—one that corresponds to one of the other generic strategies outlined in Exhibit 3–5. But because most reactors have no consistent competitive strategy, they typically underperform all other strategic types on growth and profitability dimensions.[10] Therefore, we largely ignore reactors in the remainder of this discussion.

Prospectors are also discussed as a single strategic category because the desire for rapid new product or market development is the overriding aspect of their strategy. There is little need for a prospector to consider how it will compete in the various new product-markets it develops. It usually faces little or no competition in those markets—at least not until those markets become established and other firms begin to enter. In 3M's Medical Products SBU, for example, most marketing programs are aimed at generating awareness and stimulating primary demand instead of offering low prices or finding ways to differentiate products because they are unchallenged by any competitors.

---

[9]Charles C. Snow and Lawrence G. Hrebiniak, "Strategy, Distinctive Competence and Organizational Performance," *Administrative Science Quarterly* 25 (1980), pp. 317–35.

[10]Jeffrey S. Conant, Michael P. Mokwa, and P. Rajan Varadarajan, "Strategic Types, Distinctive Marketing Competencies, and Organizational Performance: A Multiple Measures-Based Study," *Strategic Management Journal* 11 (1990), pp. 365–83.

THE UNDERLYING DIMENSIONS OF
ALTERNATIVE BUSINESS STRATEGIES

In Chapter 2 we said that all strategies consist of five components or underlying dimensions: scope (or the breadth of the strategic domain); goals and objectives; resource deployments; a basis for achieving a sustainable competitive advantage; and synergy. The generic business strategies outlined in Exhibit 3–5 are defined largely on the basis of their differences on only one of these dimensions: the nature of the competitive advantage sought. However, each strategy also involves some important differences on the other four dimensions. Those underlying differences provide some useful insights about the conditions under which each strategy is most appropriate and about the relative importance of different functional activities, particularly marketing actions, in implementing them effectively.

Differences in scope

Both the breadth and the stability of a business's domain are likely to vary with different strategies. This, in turn, can affect the variables the corporation uses to define its various businesses. At one extreme, defender businesses, whether low cost or differentiated, tend to operate in relatively well-defined, narrow, and stable domains where both the product technology and the customer segments are mature. A company can define and group related product-market entries into such business units on the basis of the three criteria discussed earlier: technical compatibility, the customer need to be satisfied, and similarity of customer characteristics and behavior patterns. For example, Pillsbury's Prepared Dough Products business unit is a differentiated defender consisting of several product-market entries, such as Hungry Jack Biscuits and Crescent Rolls. All the products in the SBU hold a commanding share of their product category, appeal to traditional households who want fresh-baked breadstuffs, and are based on the same dough-in-a-can technology. Consequently, the SBU is largely self-contained with respect to production facilities, marketing, and distribution.

At the other extreme, prospector businesses usually operate in broad and rapidly changing domains where neither the technology nor customer segments are well established. The scope of such businesses often undergoes periodic redefinition. Also, it is usually impossible to organize such units according to all three of the preceding criteria. Thus, prospector businesses are typically organized around either a core technology that might lead to the development of products aimed at a broad range of customer segments or a basic customer need that might be met with products based on different technologies. The latter is the approach taken by 3M's Medical Products SBU. Its mission is to satisfy the health needs of a broad range of patients with new products and services developed from technologies drawn from other business units within the firm. For example, it has developed a variety of innovative drug delivery systems using aerosols, adhesives, and other 3M technologies.

Analyzer businesses, whether low cost or differentiated, fall somewhere in between the two extremes. They usually have a well-established core business to defend, and often their domain is primarily focused on that business. However, businesses pursuing this intermediate strategy are often in industries that are still growing or experiencing technological changes. Consequently, they must pay attention to the emergence of new customer segments and/or new product types. As a result, managers must review and adjust the domain of such businesses from time to time.

Differences in goals and objectives

Another important difference across generic business-level strategies with particular relevance for the design and implementation of appropriate marketing programs is that different strategies often focus on different objectives. SBU and product-market objectives might be specified on a variety of criteria; but to keep things simple, we focus on only three performance dimensions of major importance to both business-unit and marketing managers:

1. *Effectiveness*—the success of a business's products and programs relative to those of its competitors in the market. Effectiveness is commonly measured by such items as sales growth relative to competitors or changes in market share.

2. *Efficiency*—the outcomes of a business's programs relative to the resources used in implementing them. Common measures of efficiency are profitability as a percentage of sales, and return on investment.

3. *Adaptability*—the business's success in responding over time to changing conditions and opportunities in the environment. Adaptability can be measured in a variety of ways, but the most common ones are the number of successful new products introduced relative to competitors, or the percentage of sales accounted for by products introduced within the last five years.

However, it is very difficult for any SBU, regardless of its competitive strategy, to simultaneously achieve outstanding performance on even this limited number of dimensions because they involve substantial trade-offs. Good performance on one dimension often means sacrificing performance on another.[11] For example, developing successful new products or attaining share growth often involves large marketing budgets, substantial up-front investment, high operating costs, and a shaving of profit margins—all of which reduce ROI. This suggests that managers should choose a competitive strategy with a view toward maximizing performance on one or two dimensions while expecting to sacrifice some level of performance on the others, at least in the short term. Over the longer term, of course, the chosen strategy should promise discounted cash flows that exceed the business's cost of capital and thereby increase shareholder value.

As Exhibit 3–6 indicates, prospector businesses are expected to outperform defenders on both new product development and market share growth. For instance, the Life Sciences sector of 3M, which includes a large proportion of prospector businesses, produced revenue growth of more than 50 percent from 1987 through 1993, and more than 40 percent of that

---

[11]Gordon Donaldson, *Managing Corporate Wealth* (New York: Praeger, 1984).

EXHIBIT 3–6

How Business Strategies Differ in Scope, Objectives, Resource Deployments, and Synergy

Dimensions	Low-cost defender	Differentiated defender	Prospector	Analyzer
• Scope	Mature/stable/well-defined domain; mature technology and customer segments	Mature/stable/well-defined domain; mature technology and customer segments	Broad/dynamic domains; technology and customer segments not well established	Mixture of defender and prospector strategies
• Goals and objectives Adaptability (new product success)	Very little	Little	Extensive	Mixture of defender and prospector strategies
Effectiveness (increase in market share)	Little	Little	Large	Mixture of defender and prospector strategies
Efficiency (ROI)	High	High	Low	Mixture of defender and prospector strategies
• Resource deployment	Generate excess cash (cash cows)	Generate excess cash (cash cows)	Need cash for product development (question marks or stars)	Need cash for product development but less so than prospectors
• Synergy	Need to seek operating synergies to achieve efficiencies	Need to seek operating synergies to achieve efficiencies	Danger in sharing operating facilities and programs — better to share technology/marketing skills	Danger in sharing operating facilities and programs — better to share technology/marketing skills

revenue was generated by new products. In contrast, 3M's total revenues grew only about 35 percent during the same period.

On the other hand, both defender strategies should lead to better returns on investment. Differentiated defenders likely produce higher returns than low-cost defenders, assuming that the greater expenses involved in maintaining their differentiated positions can be more than offset by the higher margins gained by avoiding the intense price competition low-cost competitors often face. Once again, both low-cost and differentiated analyzer strategies likely fall between the two extremes.

The validity of the expected performance differences outlined in Exhibit 3–6 is supported by some empirical evidence. One study found that businesses pursuing defender strategies significantly outperformed prospector businesses on return on investment and cash flow on investment regardless of the type of environment they faced, while prospectors generated significantly greater rates of market share growth—particularly in innovative or rapidly growing markets.[12] Similarly, a more recent study found that both prospectors and analyzers outperformed defenders on market share growth and return on equity in markets experiencing steady growth. Surprisingly, though, the same study found that defenders outperformed all other strategies on both efficiency and effectiveness dimensions in highly volatile markets.[13] This unexpected finding might be attributable to the episodic periods of both growth and contraction that volatile markets experience. Thus, while aggressive prospector and analyzer businesses may outperform the more conservative defenders during growth periods, they may also suffer greater volume and financial losses during periods of market decline.

Differences in resource deployments

Businesses following different strategies also tend to allocate their financial resources differently across product-markets, functional departments, and activities within each functional area. Prospector—and to a lesser degree, analyzer—businesses devote a relatively large proportion of resources to the development of new product-markets. Because such product-markets usually require more cash to develop than they produce in the short term, businesses pursuing these strategies often need infusions of financial resources from other parts of the corporation. In portfolio terms, they are "question marks" or "stars."

Defenders, on the other hand, focus the bulk of their resources on preserving existing positions in established product-markets. These product-markets are usually profitable; therefore, defender businesses typically generate excess cash to support product and market development efforts in other business units within the firm. They are the "cash cows."

Resource allocations among functional departments and activities within the SBU also vary across businesses pursuing different strategies. For instance, marketing budgets tend to be the largest as a percentage of an SBU's revenues when the business is pursuing a prospector strategy; they tend to be the smallest as a percentage of sales under a low-cost defender strategy. We discuss this in more detail later in this chapter.

Differences in sources of synergy

Because different strategies emphasize different methods of competition and different functional activities, a given source of synergy may be more appropriate for some strategies than for others.

At one extreme, sharing operating facilities and programs may be an inappropriate approach to gaining synergy for businesses following a prospector strategy. And to a lesser extent this may also be true for both types of analyzer strategies. Such sharing can reduce an SBU's ability to adapt quickly to changing market demands or competitive threats. Commitments to internally

---

[12]Donald C. Hambrick, "Some Tests of the Effectiveness and Functional Attributes of Miles and Snow's Strategic Types," *Academy of Management Journal* 26 (1983), pp. 5–26.

[13]Daryl O. McKee, P. Rajan Varadarajan, and William M. Pride, "Strategic Adaptability and Firm Performance: A Market-Contingent Perspective," *Journal of Marketing*, July 1989, pp. 21–35.

negotiated price structures and materials, as well as the use of joint resources, facilities, and programs, increase interdependence among SBUs and limit their flexibility. Because prospector and analyzer businesses seek growth through new product and market development, a lack of flexibility makes it difficult for them to successfully implement their chosen strategy. It is more appropriate for such businesses to seek synergy through the sharing of technology, engineering skills, or market knowledge—expertise that can help improve the success rate of their product development efforts. Thus, 3M's Medical Products SBU attempts to find medical applications for new technologies developed in many of the firm's other business units.

At the other extreme, however, low-cost defenders should seek operating synergies that will make them more efficient. Synergies that enable such businesses to increase economies of scale and experience curve effects are particularly desirable. They help reduce unit costs and strengthen the strategy's basis of competitive advantage. The primary means of gaining such operating synergies is through the sharing of resources, facilities, and functional activities across product-market entries within the business unit or across related business units. Emerson Electric, for instance, has formed an "operating group" of several otherwise autonomous business units that make different types of electrical tools. By sharing production facilities, marketing activities, and a common salesforce, the group has been able to reduce per-unit production and marketing costs.

THE FIT BETWEEN BUSINESS STRATEGIES AND THE EXTERNAL ENVIRONMENT

Because different strategies pursue different objectives in different domains with different competitive approaches, they do not all work equally well under the same environmental circumstances. The question is, Which environmental situations are most amenable to the successful pursuit of each type of strategy? Exhibit 3–7 briefly outlines some of the major market, technological, and competitive conditions—plus a business unit's strengths relative to its competitors—that are most favorable for the successful implementation of each generic business strategy. We next discuss the reasons why each strategy fits best with a particular set of environmental conditions.

Appropriate conditions for a prospector strategy

A prospector strategy is particularly well suited to unstable, rapidly changing environments resulting from new technology, shifting customer needs, or both. In either case, such industries tend to be at an early stage in their life cycles and offer many opportunities for new product-market entries. Industry structure is often unstable because few competitors are present and their relative market shares can shift rapidly as new products are introduced and new markets develop. Prospector strategies are common in industries where new applications and customer acceptance of existing technologies are still developing (such as the personal computer, computer software, and information technologies industries) and in industries with rapid technological change (such as biotechnology, medical care, and aerospace).

EXHIBIT 3–7

Environmental Factors Favorable to Different Business Strategies

External factors	Prospector	Analyzer	Differentiated defender	Low-cost defender
Market characteristics	Industry in introductory or early growth stage of life cycle, many potential customer segments as yet unidentified and/or undeveloped.	Industry in late growth or early maturity stage of life cycle, one or more product offerings currently targeted at major customer segments, but some potential segments may still be undeveloped.	Industry in maturity or decline stage of life cycle; current offerings targeted at all major segments; sales primarily due to repeat purchases/replacement demand.	Industry in maturity or decline stage of life cycle; current offerings targeted at all major segments, sales primarily due to repeat purchases/replacement demand.
Technology	Newly emerging technology; many applications as yet undeveloped.	Basic technology well developed but still evolving; product modifications and improvements—as well as emergence of new competing technologies—still likely.	Basic technology fully developed and stable; few major modifications or improvements likely.	Basic technology fully developed and stable; few major modifications or improvements likely.
Competition	Few established competitors; industry structure still emerging; single competitor holds commanding share of major market segments.	Large number of competitors, but future shakeout likely; industry structure still evolving; one or more competitors hold large shares in major segments but continuing growth may allow rapid changes in relative shares.	Small to moderate number of well-established competitors; industry structure stable, though acquisitions and consolidation possible; maturity of markets means relative shares of competitors tend to be reasonably stable over time.	Small to moderate number of well-established competitors; industry structure stable, though acquisitions and consolidation possible; maturity of markets means relative shares of competitors tend to be reasonably stable over time.
Business's relative strengths	SBU (or parent) has strong R & D, product engineering, and marketing research and marketing capabilities.	SBU (or parent) has good R & D, product engineering and marketing research capabilities, but not as strong as some competitors; has either low-cost position or strong sales, marketing, distribution, or service capabilities in one or more segments.	SBU has no outstanding strengths in R & D or product engineering; costs are higher than at least some competitors; SBU's outstanding strengths are in process engineering and quality control and/or in marketing, sales, distribution, or customer services.	SBU (or parent) has superior sources of supply and/or process engineering and production capabilities that enable it to be low-cost producer; R & D, product engineering, marketing, sales, or service capabilities may not be as strong as some competitors.

Because they emphasize the development of new products and/or new markets, the most successful prospectors are usually strong in and devote substantial resources to two broad areas of competence: (1) R & D, product engineering, and other functional areas that identify new technology and convert it into innovative products; and (2) marketing research, marketing, and sales—functions that identify and develop new market opportunities.

In addition, successful prospector SBUs usually have a higher degree of decision-making and operational autonomy. Such businesses can react quickly to new technological developments and market needs. Illinois Tool Works (ITW)—a manufacturer of a variety of tools and components—is a good example of a firm that gives substantial autonomy to its prospector business units.[14] For a description of how ITW's organizational structure and policies facilitate the success of those units, see Exhibit 3–8.

In some cases, however, even though a prospector business has strong product development and marketing skills, it may lack the resources to maintain its early lead as product-markets grow and attract new competitors. For example, Minnetonka was the pioneer in several health and beauty-aid product categories with brands like Softsoap liquid soap and Check-Up plaque-fighting toothpaste. However, because competitors like Procter & Gamble and Colgate-Palmolive introduced competing brands with advertising and promotion

EXHIBIT 3–8

Illinois Tool Works — Organizational Structure and Policies Favorable to the Performance of Prospector Businesses

Unglamorous and low-profile, ITW manufactures a diverse array of items that are typically attached to, embedded in, or swathed around somebody else's goods. It makes nails, screws, bolts, strapping, wrapping, valves, capacitors, filters, and adhesives — as well as the tools and machines to apply them.

ITW is not a firm where senior managers hog power, build empires, or bark orders. The company has 90 SBUs or divisions loosely organized into nine groups. The largest, the $420-million-a-year construction products group, has only three central administrators — a president, a controller, and a shared secretary.

While many of ITW's SBUs are defender businesses with well-established products in mature markets, a surprising number are newly developed prospector businesses. Part of the reason for this is that when engineers and marketers in an existing division develop and commercialize a highly successful new product, it is often split off to form a new business unit. This is how a unit known as Nexus came into being. A researcher in an established division invented a durable, safety-rated plastic buckle for a customer who makes life jackets. Six years later, Nexus — along with its licensees — sold $45 million of the buckles for backpacks, bicycle helmets, and pet collars.

ITW's prospector divisions are typically small, with less than $30 million in annual revenues. Most seek out, and often dominate, market niches where there are no established competitors. And to ensure their continued autonomy and flexibility, each division's chief is given control over the unit's R & D, manufacturing, and marketing operations.

SOURCE: Based on material found in Ronald Henkoff, "The Ultimate Nuts & Bolts Co.," *Fortune*, July 16, 1990, pp. 70–73. *Fortune*, © 1989 The Time Inc. Magazine Company. All rights reserved.

---

[14]Ronald Henkoff, "The Ultimate Nuts & Bolts Co.," *Fortune*, July 16, 1990, pp. 70–73.

budgets much larger than Minnetonka could match, the firm was eventually forced to change its strategy and concentrate on manufacturing products under licenses from larger firms.

Appropriate conditions for an analyzer strategy

The analyzer strategy is a hybrid. On one hand, analyzers are concerned with defending (via low costs or differentiation in quality or service) a strong share position in one or more established product-markets. At the same time, the business must pay attention to new product development in order to avoid being leapfrogged by competitors with more technologically advanced products or being left behind in newly developing application segments within the market. This dual focus makes the analyzer strategy appropriate for well-developed industries that are still experiencing some amount of growth and change due to evolving customer needs and desires or continuing technological improvements.

Commercial aircraft manufacturing is an example of such an industry. Both competitors and potential customers are few and well established. But technology continues to improve, the increased competition among airlines since deregulation has changed the attributes those firms look for when buying new planes, and mergers have increased the buying power of some customers. Thus, Boeing's commercial aircraft division has had to work harder to maintain a 50 percent share of worldwide commercial plane sales. Although the firm continues to enjoy a reputation for producing high-quality and reliable planes, it had to make price concessions and increase customer services during the late 1980s and early 1990s to stave off threats from competitors like the European Airbus consortium. At the same time, Boeing's commercial aircraft division had to engage in a $4–5 billion development effort aimed at producing the next generation of aircraft.

Boeing's experience illustrates one problem with an analyzer strategy. Few businesses have the resources and competencies needed to successfully defend an established core business while generating new products at the same time. Success on both dimensions requires strengths across virtually every functional area, and few businesses (or their parent companies) have such universal strengths relative to competitors. Therefore, analyzers are often not as innovative in new product development as prospectors. And they may not be as profitable in defending their core businesses as defenders.

Appropriate conditions for a defender strategy

A defender strategy makes sense only when a business has something worth defending. It is most appropriate for units with a profitable share of one or more major segments in a relatively mature, stable industry. A defender may initiate some product improvements or line extensions to protect and strengthen its position in existing segments; but it devotes relatively few resources to basic R & D or the development of innovative new products. Thus, a defender strategy works best in industries where the basic technology is not very complex or where it is well developed and unlikely to change dramatically over the short run. Pillsbury's Prepared Dough Products SBU, for instance, has introduced a number of line extensions over the years; but as noted earlier, most have been reconfigurations of the same basic dough-in-a-can technology, such as Soft Breadsticks.

Differentiated defenders

To effectively defend its position by differentiation, a business must be strong in those functional areas critical for maintaining its particular competitive advantage over time. If a business's differentiation is based on superior product quality, those key functional areas include production, process engineering, quality control, and perhaps product engineering to develop product improvements. Interestingly, successful differentiation of its offerings on the quality dimension has a strong impact on a business's return on investment—a critical performance objective for defenders. The positive correlation between quality and ROI holds true even after allowing for the effects of market share and investment intensity. As Exhibit 3–9 shows, the pretax return on investment is higher in all businesses for firms selling above-average- and highest-quality products than for firms selling average- or below-average-quality offerings.

Regardless of the basis for differentiation, marketing is also important for the effective implementation of a differentiated defender strategy. Marketing activities that track changing customer needs and competitive actions and communicate the product offering's unique advantages through promotional and sales efforts to maintain customer awareness and loyalty are particularly important.

Low-cost defenders

Successful implementation of a low-cost defender strategy requires the business to be more efficient than its competitors.[15] Thus, the business must establish the groundwork for such a strategy early in the growth stage of the industry. Achieving and maintaining the lowest per-unit cost usually means that the business has to seek large volume from the beginning—through some combination of low prices and promotional efforts—to gain economies of scale and experience. At the same time, such businesses must also invest in more plant capacity to anticipate future growth and in state-of-the-art equipment to minimize production costs. This combination of low margins and heavy investment can be prohibitive unless the parent corporation can commit substantial resources to the business or extensive sharing of facilities, technologies, and programs with other business units is possible.

The low-cost defender's need for efficiency also forces the standardization of product offerings and marketing programs across customer segments to achieve scale effects. Thus, such a strategy is usually not so effective in fragmented markets desiring customized offerings as it is in commodity industries such as basic chemicals, steel, or flour, or in industries producing low-technology components such as electric motors or valves. In the future, however, it may become a more widely applicable competitive strategy as

---

[15]Low-cost defenders are distinguished by the fact that efficiency and competition based on low price are *primary* elements of their business strategy. However, businesses pursuing other competitive strategies should also hold down their costs as much as possible given the functional activities and programs necessary to implement those strategies effectively. Indeed, some of the most successful businesses are those that work aggressively to simultaneously lower costs while improving quality and service. For example, see Ronald Henkoff, "Cost Cutting: How to Do It Right," *Fortune*, April 9, 1990, pp. 40–49; and David Greising, "Quality: How to Make It Pay," *Business Week*, August 8, 1994, pp. 54–59.

EXHIBIT 3-9

The Relationship between Product Quality and Pretax ROI by Business Type

	Quality level				
	Lowest	Below average	Average	Above average	Highest
Consumer durables	16%	18%	18%	26%	32%
Consumer nondurables	15	21	17	23	32
Capital goods	10	8	13	20	21
Raw materials	13	21	21	21	35
Components	12	20	20	22	36
Supplies	16	13	19	25	36

NOTE: Numbers refer to percent average ROI.

SOURCE: Robert D. Buzzell, "Product Quality," *Pimsletter* no. 4 (Cambridge, Mass.: The Strategic Planning Institute, 1986), p. 5.

computer-assisted design and manufacturing systems make "mass customization" more economically viable.[16]

Changing strategies at different stages in the industry life cycle

A business may have to change its objectives and competitive strategy as the industry and the business's competitive position within it mature and stabilize. Thus, a prospector strategy is most appropriate during the early stages of a product category's life cycle as a business attempts to build a successful product line and increase its market share. As the industry matures and the competitive environment stabilizes, analyzer and ultimately defender strategies become more appropriate as the business turns its attention to maintaining and reaping the higher ROI and cash flows of its hard-won market position.

The problem is that the effective implementation of different business strategies requires not only different functional competencies and resources but also different organizational structures, decision-making and coordination processes, reward systems, and even personnel. Because such internal structures and processes are hard to change quickly, it can be very difficult for an entire SBU to make a successful transition from one basic strategy to another.[17] For example, many of Emerson Electric's SBUs historically were successful low-cost defenders; but accelerating technological change in their industries caused the corporation to try to convert them to low-cost analyzers who would focus more attention on new product and

---

[16]Gene Bylinsky, "The Digital Factory," *Fortune*, November 14, 1994, pp. 92–110.

[17]Connie J. G. Gersick, "Revolutionary Change Theories: A Multilevel Exploration of the Punctuated Equilibrium Paradigm," *Academy of Management Review* 16 (1991), pp. 10–36; and Michael L. Tushman, William H. Newman, and Elaine Romanelli, "Convergence and Upheaval: Managing the Unsteady Pace of Organizational Evolution," *California Management Review* 29 (1986), pp. 29–44.

market development. Initially, however, this attempted shift in strategy resulted in some culture shock, conflict, and mixed performance outcomes from within those units.

In view of the implementation problems involved, some firms do not try to make major changes in the basic competitive strategies of their existing business units. Instead, they might form entirely new prospector SBUs to pursue emerging new technologies and industries rather than expecting established units to handle extensive new product development efforts. As individual product-market entries gain successful positions in well-established markets, some firms move them from the prospector unit that developed them to an analyzer or defender unit that is better suited to reaping profits from them as their markets mature. Finally, some firms that are technological leaders in their industries may divest or license individual product-market entries as they mature rather than defend them in the face of increasing competition and eroding margins. This is an approach commonly taken by such companies as 3M and DuPont.

Business-level strategies for global competitors

Businesses that compete in multiple global markets almost always pursue an analyzer strategy. They must continue to strengthen and defend their competitive position in their home country—and perhaps in other countries where they are already well established—while simultaneously pursuing expansion and growth in international markets.

When examined country by country, however, the same business unit might be viewed as pursuing different competitive strategies in different countries. For instance, while 3M's Industrial Tape Group competes as a differentiated defender in the United States, Canada, and some European countries where it has established large market shares, it competes more as a prospector when attempting to open and develop new markets in emerging economies like China and Mexico. This suggests that a single SBU may need to engage in different functional activities (including different marketing policies and programs, as described in the next section)—and perhaps even adopt different organizational structures to implement those activities—across the various countries in which it competes.

MARKETING IMPLICATIONS OF DIFFERENT BUSINESS STRATEGIES

Business units typically incorporate a number of distinct product-markets. A given entry's marketing manager monitors and evaluates the product's environmental situation and develops a marketing program suited to it. However, the manager's freedom to design such a program is constrained by the business unit's competitive strategy because different strategies focus on different objectives and seek to gain and maintain a competitive advantage in different ways. As a result, different functions within the SBU—and different activities within a given functional area, such as marketing—are critical for the success of different strategies.

Therefore, different functional key factors for success are inherent in the various generic business strategies. This constrains the individual marketing manager's freedom of action in two basic ways. First, because different functions within the business unit are more important under different strategies, they receive different proportions of the SBU's total resources.

Thus, the SBU's strategy influences *the amount of resources committed to marketing* and ultimately the budget available to an individual marketing manager within the business unit. Second, the SBU's choice of strategy influences both the kind of *market and competitive situation* that individual product-market entries are likely to face and the *objectives* they are asked to attain. Both constraints have implications for the design of marketing programs for individual products within an SBU.

Of course, it is somewhat risky to draw broad generalizations about how specific marketing policies and program elements might fit within different business strategies. While a business strategy is a general statement about how an SBU chooses to compete in an industry, that unit may comprise a number of different product-market entries facing different competitive situations in different markets. Thus, plenty of variation is likely in marketing programs, and in the freedom individual marketing managers have in designing them, across products within a given SBU. Still, a business's strategy does set a general direction for the types of target markets it will pursue and how the unit will compete in those markets. And it does have some influence on marketing policies that cut across product-markets. Exhibit 3–10 outlines some differences in marketing policies and program elements that occur across businesses pursuing different strategies, and those differences are discussed next.

Product policies

One set of marketing policies defines the nature of the products the business will concentrate on offering to its target markets. These policies concern the *breadth or diversity of product lines*, their *level of technical sophistication*, and the target *level of product quality* relative to competitors.

Because prospector businesses rely heavily on the continuing development of unique new products and the penetration of new markets as their primary competitive strategy, policies encouraging broader and more technically advanced product lines than those of competitors should be positively related to performance on the critical dimension of share growth. The diverse and technically advanced product offerings of 3M's Medical Products SBU are a good example of this.

Whether a prospector's products should be of higher quality than competitors' products is open to question. Quality is hard to define; it can mean different things to different customers. Even so, it is an important determinant of business profitability. Thus, Hambrick suggests that in product-markets where technical features or up-to-the-minute styling are key attributes in customers' definitions of quality, high-quality products may play a positive role in determining the success of a prospector strategy. On the other hand, in markets where the critical determinants of quality are reliability or brand familiarity, the maintenance of relatively high product quality is likely to be more strongly related to the successful performance of defender businesses, particularly differentiated defenders.[18]

Differentiated defenders compete by offering more or "better" choices to customers than their competitors. For example, 3M's commercial graphics business, a major supplier of sign

---

[18]Hambrick, "Some Tests of the Effectiveness and Functional Attributes of Miles and Snow's Strategic Types."

EXHIBIT 3-10

Differences in Marketing Policies and Program Components across
Businesses Pursuing Different Strategies

Marketing policies and program components	Strategy		
	Prospector	Differentiated defender	Low-cost defender
Product policies			
• Product line breadth relative to competitors	+	+	−
• Technical sophistication of products relative to competitors	+	+	−
• Product quality relative to competitors	?	+	−
• Service quality relative to competitors	?	+	−
Price policies			
• Price levels relative to competitors	+	+	−
Distribution policies			
• Degree of forward vertical integration relative to competitors	−	+	?
• Trade promotion expenses as percentage of sales relative to competitors	+	−	−
Promotion policies			
• Advertising expenses as percentage of sales relative to competitors	+	?	−
• Sales promotion expenses as percentage of sales relative to competitors	+	?	−
• Salesforce expenses as percentage of sales relative to competitors	?	+	−

KEY: Plus sign (+) = greater than the average competitor
Minus sign (−) = smaller than the average competitor
Question mark (?) = uncertain relationship between strategy and marketing policy or program component

material for truck fleets, has strengthened its competitive position in that market by developing products appropriate for custom-designed signs. Until recently, the use of film for individual signs was not economical. But the use of computer-controlled knives and a new Scotch-brand marking film produce signs of higher quality and at a lower cost than those that are hand-painted. This kind of success in developing relatively broad and technically sophisticated product lines should be positively related to the long-term ROI performance of most differentiated defender businesses. However, such policies are inconsistent with the efficiency requirements of the low-cost defender strategy. Broad and complex product lines lead to short production runs and large inventories. Maintaining technical sophistication in a business's products requires continuing investment in product and process R & D. Consequently, the adoption of such policies is apt to be less common in low-cost defender businesses.

Instead of, or in addition to, competing on the basis of product characteristics, businesses can distinguish themselves relative to competitors by the *quality of service* they offer. Such service might take many forms, including engineering and design services, alterations, installation, training of customer personnel, or maintenance and repair services. A policy of high service quality is particularly appropriate for differentiated defenders because it offers a way to maintain a competitive advantage in well-established markets.

The appropriateness of an extensive service policy for low-cost defenders, though, is more questionable if higher operating and administrative costs offset customer satisfaction benefits. Those higher costs may detract from the business's ability to maintain the low prices critical to its strategy, as well as lowering ROI—at least in the short term. On the other hand, even low-cost defenders may have difficulty holding their position over the long term without maintaining at least competitive parity with respect to critical service attributes.[19]

Pricing policies

Success in offering low prices relative to competitors should be positively related to the performance of low-cost defender businesses because low price is the primary competitive weapon of such a strategy. However, such a policy is inconsistent with both differentiated defender and prospector strategies. The higher costs involved in differentiating a business's products on either a quality or service basis require higher prices to maintain profitability. Differentiation also provides customers with additional value for which higher prices can be charged. Similarly, the costs and benefits of new product and market development by prospector businesses require and justify relatively high prices. Thus, differentiated defenders and prospectors seldom adhere to a policy of low competitive prices.

Distribution policies

Some observers argue that prospector businesses should show a greater degree of *forward vertical integration* than defender businesses.[20] The rationale for this view is that the prospector's focus on new product and market development requires superior market intelligence and frequent reeducation and motivation of distribution channel members. This can best be accomplished through tight control of company-owned channels. However, these arguments seem inconsistent with the prospector's need for flexibility in constructing new channels to distribute new products and reach new markets.

Attempting to maintain tight control over the behavior of channel members is a more appropriate policy for defenders who are trying to maintain strong positions in established markets. This is particularly true for defenders who rely on good customer service to differentiate themselves from competitors. Thus, it seems more likely that a relatively high

---

[19] For additional arguments in the debate about the relative costs and competitive benefits of superior customer service, see Frank Rose, "Now Quality Means Service Too," and Rahul Jacob, "Beyond Quality and Value."

[20] Miles and Snow, *Organizational Strategy, Structure, and Process*; and Hambrick, "Some Tests of the Effectiveness and Functional Attributes of Miles and Snow's Strategic Types."

degree of forward vertical integration is found among defender businesses, particularly differentiated defenders, while prospectors rely more heavily on independent channel members—such as manufacturer's representatives or wholesale distributors—to distribute their products.[21]

Because prospectors focus on new products where success is uncertain and sales volumes are small in the short run, they are likely to devote a larger percentage of sales to *trade promotions* than defender businesses. Prospectors rely on trade promotion tools such as quantity discounts, liberal credit terms, and other incentives to induce cooperation and support from their independent channel members.

Promotion policies

Extensive marketing communications also play an important role in the successful implementation of both prospector and differentiated defender strategies. The form of that communication, however, may differ under the two strategies. Because prospectors must constantly work to generate awareness, stimulate trial, and build primary demand for new and unfamiliar products, high advertising and sales promotion expenditures are likely to bear a positive relationship to the new product and share-growth success of such businesses. 3M's Medical Products SBU, for instance, devotes substantial resources to advertising in professional journals and distributing samples of new products, as well as to maintaining an extensive salesforce.

Differentiated defenders, on the other hand, are primarily concerned with maintaining the loyalty of established customers by adapting to their needs and providing good service. These tasks can best be accomplished—particularly in industrial goods and services industries—by an extensive, well-trained, well-supported salesforce.[22] Therefore, differentiated defenders are likely to have higher salesforce expenditures than competitors.

Finally, low-cost defenders appeal to their customers primarily on price. Thus, high expenditures on advertising, sales promotion, or the salesforce would detract from their basic strategy and may have a negative impact on their ROI performance. Consequently, such businesses are likely to spend little as a percentage of sales on those promotional activities.

SERVICE BUSINESSES: DO THEY REQUIRE DIFFERENT STRATEGIES?

The service component of the U.S. economy accounts for roughly two-thirds of all economic activity in this country, and services are the fastest-growing sector of most other developed economies around the world. Expansion in the number of two-wage-earner families and single-person households has made time a more scarce and valuable commodity

---

[21] Although Hambrick argued for the reverse relationship, data from his study of 850 SBUs actually support our contention that defenders have more vertically integrated channels than prospectors. See Hambrick, "Some Tests of the Effectiveness and Functional Attributes of Miles and Snow's Strategic Types."

[22] Jaclyn Fierman, "The Death and Rebirth of the Salesman," *Fortune*, July 25, 1994, pp. 80–91.

for many people. This, coupled with increasing household incomes and other factors, suggests that demand for services in the global economy is likely to be robust for the foreseeable future.

But what is a service? Basically, services can be thought of as **intangibles** and goods as **tangibles**. The former can rarely be experienced in advance of the sale, while tangible products can be experienced, even tested, before purchase.[23] Using this distinction, a **service** can be defined as "any activity or benefit that one party can offer to another that is essentially intangible and that does not result in the ownership of anything. Its production may or may not be tied to a physical product."[24]

We typically associate services with nonmanufacturing businesses, even though service is often an indispensable part of a goods producer's offering. Services like applications engineering, system design, delivery, installation, training, and maintenance can be crucial for building long-term relationships between manufacturers and their customers, particularly in consumer durable and industrial products businesses. Thus, almost all businesses are engaged in service to a greater or lesser extent.

On the other hand, many organizations are concerned with producing and marketing a service as their primary offering rather than as an adjunct to a physical product. These organizations include firms providing personal services, such as health care, communications, retailing, and finance companies; commercial service organizations, such as accounting, legal, and consulting firms; public sector services like the military, police and fire departments, and schools; and not-for-profit service organizations, such as churches, hospitals, universities, and arts organizations. The crucial question is whether such organizations must employ different strategies and functional programs than goods manufacturers to be successful.

There are substantial similarities in the strategic issues both goods and service producers face, especially when deciding how to compete at the business level. However, the intangibility, as well as some other special characteristics, of services can cause unique marketing and operational problems for service organizations, as discussed next.

Business-level competitive strategies

The framework we used to classify the business-level competitive strategies pursued by goods producers is equally valid for service businesses. Some service firms—such as Super 8 or Days Inn in the lodging industry—attempt to minimize costs and compete largely with low prices. Other firms, like Marriott, differentiate their offerings on the basis of high service quality or unique benefits. Similarly, some service businesses adopt prospector strategies and aggressively pursue the development of new offerings or markets. For instance, American Express's Travel Related Services division has developed a variety of new services tailored to specific segments of the firm's credit-card holders. Other service businesses focus narrowly on defending established positions in current markets. Still others can best be described as analyzers pursuing both established and new markets or as reactors who lack any consistent strategy.

---

[23]Theodore Leavitt, *The Marketing Imagination* (New York: The Free Press, 1986), pp. 94–95.

[24]Philip Kotler and Gary Armstrong, *Principles of Marketing* (Englewood Cliffs, N.J.: Prentice Hall, 1989), p. 575.

A recent study of the banking industry provides some empirical evidence that service businesses actually do pursue the same types of competitive strategies as goods producers. The 329 bank CEOs who responded to the survey had little trouble categorizing their institutions' competitive strategies into one of Miles and Snow's four types. Fifty-four of the executives reported that their banks were prospectors, 87 identified their firms as analyzers, 157 as defenders, and 31 as reactors.[25]

The impact of service characteristics on marketing[26]

The business-level competitive strategy pursued by a service business has the same implications for marketing policies and program elements as those discussed earlier for goods producers. For example, a bank pursuing a prospector strategy likely offers a broader range of services, promotes them more extensively, has broader distribution (more branch offices), and charges more for its services than one following a defender strategy. However, services have some characteristics that often give rise to special marketing problems and therefore demand special marketing policies and actions. These characteristics are that services are intangible and perishable, they often require substantial customer contact, and their quality can vary from one transaction to the next.

Intangibility

The intangibility of services can make it more difficult to win and hold onto customers. Because prospective customers have difficulty experiencing (seeing, touching, smelling, feeling) the service offering in advance, they are forced to buy promises. But promises are also intangible; hence, metaphors and similes become surrogates for the tangibility that is lacking. This helps explain the solid, reassuring decor of most banks and law offices; the neat, cheerful uniforms worn by employees at McDonald's or Burger King; and the elegant decor and atmosphere of upscale shops and hotels. These things become the tangible symbols of the intangible services being offered.

A further difficulty with intangibility is that customers often don't know what criteria to use in evaluating a service. How do you rate a stockbroker's advice *before* you follow it? Or a doctor's? Typically, customers approach the purchase of services with optimistic expectations. Disappointment is all too easy to come by under these conditions.

One special marketing challenge facing most service businesses, then, is to find ways to make their offerings more tangible to potential customers. Some methods for accomplishing this included the following:

[25]Daryl O. McKee, P. Rajan Varadarajan, and William Pride, "Strategic Adaptability and Firm Performance: A Market-Contingent Perspective."

[26]For a more detailed discussion of the unique marketing problems faced by service businesses, see Valarie A. Zeithaml, A. Parasuraman, and Leonard L. Berry, "Problems and Strategies in Services Marketing," *Journal of Marketing*, Spring 1985, pp. 33–46; Valarie A. Zeithaml, A. Parasuraman, and Leonard L. Berry, *Delivering Quality Service: Balancing Customer Perceptions and Expectations* (New York: The Free Press, 1990); and James L. Heskett, Thomas O. Jones, Gary W. Loveman, W. Earl Sasser, Jr., and Leonard A. Schlesinger, "Putting the Service-Profit Chain to Work," *Harvard Business Review*, March–April 1994, pp. 164–74.

- *Designing facilities and products and training personnel to serve as symbols of service quality.* As just mentioned, the firm should attempt to design all aspects of the physical environment surrounding the delivery of its service—including its facilities, advertising, promotional materials, and so forth—to act as tangible symbols of the quality and reliability of its service offering. Such actions are particularly important for prospector businesses attempting to develop new markets for new service offerings. Because new offerings are both intangible and unfamiliar to most customers, potential buyers have a doubly hard time judging whether the benefits they offer justify their cost.

  The service firm's personnel can also be important tangible symbols of service quality. Everyone who comes in contact with customers should be carefully trained to project an appropriate image, as well as to actually provide a high-quality experience for the customer. This is especially true in differentiated defender businesses where superior employee training and performance can provide a premium image and an important advantage over competitors. For instance, American Express devotes much effort to training, measuring, and rewarding the service performance of its employees as a primary element of its strategy for defending its strong position in the highly competitive credit-card industry.

- *Creating a tangible representation of the service.* American Express has done this, for instance, with its prestigious Gold and Platinum Cards.

- *Tying the marketing of services to the marketing of goods.* For example, H & R Block tax preparation services and Allstate Insurance benefit substantially from their association with Sears.

Perishability

Because a service is an experience, it is perishable and cannot be inventoried. Motel rooms and airline seats not occupied, idle telephone capacity, and the unused time of physicians and lawyers cannot be reclaimed. Further, when demand exceeds capacity, customers must be turned away because no backup inventory is available. Thus, service organizations must do everything possible to anticipate peak loads and to fit capacity to demand. Here are some possible approaches to this problem:

- *Smoothing out the variability in demand.* One way firms attempt to accomplish this is by offering lower prices during off-peak periods, as when hotels offer lower rates on the weekends and theaters charge less for tickets to matinee performances. Other firms advertise extensively to get customers to change their habits, as in the case of the U.S. Postal Service's campaign to encourage early mailing of Christmas cards and packages. And some service firms have added additional services or goods to make more complete use of their facilities and personnel during slow periods, as with the addition of breakfast items at fast-food chains.

- *Lowering fixed costs by making capacity more flexible.* Firms have attempted to accomplish this in a variety of ways, such as training employees to handle multiple tasks, substituting machines for labor (as with automatic teller machines at banks), sharing facilities, equipment, or personnel with other similar service organizations, and using part-time or paraprofessional employees.

Customer contact

The physical presence of the customer is another characteristic of many service organizations. Many services are sold, produced, and consumed almost simultaneously. The amount of customer contact during the production process is especially important because it affects service design, production, and delivery decisions. High-contact service systems are more difficult to manage than low-contact systems because the greater involvement of the customer in the process affects the timing of demand and the nature and quality of the service itself.[27]

Exhibit 3–11 shows how a variety of decisions are influenced by high and low levels of customer contact in a service system. Some of the general conclusions suggested by the exhibit follow:

- There is a high degree of uncertainty in the day-to-day operations of high-contact systems because the customer can disrupt the production system in a variety of ways. For instance, an unexpected need for emergency service from a hospital can overload operating room facilities.

- Rarely does the demand for a high-contact service equal capacity at any one time— not only because of the difficulty of making reliable forecasts, but also because of last-minute changes by the customer, as in the case of cancellations of hotel reservations. Low-contact systems can better match supply and demand by structuring a resource-oriented schedule and lengthening delivery times when necessary.

- It is difficult to set up an efficient production schedule for high-contact services because customers cannot be programmed.

- Because employees interact directly with customers in high-contact service systems, their appearance and behavior can directly affect customer satisfaction with the service.

Variability

A final, closely related characteristic, particularly of high-contact services, has to do with variability, or the difficulty of maintaining quality control. Because of the human element, service quality can vary substantially depending on who provides it and when. In some respects, this can be viewed as a positive opportunity for the service organization. The personal nature of many services enables firms to customize their services and thus attain a better fit with customer needs. For example, travel agencies can prepare special itineraries

---

[27]Richard B. Chase, "Where Does the Customer Fit into a Service Operation?" *Harvard Business Review*, November–December, 1978, pp. 139–73.

EXHIBIT 3–11

Major Design Considerations in High- and Low-Contact Service Systems

Decision	High-contact system	Low-contact system
Facility location	Operations must be near the customer.	Operations may be placed near supply, transportation, or labor.
Facility layout	Facility should accommodate the customer's physical and psychological needs and expectations.	Facility should enhance production.
Product design	The environment as well as the physical product define the nature of the service.	Customer is not in the service environment, so the product can be defined by fewer attributes.
Process design	Stages of production process have a direct immediate effect on the customer.	Customer is not involved in majority of processing steps.
Scheduling	Customer is in the production schedule and must be accommodated.	Customer is concerned mainly with completion dates.
Production planning	Orders cannot be stored, so smoothing production flow results in loss of business.	Both backlogging and smoothing are possible.
Worker skills	Direct workforce comprises a major part of the service product and so must be able to interact well with the public.	Direct workforce needs only to have technical skills.
Quality control	Quality standards are often in the eye of the beholder and hence variable.	Quality standards are generally measurable and hence fixed.
Time standards	Service time depends on customer needs, and therefore time standards are inherently loose.	Work is performed on customer surrogates (e.g., forms), and time standards can be tight.
Wage payment	Variable output requires time-based wage systems.	"Fixable" output permits output-based wage systems.
Capacity planning	To avoid lost sales, capacity must be set to match peak demand.	Storable output permits setting capacity at some average demand level.
Forecasting	Forecasts are short term, time-oriented.	Forecasts are long term, output-oriented.

SOURCE: Reprinted by permission of the *Harvard Business Review*. An exhibit from "Where Does the Customer Fit into a Service Operation?" by Richard B. Chase (November–December 1978). Copyright © 1978 by the President and Fellows of Harvard College; all rights reserved.

for individual travelers, and stockbrokers can recommend individualized portfolios for their clients.

On the other hand, variability can lead to inconsistent experiences for the customer and result in dissatisfaction. Variations in quality can be a particularly difficult problem for firms that operate multiple outlets, such as banks, hotels, airlines, and retail chains. Delivering a uniform experience to customers of the Marriott Hotel group is much more difficult than producing and selling Zenith TVs of consistent quality.

To overcome these quality control problems, as well as to increase supplier productivity, Leavitt suggests that firms should attempt to "industrialize" their services.[28] Here are some means of accomplishing this:

- *Use of hard technologies.* This involves finding ways to control service production and delivery processes by substituting machinery and/or tools for people where possible. Examples include automatic teller machines, automatic toll collectors, vending machines, and bankcards that enable loans to be preapproved for reliable customers.

- *Use of soft technologies.* This is primarily concerned with improving the quality and consistency of employee performance through the development of standardized job procedures, detailed training, and close supervision. This approach, used by McDonald's, Marriott, H & R Block, and many other firms, helps ensure the delivery of consistently high-quality service regardless of the employee or situation involved.

- *Use of hybrid technologies.* These function by using hard equipment in conjunction with carefully planned job procedures to control service quality and gain efficiency. Leavitt cites as examples specialized, limited-service, fast, low-priced automobile repair businesses such as Midas Muffler and Jiffy-Lube.

On the other hand, Heskett and his colleagues recommend a different approach for improving quality in high-contact service systems. Instead of standardizing or "industrializing" the service, they suggest hiring well-qualified employees, training them extensively, and then giving them substantial *autonomy to customize* the service to the needs and preferences of individual customers. In their view, such an approach both reduces employee turnover and increases customer satisfaction and loyalty, thereby producing greater profitability over the long term even though it may lead to higher wages and other costs in the short run.[29]

Finally, though, it is important to keep in mind that the marketing programs for individual product-market entries within a particular business unit—whether services or goods—may vary a good deal on some or all of the four Ps: product, price, promotion, and place of distribution. Within the constraints imposed by the characteristics of the offering and the business's strategy, individual marketing managers usually have a range of strategic options to choose from when developing a marketing plan. The nature of those options, their relative advantages and weaknesses, and the environmental conditions in which each is most appropriate are the focus of the rest of this book.

SUMMARY

To be implemented successfully, the marketing program for a given product-market entry must be compatible with the internal capabilities, resources, management processes, and

---

[28]Theodore Levitt, *The Marketing Imagination*, pp. 38–61.

[29]James L. Heskett, Thomas O. Jones, Gary W. Loveman, W. Earl Sasser, Jr., and Leonard A. Schlesinger, "Putting the Service-Profit Chain to Work."

procedures of the firm. It should also fit with the corporation's higher-level strategies, particularly the competitive strategy of the entry's business unit.

When formulating a business-level strategy, managers must make recommendations about (1) the SBU's objectives and scope, (2) how resources should be allocated across product-markets and functional departments within the SBU, and (3) which competitive strategy the unit should pursue in attempting to build a sustainable competitive advantage in its product-markets. Decisions about an SBU's scope, objectives, and resource deployments are similar to and should be consistent with those made at the corporate level. However, the major question to be addressed by a business-level strategy is, How are we going to compete within our industry? Thus, an SBU's competitive strategy should take into account the unit's unique strengths and weaknesses relative to competitors and the needs and desires of customers in its target markets.

Researchers have identified general categories of business-unit strategies based on observations of how those SBUs compete within their industries. We combined the classification schemes of Porter and Miles and Snow to arrive at a typology of six different business-level competitive strategies: (1) prospector, (2) differentiated analyzer, (3) low-cost analyzer, (4) differentiated defender, (5) low-cost defender, and (6) reactor.

Businesses pursuing a **prospector** strategy are primarily concerned with attaining rapid volume growth by developing and introducing new products and by attaining a leading share of new markets. This strategy is particularly appropriate for industries in the introductory or early growth stages of their life cycle.

At the other extreme, **defender** businesses are primarily concerned with maintaining an already strong position in one or more major market segments in industries where the technology, customer segments, and competitive structure are all relatively well developed, stable, and mature. Their major objective is usually to gain and sustain a substantial return from their businesses. **Differentiated defenders** try to do this by maintaining an advantage based on either premium product quality or superior customer service. **Low-cost defenders** seek economies of scale, attempt to minimize unit costs in production and marketing, and compete largely on the basis of low price.

The **analyzer** strategies fall in between prospectors and defenders. Such strategies are most commonly found in industries that are in the late growth or early maturity stages of their life cycles where, although the industry is largely developed, some technological changes, shifts in customers needs, or adjustments in competitive structure are still occurring. Because the analyzer is a hybrid strategy, it is difficult to make many generalizations about its implications for the allocation of resources across functional departments or for the design of marketing programs for individual product-market entries within such businesses.

Reactors are businesses that operate without any well-defined or consistently applied competitive strategy. They react to changing circumstances in an ad hoc, unsystematic way. Consequently, they tend not to perform as well on any dimension as units with more consistent strategies, and it is impossible to draw conclusions about how such businesses are likely to market their products.

Most business units incorporate multiple product-market entries. Although those entries often face different market and competitive situations, their marketing programs are all likely to be influenced and constrained by the SBU's overall competitive strategy.

Successful prospector businesses tend to be competent in, and allocate a relatively large proportion of their resources to, functional areas directly related to new product and market development, such as R & D, product engineering, marketing, sales, and marketing research. Differentiated defenders also spend substantial resources on marketing and sales to maintain a strong product quality or customer service position. But low-cost defenders usually allocate relatively few resources to any of these functions to hold down costs and prices.

The competitive thrust of a business unit's strategy influences and constrains marketing policies and programs, such as the breadth of the product line, pricing policies, and the size of advertising and promotion budgets. Thus, while marketing managers often play a crucial role in formulating the SBU's strategy, that strategy subsequently imposes constraints and direction on the marketer's decisions about the marketing program for a specific product-market entry within the SBU.

Finally, service businesses tend to pursue the same kinds of business-level strategies as goods producers, and those strategies impose the same kinds of influences and constraints on their marketing policies and programs. However, service offerings often have some unique characteristics, including (1) intangibility, (2) perishability, (3) close customer contact, and (4) variability, which can create special marketing and operational challenges.

OPPORTUNITY ANALYSIS

Environmental and Competitive Analysis

THE GLOBAL ECONOMY IN TRANSITION[1]

Within the next 20 or so years, the world will witness the biggest shift in economic power since the mid-1800s. The scenario calls for the newly emerging economies to collectively surpass the now-dominant industrial economies of Europe, the United States, and Japan. Literally dozens of third world countries (most in East and South Asia as well as in Latin America) have adopted a market-oriented economic system, thereby opening their borders to increased trade and investment.

Despite the rather grim economic prospects for most of Africa, Brazil, and Russia, the overall growth rate for the next 10 years in the developing countries is expected to be about twice that of the developed countries (5 percent annually versus 2.5 percent). If output is based on purchasing power parity measures (as opposed to exchange rates), the developing nations will account for more than half of the world's output by the year 2000. By 2020 China will overtake America as the world's biggest economy, and 6 of the leading 10 economies will be from the third world (in 1992 that number was 4). Interestingly, manufactured goods now account for about 60 percent of the exports of these countries versus 5 percent in 1955. This has understandably caused concern among politicians and businesspeople in the developed countries, who fear that such an outpouring of manufactured goods will damage their economies.

However, longer-term forecasts of the developing countries' growth rate are no doubt exaggerated; success will probably slow these rates. Even so, there is no question that the size of the middle classes is exploding throughout the developing world, opening new markets and untold opportunities to the world's business community. As of this writing the numbers of

[1]Based on "The Global Economy," *The Economist*, October 1, 1994, special section; Rahul Jacob, "The Big Rise," *Fortune*, May 30, 1994, p. 74; and "The New Global Consumer," *Fortune*, Autumn–Winter 1993, p. 68.

middle-class workers earning between $10,000 and $40,000 (based on purchasing power parity) are 83 million in China, 30 million in India, and 17 million in Brazil. By the turn of the century Asia will have 259 million people earning at least $18,000 annually; China alone will account for 150 million.

These purchasing power parity–based incomes take into account that living costs are much lower in the developing countries (with the possible exception of food). Chinese consumers are estimated to spend less than 5 percent of their incomes on rent, transportation, health, and education because of high government subsidies, whereas a typical American family spends 40 to 50 percent of its income on these

areas. Thus, an annual Shanghai household income of about $2,000 supports considerable purchasing power; 85 percent of the households there own washing machines and 93 percent own color TVs.

Some multinational firms are already taking advantage of this growth of the middle classes. Citicorp earns more money in the developing world than in the developed countries, and Gillette had operating profits of $178 million in Latin America in 1992. Many members of the new middle class are willing to pay more for foreign brands, which they believe will provide better quality than the local brands. And the growth in manufacturing is providing a substantial market for all sorts of business goods and services (especially financial).

COMPONENTS OF THE MARKETING MACROENVIRONMENT

This description of the changes under way in much of the developing world is primarily concerned with the demographic and economic environment, which is just one of the five components of marketing's macroenvironment. The other four components are the physical, political/legal, technological, and sociocultural environments. These five components typically interact to set off a chain reaction. For example, problems in the physical environment (air pollution) lead to U. S. legislation (Clean Air Act) that affects the economics of various industries (alternative fuels), stimulating the development of new technologies (catalytic converters), changing consumer attitudes in support of government actions to reduce pollution, which leads to demands for even more stringent laws to protect the environment, and so on (see Exhibit 4–1).

We will discuss each of these five environments, primarily in terms of how changes in each affect marketing strategies and programs. We then discuss competitor analysis and the strategic issue management process required to evaluate environmental factors important in targeting market segments and in formulating strategic marketing programs.

The physical environment

An obvious but frequently overlooked factor in the marketing environment is a market's physical location. Special conditions such as extreme hot or cold temperatures or high humidity can affect the design of conventional products. For example, vehicles operating in the Middle East require elaborate rustproofing.

EXHIBIT 4–1

Components of the Macroenvironment and Their Interaction

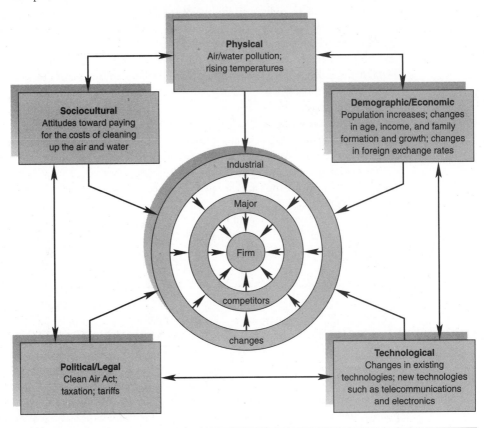

One of the more frightening environmental scenarios concerns the buildup of carbon dioxide in the atmosphere that has resulted from heavy use of fossil fuels. This carbon dioxide "blanket" traps the sun's radiation and is predicted to raise the earth's mean temperature. A recent study commissioned by the U. S. Environmental Protection Agency found that global warming will probably decrease food output and thus make the problem of feeding the earth's growing population even more difficult.[2]

Mild temperatures over the past decade have permitted killer bees to fly north from South America and insects from the southern U. S. to migrate northward (for example, large

---

[2]"And Maybe Worse to Come," *The Economist*, May 23, 1992, p. 49. Also see "Hot Stuff," *The Economist*, July 11, 1992, p. 67; and Gary S. Becker, "On Global Warming, Let Coolest Heads Prevail," *Business Week*, July 20, 1992, p. 166.

cockroaches from Florida have taken up residence in Boston, Chicago, and New York). Pesky plants like kudzu, a southern vine that smothers other flora, can now be found in the suburbs of New York City.[3] The greenhouse effect could also help to infect nontropical human populations—especially older people—with such tropical diseases as malaria, hepatitis, yellow fever, cholera, and meningitis.[4]

Another example of the physical environment's impact can be found in Southern California, where the high cost of municipal water has, after considerable debate, forced the use of "reclaimed" sewage water on parks, golf courses, and roadside landscaping, but not for drinking. However, in some European cities tertiary sewage treatment purifies water that is then considered potable for up to five or six trips through the plumbing.[5]

Response to physical environmental problems

To this point the discussion of the physical environment has stressed threats to business throughout the world. But businesses can often turn problems into opportunities, such as by investing in research to find ways to save energy in heating and lighting. Another method is to find new energy sources, such as new, low-cost wind farms like the one being developed by Iowa-Illinois Gas and Electric Company and U. S. Windpower, Inc.[6] DuPont is working on substitutes for chlorofluorocarbons (CFCs), which are aerosol propellants that deplete the ozone layer, and Weyerhauser is developing drought-resistant loblolly pines.[7]

Businesses have also found opportunities to develop environmentally friendly (green) products such as phosphate-free detergents, recycled motor oil, tuna caught without the netting of dolphins, organic fertilizers, high-efficiency light bulbs, recycled paper, and men's and women's casual clothes made from 100 percent organic cotton and colored with nontoxic dyes.[8] Other improvements include using smaller packages for many consumer goods (such as compact containers for superconcentrated soaps and the use of collapsible pouches for cleaners once packed in plastic jugs), eliminating the use of cardboard packages for deodorants, and selling teabags without tags and strings.[9]

The political/legal environment

The major element of this component of the macroenvironment is legislation, which defines the regulatory environment within which both local and foreign firms must operate. As with any other external force, the political/legal environment presents a firm with strategic opportunities as well as threats. New regulations or deregulation may open new markets, as

---

[3]Robert Johnson, "Warmer Weather Has Florida Roaches Moving to Chicago," *The Wall Street Journal*, June 23, 1992, p. A1.

[4]George F. Sanderson, "Climate Change: The Threat to Human Health," *The Futurist*, March–April 1992, p. 34.

[5]"California Water—Want Some More?" *The Economist*, October 8, 1994, p. 30.

[6]David Stipp, "'Wind Farms May Energize the Midwest," *The Wall Street Journal*, September 16, 1991, p. B1.

[7]Peter Nulty, "Global Warming: What We Know," *Fortune*, April 9, 1990, p. 101.

[8]Pat Sloan, "Where-o-where Can You Get 'Green' Garb?" *Advertising Age*, June 5, 1992, p. 3.

[9]Gary Strauss, "Big Trend: Smaller Packaging," *USA Today*, April 1, 1993, p. B1.

has occurred in the pollution and energy-control markets; or the political environment can destabilize an industry. The most important question about a country's political/legal environment concerns its stability—to what extent present regulations will endure.[10] A change in government often signals a change in regulations pertaining to a foreign company. However, the same government can change its political posture, as was the case recently in Mexico when the government reversed itself by encouraging foreign investment.

Political risk

Corporations face many types of political risk including confiscation (seizure without compensation, as occurred in Iran a few years ago), expropriation (seizure with some compensation), and domestication (requiring transfer of ownership in favor of the host country and local management and sourcing.). Other risks include changes in exchange control (which can take a variety of forms), local content laws, import restrictions, discrimination, taxes, and price controls—all of which usually operate to the advantage of local industry. Clearly, many third world countries present an array of political risks to companies seeking to do business there.

Governments can encourage foreign investment through policies such as tax concessions and tariff protection. Indeed, countries commonly encourage certain kinds of investments while simultaneously restricting others. For example, governments may encourage local firms to export to countries having considerable political risk by providing insurance against losses from such risks (such as through the U. S. Export-Import Bank).

Government regulation

The number and intricacies of international laws and regulations make it difficult to understand the regulatory elements affecting marketing. Most countries have regulations concerning food and drugs as well as prices, products, promotion, and distribution, but these laws vary considerably in their applicability to marketing. The EC is phasing in thousands of rules designed to provide uniform safety, health, and environmental standards for its member countries. These rules favor companies now producing different products for different countries, but some exporters will be required to make costly design changes, to substantially retool, and to add new quality control systems.[11]

Government deregulation

Government, business, and the general public throughout much of the world have become increasingly aware that overregulation protects inefficiencies, restricts entry by new competitors, and creates inflationary pressures. As a result, industries have been deregulated in many countries. In the United States airlines, trucking, railroads, telecommunications, and banking

---

[10] This discussion of political stability and political risk is based on Cateora, *International Marketing*, 8th ed. Burr Ridge, Ill.: Irwin, 1993, pp. 159–68.

[11] "10,000 New EC Rules," *Business Week*, September 7, 1992, p. 48.

have been deregulated, while cable TV has been reregulated. Markets are also being liberated in Western Europe, Eastern Europe, Asia, and many of the developing countries. Trade barriers are crumbling due to political unrest and technological innovation.

In discussing the opportunities resulting from deregulation, Bleeke notes that strategies of the firms in the affected industry change immediately following deregulation and again about five years later. The early actions of such firms include improving pricing capabilities, cutting structural costs, finding new ways to differentiate their services, conserving capital to maintain flexibility, and increasing their marketing skills, especially those relating to new products. Five years later, strategies of the surviving companies center on fine-tuning their pricing capabilities, preempting competitors via strategic alliances, and developing market power.[12]

Other government influences and actions

Worldwide there is a strong and growing public sentiment to do something about air and water pollution, hazardous waste, garbage, and toxic substances. The publicity concerning acid rain, toxic landfills, water and air pollution, droughts, and oil spills has led to strong activism by the general public.

The United States has a tough Clean Air Act that strongly affects producers of automobiles and trucks, farm machinery, gasoline, alternative fuels such as coal and natural gas, chemicals, electricity, and smokestack industries in general. The act has revived interest in the production of electric cars and public transportation.[13] The billions of dollars spent annually to clean up America's air provide opportunities for many firms. For example, the bill's requirement to cleanse exhaust fumes benefits producers of catalytic converters, additives to make gasoline burn cleaner, baking soda (which removes sulfur dioxide emissions from utility boilers), precious metals used to meet the new exhaust standards, and corn used to make ethanol (a substitute fuel).

The technological environment

Technology can substantially affect an industry's performance; for example, consider the impact of genetic engineering on pharmaceuticals, of transistors on telecommunications, and of plastics on metals. Identification of the commercial potential of technological developments has dramatically accelerated, and the lag between ideas, invention, and commercialization has decreased. In addition to creating new products, technological developments affect all marketing activities, including communication (making available new media or new selling tools), distribution (opening new channels or modifying the operations and performance of existing ones), packaging (using new materials), and marketing research (monitoring food store sales via scanners).

---

[12]Joel A. Bleeke, "Strategic Choices for Newly Opened Markets," *Harvard Business Review*, September–October 1990, p. 163.

[13]Gill Andrews Pratt, "EVS: On the Road Again," *Technology Review*, August–September 1992, p. 48.

Intensification of technological development

In the past 10 to 12 years an amazing number of new technologies have brought forth such products as videocassette recorders, compact disks, ever-more-powerful and ever-smaller computers, fax machines, and highly effective genetically engineered drugs. Technological progress over the next 10 years is predicted to be several times that experienced during the past 10 years; much of it will be spurred by the need to solve our environmental problems. Major technological innovations can be expected in a variety of fields, especially in biology, electronics, telecommunications, and manufactured materials.

Trends in biology   The *biological revolution* is of fairly recent origin. By modifying the hereditary characteristics of bacteria, biologists have opened new areas of research concerned with such subjects as enhancing the body's ability to heal itself. An international project is under way to map all human genes—some 50,000 to 100,000—by the year 2005. This undertaking would include identifying each gene's function and how it learns to follow instructions. Anticipated applications of the resulting technologies in the pharmaceutical and agricultural areas include such exciting areas as these:

- *Pharmaceuticals*: production of human growth hormones to cure dwarfism and prevent muscle wasting, and introduction of powerful genetically engineered vaccines to eliminate many infectious diseases, including AIDS and possibly certain cancers. Replacement of defective genes that cause about 4,000 diseases (such as cystic fibrosis) is fast becoming a reality.[14]

- *Agriculture*: production of more disease-resistant livestock and plants; nonpolluting biological pesticides and insecticides; and protein by fermentation of algae or by the action of yeasts on hydrocarbons.

Trends in electronics   Electronics have played an important role in our society since the 1950s. They were first used primarily in such areas as radio and television and later aided in the development of new products such as digital watches, automatic cameras, video games, and microcomputers. Probably nothing has changed the workplace more in recent years than the personal computer. By the year 2000 we can expect that personal computers will be 10 times more powerful, will understand verbal **and** written messages, will be able to access a far greater volume of data, and will provide TV-quality displays.[15]

With regard to computers in general, the next decade will see even faster machines capable of handling billions—perhaps trillions—of calculations a second; dramatic improvements in storage capacity and speed of access; and continuing miniaturization at ever-lower costs. Perhaps the biggest changes will result from the conversion of previously analog data,

---

[14]"Science and Technology: The Tiniest Transplants," *The Economist*, April 25, 1992, p. 95. Also see "Science and Technology: The End of the Beginning," *The Economist*, October 24, 1992, p. 96.

[15]William F. Buckley, "A Brave New World: Streams of 1s and 0s," *The Wall Street Journal Centennial Edition*, p. A15. Also see Mark Lander, Bart Ziegler, Mark Lewyn, and Leah Lewyn, "Bell-Ringer," *Business Week*, October 25, 1993, p. 32.

such as sound, to digital bits (0s and 1s), which can then be handled like data in a computer; among other possibilities, this will create the much-discussed information superhighway. Telephone calls, television, and movies are being digitalized. Phone companies, cable operators, and utilities are competing to service homes and offices with an array of traditional services plus access to libraries comprised of books and films.[16] In late 1994 consumer testing of multimedia technology (the marriage of cable TV, the computer, and the telephone) began. In these trials consumers used their TVs to scan updated catalogs providing images and data about a host of products, order goods via remote control or a mouse, and have these orders delivered to their homes. These trials gave consumers control over what image was on the screen, which is not possible with existing home shopping TV channels. This new technology raises questions about the future structure of America's $2 trillion retailing industry.[17]

Trends in manufactured materials   A third and increasingly important megatechnology has to do with the development of new materials. Using a variety of new technologies, researchers are literally designing new materials atom by atom. To date the results have mainly improved existing materials, such as the development of extra-tough steel that can be used in a variety of ways, including the building of space shuttle engines.

Researchers have recently developed lightweight silicon mixtures that are used to make pliable ceramics that tolerate extremely high temperatures. These can be used in cars, jet engines, and airplane frames. Such materials should make possible more fuel-efficient cars, planes capable of crossing the Pacific in two hours, and much faster computer chips that will lead to handheld supercomputers.[18] (Exhibit 4–2 describes a recently developed lightweight product.)

The sociocultural environment

This environmental component represents the values, attitudes, and general behavior of individuals in a given society, and it evolves more slowly than do the other components. Transformations in a society's culture, especially in its structure, its institutions, and its distribution of wealth, typically occur gradually in democratic countries. Two such transformations that have had particular impact on the U. S. market in recent years are changes in individual values and shifts in family structure. These changes have affected the sale of personal consumer products; the development of advertising programs to accommodate more joint decision making; the creation of special marketing programs for minority groups; the popularity of fast-food outlets; and the emergence of more energy-saving, reliable, and

---

[16]Kathy Rebello, Richard Brandt, Peter Coy, and Mark Lewyn, "Your Digital Future," *Business Week*, September 1, 1992.

[17]"The Interactive Bazaar Opens," *The Economist*, August 20, 1994, p. 49. Also see Neil Weinstock, "Future Seen: It's Interactive," *Advertising Age*, September 29, 1993, p. T12.

[18]Naomi Freundlech, Neil Gross, John Carey, and Robert D. Hof, "The New Alchemy," *Business Week*, July 29, 1991, p. 48.

EXHIBIT 4-2

Solid Magic

Silica aerogels (referred to as frozen smoke) are the lightest solids made by humans (spider webs are lighter). They can be made so light that a chunk comparable to an average refrigerator weighs only a pound. Aerogels not only are lightweight but are so strong they can support thousands of times their weight — and they provide superior insulation. They have numerous applications, especially in coatings, insulations, and packaging.

SOURCE: David Kirkpatrick, "Solid Magic," *Fortune*, November 4, 1991, p. 155.

longer-lasting products. Similar shifts are occurring with the middle class in many emerging economies.[19]

Changing individual values

Religions influence buyer behavior by emphasizing different material and spiritual beliefs and values. Islam, for example, details how one should behave under a variety of conditions, defines the roles of men and women, and is essentially fatalistic and nonmaterial.[20] It will be interesting to see whether these Islamic tenets will affect the materialistic behavior of the many increasingly prosperous Muslim consumers in East Asia.

Protestantism, on the other hand, emphasizes individualism and has facilitated the development of the Puritan ethic of hard work, thriftiness, and faith in others and in institutions. This was particularly true in North America until the 1960s, when a new social force emerged that did not entirely share these values. Instead of leaving the destiny of their country in the hands of their elders and institutions, the young—particularly college students—collectively fought for causes such as civil rights, the end of the Vietnam war, and individual nonconformism. The young emerged as a new social force, sharing and defending a common set of new values even across national borders.

More recently, individual values have shifted again for a variety of reasons, including a new sense of lowered expectations, apprehensions about the future, mistrust of institutions, and a growing sense of limits. Thus, individuals are becoming more concerned about individualism that devalues self-restraint and rewards competitive drive more than cooperation, personal skills more than team work.[21] The meaning of work, relations with the opposite sex, and the importance of inner harmony underwent change as more people questioned the traditional ways of defining success. As a consequence of this trend, marriages were postponed, birthrates dropped, divorce rates skyrocketed, and young women in the millions joined the labor force. Increasingly, marketers find that consumers are preoccupied with maintaining economic stability in an environment perceived as hostile. Other changes include more

[19]Jacob, "The Big Rise," p. 74.

[20]For an interesting discussion of the problems international media companies face in servicing Asian populations because of their diverse cultures, see "Aliens Invade Asia," *The Economist*, October 8, 1994, p. 33.

[21]Cheryl Russell, "The Master Trend," *American Demographics*, October 1993, p. 28.

concern about education, health and its costs, the environment, dependent care, and personal safety.[22]

Changing family structure

The traditional husband-dominated, closely structured family is growing less and less typical of North American society. Children are becoming more autonomous and participate at an earlier age in many family decisions. A more balanced allocation of power between husband and wife has also emerged. Working parents' absence from home has substantially reduced the interactions among family members, eroding cohesiveness. The rising divorce rate has made one-parent households commonplace. Such changes are also occurring in Europe, Japan, and Pacific Rim countries but not to the same extent as in the United States.

This evolution of the family has considerably changed the buying process for many goods. It is now commonplace for all family members to influence the purchase of such major durables as housing, cars, furniture, and appliances. The influence of men on food purchases compared with that of women has risen in households where both spouses work outside the home. Consequently, many food firms are redirecting some of their marketing communications from media aimed primarily at women to those appealing to men and children.

The demographic/economic environment

In an uncertain economic climate, the variables most likely to affect marketing strategies and programs are population demographics, rates of economic growth, interest rates, currency exchange rates, and international competition.

Demographic trends

The world's population is estimated at 5.5 billion and is expected to grow to 7.2 billion by 2010, with 60 percent residing in Asia. Thus, the distribution of the world's population continues to shift to the less developed countries that are already overpopulated. In contrast, the developed nations have a relatively stable population; Europe even has a declining birth rate. A further difference between less developed and industrialized nations is that in the former about 40 percent of the population is under 44 years of age, versus 25 percent in the latter. The percentage of citizens in the industrialized nations in the over-65 age group is about twice that of the developing countries.[23]

---

[22]Elizabeth Emlich, John Hoenr, Michael J. Mandel, David Castellon, Antonio N. Fins, and Todd Mason, "How the Next Decade Will Differ," *Business Week*, September 25, 1989, p. 142.

[23]*World Population Prospects* (New York: United Nations, 1990), pp. 22–28; and "Trends in Total Population: International Estimates 1977–1991 (Mid-year)," *International Marketing Data and Statistics* (London: Euromonitor, 1993), pp. 164–225. Also see Eugene Linden, "Population: The Uninvited Guest," *Time*, June 1, 1992, p. 54; Robert S. McNamara, "The Population Explosion," *The Futurist*, December, 1992, p. 6; and Robert W. Fox, "The Population Explosion: Threatening the Third World," *The Futurist*, January–February 1992, p. 60. For an interesting discussion of the consequences of the world's population explosion, see Paul Kennedy, *Preparing for the Twenty-first Century* (New York: Random House, 1993), chs. 1 and 2.

Another major world population trend is the shift from rural to urban living. At present some 35 percent of the world's population lives in urban areas, and by 2025 this percentage is expected to reach 60 percent. By the year 2000 three cities will have populations in excess of 20 million: Mexico City (24.4 million), Sào Paulo (23.6 million), and Tokyo/Yokohama (21.3 million).[24]

U. S. demographics[25]   The total U. S. population is expected to grow from 250 million in 1990 to over 300 million by 2020. One of the more important demographic trends increasingly affecting business is that the U. S. population is becoming older. Americans over 50 represent a very substantial market: They have total annual incomes in excess of $800 billion, account for 40 percent of total consumer demand, and have 51 percent of all discretionary income. They own half of all luxury cars and one-third of all spa and health club memberships. As the baby boomers age, the over-50 market will become even larger—especially for home products offering convenience, security, home entertainment and comfort (such as air conditioning), health care products and services, wellness and youth-enhancing products, financial services, and recreational and leisure services.[26]

Another major trend is that the United States is becoming more ethnically diverse. By the year 2000 Asians will represent 4 percent of the population with Hispanics at 10 percent and blacks at 12 percent. By 2015 Hispanics are expected to replace blacks as the largest minority group. Such growth will further internationalize the United States—especially such major cities as Los Angeles, Miami, and New York. Products with high ethnic appeal such as food and clothing should be in high demand in such areas.[27]

Economic performance

Economic performance is usually measured by a country's per capita gross national product (GNP).[28] But in order to realistically compare incomes between countries, it is necessary to adjust for what a given sum of money will buy in each (purchasing power parity). Exhibit 4–3 shows such data for select countries in terms of purchasing a hamburger.

Interest rates in the United States are currently between 8 and 9 percent, and many economists believe that U. S. interest rates will remain in that range for some time. High interest rates adversely affect the market by restricting capital spending and customers' financing capabilities—particularly for such consumer durables as housing, cars, and major appliances.

---

[24]*Prospects of World Urbanization* (New York: United Nations, 1988), pp. 19–21. Also see Eugene Linden, "Megacity," *Time*, January 11, 1993, p. 25.

[25]Much of this section is based on William Dunn's article entitled "Survival by the Numbers," *Nation's Business*, August 1991, pp. 14–21.

[26]Kenneth J. Doka, "When Gray Is Golden," *The Futurist*, July–August, 1992, p. 16. Also see Margaret Ambry, "The Ages of Spending," *American Demographics*, November 1990, p. 16.

[27]"American Diversity," *American Demographics*, Desk Reference, no. 1, July 1991, pp. 4–7.

[28]For a discussion of other data used to measure a nation's economic performance, see Brian Toyne and Peter G. Walters, *Global Marketing Management* (Boston, Mass.: Allyn and Bacon, 1993), ch. 7.

EXHIBIT 4–3

The Big Mac Hamburger Index

> *The Economist* annually publishes a McDonald's Big Mac hamburger index based on an exchange rate that leaves hamburgers costing the same in all countries. The Swiss Big Mac is the most expensive, while that of China is the least expensive. Dividing Switzerland's price of SFR 5.70 by the average American price of $2.30 gives a Big Mac purchasing power parity for the dollar of SFR 2.48 (at this exchange rate a Swiss Big Mac would cost the same as an American one). But the current exchange rate is only SFR 1.44, indicating that the Swiss franc is overvalued versus the dollar by 72 percent. Using the same reasoning, the Chinese yuan is undervalued by 55 percent while the yen is overvalued by 64 percent, the D-marc by 17 percent, and the French franc by 38 percent.

Source: "Big Mac Currencies," *The Economist*, April 9, 1994, p. 88.

Fluctuating *exchange rates* may significantly change the relative price competitiveness of firms manufacturing in different countries. For example, the sharp appreciation of the yen over the dollar (from 264.45 in February 1985, to less than 100 to the dollar in April, 1995) has forced Japanese automakers (despite reducing costs by moving some production to lower-cost countries) to raise prices to a point where they are on average about $2,000 more expensive than comparably equipped American cars.[29]

International competition

Increasingly, countries have become more economically interdependent. Free trade agreements in various stages of completion embrace a high percentage of the major industrialized nations of the world. Such agreements include a single European market (EC); a merging of the European community (EC) with the European Free Trade Area (EFTA) to form the European Economic Area (EEA); and the North American Free Trade Agreement (NAFTA) between the United States, Canada, and Mexico, which will eventually embrace most Latin American countries. These developments provide a host of opportunities and threats for companies located everywhere.

The United States is the largest *national* market, representing about 25 percent of the total world market for goods and services (Japan is second with 10 percent). As such, the U. S. market is a high-priority target for the businesses of most countries—especially those of Japan and Western Europe. The United States is not only the biggest importer of goods and services but also the biggest exporter, with Germany a close second.

Today nearly 30 percent of all automobiles sold in the United States are of Japanese origin. A large percentage of all TVs and radios, handheld calculators, motorcycles, binoculars, cameras, VCRs, tape players, and digital watches sold in the United States are foreign made. Many U. S. companies are now foreign owned—for example, Pillsbury (English), Carnation (Swiss), Firestone (Japanese), Brooks Brothers Clothing (Canadian), and CBS Records (Japanese). American firms increasingly compete aggressively for

---

[29]"Japanese Firms Adjust to Strong Yen," *USA Today*, April 6, 1993, p. A1.

foreign markets; companies such as Boeing, General Electric, McDonnell Douglass, and the big three automakers each export over $5 billion annually.[30] Most of the export problems faced by both large and small firms are concerned with marketing—a failure to understand and take advantage of the fundamental changes taking place in the global market environment.[31]

COMPETITIVE ANALYSIS

The competitive environment is typically of more immediate importance to most managers than the other environments; hence, it is treated as a separate and distinct subject area. More and more large firms are setting up in-house organizations to gather and analyze competitive intelligence largely because competition has intensified as well as become global. As industries mature and growth slows, increased volume comes primarily at the expense of competitors. Thus, companies are forced to pay more attention to strategies designed to exploit their competitors' weaknesses. Any analysis of the competitive environment must consider industry structure and how the interplay of various competitive forces affects the industry's long-term profitability and the competitive position, strategy, and strengths and weaknesses of a firm's close rivals. We are primarily concerned here with the second subject area—**competitor analysis**. Industry structure is discussed in the next chapter. The major steps in an analysis of individual competitors are shown in Exhibit 4–4.

Competitor's objectives

Analyzing a competitor's objectives provides important insights into whether the competitor is satisfied with its current profitability and market position and thus how likely it is to retain its present strategy. Objectives include financial goals, competitive position (market share), and such qualitative objectives as industry leadership in price, product technology, and social responsibility. Managers must know which trade-offs the competitor will make between profitability objectives and its other objectives during times of stress. For example, at the *business-unit level* managers typically seek answers to the following questions:[32]

- What are the competitor's financial and market position objectives? How are trade-offs made between these objectives? How does the competitor balance its rate of growth and return on managed assets?

- What are the competitor's expectations for some of its activities, and how do they affect its objectives? Does it think of itself as the market leader? The price leader?

---

[30]Therese Euben, "U. S. Exporters on a Roll," *Fortune*, June 29, 1992, p. 94.

[31]Edene Kaynak, "Editorial Comments," *Journal of Global Marketing* 3, no. 4, 1990, p. 3. Also see Sacred Samiee and Peter G. P. Walters, "Rectifying Strategic Gaps in Export Management," *Journal of Global Marketing* 4(1), 1990, p. 7.

[32]Based on Michael E. Porter, *Competitive Strategy* (New York: Free Press, 1980), pp. 51–57.

EXHIBIT 4-4

Competitor Evaluation Process

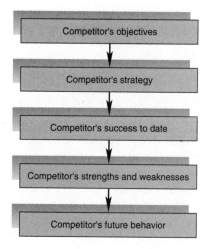

The technological leader? Is the competitor, in fact, the leader it perceives itself to be in a given field? What will it pay to remain the leader?

- What incentive and control systems does the competitor use? How do these affect management's response to competitive action?

- What is the background of the competitor's key executives? What functional areas have they managed? What companies have they worked for?

- What successes or failure of consequence has the competitor had recently? Will these affect future behavior? How?

- Does the competitor have any commitments that may inhibit action? (Commitments may or may not be contractual and include licensing, debt, and joint ventures.)

- Does the competitor have any regulatory constraints on its behavior? (This constraint can often be inferred when a large firm is reluctant to respond to the price moves made by a small competitor.)

In addition to these, a firm needs to inquire about the competitor's parent organization because it may directly or indirectly impose constraints on the behavior of its SBUs. Thus, the following questions need to be asked at the *corporate level* of the competitor:

- What are the parent company's objectives and how important is the SBU in attaining these objectives?

- How successful has the parent been, and how does this affect its reaction to the SBU's performance?

- What strategic value does the SBU have in the parent's overall strategy? A large and successful parent that has assigned an important strategic role to an SBU is likely to react strongly to any action by a competitor it perceives as threatening.
- What are the economic relationships between the SBU and other SBUs? Do they involve shared costs or complementary products?

Competitor's strategy

This analysis reviews past and present strategies of each major competitor. Past strategies provide insights into failures and reveal how the firm engineered changes, especially in new product-market relationships. Such historical information helps anticipate which strategic marketing programs the competitor might use in the future. For example, Philip Morris has traditionally emphasized programs that stressed heavy brand advertising, low costs, and maximum product availability with its cigarette, beer, and food products.

Competitor's success to date

The next step is to evaluate how successful the competitor has been in achieving its objectives and carrying out its strategies. Profitability measures may be difficult when the competitor is part of a large corporate entity and even more difficult where specific product-market entries are concerned. It is often possible, however, to obtain reliable estimates of sales and market share even at the segment level from a variety of sources, including annual reports and syndicated commercial service organizations.

Another important factor is the number of times the competitor has failed or succeeded in recent years. These can affect a competitor's confidence for better or worse. In a similar vein, a firm should examine how the competitor responded over the years to market and industry changes, including strategy moves made by other firms. Was there a response? How quickly? Was it a rational or emotional response? Was it successful?

Competitor's strengths and weaknesses

To a considerable extent, knowledge of a competitor's strengths and weaknesses derives from the previous steps in the competitor analysis. This information is important, especially when tied to the competitor's objectives and strategies. Any evaluation of strengths and weaknesses must take into account the relative importance of the major components of the strategic marketing program required to exploit the situation. Ideally, a firm would take advantage of a competitor's weakness using its own strength.

Competitor's future behavior

The objective of the analysis thus far has been to assess the competitor's likely future behavior in terms of its objectives and strategies. To develop a response profile for each key competitor, the following questions need to be asked. The answers should help a firm decide which competitors to target within each major segment and which strategies to use.

- How satisfied is the competitor with its current position?
- How likely is the competitor to change its current strategy? What specific changes will it likely make?
- How much weight will the competitor put behind such changes?
- How will other competitors respond to these moves? How will those responses affect the competitor initiating the changes?
- What opportunities does the competitor provide its close rivals? Will these opportunities endure for some time or will they close down shortly?
- How effective will the competitor be in responding to environmental change, including moves made by its competitors? Which events and moves can it respond to well and which poorly? For each event or move, what retaliatory actions are most likely?

STRATEGIC ENVIRONMENTAL ISSUE MANAGEMENT

Managers need a system that enables them to identify, evaluate, and respond to environmental issues that may affect the firm's long-term profitability and market position. One such approach, termed **strategic environmental issue management**, is used by many well-known companies, including Coca-Cola, Bank of America, General Electric, Whirlpool, and Travelers Insurance. Basically, it consists of a four-stage process consisting of environmental scanning, key environmental issue identification, impact evaluation, and formulation of a response strategy.[33] Each of these is discussed in the following sections.

Environmental scanning

A business has three ways of organizing its scanning activities: via line managers, a strategic planning group, or a special scanning office. The first alternative is more of an ad hoc approach rather than continuous activity. When either scanning or strategic planning officers are present, the environment is likely to be monitored continuously, and ad hoc studies are made on request from an SBU. The more complex and dynamic the environment (consider the Pacific Rim, for example), the more a complete scanning system is needed.

Key environmental issue identification

In any given period many issues may be detected that could change the environment. Somehow the scanning system must determine (1) the *probability* that an issue can materialize into an opportunity or a threat and (2) the *degree of impact* it can have on the firm.

---

[33]See H. Igor Ansoff, "Strategic Issue Management," *Strategic Management Journal* 1 (1980), pp. 131–48. For a discussion of risks faced by international companies, see John Daniels and Lee H. Radebaugh, *International Dimensions of Contemporary Business* (Boston, Mass.: PWS-Kent Publishing Company, 1993), chs. 3 and 4; also pp. 85–87.

EXHIBIT 4-5

Opportunity/Threat Matrix for Electric Utility Company

		Probability of occurrence	
		High	**Low**
Level of impact	**High**	4	1
	Low	2	3

1. Fluidized-bed combustion technology, which can remove 95 percent of coal's sulfur without a scrubber.
2. Compressed-air energy storage technology will become available at an affordable cost for the storage of electricity.
3. New, small modular nuclear reactors that cannot release radioactivity into the environment.
4. Given present trends in the demand for electricity and the rate at which new capacity is being added, a wave of blackouts can be expected.

Initially environmental issues are judged on these two dimensions. The issues are then plotted on an **opportunity/threat matrix** that graphically shows their relative importance. The matrix in Exhibit 4–5 contains four potential events a large electrical utility might have identified in the early 1990s. The probability of each occurring by 1997 was rated, as was its impact on the utility's profitability. Those events likely to have the greatest impact appear in the upper left box of the exhibit.

The opportunity/threat matrix enables management to focus on the most important events. Thus, events with a high probability of occurring *and* a high impact on the business should be monitored with great care and frequency. Those with a low probability of occurring and a low impact should probably be ignored, at least for the time being. Events with a low probability but a high impact should be reexamined at frequent intervals, while those with a high probability but a low impact should be reexamined less frequently to determine whether their impact rating remains sound.

Impact evaluation

Determining the impact of a key environmental issue requires answering four basic questions:

- Does the issue represent an opportunity or a threat to the firm?
- How significant will its impact be on the operations and performance of the firm?
- What is the likely timing of its impact?
- What specific marketing areas will it affect?

Analysts can chart the first three considerations for key environmental issues on a graph called an **opportunity/threat profile** (see Exhibit 4–6). The horizontal axis of the graph corresponds to the estimated timing of the environmental event. (The width of the box indicates the extent of uncertainty about the timing.) The vertical axis represents its impact

EXHIBIT 4–6

Opportunity/Threat Profile

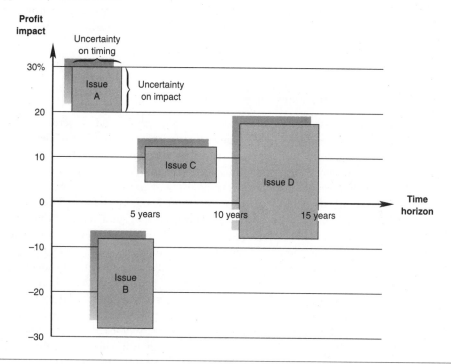

SOURCE: Copyright 1975 by The Regents of the University of California. Reprinted from the *California Management Review*, vol. 18, no. 2. By permission of The Regents.

on a performance measure such as profits or market share. (The height of the box indicates the extent of uncertainty about the profit impact.) Environmental issues below the time horizon imply potential losses in performance; those above indicate gains.[34]

In Exhibit 4–6 issues A and C are opportunities, although A is more immediate and significant. Issue B represents a definite threat, but there is substantial uncertainty about its impact level. Issue D is remote in the future, and there is considerable uncertainty concerning both its timing and impact. It could either be a substantial opportunity or have a limited negative effect on the firm's profitability.

A cross-impact analysis is often desirable in an effort to forecast the occurrence of an event. For example, will electric cars account for 2 percent of the new cars sold in the United States by the year 2000? The probability of this occurring would be estimated by considering the simultaneous impact of certain events, such as the development of longer-lasting and

---

[34]The opportunity/threat profile representation was proposed by H. Igor Ansoff in "Managing Strategic Surprise by Response to Weak Signals," *California Management Review*, Winter 1975, pp. 21–33.

faster-charging batteries; the availability of lighter-weight materials (one-third as heavy as those now used in producing car bodies); and the cost of a gallon of gasoline by the year 2000. Of particular interest to a firm is the *relative* impact of a key environmental issue. That is, within the same industry some firms will perceive a given issue as an opportunity while others see it as a threat.

Formulation of response strategies

A firm's **response strategy** includes both reactive and proactive strategic responses to an environmental issue. This assumes a time interval between the identification of a key issue and the event it triggers. A **reactive strategy** is undertaken in response to a major environmental event, often in a crisis situation. For example, some years ago in the United States Tylenol capsules were tampered with by someone unconnected with Johnson & Johnson, the manufacturer, or its channels of distribution. The company responded by recalling all Tylenol capsules and destroying them at a cost of $150 million.[35]

A **proactive strategy** is formulated in response to a key environmental issue in anticipation of its becoming an event. For example, in early 1993 the Clintons labeled the pharmaceutical industry as the major health care villain. Threatened with price control legislation that would dramatically lessen its profitability, the industry has to date delayed the passage of such legislation, perhaps even permanently. It did so by spending millions in lobbying, advertising, and public relations to create an image of themselves as researchers dedicated to improving health care and saving millions of lives at a cost of only 7 cents out of every health care dollar.[36] A proactive strategy is usually more desirable than a reactive one because it avoids pressure decisions and enables the firm to perform more in-depth analyses. Further, the greater the lead time, the broader the array of options. Exhibit 4–7 discusses examples of six response strategies that can be fashioned in either reactive or proactive modes.

ETHICAL ISSUES ARISING FROM THE ENVIRONMENT[37]

Some firms have responded to the environmental concerns of consumers by developing and promoting environmentally friendly products. For example, Kimberly-Clark uses recycled paper; Coca Cola, Heinz, and Pepsi Cola use recycled plastic bottles; and DuPont has suspended production of chlorofluorocarbons. In some (but not all) cases firms have benefited from such actions. In cases involving voluntary action a major issue is how to

---

[35] N. Craig Smith and John A. Quelch, *Ethics in Marketing* (Homewood, Ill.: Irwin, 1993), p. 291.

[36] Rick Wartzman, "Drug Firms' Lobbying to Defuse Criticism by Clintons Pays Off," *The Wall Street Journal*, August 16, 1994, p. A1. For a discussion of proactive marketing in the international arena, see Magorah Marie Yama, "International Proactive Marketing," *Journal of International Consumer Marketing* 4, no. 3 (1992), p. 95.

[37] This section has benefited from Melvyn A. J. Menezes, "Ethical Issues in Product Policy," in N. Craig Smith and John A. Quelch (eds.), *Ethics in Marketing* (Burr Ridge, Ill.: Irwin, 1993), pp. 294–98.

EXHIBIT 4-7

Response Strategies to Environmental Issues

1. **Opposition strategy:** The effectiveness of this strategy is limited because environmental factors are largely beyond the control of a firm. In some situations, a firm may, however, try to delay, attenuate, or otherwise influence an environmental force. Lobbying and corporate issue advertising are examples of opposition strategy used by some large firms.

2. **Adaptation strategy:** Adaptations are often compulsory as, for example, is the case with legislation on product specifications, packaging, and labeling. Choices often exist, however, in the type and extent of adaptation. The danger is that if an adaptation strategy is pursued to the extreme, the environment (not management) sets the pace and scope of strategic change.

3. **Offensive strategy:** Such a strategy uses the environmental issue to improve the firm's competitive position. A key environmental issue may have a destabilizing effect on an industry, which may create opportunities for the more aggressive firms. This was the type of strategy used by Merck in its offer to cut its prices to Medicaid programs. Merck's discounts would be 7 to 13 percent less than the company's regular wholesale prices. Some competitors would likely respond by offering deeper discounts on bulk purchases. Whether Merck would respond is problematical.★

4. **Redeployment strategy:** Faced with major environmental issues in one market, a firm may decide to redeploy its resources in other, less exposed areas. For example, tobacco companies such as Philip Morris and R. J. Reynolds have diversified into other consumer goods because of the environmental pressures concerning the health effects of cigarette smoking.

5. **Contingency strategies:** One such strategy decreases the risk of being exposed to potentially harmful environmental events. For example, a search may be launched for substitutes for raw materials with volatile prices. Another contingency strategy designs alternative courses of action corresponding to the different possible evolutions of the environment. This involves isolating discrete environmental scenarios the firm may have to face in the future and designing appropriate responses for each. For example, gasoline-fueled cars may be restricted in certain localities (e.g., Los Angeles) and, thus, some automobile companies are experimenting with electric cars and natural gas–powered vehicles.†

6. **Passive strategy:** This strategy calls for not responding to an environmental threat or opportunity. For example, in the early days of modern consumerism, some corporations took major public action to oppose their critics — which only provided greater exposure to the issue and worsened their images. A better alternative would have been not to have taken *any* action until performing more complete analyses and formulating an appropriate response.

★Ron Winslow. "Merck Plans Medicaid Price Cut." *The Wall Street Journal*, April 23, 1990, p. B5.

†"Cars and Truck Fleets Turn to Cleaner Fuels," *The Wall Street Journal*, July 24, 1992, p. B1. Both reprinted by permission of *The Wall Street Journal*. © 1990, 1992 Dow Jones & Company, Inc. All Rights Reserved.

handle the trade-off between profits and what's best for the environment.[38] A closely related issue is when to take action to avoid liability because it will likely take years before one can tell whether any management decisions concerning the environment will turn out to be good or bad.

---

[38]Some companies find themselves in the awkward position between having to appease a growing number of environmentally concerned customers and lobbying against certain state and federal measures that adversely affect their best-selling brands. See Alecia Swazy, "P & G Gets Mixed Marks as It Promotes Green Image but Tries to Shield Brands," *The Wall Street Journal*, August 26, 1991, p. B1.

Another concern is how a company's attempt to produce and promote environmentally friendly products will be received by consumers and the government. Some overly enthusiastic green-marketing campaigns in Britain and Canada have been criticized by environmental groups for making claims that were either inappropriate or incapable of being substantiated.[39] For instance, Revlon and Gillette made false claims about the environmental benefits of their aerosol products, and Alberto-Culver claimed its Alberto VO5 spray was environmentally safe, although 10 states had charged that it contained ozone-damaging contents.[40]

ETHICAL ISSUES IN GATHERING COMPETITIVE INTELLIGENCE

There is nothing inherently wrong with gathering information about a competitor's activities. Indeed, a surprising amount of detail about a competitor's objectives, strategies, and tactics is available from public sources. Admiral Ellis Zacharias, Deputy Chief of U. S. Naval Intelligence during World War II, said that 95 percent of all necessary intelligence, corporate or military, could be found in the public arena.[41] Since then, there has been an ever-increasing flow of freely available information (some in surprising detail) about industries and companies.

But despite the public availability of much competitive information, there are ethical issues about the methods used by some companies to obtain certain intelligence data. These questionable practices fall into three categories:[42]

1. Those involving deceit or misrepresentation. Examples include administering a questionnaire while posing as a graduate student, a private research firm, or a supplier.

2. Influencing potential informants to reveal confidential information. Examples include inducements of cash or the promise of a better job.

3. Those involving covert or unconsented-to surveillance. Examples include information from disgruntled former employees. The question here is whether such information should be regarded as private and therefore should not be used.

One of the difficulties concerning questionable ways of gathering competitive information is the lack of codes of conduct on this subject by most companies of any nationality. The ethics code of the Society of Competitor Intelligence Professionals does require its members to fully disclose their identity and company affiliation before their interviews and to respect all requests for confidentiality.

---

[39]David Kirkpatrick, "Environmentalism: The New Crusade," *Fortune*, February 12, 1990.

[40]See Alicia Swazy, "P & G Gets Mixed Marks." Also see Carl Frankel, "Blueprint for Green Marketing," *American Demographics*, April, 1992, p. 34.

[41]Ellis Zacharias, *Secret Missions: The Story of an Intelligence Officer* (New York: Putnam, 1946), pp. 117–18.

[42]Lynn Sharp Paine, "Corporate Policy and the Ethics of Competitor Intelligence Gathering," in Smith and Quelch (eds.), *Ethics in Marketing*, pp. 265–78.

SUMMARY

An analysis of the firm's external environment is concerned not only with the relevant industry and marketplace but also with the environmental trends affecting them. The deteriorating physical environment is rightly a cause of considerable concern, although the effects may be long-term. The demographic/economic environment has the most pervasive impact on marketing. The elements most likely to affect marketing strategies are demographics, economic growth, interest rates, and currency exchange rates. The political/legal environment includes all those factors controlled by authorities. The major factor here is legislation that defines the regulatory environment within which businesses must operate. The influence of the political/legal environment is not necessarily negative—opportunities may also be provided.

Technology can have a substantial impact on the performance and competitive structure of an industry. The pace of technological development has been increasing and promises to become even more intensive in the future. Three of the more important technologies having a significant influence on the future of our society are electronics/telecommunications, biology, and manufactured materials.

The sociocultural environment, which evolves slowly, represents the values, attitudes, and general behavior of people in a given society. Some of the more significant trends involve shifts in individual values toward self-realization and fulfillment, recognition of the human rights of diverse populations, changes in family structure, and concern about the environment.

Competitive analysis involves both an industry and individual close competitors. Only the latter were discussed in this chapter. The process consists of analyzing present and potential key competitors in an effort to better anticipate their future moves. The major steps in the competitor-evaluation process are the analyses of competitors' objectives, strategies, success to date, and strengths and weaknesses.

Firms should also assess the objectives and success to date of a competitor's parent company, the strategic value of the competitor SBU to the parent, and the economic relations between the competitor SBU and other SBUs within the parent firm.

The strategic environmental issue management process consists of scanning the environment, identifying key environmental issues, evaluating their impact, and formulating a response strategy. The latter can be fragmented into six response strategies having to do with opposition, adaptation, offensive action, redeployment, contingency planning, and doing nothing.

A number of ethical issues are involved in the development and marketing of environmentally friendly products. Ethical issues also arise in the gathering of competitive intelligence; questionable practices center on the need to disclose identity before soliciting information, on not exerting undue influence on respondents to reveal confidential data, and on honoring requests for confidentiality.

Industry Dynamics and Strategic Change

CELLULAR PHONES: HOT PRODUCTS![1]

Sales of cellular phones in America are exploding. At the end of 1993 an estimated 16 million people had such phones—up from 5.3 million in 1990. Industry analysts report that an average of 14,000 people a day are signing up for wireless phone service. Industry members are spending $11 billion annually to keep pace with demand. Sales are also increasing dramatically in Japan and Europe, and one industry forecaster expects the number of users worldwide to be about 100 million by the year 2000, up from around 30 million now.

Initially growth was fueled largely by businesspeople seeking improved productivity by making phone calls from their cars. But cellular phones are increasingly becoming a consumer product just as personal computers, small copiers, and faxes

have. Consumers buy cellular phones for many reasons including to improve their safety, increase their social contacts, and enhance their status.

The demographics of U. S. cellular phone owners show that in the late 1980s some 80 percent were men, but by 1993 this figure had dropped to two-thirds. During this same period the percentage who used their cellular phones primarily for business dropped from 74 percent to 34 percent. Other demographics of cellular consumers show them to be well-educated, with more than half having attended college. As for occupation, 24 percent report they are managers, professionals, or executives, while another quarter say they hold sales, clerical, or technical positions.

While some 5 percent of U. S. households owned a cellular telephone in 1993,

[1]Peter Francese, "Cellular Consumers," *American Demographics,* August 1994, p. 30. Also see William Echikson, "How to Win Markets Fast," *Fortune,* May 30, 1994, p. 114; Neil Gross, "Come One, Come All to the Cellular Sweepstakes," *Business Week,* April 25, 1994, p. 50; and G. Christian Hill, "Wanna Bet?" *The Wall Street Journal,* February 11, 1994, p. B12.

about 14 percent of all households with an annual income of $45,000 and over were subscribers. Ownership is most common among households with members between 24 and 45 years of age. As this group passes into the highest-income age group, millions will be able to afford luxuries like the cellular phone. As time passes and users become accustomed to this type of communication, its luxury will increasingly be perceived as a necessity.

STRATEGIC VALUE OF INDUSTRY EVOLUTION

Firms can benefit greatly if they are among the first to adjust to environmental change, especially where new products are involved. This was the case with Noika, a Finnish company, which, by focusing on telecommunications in the 1980s, parlayed a small telephone business into being number one in cellular phones in Europe and second only to Motorola in the United States.[2]

On the other hand, companies that delay in taking advantage of an environmental opportunity—especially in product development—often find themselves at a severe disadvantage later because the leader's products are likely to become the standard against which others are compared. Also, the leader may appropriate important ways of accessing the market as well as the major promotion appeals.

As we shall see in Chapter 8, some evidence suggests that the first firm to exploit an environmental opportunity for a new product-market tends to retain a market share and profitability advantage over followers.[3] It would be a mistake, however, to assume that the simple act of being first leads to a strong advantage over time. A recent study found that because some firms excel at leading and others at following, entry timing should depend on the firm's ability to assess its internal skills and resources in light of the market's requirements.[4]

For a variety of reasons, products and markets are constantly evolving. On the product side, the growing commonality of technology increases the difficulty of maintaining strong product differentiation. Over time, costs per unit tend to decline because of scale and learning effects. On the market side, demand eventually slows, and consumers become more knowledgeable about the product, forming attitudes about the attractiveness of competing brands. And over time, industry structure and rivalry among established companies change.

These evolutionary forces interact to affect not only a market's attractiveness but also the success requirements for a firm's various product-market entries. The management implications of this evolutionary process are as follows:

---

[2]Echikson, "How to Win Markets Fast," p. 114.

[3]William T. Robinson and Claes Fornell, "Sources of Market Pioneering Advantages in Consumer Goods Industries," *Journal of Marketing Research,* August 1985, pp. 305–17.

[4]Michael J. Moore, William Boulding, and Ronald C. Goodstein, "Pioneering and Market Share: Is Entry Time Indigenous and Does It Matter?" *Journal of Marketing Research,* February 1991, p. 97.

- At the *portfolio level* the firm must generate new products or enter new markets to sustain its profitability over time. This has been the case in the coffee industry, where gourmet blends are the only growth segment and are the younger generation's most popular kind of coffee.[5]

- At the *product level* the objectives and strategy change as the product passes through various evolutionary stages. For example, in the fax business machines using plain paper are increasingly more popular than those that use the thermal print process. Fujitsu made only thermal print units and was at a further disadvantage because the plain paper process depends heavily on office copier technology, which Fujitsu had ignored. In April 1992 the company closed its U. S. facsimile operation.[6]

- At the *marketing program level* the evolutionary process typically generates significant changes. For example, sales of camcorders (lightweight video cameras) have plateaued, and the industry is beginning to realize that it has to find new markets beyond young parents. In an effort to reach new customers, camcorder firms are downplaying the high-tech nature of their product by simplifying its design, cutting prices, and changing advertising appeals and media vehicles.[7]

Hamel and Prahalad argue that most high-level managers spend too little time developing an understanding of their industry's future, including its opportunities and threats. They estimate that senior management spends, on average, only about 2.5 percent of its time in forging a corporate understanding of its future. The lack of viable foresight inhibits the company from exploiting its potential to define a leadership position that would control its own destiny.[8]

But no matter how much time is spent trying to anticipate change, it is a very difficult undertaking. A systematic framework is needed to help managers better understand the major components of the product-market evolutionary process. This is especially the case as more and more markets become internationalized. This chapter first discusses the product life cycle, which is a generalized model of the sales history of a given product over a long time. It then discusses the major components of the evolutionary process—the market, the product, and the competitive (supply side) environment—in an effort to provide a better understanding of the forces at work.

DEFINING PRODUCTS AND MARKETS: THE UNITS OF ANALYSIS

Specifying a framework for understanding product-market evolution—including the product life-cycle concept—requires understanding what is meant by a product and a market. Thus, a product may have several life cycles depending on how its markets are defined.

---

[5]Carrie Goerne, "Coffee Consumption Down but Sales of Exotic Blends Perk Up," *Marketing News,* July 20, 1992, p. 1.

[6]John J. Keller, "Fujitsu to Close Its U. S. Business of Fax Machines," *The Wall Street Journal,* April 10, 1992, p. 34.

[7]Patrick M. Reilly, "Camcorder Makers, with Growth Easing, Try to Bring New Markets into the Picture," *The Wall Street Journal,* December 26, 1991, p. B1.

[8]Gary Hamel and C. K. Prahalad, "Seeing the Future First," a *Managing/Fortune* book excerpt, *Fortune,* September 5, 1994, p. 64.

Defining products and markets is even more difficult because they can be summed to form several different levels of aggregation. For example, Gillette, which has long employed the strategy of introducing its new products in the United States and marketing its older products overseas, recently introduced its Sensor Razor in the United States while marketing its Platinum Plus blade, which was first sold in the United States in 1967, in Pakistan.[9]

Product definitions

Products can be defined at the industry, product class, product type, and brand level. The problem with using the industry level is that it typically includes an array of noncompeting products. For example, within the automotive industry, is a Ford Fiesta in competition with a BMW? Within the chemical industry, do polymers that substitute for natural materials compete with gasoline additives, dye stuffs, and industrial coatings?

Product class suffers from this same type of problem because the products involved may serve diverse markets. The more generic the definition of a product class, the higher the aggregation level of products (for example, all desserts versus pastries) and the more stable the product life-cycle curve. Basic needs change slowly, and the effect of substitution, or *cross elasticity,* is lessened by the level of aggregation used; further, the more the product class is defined by generic need, the less useful it is for strategic planning, which seeks to identify opportunities and threats for specific product-market relationships.

Brands, which are at the bottom of the aggregation hierarchy, are also inappropriate units of analysis. Their sales are largely a function of management's strategic decisions, marketing expenditures, and competitive action.

Product types are subsets of a product class and contain items that are technically the same, although they may vary in such aspects as appearance and price. We have selected this level as our unit of analysis because product types, while serving different subsets of needs, are often close substitutes for one another. The product-type level of aggregation is considerably more sensitive to environmental changes that lead to opportunities and threats for individual product-market entries.

Market definitions

A market hierarchy is more complex than that of a product because of the numerous ways markets can be segmented. At the outset we need to link products and markets. This should be done by defining customer needs in terms of usage requirements related to product attributes. Since choice criteria ordinarily discriminate on the basis of several product characteristics, we can define the market for a given product type or subtype as those consumers with similar choice criteria. However, knowing what choice criteria consumers have is insufficient because we need to identify consumers with certain criteria and potential for targeting purposes. The resulting customer groups are referred to as *market segments,* which need to be described in terms of such factors as demographics, lifestyle, and location. As Exhibit 5–1 shows, the market hierarchy can vary substantially in the number of levels involved.

---

[9]Eric D. Randall, "Gillette Strategy Rides Cutting Edge," *USA TODAY,* September 16, 1992, p. 3B.

EXHIBIT 5–1

Illustration of a Market Hierarchy for a Consumer Product

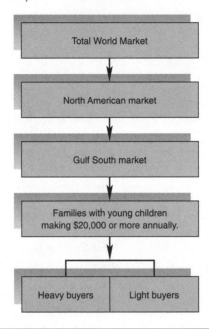

Firms differ in the levels they target; but the trend clearly is toward greater specificity—that is, targeting more precisely defined segments at the lower levels in the hierarchy. Thus, Johnson & Johnson targets children aged two to six years old with a special line of Winnie-the-Pooh shampoo products that includes Pooh's shampoo, Eeyore's conditioning detangler, Tigger bath bubbles, and Piglet liquid bath. These products use a thicker formula than do Johnson & Johnson baby products, and they have a new fruity fragrance.[10] Similarly, given the demographic information available to cellular phone companies, it is almost a certainty that they are defining their target markets with considerable precision.

As with the product hierarchy, product life-cycle curves vary depending on which market level is the basis for defining the target market—the higher the level of aggregation, the more apt the curve is to change slowly.

The product life cycle

The product life cycle concept holds that a products' sales change predictably over time and that products go through a series of five distinct stages: introduction, growth, shakeout,

---

[10]Jennifer Lawrence and Pat Sloan, "P & G Heads Shampoo into Preteen Segment with Pert Line Extension," *Advertising Age,* April 26, 1992, p. 3.

EXHIBIT 5–2

Generalized Product Life Cycle

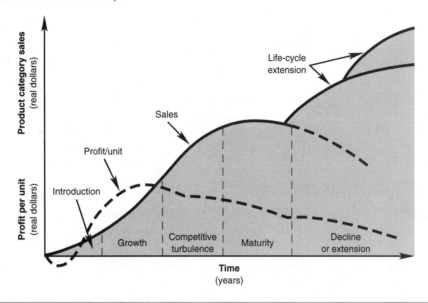

maturity, and decline (see Exhibit 5–2). At the beginning (the **introductory stage**), a product's purchase is limited because members of the target market are insufficiently aware of its existence; further, the product often lacks easy availability. As more people learn about the product and it becomes more readily available, sales increase at a progressively faster rate (the **growth stage**). Growth slows as the number of buyers nears the maximum and repeat sales become increasingly more important than trial sales. As the numbers of both buyers and their purchases stabilize, growth becomes largely a function of population growth in the target market.

At the end of the growth period—just before the advent of maturity—the **shakeout** or **competitive turbulence** stage occurs. This is characterized by a decreasing growth rate that results in strong price competition, forcing many firms to exit the industry or sell out. The **mature stage** is reached when the net adoption rate holds steady—that is, when adopters approximate dropouts. When the latter begin to exceed new first-time users, the sales rate declines and the product is said to have reached its final or *decline stage.*[11]

---

[11] For an interesting discussion of the application of the life-cycle concept to almost anything besides products (e.g., the fall of the Berlin Wall, the unification of Europe, and the demise of Communism), see Theodore Modes, "Life Cycles," *The Futurist,* September–October 1994, p. 20.

Life-cycle curves

Many products do not go through a product life-cycle curve because a high percentage are aborted after an unsatisfactory introductory period. Other products seemingly never die (Scotch whiskey, TVs, automobiles). The shape of the life-cycle curve varies considerably between and within industries. For example, one study identified 12 different types of curves (see Exhibit 5–3).

In general, only one or a very few curves typify an industry. The most common curve is the classical type, followed by the cycle-recycle curve. Consumer durables tend to follow the classical curve, although many major household appliances, such as refrigerators and washing machines, have never entered the decline stage. Drug products present the most complex patterns, involving almost all cycles. Even here, however, the cycle-recycle curve seems most common. Industrial products typically follow the pattern of sales depicted by the classical curve. Product life cycles for industrial goods are usually longer than those for consumer goods.

A surge in demand during the mature period—or recycling—can occur for many reasons. These include an increase in the price of a close substitute, a disproportionate increase in the size of a prime market segment caused by demographic shifts (as in the case of cellular phones) or increased purchases by one or more end-user industries, reduced prices resulting from lower raw material costs, the development of new applications (for example, nylon was first used in parachutes, next in women's stockings, and then in tires), or a basic shift in derived demand. Innovation maturity occurs when new product types or subtypes introduced within a product class experience considerable sales success (such as more nutritional and natural ready-to-eat cereals).

CHARACTERISTICS AND IMPLICATIONS
OF PRODUCT LIFE-CYCLE STAGES

The various stages of the product life cycle present different opportunities or threats to the firm. By understanding the characteristics of the major stages in the product life cycle, the firm can make better decisions not only about its objectives and strategies but also about its action plans. However, our discussion here is only a broad overview (see Exhibit 5–4). In later chapters we present a more comprehensive examination of specific marketing strategy programs to pursue at each stage in a product-market evolution.

Introductory stage

There is a vast difference between pioneering a product class and a product type. The former is more difficult, time-consuming, expensive, and risky, as must have been the case when the telephone was introduced versus the introduction of the cellular phone. The introductory period, in particular, is apt to be long—even for relatively simple product classes such as packaged food products. Because product type and subtype entries usually emerge during the late-growth and maturity stages of the product class, they have shorter introductory and

EXHIBIT 5–3

Product Life-Cycle Curves

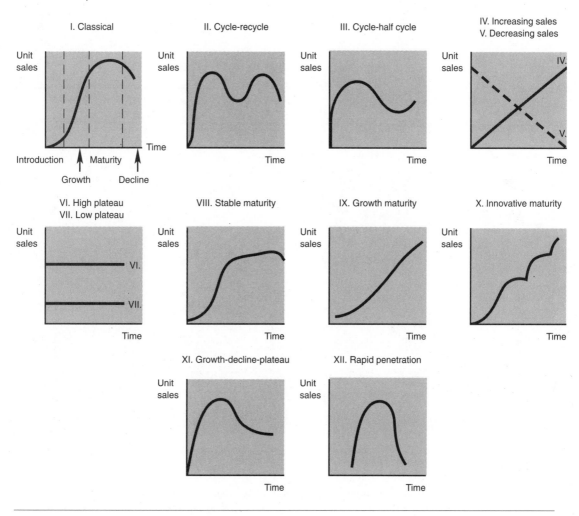

Reprinted from J. E. Swan and D. R. Rink, "Effective Use of Industrial Product Life-Cycle Trends," in *Marketing in the 80s* (New York: American Marketing Association, 1980), pp. 198–99.

growth periods. For example, the sales of cellular phones reached an annual growth rate of some 25 percent in 1994.

Once the product is launched, the firm's goal should be to move it through the introductory stage as quickly as possible. Research, engineering, and manufacturing capacity are critical to ensure quality products. Where service is important, the firm must be able to provide it promptly (as in postpurchase service and spare-parts availability). The length of the product line should be relatively short to reduce production costs and hold down inventories.

EXHIBIT 5–4

Expected Characteristics and Responses by Major Life-Cycle Stages

Stage characteristics	Stages in product life cycle				
	Introduction	**Growth**	**Shakeout**	**Mature**	**Decline**
Market growth rate (constant dollars)	Moderate	High	Leveling off	Insignificant	Negative
Technical change in product design	High	Moderate	Limited	Limited	Limited
Segments	Few	Few to many	Few to many	Few to many	Few
Competitors	Small	Large	Decreasing	Limited	Few
Profitability	Negative	Large	Low	Large for high market-share holders	Low
Firm's normative responses					
Strategic marketing objectives	Stimulate primary demand	Build share	Build share	Hold share	Harvest
Product	Quality improvement	Continue quality improvements	Rationalize★	Concentrate on features	No change
Product line	Narrow	Broad	Rationalize★	Hold length of line	Reduce length of line
Price	Skimming versus penetration	Reduce	Reduce	Hold or reduce selectively	Reduce
Channels	Selective	Intensive	Intensive	Intensive	Selective
Communications	High	High	High	High to declining	Reduce

★Eliminate weaker items.

For sophisticated industrial products the initial market consists mainly of large companies with enough resources to risk adoption, the technical capabilities to objectively evaluate the merits of the new product, and the most to gain if it works out well. To encourage consumers to try and keep buying their products, U. S. marketers of consumer products use a combination of methods, including heavy demonstration-oriented TV advertising, in-store demonstrations, free samples, coupons, and special introductory prices. The firm must also obtain distribution, in-store displays, and ample shelf space to provide product availability—particularly in supermarkets.

Pricing   The price level is strongly affected by a variety of factors: the product's value to the end user; how quickly it can be imitated by competitors; the presence of close substitutes; and the effect of price on volume (elasticity) and thus, in turn, on costs. Basic strategy choices involve skimming and penetration. **Skimming** is designed to obtain as much margin per unit as possible. This enables the company to recover its new product investments more quickly. Such a strategy is particularly appropriate in niche markets and where consumers are relatively insensitive to price, as was the case in the sale of cellular phones to business executives early in that product life cycle. **Penetration pricing** enables the firm to strive for quick market development and makes sense when there is a steep experience curve, a large market, and abundant potential competition.

Promotion   During the introductory period, advertising and salesforce expenditures are typically a high percentage of sales, especially for a mass market, small-value product. For industrial goods, personal selling costs are apt to be much higher than advertising costs.

The communications task at the outset is to build awareness of the new product's uniqueness, which is typically an expensive undertaking. Further, the promotional expenditures (such as in-store displays, premiums, coupons, samples, and off-list pricing) required to obtain product availability and trial are substantial. For industrial products, the time required to develop awareness of the product's uniqueness is often extensive due to the number of people in the buying center and the complexity of the buying systems.

Distribution   The importance of channel intermediaries during the introductory stage varies substantially from consumer to industrial goods. The latter are often sold directly, but with few exceptions consumer goods use one or more channel intermediaries. Product availability is particularly important with consumer goods because of the large amounts spent on promotion to make consumers aware of the product and to induce usage.

Growth stage

This stage starts with a sharp increase in sales. Important product improvements continue in the growth stage, but at a slower rate. Increased brand differentiation occurs primarily in product features. The product line expands largely because of the addition of new segments through lower prices and product differentiation. During the latter part of the growth stage, the firm—especially the dominant one—makes every effort to extend the growth stage by adding new segments, lowering costs, improving product quality, adding new features, and trying to increase product usage among present users.

Pricing   Prices tend to decline during the growth period (the average cost of servicing cellular subscribers has been dropping by about 20 percent annually), and price differences between brands decrease. The extent of the decline depends on cost–volume relationships, industry concentration, and the volatility of raw material costs.

Promotion   Advertising and personal selling in the growth stage become more concerned with building demand for a company's brand (selective demand) rather than demand for the product class or type (primary demand). Firms strive to build favorable attitudes toward their brand on the basis of its unique features. Even though promotion costs remain high, they typically decline as a percentage of sales.

Distribution   During this period sellers of both industrial and consumer goods hope to build a channel or a direct-sales system that provides maximum product availability and service at the lowest cost. If this can be accomplished, rivals can be placed at a disadvantage, even to the extent of excluding them from some markets. A brand must attain some degree of success before the mature stage, because during that stage channel members tend to disinvest in less successful brands.

Shakeout period

The advent of this period is signaled by a drop in the overall growth rate and is typically marked by substantial price cuts. Weaker competitors exit the market, and thus major changes in the industry's competitive structure occur. During shakeout the firm must rationalize its product line (that is, eliminate weaker items), emphasize creative promotional pricing, and strengthen its channel relationships.

Mature stage

When sales plateau, the product enters the mature stage, which typically lasts for some time. Most products now on the market are in the mature stage. Stability in terms of demand, technology, and competition characterizes maturity. Strong market leaders, because of lower per-unit costs and the lack of any need to expand their facilities, should enjoy strong profits and high positive cash flows. But there is always the possibility of changes in the marketplace, the product, the channels of distribution, the production processes, and the nature and scope of competition.

The longer the mature stage lasts, the greater the possibility of change. If the firm does not respond successfully to a change but its competitors do, then a change in industry structure of some significance may occur. Because of technical maturity, the various brands in the marketplace become more similar; therefore, any significant breakthroughs by R & D or engineering can have a substantial payout. One option is to add value to the product that benefits the customer: by improving the ease of use (voice-activated dialing with cellular phones), by incorporating labor-saving features, or by selling systems rather than single products (adding extended service contracts).[12] Increasingly, service (including prompt delivery) becomes a way of differentiating the offering.

Marketing mix changes   Promotion expenditures and prices tend to remain stable during the mature stage. But the nature of the former is apt to change; media advertising for consumer goods declines and in-store promotions, including price deals, increase. The price premium attainable by the high-quality producer tends to erode. The effect of experience on costs and prices becomes smaller and smaller. Competition may force prices down—especially when the two leading competitors hold similar shares. For consumer goods,

---

[12]"PCs—What the Future Holds," *Business Week,* August 12, 1991, p. 64.

distribution and in-store displays (shelf facings) become increasingly important, as does effective cost management.

Decline stage

Eventually most products enter the decline stage, which may be gradual (canned vegetables/hot cereals) or extremely fast (some prescription drugs). The sales pattern may be one of decline and then petrification as a small residual segment still clings to the use of the product (tooth powder versus toothpaste). Products enter this stage primarily because of technologically superior substitutes (jet engines over piston engines) and a shift in consumer tastes, values, and beliefs (cholesterol-free margarine over butter).

As sales decline, costs increase, and radical efforts are needed to reduce costs and the asset base. Even so, if exit barriers are low many firms vacate the market, which increases the sales of remaining firms, thereby delaying their exit. Stronger firms may even prosper for a time. If the curve is a steep decline followed by a plateau, then some firms can adjust. If the firm is strong in some segments vacated by its competitors, then it may experience a sufficient increase in market share to compensate for loss of sales elsewhere.

Marketing mix changes   Marketing expenditures, especially advertising, usually decrease as a percentage of sales in the decline stage. Prices tend to remain stable if the rate of decline is slow; there are some enduring profitable segments and low exit barriers; customers are weak and fragmented; and there are few single-product competitors. Conversely, aggressive pricing is apt to occur when decline is fast and erratic; there are no strong unique segments; there are high exit barriers; a number of large single-product competitors are present; and customers have strong bargaining power. For consumer goods, marketing activity centers on persuading distributors and dealers to continue to stock the item even though they may not promote it. For industrial products the problem may center around maintaining the interest of the salesforce in selling the item.

Harvesting or withdrawal   Harvesting has as its objective an increase in cash flow, which can be accomplished by milking (making only the essential investments), internal transfer of assets, and sale of the business or its assets. In any milking operation management looks for ways to reduce assets, costs, and the number of items in the product line.

Strategic implications of the product life cycle

The product life-cycle model is a framework that signals the occurrence of opportunities and threats in the marketplace and the industry, thereby helping the business change a product's strategic market objective, its strategy, and its marketing program. By matching the entry's market position objective with the investment level required and the profits and cash flows associated with each stage in the product life cycle, we can better visualize the interrelationships (see Exhibit 5–5). As would be expected, there is a high correlation between the market and industry characteristics of each stage, the market share objectives, and the level of investment, which, in turn, strongly affects cash flow.

EXHIBIT 5-5

Relationship of Strategic Market Position Objective, Investment Levels, Profits, and Cash Flow to Individual Stages in the Product Life Cycle

Stage	Strategic market objective	Investments	Profits	Cash flow
Introduction	For both innovators and followers, accelerate overall market growth and product acceptance through awareness, trial, and product availability	Moderate to high for R & D, capacity, working capital, and marketing (sales and advertising)	Highly negative	Highly negative
Growth	Increase competitive position	High to very high	High	Negative
Shakeout	Improve competitive position	Moderate	Low to moderate	Low to moderate
Mature	Maintain position	Low	High	Moderate

Investment strategy during introductory and growth stages

Because the introduction of a new product requires large investments, most firms sustain a rather sizable short-term loss. As the product moves into the growth stage, sales increase rapidly; hence, substantial investments continue. Profitability is depressed because facilities have to be built in advance to ensure supply. The firm with the largest share during this period should have the lowest per-unit costs due to scale and learning effects. If it chooses to decrease its real price proportionate to the decline in its costs, it dries up the investment incentives of would-be entrants and lower-share competitors. The innovating firm's share is likely to erode substantially during the growth stage. Nevertheless, it must still make large investments, for even though it is losing share, its sales are increasing. New entrants and low-share sellers are at a substantial disadvantage here. They must invest not only to accommodate market growth but also to gain market share.

Investment strategy during mature and declining stages

As the product enters the mature stage, the larger-share sellers should be able to reap the benefits of their earlier investments. Given that the price is sufficient to keep the higher-cost sellers in business, that growth investments are no longer needed, and that most competitors may no longer be striving to gain share, the leader's profitability and positive cash flow can be substantial. But the leader needs to continue investing to improve manufacturing, marketing, and physical logistics efficiency.

The generalized product life-cycle model portrays a profitability peak during the latter part of the growth stage. But one study of over 1,000 industrial businesses found that despite declining margins, overall profitability did not decline during maturity mainly because less money was spent on marketing and R & D.[13]

---

[13]Hans B. Thorelli and Stephen C. Burnett, "The Nature of Product Life-Cycles for Industrial Goods Businesses," *Journal of Marketing,* Fall 1981, p. 108.

The product life-cycle model's major weakness lies in its normative approach to prescribing strategies based on assumptions about the features or characteristics of each stage. It fails to take into account that the product life cycle is, in reality, driven by market forces concerned with the evolution of consumer preferences (the market), technology (the product), and competition (the supply side).[14] Mary Lambkin and George Day in particular argue strongly that greater emphasis on supply-side issues helps to better explain the evolution of a product-market. This is especially the case in understanding the dynamics of competitive behavior in evolving market structures.[15] We discuss these three driving forces in the remainder of this chapter.

MARKET EVOLUTION

The product life-cycle concept owes much to the **diffusion of innovation** theory, which seeks to explain adoption of a product or a service over time among a group of potential buyers. Thus, lack of awareness initially limits adoption. As word about the product spreads, the product enters the growth stage. When the net adoption rate holds steady, the mature stage is reached; and when the rate begins to decline, the product has reached its final or decline stage. While diffusion theory emphasizes the behavior of individuals, their demographics, and how they respond to various kinds of communication, it also considers product attributes and the competitive environment as determinants of the adoption rate.[16]

The adoption process

The **adoption process** involves the attitudinal changes experienced by individuals from the time they first hear about a new product, service, or idea until they adopt it. As might be expected, not all individuals respond alike—some tend to adopt early, some late, and some never. Thus, the market for a new product tends to be segmented over time.

The five stages in the adoption process include awareness, interest, evaluation, trial, and adoption. Each of these is discussed briefly here.

1. *Awareness.*   In this stage the person is only aware of the existence of the new product and is insufficiently motivated to seek information about it.

2. *Interest.*   Here the individual becomes sufficiently interested in the new product but is not yet involved.

3. *Evaluation.*   This is sometimes referred to as the *mental rehearsal stage.* At this point the individual is mentally applying the new product to his or her own use requirements and anticipating the results.

---

[14]Frederick E. Webster, Jr., *Industrial Marketing Strategy* (New York: John Wiley & Sons, 1991), p. 128.

[15]Mary Lambkin and George S. Day, "Evolutionary Processes in Competitive Markets beyond the Product Life Cycle," *Journal of Marketing,* July 1989, pp. 8–9.

[16]For an excellent discussion of the application of diffusion theory to industrial products, see Webster, *Industrial Marketing Strategy,* pp. 158–72.

EXHIBIT 5–6

Percentage of People Adopting over Time

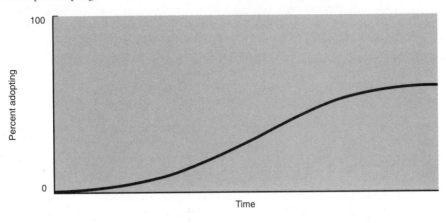

4. *Trial.* Here the individual actually uses the product but, if possible, on a limited basis to minimize risk. Trial is not tantamount to adoption because only if the use experience is satisfactory will the product stand a chance of being adopted.

5. *Adoption.* In this stage the individual not only continues to use the new product but adopts it in lieu of substitutes.

The rate of adoption

If plotted on a cumulative basis, the percentage of people adopting a new product over time would have a curve like that shown in Exhibit 5–6. Although the curve tends to have the same shape regardless of the product involved, the amount of time differs among products, often substantially.

The time dimension is a function of the rate at which people in the target group (those ultimately adopting) move through the five stages in the adoption process. Generally speaking, the speed of the adoption process depends on the following factors: (1) the risk (cost of product failure or dissatisfaction), (2) the relative advantage over other products, (3) the relative simplicity of the new product, (4) its compatibility with previously adopted ideas, (5) the extent to which its trial can be accomplished on a small scale, and (6) the ease with which the central idea of the new product can be communicated.[17] Some new products move quickly through the adoption process (a new breakfast cereal), while others take years (robots). For an interesting, if tragic, example of the importance of speeding up the adoption process, see Exhibit 5–7.

[17]Everett M. Rogers, *Diffusion of Innovations* (New York: The Free Press, 1983).

EXHIBIT 5–7

Slow Adoption of Lifesaving Medical Treatments May Be Costing Lives

> A new research study that focused on heart disease treatments reports that influential medical experts too often fail to recommend lifesaving treatments until years after clinical data support their use. The result is that thousands of lives are lost each year because such influential people are not "keeping up" with the increasing flow of research results on new remedies. For example, there was sufficient data available by 1973 to reveal that the use of blood clot dissolving drugs would significantly reduce death rates caused by heart attacks. But most "expert reviewers" didn't begin to recommend the use of such drugs until 1986 — some 13 years later. According to one medical researcher, 10,000–12,000 lives would have been saved each year if clot dissolvers had been widely used.

SOURCE: David Stipp, "Medical Experts Slow to Adopt New Remedies," *The Wall Street Journal,* July 8, 1992, p. B1.

The rate at which a product passes through the adoption process is also a function of the actions taken by the product's supplier. Thus, the diffusion process is faster when there is strong competition among members of the supplier group, when they have favorable reputations, and when they allocate substantial sums to R & D (to improve performance) and marketing (to build awareness).[18] The cellular phone industry should score high on these adoption factors.

Adopter categories

Early adopters differ from later adopters. Using time of adoption as a basis for classifying individuals, five major groups can be distinguished: innovators, early adopters, early majority, late majority, and laggards. (Note that these types of adopters differ from the five stages of adoption just discussed.) Because each category comprises individuals who have similar characteristics and because individuals differ substantially across categories, these adopter groups can be considered market segments. Thus, one would use a different set of strategies to market a new product to the early adopter group than to market it to the late majority group. See Exhibit 5–8 for the approximate size of each group.[19]

Implications for marketing strategy

The differences cited in Exhibit 5–8 are important because they provide guidelines for the development of strategic marketing programs. In organizational markets, suppliers can identify innovative firms by reputation, profitability, size, and the suppliers' experiences in dealing with them. As is evident from earlier discussion, information alone is not usually sufficient for adoption. Commercial sources of information (such as salespeople and mass

---

[18]Thomas S. Robertson and Hubert Gatignon, "Competitive Effects on Technological Diffusion," *Journal of Marketing,* July 1986, pp. 1–12.

[19]Rogers, *Diffusion of Innovations.*

EXHIBIT 5–8
Size of Individual Adopter Groups

- **Innovators** represent the first 2.5 percent of all individuals who ultimately adopt a new product. They are more venturesome than later adopters, more likely to be receptive to new ideas, and tend to have high incomes, which reduces the risk of a loss arising from an early adoption.
- **Early adopters** represent the next 13 to 14 percent who adopt. They are more a part of the local scene, are often opinion leaders, serve as vital links to members of the early majority group (because of their social proximity), and participate more in community organizations than do later adopters.
- The **early majority** includes 34 percent of those who adopt. These individuals display less leadership than early adopters, tend to be active in community affairs (thereby gaining respect from their peers), do not like to take unnecessary risks, and want to be sure that a new product will prove successful before they adopt it.
- The **late majority** represents another 34 percent. Frequently these individuals adopt a new product because they are forced to do so for either economic or social reasons. They participate in community activities less than the previous groups and only rarely assume a leadership role.
- **Laggards** comprise the last 16 percent of adopters. Of all the adopters, they are the most "local." They participate less in community matters than members of the other groups and stubbornly resist change. In some cases, their adoption of a product is so late it has already been replaced by another new product.

media advertising) are important at the outset. However, less commercial and more professional sources are sought to validate the proclaimed merits of the new product—especially during the evaluation stage. Advice from opinion leaders is more critical as a legitimizing agent than as a source of information. A classic study of how doctors reacted to the introduction of a new "miracle drug" found that only 10 percent adopted on the basis of data provided by their initial source of information, indicating that data alone will not cause widespread adoption.[20]

Thus, commercial sources are most important at the awareness stage in the adoption process, while personal influence is most important at the evaluation stage. In the interest stage, both are important. In the trial stage, marketers should attempt to make it relatively easy for a prospect to try a product under conditions that minimize risk. Therefore, strategic marketing programs should accommodate the various stages in the adoption process as well as the different adoption audiences.

PRODUCT EVOLUTION

Our discussion of the diffusion process described the impact of the product and its characteristics on the rate of diffusion; for example, the more complex and expensive the product, the slower this rate. As product characteristics evolve over time they generate

---

[20]Webster, *Industrial Marketing Strategy,* pp. 158–74.

opportunities and threats, which in turn affect product differentiations, which are key variables in determining the intensity and form of rivalry among existing firms within an industry and the ease of entry into it.

Product differentiation over time

The **PIMS (profit impact of market strategy)** research on competitive strategy has studied how a product-market's characteristics change as the market evolves.[21] As might be expected, average innovation diminishes over time. This tendency is revealed in a number of ways. First new product sales as a percentage of total market volume decline from 10.2 percent during the growth stage of evolution to 5.4 percent during growth maturity, to 3.5 and 3.7 percent during stable maturity and declining maturity, and to 2.8 percent in the decline stage.

R & D, expressed as an average percentage of sales, also declines over time. Rates fall from 3.1 percent during the growth period to 2.0 percent during the maturity period and to only 1.2 percent during the decline phase. An important point here is that product R & D declines from 72 percent of total R & D costs during growth to 60 percent during the decline period. Thus, the proportion of the R & D expenditure spent on process (rather than on product) R & D increases over time in an effort to decrease per-unit costs as the product matures.

The type and amount of R & D also appear to affect the evolutionary process by increasing the rate and level of diffusion. The more standardized the technology, the higher the diffusion rate. Thus, the more the industry spends on product R & D, the faster standardization is achieved.[22] Assuming that process R & D leads to lower manufacturing costs, which in turn are translated into lower prices, then the more money spent on this activity, the faster the diffusion rate.

An analysis by PIMS indicates that over time competitors become more alike. The index of product differentiation drops substantially (from 51 to 32) from the growth to the decline stage.[23] It is understandable why price differences between competing products also decline. And, as the market evolves, more major competitors have similar lines and serve the same types of customers. As would be expected when differentiation declines, so do margins and ROI. According to PIMS, margins drop from 30.5 percent during the growth period to 26.0 percent in stable maturity and to 21.8 percent in the decline stage. The decline in marketing expenditures for consumer goods declines from 14.1 percent in the growth period to 10.9

---

[21] The PIMS program involves data relating to the strategies and financial results of about 3,000 strategic business units from 450 companies (many of which are international) for periods of from 2 to 12 years. For more information about PIMS, see Robert Buzzell and Bradley Gale, *The PIMS Principles* (New York: The Free Press, 1987), ch. 3. This section of our discussion is based largely on ch. 10 of that book. For an interesting discussion of how Japanese executives perceive the validity of PIMS principles, see Marsaeky Kotable and Dale Durham, with David Smith, Jr., and R. Dale Wilson, "The Perceived Veracities of PIMS Strategy Principles in Japan: An Empirical Inquiry," *Journal of Marketing,* January 1991, p. 16.

[22] Robertson and Gatignon, "Competitive Effects," pp. 4–6.

[23] The relative superiority of a company's product was determined by asking managers to rate their product's performance versus those of leading competitors on a scale of 1 to 10 for each product attribute. For further information on how this rating takes place, see Buzzell and Gale, *The PIMS Principles,* chs. 3 and 6.

EXHIBIT 5–9

The Major Forces That Determine Industry Competition

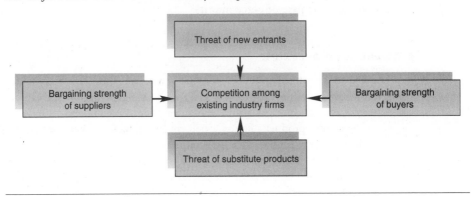

SOURCE: Adapted with the permission of The Free Press, an imprint of Simon & Schuster Inc., from *COMPETITIVE STRATEGY: Techniques for Analyzing Industries and Competitors* by Michael E. Porter. Copyright © 1980 by The Free Press.

percent in the decline period. Similar figures for industrial goods are 9.9 percent and 5.9 percent.

PIMS indicates very clearly that as the market moves from one stage of evolution to the next, some strategic marketing program changes are appropriate. Thus, in the later evolutionary stages, managers should anticipate more market share stability, fewer new products of any real significance, increased direct competition from chief rivals, and a greater price sensitivity.[24]

COMPETITIVE (SUPPLY-SIDE) EVOLUTION

This part of the evolutionary framework is primarily concerned with supply-side issues: that is, the effect of evolving industry structures on competitive behavior among firms serving much the same market(s). There seems little doubt that an industry's structural attributes affect not only the degree of competitive intensity but the bases of competition as well. Industry evolution can best be judged by analyzing changes that affect the interplay of five competitive forces over time: present competitors, potential competitors, the bargaining power of suppliers *and* buyers, and substitute products (see Exhibit 5–9).

Collectively these forces determine an industry's long-term attractiveness as measured by return on investment. The mix of forces explains why some industries are consistently more profitable than others and provides insights into what resources are required and which strategies should be adopted if the business is to be successful.[25]

---

[24]Buzzell and Gale, *The PIMS Principles,* pp. 204–9.

[25]See Michael E. Porter, *Competitive Strategy* (New York: The Free Press, 1980), pp. 30–41.

The strength of the individual forces varies from industry to industry and, over time, within the same industry. In the fast-food industry the key forces are present competitors (for example, Wendy's versus Burger King versus McDonald's), substitute products (neighborhood delis, salad bars, all-you-can-eat buffet restaurants, and frozen meals), and buyers who are concerned about health and nutrition and who see fast foods as a symbol of a throw-away society.

Present competitors

Rivalry occurs among firms that produce products that are close substitutes for each other—especially when one competitor acts to improve its standing or protect its position. Thus, firms are mutually dependent: what one firm does affects others and vice versa. Ordinarily, profitability decreases as rivalry increases. Competition is greater in these conditions:

- *There is high investment intensity; that is, the amount of fixed and working capital required to produce a dollar of sales is large.* High intensity requires firms to operate at or near capacity as much as possible, thereby putting strong downward pressure on prices when demand slackens. Thus, high investment-intensity businesses are, on average, much less profitable than those with a lower level of investment. Bob Crandall, the CEO of American Airlines, once described the airlines business as being "intensely, vigorously, bitterly, savagely competitive."[26]

- *There are many small firms in an industry or no dominant firms exist.* In recent years hundreds of pharmaceutical companies have started up, all hoping to produce new wonder drugs. In such crowded segments as neurosciences, inflammatory diseases, and drug delivery, competition is keen, and some companies are considering preemptive steps in an effort to dominate their niches.[27]

- *There is little product differentiation*—for example, major appliances, TV sets, and passenger car tires.

- *There is a high cost to changing suppliers (switching costs).* Walter Wriston, former CitiCorp CEO, notes that once you get a customer locked into your system, it's difficult for another supplier to get in.[28]

Threat of new entrants

A second driving force affecting competition is the threat of new entrants. This has been the case in recent years in many industries because of international competition, as in the invasion of the United States by Japanese firms producing a variety of home electronics products, automobiles, cameras, watches, and robots. New competitors add capacity to the

---

[26]Windy Zellner, Andrea Rothman, and Eric Schine, "The Airlines Mess," *Business Week,* July 6, 1992.

[27]Vdayan Gupta, "Consolidation in Biotechnology Industry Accelerates," *The Wall Street Journal,* July 27, 1992, p. B2.

[28]Myron Magnet, "Meet the New Revolutionaries," *Fortune,* February 24, 1992, pp. 98–99.

industry and bring with them the need to gain market share, thereby making competition more intense. Entry is more difficult under the following conditions:

- *When strong economies of scale and learning effects are present,* entry is much more difficult because it takes time to obtain the volume and learning required to yield a low relative cost per unit. If firms already present are vertically integrated, entry becomes even more expensive. Also, if the exiting firms share their output with their related businesses, the problem of overcoming the cost disadvantage is made more difficult.
- *If the industry has strong capital requirements at the outset.*
- *When strong product differentiation exists.*
- *If gaining distribution is particularly difficult.*
- *If a buyer incurs switching costs in moving from one supplier to another.*

Bargaining strengths of suppliers

The bargaining power of suppliers over firms in an industry is the third major determinant of industry competition. It is exercised largely through increased prices. Its impact can be significant, particularly when a limited number of suppliers service a number of different industries. Their power is increased if switching costs and prices of substitutes are high. Suppliers are especially important when their product is a large part of the buyer's value added—as is the case with metal cans, where the cost of tinplate is over 60 percent of the value added. In recent years the bargaining strength of suppliers in many industries has changed dramatically as more companies seek a partnership relationship with their suppliers. What was once an arm's-length adversarial relationship has turned into a cooperative one, resulting in lower transaction costs, improved quality derived primarily from using a supplier's technological skills to design and manufacture parts, and decreased transaction time.[29]

Bargaining strengths of buyers

An industry's customers constantly look for reduced prices, improved product quality, and added services and thus can affect competition within an industry. Buyers play individual suppliers against one another in their efforts to obtain these and other concessions. This is certainly the case with some large retailers in their dealings with many of their suppliers.

The extent to which buyers succeed in their bargaining efforts depends on (1) the extent of buyer concentration, as when a few large buyers that account for a large portion of industry sales facilitate gaining concessions; (2) switching costs that reduce the buyer's bargaining power; (3) the threat of backward integration, thereby alleviating the need for the supplier; (4) the product's importance to the performance of the buyer's product—the greater the importance, the lower the buyer's bargaining power; and (5) buyer profitability—if buyers

---

[29]Myron Magnet, "The New Golden Rule of Business," *Fortune,* February 21, 1994, p. 60.

EXHIBIT 5-10

Railroads Are Giving Trucks a Run for Their Money

> Railway managers are optimistic about increasing their 15 percent share of the $200 billion U. S. intercity freight market. This revival of fortunes has resulted from improved service and productivity, the latter mainly from a reduction in the size of freight train crews, larger and lighter freight cars, and consolidations. This is in contrast to trucking companies, which are facing higher costs and a shortage of long-haul drivers. In an effort to reduce costs, some truckers are even putting their freight (in the form of containers) on the rails.

SOURCE: Daniel Machalaba, "Railroads Merging to Give Trucks a Run for the Money," *The Wall Street Journal,* August 11, 1994, p. B6; and Randy Tardy, "Rail Industry on a Roll Again," *Arkansas Democrat-Gazette,* October 9, 1994, p. G1.

earn low profits and the product involved is an important part of their costs, then bargaining will be more aggressive.

Threat of substitute products

Substitutes are alternative product types (not brands) that perform essentially the same functions. Substitute products put a ceiling on the profitability of an industry by limiting the price that can be charged, especially when supply exceeds demand (see Exhibit 5–10).

Changing competition and industry evolution

All five competitive forces just discussed are affected by the passage of time; therefore, their strength varies as the industry passes from its introductory stage to its growth stage and on to maturity, followed by decline. Competitive forces are apt to be weakest during the fast-growth period; thus, there are substantial opportunities for gaining market share. During the shakeout period, competitive forces are at their strongest, and many competitors are forced to exit the industry. During industry maturity, competition typically slackens, but only if the industry leader holds a strong relative share position. Increasing international competition has shortened the time when opportunities exist for gaining market share. In recent years the United States has witnessed an impressive array of mergers and strategic alliances triggered to a considerable extent by strong foreign competition. Industry after industry is being restructured. For example, 5 of America's top 10 banks have announced megamergers; the big three airlines—United, Delta, and American—are becoming supercarriers as they buy up routes from such troubled airlines as TWA and Pan Am; and Apple and IBM have announced a cooperative research undertaking.[30]

An industry will experience more price competition during maturity if the leader holds a weak *relative* share position. Kellogg and General Mills holds two-thirds of the U. S. domestic

---

[30]Brian Brenner, Kathy Rabello, Zachary Schiller, and Joseph Weller, "The Age of Consolidation," *Business Week,* October 14, 1991, p. 86. Also see Bradley A. Stertz, "In a U-Turn from Past Policy, Big Three of Detroit Speed into Era of Cooperation," *The Wall Street Journal,* June 28, 1991, p. B3.

cereal market, but since Kellogg does not hold a dominant relative share, the industry experiences considerable price competition. A declining industry usually witnesses considerable rivalry, the extent of which depends on the strength of the exit barriers and the rate of decline.

Industry evolution and potential competitors

During the early stages of industry evolution, technology is a major entry barrier along with scale economies and product differentiation. Thus, an existing company can take advantage of technology barriers to build sales and customer loyalty. This is what Gillette did with its high-tech Sensor razor, and Federal Express did the same thing in the overnight express business it created 20 years ago.

As the industry passes through its high-growth period, technology as a barrier to entry declines; witness UPS's entry into the overnight express business formerly dominated by Federal Express. As an industry passes through the shakeout stage and enters maturity, entry barriers increase because firms focus on reducing costs and developing a favorable brand image, which both constitute entry barriers. When the decline stage is reached, entry is further inhibited by the industry's low profits.

Industry driving forces

Industries, or subsets thereof, are rarely static for any length of time. A change in any of the five forces that determine the nature and scope of industry competition—suppliers, buyers, potential entrants, substitute products, and industry competitors—affects industry structure and hence a firm's strategy and marketing program for a product-market entry. Thus, it is important to look at the forces driving an industry to see how they will affect any of these. Michael Porter identifies a number of such driving forces that to a greater or lesser degree are present in the evolution of any industry.[31] These include (1) changes in the market's long-term growth rate, which directly affect investment decisions and intensity of competition; (2) changes in buyer segments, which affect demand and strategic marketing programs; (3) diffusion of proprietary knowledge, which controls both the rate at which products become more alike and the entry of new firms; (4) changes in the cost and efficiency, derived from scale and learning effects, which have the potential of making entry more difficult; and (5) changes in government regulations, which can affect entry, costs, bases of competition, and profitability.

SUMMARY

Firms benefit greatly if they are among the first to identify and take advantage of environmental change. This is especially true when a new product-market is involved. Early entrants tend to attain higher market share and profitability than later entrants. In addition to

---

[31] Michael E. Porter, *Competitive Strategy,* ch. 3.

analyzing the several dimensions of the macroenvironment, firms must also consider the evolution of their product-market entries.

The product life cycle is the traditional model used to explain the evolution of product-market entries. Essentially, it is a generalized model of the sales history of a given product category over a long period. This concept holds that a product's sales change over time in a predictable way and that the product goes through a series of distinct stages. The product life-cycle concept has been used as a framework that, by signaling the timing of opportunities and threats, prescribes the strategies and marketing programs most appropriate for each stage of the cycle. The major weakness of the concept lies in its normative approach to prescribing strategies based on assumptions concerning the features or characteristics of each stage. Hence, a firm must also consider forces relating to the product, the market, and the competitive environment.

Diffusion theory seeks to explain the adoption process for a given product, service, or idea over time and thus relates directly to market evolution. It emphasizes the behavior of individuals, their demographics, and how they respond to various kinds of communication. The process is defined as the attitudinal changes experienced by individuals from the time they first hear about a new product until they adopt it. It consists of five stages: awareness, interest, evaluation, trial, and adoption. Adopter categories are innovators, early adopters, early majority, late majority, and laggards. There are substantial demographic differences between early and late adopters.

Product evolution is mainly affected by changes in a firm's product differentiation. PIMS research shows that innovation diminishes over time, based on such measures as new product sales as a percentage of all firms' sales. R & D expenditures, a switch from product R & D to process R & D, and the percentage change in markets experiencing a major change in technology. As time passes, competitors become more alike with respect to product, the breadth of product line, and the type of customers served.

Competitive environment evolution is mainly concerned with supply-side issues and can best be studied by analysis of changes affecting the interplay of five competitive forces over time: present competitors, potential competitors, bargaining power of buyers and suppliers, and substitute products. The strength of these individual forces varies from industry to industry and, over time, within the same industry. Competitive forces are apt to be at their weakest during the fast-growth and mature periods and at their strongest during the shakeout and decline stages. The forces of present and potential competitors are the two most affected by industry evolution.

A number of driving forces are typically present in the evolution of any industry. These include changes in the market's long-term growth rate, changes in buyer segments, diffusion of proprietary knowledge, changes in costs and efficiency and in entry and exit, and changes in government policies and regulations.

Market Segmentation and Market Targeting

DUDLEY RIGGS AND THE BRAVE NEW WORKSHOP[1]

Dudley Riggs is the fourth generation of a British circus family. Riggs joined the family flying trapeze act at the age of five and performed with circuses around the world. After a bad fall, he left the circus and shortly thereafter opened a coffeehouse near the University of Minnesota campus. There, he and some friends formed an acting group, the Dudley Riggs Brave New Workshop, which specialized in satirical reviews and improvisational humor.

Over the years, the venture survived and prospered, largely on the strength of the talented young actors and writers Riggs discovered and developed. Several of those went on to become well known nationally. But despite his success, Riggs was not satisfied—there were too many empty seats and too many Twin City residents who had never seen a performance at his theater.

In an effort to learn more about his prospective audiences, Riggs commissioned a marketing research study. From their findings, the researchers recommended that he concentrate his marketing efforts on people most likely to be theatergoers— people who were young to middle-aged (26 to 45), with a high household income, who had a good education (at least some college) and a white collar/professional/ student occupation. The data also found three types of theatergoers who attended the theater for different reasons (see Exhibit 6–1).

As might be expected, the researchers found that the Brave New Workshop attracted primarily hedonist theatergoers. Thus, they recommended that Riggs' strategy should be to expand his audience within this group—especially because there was little competition for the group's

[1]Based on Shelly Braden, Catherine Brink, and Randall Hansen, "Live from Minneapolis: A Survey of the Potential Audiences of Dudley Riggs' Theaters," research paper (Minneapolis: University of Minnesota, 1978); and D. Hill, "Dudley Riggs: More Than Just That Coffeehouse Man," *Sun Weekender,* January 21, 1987, pp. 6–7.

EXHIBIT 6-1

Three Types of Theatergoers

1. The *sociables,* who go to the theater primarily as a social event. They prefer musicals or comedies and often go to good, professional community theaters.
2. The *intellectuals,* who see theatergoing as an educational experience. They want to see the classics or serious contemporary plays and prefer repertory and experimental theaters or national touring companies.
3. The *hedonists* who go to the theater primarily to have fun. They prefer comedies, satirical reviews, and humorous improvisations.

patronage. More specifically, they suggested that the attitudes and awareness of the hedonists toward the Brave New Workshop could be improved via a promotional campaign explaining and demonstrating the satirical humor presented there. They also suggested Riggs charge relatively low prices, promote the fact that people could attend a live performance for about the same price as going to a movie, and use newspaper ads and radio spots on rock and contemporary stations to communicate these messages.

SEGMENTATION, TARGETING, AND POSITIONING

The Dudley Riggs example illustrates three interrelated marketing concepts—market segmentation, market targeting, and product positioning. **Market segmentation** is the process by which a market is divided into distinct customer subsets of people with similar needs and characteristics that lead them to respond in similar ways to a particular product/service offering and strategic marketing program. In the Brave New Workshop example, the researchers divided the total population into theatergoers and nontheatergoers. They then segmented the theatergoers into three groups according to the benefits each group sought from attending a theater and the relative importance they attached to various choice criteria (such as price and location) they might use in deciding which theater to attend. Then they described each segment's demographic characteristics (age, income, and education).

Since no single theater could satisfy the needs of all three segments, Riggs had to decide which segment to target. After evaluating the relative attractiveness of each segment (size, revenue potential, and growth rate), the benefits sought by each, and the relative resources of his workshop, he decided to target the hedonist segment. This process is called **market targeting.**

Finally, **product positioning** involved designing a product offering and marketing program that creates a competitive advantage in the target market. In the case of the Brave New Workshop, Riggs followed—with considerable success—the researchers' recommendations in the development of a marketing program that would appeal to members of the

EXHIBIT 6–2

Market Segmentation, Market Targeting, and Product Positioning

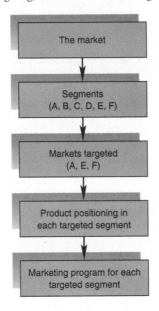

target segment (low prices, audience participation, and an informal atmosphere) and used radio and newspapers to communicate those benefits.

These three decisions—market segmentation, market targeting, and positioning—are closely linked and have a strong interdependence. All must be properly made and implemented if the firm is to succeed in managing a given product-market relationship (see Exhibit 6–2). More often than not, successful companies have been able to finesse this relationship and in so doing distance themselves from their competitors. Consider the following international example.[2]

> In England, Japanese companies have outperformed their British rivals across a range of industries. A major reason for this was that the Japanese were better at managing the segmentation, targeting, and positioning relationships. Thus, only 13 percent of the Japanese firms versus 47 percent of the British were unclear about their target segment of customers and their special needs.
>
> All too often the marketing directors of the British companies remarked that they see their market as being the whole industry and since their products had wide appeal, there was no need to segment the market. As a consequence, the Japanese concentrated their resources in specific high-potential segments while the British tended to spread theirs thinly across the entire

---

[2]Peter Doyle, "Managing the Marketing Mix," in Michael J. Baker (ed.), *The Marketing Book* (Oxford, England: Butterworth-Heinemann, Ltd., 1992), p. 273.

market. When British companies did segment, they did so at the lower, cheaper end of the market. This resulted in customers increasingly perceiving the Japanese, in contrast to the British, as offering quality and status.

The above example indicates clearly that however large the firm, its resources are usually limited compared to the number of alternative marketing investments available. Thus, a firm must make choices. For a given market the marketing investment options are expressed in terms of market segments. Even in the unusual case where a firm can afford to serve all market segments, it must determine the most appropriate allocation of its marketing effort *across* segments.

The remainder of this chapter examines market segmentation and market targeting, while the following chapter covers positioning. Our concern here is severalfold. First we take a closer look at the rationale for segmenting. Next we examine the various ways to segment consumer and organizational markets. Finally, we discuss the criteria and procedures for evaluating the long-run attractiveness of different segments and the firm's business strengths relative to customer needs and competitors. The outcome of this analysis should make it possible for a manager to decide which segments to target.

MARKET SEGMENTATION

Because markets are rarely homogeneous in benefits wanted, purchase rates, and price and promotion elasticities, their response rates to products and marketing programs differ. Variations among markets in product preferences, size and growth in demand, media habits, and competitive structures further affect the differences and response rates. Thus, markets are complex entities that can be defined (segmented) in a variety of ways. The critical issue is to find an appropriate segmentation scheme that will facilitate market targeting, product positioning, and the formulation of successful marketing strategies and programs.

A firm has the option of adopting a market aggregation strategy or a segmentation strategy. Most companies adopt the latter. A market aggregation strategy is appropriate where the total market has few differences in customer needs or desires, especially when the product can be standardized. It is also appropriate where it is operationally difficult to develop distinct products or marketing programs to reach different customer segments; that is, not all segmentation schemes are actionable. Because customers and their needs are diverse, relatively few product-markets meet these conditions. Even so, some firms have pursued at least a partial aggregation strategy—for example, Lever's 2000 multipurpose soap with annual sales in excess of $100 million enabled the company to push ahead of archrival P&G in toilet soap revenues. It was designed to appeal to both sexes regardless of the individual's skin condition (dry versus oily), fragrance preferences, and deodorant needs.[3]

While most retailers segment their market, there is some evidence that the large discount stores (including warehouse club operators) are seeking to grow sales by embracing "almost

---

[3]Valerie Reitman, "Buoyant Sales of Lever 2000 Soap Bring Sinking Sensation to Procter & Gamble," *The Wall Street Journal*, March 19, 1992, p. 89.

everyone." Increasingly consumers welcome low prices derived from large-scale buying. In the case of warehouse clubs, sales cover operating expenses while annual membership dues of $25 to $50 go straight into profits according to some industry analysts. Such organizations appear to have an opportunity to increase sales substantially.[4]

Growing importance of segmentation

Market segmentation has become increasingly important in the development of marketing strategies for several reasons. First, population growth has slowed in the industrialized countries, and more product-markets are maturing. This, in turn, sparks more intense competition as firms seek growth via gains in market share (consider the situation in the automobile industry) as well as in an increase in brand extensions (for example, Mr. Coffee's coffee, Colegate toothbrushes, and Visa travelers checks).[5]

Second, such social and economic forces as expanding disposable incomes, higher educational levels, and more awareness of the world have produced customers with more varied and sophisticated needs, tastes, and lifestyles than ever before. This has led to an outpouring of goods and services that are competing with each other for the opportunity of satisfying some group of consumers.

Third, new technology such as computer-aided design has enabled firms to customize many products as diverse as designer jeans and cars. For example, Mazda uses a flexible production system that can produce as many as eight different models on the same production line. This enables the company to produce cars made to order.[6]

Finally, many marketing organizations have facilitated the implementation of specialized marketing programs by broadening and segmenting their own services. For example, new advertising media have sprung up to appeal to narrow-interest groups. These include special-interest magazines, radio programs, and cable TV. Also, more and more broad-based magazines (such as *Time, Southern Living,* and *Sports Illustrated*) offer advertisers the opportunity to target specific groups of people within their subscription base. This approach relies heavily on zip codes and permits businesses to target not only specific regions and cities for their advertising but selected income groups as well. Increasingly, there will be the opportunity to exploit data banks made up of billions of data bytes on how consumers spend their money (see Exhibit 6–3).

Benefits of market segmentation

In addition to forcing firms to face the realities of the marketplace, segmentation offers the following benefits:

---

[4]Howard Schlossberg, "Warehouse Club Owners Hope to Sign Up Everybody Eventually," *Marketing News,* September 13, 1993, p. 1.

[5]David A. Aaker, *Managing Brand Equity* (New York: The Free Press, 1991), pp. 211–12.

[6]Micheline Maynard, "Mazda Paves Road to Profit with Flexibility," *USA Today,* December 30, 1991, p. 31. Also see Joseph Pine II, Bart Victor, and Andrew C. Boynton, "Making Mass Customization Work," *Harvard Business Review,* September–October 1993, pp. 108–19, which discusses some of the problems involved in the implementation of a highly segmented, customized strategy.

EXHIBIT 6-3

Data Mining—Developing New Views of Customers

American Express has a data bank consisting of over 500 billion bytes of data describing how some 35 million customers have used its credit cards to spend $350 billion since 1991. Others who have similar data banks (in type if not in size) include banks, insurers, Wall Street firms, and of course other credit card companies. But until recently large mainframe computers could not cope with processing such large quantities of data.

It now seems possible to break the data gridlock by using large parallel supercomputers that link hundreds of standard microchips from personal computers. The result is that parallel processors can accomplish in a matter of minutes what a mainframe would need weeks to do. American Express is currently testing a system that will tell them how cardholders shop—how often and how much they spend for what at which stores. With such information American Express could tailor a discount package for women who buy dresses at Saks Fifth Avenue featuring Saks's shoes as a reward for using their card. The hope is that such customers would charge more purchases and the store would handle more American Express business.

Other companies are planning extensive "data mining." The Rover group (automobiles) hopes to track which parts go into which production runs, thereby narrowing recalls when only one batch has a flaw. Airlines are already targeting frequent flyers but want to identify customers when they begin to travel less. Insurers hope to reduce fraud by matching multiple claims from the same individual or doctor. A large mail order firm hopes to determine which of its 25 million customers recently bought patio furniture so it can offer them a "deal" on a gas grill. But as much as the new technology gives marketing managers an ability heretofore never considered, it may represent a serious problem to consumers. The potential for abuse is enormous—especially if companies sell their data to other companies and even to the Internal Revenue Service.

SOURCE: Reprinted by permission of *The Wall Street Journal,* © 1994 Dow Jones & Company, Inc. All Rights Reserved Worldwide.

- *It identifies opportunities for new product development.* Often a careful analysis of various segments of potential customers reveals one or more groups whose specific needs and concerns are not being well satisfied by existing competitive offerings. Such uncovered segments may represent attractive opportunities for development of new products or innovative marketing approaches. Thus, for example, Toshiba entered the North American and European CAT diagnostic medical scanner market by targeting customers who had simple needs involving standard diagnoses, requiring low-power versus fully featured units made by GE and Siemens. Competitors were slow to respond because they did not believe that such a segment existed.[7]

- *Segmentation helps in the design of marketing programs that are most effective for reaching homogeneous groups of customers.* For example, by identifying and focusing on the hedonistic theatergoers, Dudley Riggs developed a pricing policy geared to their economic circumstances, selected advertising media to effectively reach them, and designed advertising appeals tailored to their unique interests.

---

[7]George S. Day, *Market Driven Strategies* (New York: The Free Press, 1990), p. 98.

- *It improves the strategic allocation of marketing resources.* The strategic benefits of segmentation are sometimes overlooked. Well-defined segments, when coupled with specific products, serve as potential investment centers for a business. Few businesses have the resources or competitive strengths to pursue all segments within a given market. Even when they do, they must still determine the appropriate allocation of resources across segments. Most dramatically successful business strategies are market segmentation–based and concentrate resources in the more attractive segments. Segmentation should focus on subdividing markets into areas in which investments can gain a long-term competitive advantage. Thus for example, Dr. Scholl has developed an array of new antifungus footware products to take advantage of the growing athlete's foot business, which has steadily increased over the past several years. These will be sold in sports and specialty stores in addition to traditional outlets such as drug and mass merchandiser retailers.[8]

IDENTIFICATION OF MARKET SEGMENTS

The objective of the segmentation process is to divide the market into groups of prospective buyers of a product or service who are relatively homogeneous with regard to their demands. Ideally, the variances within these individual groups would be small compared to the differences between groups. The process must also describe these groups so that members can be readily identified, determine the size and value of each group, and describe the differences in customer needs. The segmentation criteria (termed **descriptors**) should facilitate these objectives.

Marketers divide segmentation descriptors into four major categories for consumer and industrial markets—physical descriptors, person- or firm-related behavioral descriptors, product-related behavioral descriptors, and customer needs descriptors.[9] These categories are discussed next.

Physical descriptors

These are used mainly to describe consumers (in contrast to organizations), largely on the basis of such demographics as those shown in Exhibit 6–4. Here are some examples of their use:

Age.   Hyatt recently announced a program at its resort hotels featuring sports, excursions, and social events for teenagers.[10]

Sex.   Phillips–Van Heusen targets women in about 50 percent of its advertising because they buy 60 to 70 percent of men's shirts and are thought to be more brand loyal.[11]

---

[8]Emily Denitte, "Dr. Scholl's Steps Up Intro, Aims Younger," *Advertising Age,* July 12, 1993, p. 8.

[9]For an excellent discussion of the segmentation of industrial markets, see Frederick E. Webster, *Industrial Marketing Strategy* (New York: John Wiley & Sons, 1991), ch. 4.

[10]Ira Teinowitz, "Hyatt Thinks a Little Older as It Eyes Teens with New Program," *Advertising Age,* June 2, 1992, p. 46. Also see "How Spending Changes during Middle Age," *The Wall Street Journal,* January 14, 1992, p. B1.

[11]Terry Akins, "Women Help Van Heusen Collar Arrow," *The Wall Street Journal,* May 22, 1992, p. B1.

EXHIBIT 6–4

Some of the More Commonly Used Demographic Descriptors

Demographic descriptors	Examples of categories
Age	Under 2, 2–5, 6–11, 12–17, 18–24, 25–34, 35–49, 50–64, over 64
Sex	Male, female
Family life cycle	Young, single; newly married, no children; youngest child under 6; youngest child 6 or over; older couples with dependent children; older couples without dependent children; older couples retired; older, single
Income	Under $10,000; $10,000–$14,999; $15,000–$24,999; $25,000–$49,999; $50,000 or over
Occupation	Professional, manager, clerical, sales, supervisor, blue-collar, homemaker, student, unemployed
Education	Some high school, graduated high school, some college, graduated college
Geography	Regions, countries, cities, metropolitan areas, counties, zip codes, and blocks
Race and ethnic origin	Anglo-Saxon, black, Italian, Jewish, Scandinavian, Hispanic, Asian

Family life cycle.   The cycle describes the stages in the formation, growth, and decline in the family unit. Each stage differs in its purchasing behavior. Young marrieds, for example, are heavy buyers of small appliances, furniture, and linens, and with the arrival of children, purchases include insurance, baby food, and washers and dryers.

Income.   Higher-income families purchase a disproportionate number of cellular phones, expensive cars, and theater tickets. But low-income consumers are an important market (40 percent of all U. S. households have incomes of $25,000 or less, as the discounters have known all along).[12]

Occupation.   The sales of certain kinds of products (such as work shoes, automobiles, uniforms, and trade magazines) are tied closely to occupational type. The increase in the number of working women has created needs for goods and services such as financial services, business wardrobes, convenience foods, automobiles, and special interest magazines.

Education.   There is a strong, positive correlation between the level of education and the purchase of travel, books, magazines, insurance, theater tickets, and photographic equipment.

Geography.   Different locations vary in their sales potential, growth rates, customer needs, cultures, climates, servicing costs, and competitive structures. For example, more pickup trucks are sold in the Southwest United States, more vans in the Northeast, and more high-priced imports in California. More and more advertisers are taking advantage of geographic media buys. For example, Ford and General Motors increased their regional promotions to try to win back import buyers. Ford's campaign consisted of three regional ads with

---

[12]Cyndee Miller, "The Have-Nots," *Marketing News,* August 1, 1994, p. 1.

personalized direct response cards in three Time-Warner publications, 125,000 Taurus videocassettes mailed to Toyota and Honda owners, three different test drive incentives, and spot TV and radio ads.[13]

Race and ethnic origin.   More and more companies are targeting ethnic segments via specialized marketing programs that often include unique products such as cosmetics formulated for Asian-Americans, radio and TV commercials in Spanish, and magazines published in a variety of languages, including Chinese. American automakers are increasing their efforts via advertising to win back black consumers, who to a greater extent than whites have purchased imports.[14]

Physical descriptors are also important in the segmentation of industrial markets, which are segmented in two stages. The first, *macrosegmentation,* divides the market according to the characteristics of the buying organization, using such descriptors as geographic location, company size, and industry affiliation (SIC code). The international counterpart of SIC is the trade category code.

The second stage, *microsegmentation,* groups customers by the characteristics of the individuals who influence the purchasing decision (such as age, sex, and position within the organization). International markets are segmented in a similar hierarchical fashion, starting with countries followed by groups of individuals or buying organizations.

General behavioral descriptors[15]

General behavioral descriptors seek to produce a better understanding of how a consumer behaves in the marketplace and why. The most common behavioral descriptors in consumer markets are **lifestyle** (psychographics) and **social class,** both of which are described briefly next.

Lifestyle

Segmentation by lifestyle, or psychographics, groups consumers on the basis of their activities, interests, and opinions. From such information it is possible to infer, on a general basis, what types of products and services appeal to a particular group, as well as how best to communicate with individuals in the group. Such segmentation recognizes the fact that two people with similar demographics do not necessarily live the same way.

Stanford Research Institute (SRI) has developed a U. S. segmentation scheme (called VALS) that has a conceptual framework consisting of two dimensions—self-orientation and

---

[13]Raymond Serafin, "Regional Assault," *Advertising Age,* April 27, 1992, p. 4.

[14]William Dunn, "The Move toward Ethnic Marketing," *Nations Business,* July 1992, p. 39; Stuart Livingston, "Marketing to the Hispanic Community," *Journal of Business Strategy,* March–April 1992, p. 54; William O'Hare, "A New Look at Asian-Americans," *American Demographics,* October 1990, p. 26; and Christy Fisher, "Ethnics Gain Marketing Clout," *Advertising Age,* August 5, 1991, p. 12; and see Raymond Serafin and Ricardo A. Davis, "Detroit Moves to Woo Blacks, *Advertising Age,* April 1, 1994, p. 10.

[15]For a discussion of the growing importance of such descriptors, see Joe Mandese, "Death Knell for Demos? Buyers Set to Move On," *Advertising Age,* July 25, 1994, p. S2.

EXHIBIT 6–5

Description of VALS Eight Consumer Segments

- *Actualizers:* Successful, sophisticated, active, take-charge people with high self-esteem and abundant resources.
- *Fulfilleds (principle-oriented):* Mature, satisfied, well-informed, reflected, and, for the most part, well-educated. They are conservative, practical consumers who want value, durability, and functionality in the products they buy.
- *Believers (principle-oriented):* These are conservative, conventional people with concrete beliefs based on traditional codes: family, church, community, and the nation. As consumers, they are conservative and predictable and favor American products and established brands.
- *Achievers (status-oriented):* People in this segment are successful and work-oriented and in control of their lives. They value structure, predictability, and stability and favor established products and services.
- *Strivers (status-oriented):* They seek motivation, self-definition, and approval from the world around them. They are deeply concerned about the opinions and approval of others. Strivers are impulsive and easily bored.
- *Experiencers (action-oriented):* These are young, enthusiastic, impulsive, and rebellious people who want variety and excitement. They enjoy exercise, sports, and social activities and are avid consumers, especially with respect to clothing, music, movies, and fast foods.
- *Makers (action-oriented):* These are practical and self-sufficient people with constructive skills. They live within a traditional context of family, practical work, and physical recreation — and have little interest in anything else
- *Strugglers:* They are poor, low-skill, ill-educated, aging, and concerned about their health. They are often despairing, passive, and primarily concerned with security.

SOURCE: Adapted from materials received from Stanford Research Institute International, Menlo Park, California.

resources. The first describes how people search for and acquire products and services via self-oriented beliefs, behavior of others, and the need for social or physical activity, variety, or risk taking. Resources include the full range of physical, psychological, and material means as well as the capacities consumers can draw on such as income, education, health, self-confidence, intelligence, energy level, and eagerness to buy. By combining the two dimensions, VALS generates eight consumer segments of about equal size (see Exhibit 6–5).

In the international area, Goodyear Tire and Rubber and Ogilvy and Mather (an advertising agency), working separately, have developed several classifications for global lifestyle segments. The Goodyear effort consists of six groups—the prestige buyer, the comfortable conservative, the value shopper, the pretender, the trusting patron, and the bargain hunter. Ogilvy and Mather proposes 10 global segments based on lifestyle characteristics—basic needs, fairer deal, traditional family life, conventional family life, look-at-me, somebody better, real conservatism, young optimist, visible achiever, and socially aware.[16]

---

[16]Salah S. Hassan and Lea P. Katsnis, "Identification of Global Consumer Segments: A Behavioral Framework," *Journal of International Consumer Marketing* 3, no. 2 (1991), p. 16.

Social Class

Every society has its status groupings based largely on similarities in income, education, and occupation.[17] Because researchers have long documented the values of the various classes, it is possible to infer certain behavior concerning a given product. For example, the middle classes tend to place more value on education, family activities, cleanliness, and being up-to-date than do lower class families. In the international field one has to be careful in using social class as a segmentation variable because the difference among classes can become blurred (for example, in Scandinavian countries).[18] In America many of the criteria used to define class status seem to some to be no longer applicable as the nation becomes increasingly fragmented into dozens of distinct subcultures, each with its own unique tastes and ambitions. Claritas, Inc., has identified 62 distinct classes in the U. S., each with its own set of beliefs and aspirations.[19]

Industrial behavioral descriptors

Purchasing structure and buying situation segmentation descriptors are unique to industrial markets. **Purchasing structure** is the degree to which the purchasing activity is centralized. In such a structure the buyer is likely to consider all transactions with a given supplier on a global basis, emphasizing cost savings and minimal risk. In a decentralized situation, the buyer is apt to be more sensitive to the user's need, emphasize product quality and fast delivery, and be less cost conscious.

The **buying situation** descriptor includes three distinct types of situations: *straight rebuy*, a recurring situation handled on a routine basis; *modified rebuy*, which occurs when some element, such as price or delivery schedules, has changed in a client–supplier relationship; and a *new buying situation*, which may require the gathering of considerable information and an evaluation of alternative suppliers.

Product-related behavioral descriptors

These descriptors reflect the behavior of customers toward a specific product. They include product usage, loyalty, purchase predisposition, and purchase influence, all of which can be used to segment both consumer and industrial markets. **Product usage** is important because in many markets a small proportion of potential customers makes a high percentage of all purchases. In industrial markets the customers are better known, and heavy users (often called *key accounts*) are easier to identify.

---

[17]The relative weight of these vary across countries. In China, for example, more weight is given to occupation and education, whereas Western countries emphasize residence, income, and family background. See John D. Daniels and Lee H. Radebaugh, *International Dimensions of Contemporary International Business* (Boston: PWS-Kent Publishing Company, 1993), p. 136.

[18]Simon Majaro, "International Marketing—the Major Issues" in Michael J. Baker (ed.), *The Marketing Book* (Oxford, England: Butterworth-Heineman, Ltd., 1992), p. 430.

[19]Kenneth Labech, "Class in America," *Fortune,* February 7, 1994, p. 14.

With respect to **loyalty**—reflected by the numbers of successive purchases made over time—current users can vary considerably in their purchases of a given brand or patronage of a particular supplier. In industrial markets sellers can often observe this directly; in consumer markets identifying loyal customers requires marketing research.[20]

Consumers hold different predispositions toward the purchase of a product. A market segmentation scheme based on product knowledge (are they aware of it?) and **purchase predisposition** can identify the nonusers who are most likely to become future buyers. For example, knowledgeable nonusers who state intentions to buy, say, a high-fiber cereal are most likely to become future users. Knowledgeable nonusers who do not intend to buy, on the other hand, would probably represent a low potential.

Market segmentation based on sources of **purchase influence** is relevant for both consumer and industrial markets. Many products used by various family members are purchased by the wife, but joint husband–wife decisions are becoming more common. Children's products, prescription drugs, and gifts are clearly influenced by a variety of individuals. In industrial markets several individuals or organizational units with varying degrees of influence participate in the buying center.

Innovativeness is concerned with how individuals and organizations vary in their capacity and desire to innovate. This is particularly so for the adoption of new products. As we noted earlier, there are substantial differences between early and late adopters in terms of age, income, education, occupation, and social status. Thus, each of the various adopter groups (innovators, early adopters, early majority, late majority, and laggards) can be considered a segment.

Customer needs

Customer needs are expressed in **benefits sought** from a particular product or service. Individual customers do not have identical needs and thus attach different degrees of importance to the benefits offered by different products. In the end, the product that provides the best bundle of benefits—given the customer's particular needs—is most likely to be purchased.

Because purchasing is a problem-solving process, consumers evaluate product or brand alternatives on the basis of desired characteristics and how valuable each characteristic is to the consumer—**choice criteria.** Marketers therefore can define segments according to these different choice criteria in terms of the presence or absence of certain characteristics and the importance attached to each. Firms typically single out a limited number of benefit segments to target. Thus, for example, different automobile manufacturers have emphasized different benefits over the years, such as safety (presence of airbags), reliability, and high mileage versus styling, quickness, and status.

In industrial markets, customers consider relevant benefits that include product performance in different use situations. For example, Cray Computers are bought because they

---

[20]For a detailed discussion of the implications of customer loyalty for both market share leaders and challengers, see Adrian J. Slywatzky and Benson P. Shapiro, "Levering to Beat the Odds: The New Marketing Mind-Set," *Harvard Business Review*, September–October 1993, pp. 97–107.

meet the high-speed computational requirements of a small group of customers such as governments, universities, and research labs. Other considerations in the purchase of industrial products and services include on-time delivery, credit terms, economy, spare parts availability, and training. And different customers have different choice criteria; for instance, in the office supply market, some industrial buyers want service, while others are primarily concerned with cost and credit terms.

Note that benefits sought must often be linked to usage situations. There is ample evidence that usage often strongly affects product choice and substitutability. Thus, the appropriateness of product attributes varies across different usage environments. Any attempt to define viable segments must recognize this fact—particularly with consumer goods. For example, the appropriateness of drinking beer versus a soft drink, coffee, or gin and tonic varies substantially across such usage situations as with or after a meal, immediately following work, while watching TV, or at a formal dinner party.

As we move from physical to general behavioral to product-related to customer needs (benefits wanted) descriptors, the implications for the formulation of marketing strategies and programs become more apparent and meaningful. But all the various descriptors are important and would likely be used to some extent in the segmentation of a given market. For a summary listing of these various descriptors, see Exhibit 6–6.

THE SEGMENTATION PROCESS

As we have noted, selection of meaningful descriptors in a given market situation is the first step in the market segmentation process. The next step is to determine whether and to what extent there are differences in the needs or benefits being sought by customers in the various segments. The first and second steps in the process are sometimes reversed. Thus, a firm can first segment a market on the basis of different benefits sought and then identify it on the basis of physical descriptors.

Determining differences in needs

The segmentation descriptors used should describe the differences in customers' buying behavior in such a way that management can determine which segments require differentiated marketing programs involving different products and/or marketing activities. This is why benefits sought and product-specific behavioral variables are particularly useful for answering strategic questions like these:

- How many distinct product-markets are there within a particular industry? In the case of theatergoers, several distinct segments have different needs, including the sociables, intellectuals, and hedonists.

- Which segments represent attractive opportunities in view of the customers' needs and the firm's competitive strengths and weaknesses? Dudley Riggs determined that hedonists wanted comedies, satirical revues, and improvisations, which matched what he could provide at an affordable price.

- Which segments are not currently being satisfied and therefore represent opportunities?

EXHIBIT 6–6

Descriptors Used to Segment Consumer and Industrial Markets

Descriptors	Industrial		Consumer
	Macro	Micro	
Physical:			
Demographics	—	X	X
Company size	X	—	—
Industrial sector	X	—	—
General behavioral:			
Innovative★	—	X	X
Lifestyle	—	—	X
Social class	—	—	X
Purchase structure	X	—	—
Buying situation	X	—	—
Product-related behavior:			
Product usage	X	—	X
Loyalty	X	—	X
Purchase predisposition	—	X	X
Purchase influence	—	X	X
Customer needs	X	—	X

★Adopter group (such as innovators or early adopters).

Benefit segmentation further enhances the resource allocation process by helping the firm better understand the relative standing accorded its product compared to competitors. It also provides insights into the extent to which different segments will respond to various elements in the marketing mix, a critical part of the firm's plan of action.

General behavioral and physical descriptors are useful for answering many of the operational questions that arise during design of a marketing program to reach a particular product-market. For example:

- Which retail outlets or distributors should be included in the distribution channel?

- How should sales territories be designed and how frequently should salespeople call on different customers?

- What advertising media should be used?

- Which promotional appeals should be emphasized?

- What is the size of the segment(s)?

Marketers thus try to define segments using a combination of benefit, behavioral, and physical factors, even though this often requires collection of marketing research data and use of sophisticated statistical analyses.[21]

---

[21]For a useful discussion of one type of analysis for implementing market segmentation, see Paul E. Green and Abba M. Krieger, "Segmenting Marketings with Conjoint Analysis," *Journal of Marketing,* October 1991, p. 20. Also see Thomas P. Novak, Jan de Leévu, and Bruce MacEvay, "Richness Curves for Evaluating Market Segmentation," *Journal of Marketing Research,* May 1992, p. 254.

Requirements for effective segmentation

An effective and useful segmentation scheme should define market segments that meet four criteria: *adequate size, measurability, accessibility,* and *differential response to marketing variables.* These criteria are further defined as follows:

1. Adequate size—sufficient potential customers in each segment. This criterion involves trade-offs between customer homogeneity and scale effects.

2. Measurability—use of measurable variables as bases for segmentation. Here marketers need to combine concrete (such as age) and abstract descriptors.

3. Accessibility—segments defined to facilitate targeting of marketing efforts. Segmentation variables must identify members in ways that facilitate their contact.

4. Different response—segments must respond differently to one or more marketing variables. Segmentation variables must maximize behavioral differences between segments.

Global market segmentation

The traditional approach to global market segmentation has been to view a country or a group of countries as a single segment made up of all consumers living in that country. As Salah Hassan and Lea Katsnis note, this approach is seriously flawed because it relies on country variables rather than consumer behavior, assumes homogeneity *within* the country segment, and ignores the possibility of the existence of homogeneous groups of consumers *across* country segments.[22]

More and more companies are approaching global market segmentation by attempting to identify consumers with similar needs and wants in a range of countries and group them by their behavior in the marketplace. This intercountry segmentation enables a company to develop reasonably standardized programs that require little change across local markets, thereby resulting in scale economies.

Theodore Levitt has long been a proponent of globalization of a homogeneous marketplace for certain goods (such as consumer durables) based on price and high quality. He argues that similar segments have emerged in different countries at the same time due to technological developments affecting communications, transportation, and travel.[23] Hassan and Katsnis, using much the same reasoning, believe there are two emerging international segments—the **global elite** consumer and the **global teen-age** segment. The former is targeted by producers of products and services that fit an image of exclusivity (for example, Mercedes Benz, American Express Gold Card, and Joy perfume).[24]

---

[22]Hassan and Katsnis, "Identification of Global Consumer Segments," p. 17.

[23]Theodore Levitt, "The Globalization of Markets," *Harvard Business Review,* May–June 1983, pp. 92–102. Also see Sundar G. Bharadway and P. Rajan Varadarajan, "Standardization versus Adaptation of International Marketing Strategy: An Empirical Investigation," *Journal of Marketing,* October 1993, p. 1; and a review of the global segmentation literature in Salah S. Hassan and Lea Katsnis, "Identification of Global Consumer Segments," p. 12.

[24]For an interesting discussion of how Unilever takes advantage of Asian consumers, see "Poor Countries, Rich in Wealthy People," *The Economist,* August 15, 1992, p. 56.

The global teenage segment assumes a minimum of differences in cultural norms and lifestyles for teenagers across countries.[25] Empirical evidence supports this view for certain kinds of products such as Swatch watches, Sony's line of audio products for children, and Benetton's colorful knitwear. Even in Japan, typed as a homogeneous culture featuring the "Japan First" viewpoint, there is considerable evidence that younger generations are becoming more positive about U. S. and European products.

Clearly, many global trends influence the behavior of consumers, including increased per capita GNP, increased literacy and education, growth in urbanization, greater availability of TV, and more travel. Many consumer products are becoming more commonplace (automobiles, major home appliances, TV). Thus, the global market for many products can be thought of as in transition. This development will require global marketers to continuously monitor their markets to identify emerging segments.

MARKET ATTRACTIVENESS

Most firms no longer aim a single product and marketing program at the mass market. Instead, they break that market into homogeneous segments on the basis of meaningful differences in the benefits sought by different groups of customers. Then they tailor products and marketing programs to the particular desires and idiosyncrasies of each segment. But not all segments represent equally attractive opportunities for the firm. To prioritize segments by their potential, marketers must evaluate their future attractiveness and their firm's strengths and capabilities relative to the segments' needs and competitive situations.

Analyzing and prioritizing potential target markets

Rather than allowing each business unit or product manager to develop an approach to evaluate the potential of alternative market segments, it is often better to apply a common analytical framework across segments. With this approach managers can compare the future potential of different segments using the same set of criteria and then prioritize them to decide which segments to target and how resources and marketing efforts should be allocated. One useful analytical framework managers can use for this purpose is the **market attractiveness/business position matrix.** Managers use such models at the corporate level to allocate resources across businesses, or at the business-unit level to assign resources across product-markets. We are concerned here with the second application.

Exhibit 6–7 outlines the steps involved in developing a market attractiveness/business position matrix for analyzing current and potential target markets. Underlying such a matrix is the notion that managers can judge the attractiveness of a market (its profit potential) by examining market, competitive, and environmental factors that may influence that profitability. Similarly, they can estimate the strength of the firm's competitive position by looking at

---

[25]Marte J. Rhea, Barbara C. Garland, and John C. Crawford, "International Market Segmentation: The U.S.–Japanese Markets," *Journal of International Consumer Marketing* 2 (2), 1989, pp. 75–90. Also see Robert M. March, *The Honorable Consumer* (London: Pitman, 1990), p. 150.

EXHIBIT 6-7

Steps in Constructing a Market Attractiveness/Business Position Matrix for Evaluating Potential Target Markets

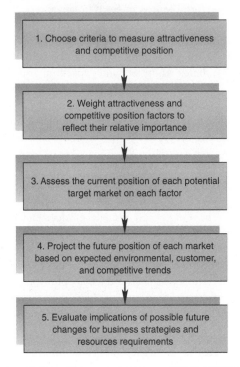

the firm's capabilities or shortcomings relative to the needs of the market and the competencies of likely competitors.

The first steps in developing a matrix, then, are to identify the most relevant variables for evaluating alternative market segments and the firm's competitive position regarding them, and to weight each variable in importance. Note, too, that Exhibit 6-7 suggests conducting a forecast of future changes in market attractiveness or competitive position in addition to, but separately from, an assessment of the current situation. This reflects the fact that a decision to target a particular segment is a strategic choice that the firm will have to live with for some time into the future.

Step 1: Select market attractiveness and business strength factors

An evaluation of the attractiveness of a particular market and of the strength of the firm's current or potential competitive position in it builds naturally on the kind of opportunity analysis discussed earlier. Managers can assess both dimensions on the basis of information obtained from analyses of the environment, customer segments, the competitive situation, and market potential estimates.

EXHIBIT 6-8

Factors Underlying Market Attractiveness and Competitive Position

Market attractiveness factors	Competitive position factors

Market/customer factors:
    Size (dollars, units)
    Market potential
    Market growth rate
    Stage in life cycle
    Diversity of competitive offerings (potential
        for differentiation)
    Customer loyalty/satisfaction with current
        offerings
    Price elasticity
    Bargaining power of customers
    Cyclicality/seasonality of demand
	Market position factors:
	    Relative market share
	    Rate of change in share
	    Perceived actual or potential differentiation
	        (quality/service/price)
	    Breadth of current or planned product line
	    Company image

Economic and technological factors:
    Investment intensity
    Industry capacity
    Level and maturity of technology utilization
    Ability to pass through effects of inflation
    Barriers to entry/exit
    Access to raw materials
	Economic and technological factors:
	    Relative cost position
	    Capacity utilization
	    Technological position
	    Patented technology (product or
	        manufacturing)

Competitive factors:
    Industry structure
    Competitive groupings
    Substitution threats
    Perceived differentiation among competitors
    Individual competitors' strengths
	Capabilities:
	    Management strength and depth
	    Financial
	    R & D/product development
	    Manufacturing
	    Marketing
	    Salesforce
	    Distribution system
	    Labor relations
	    Relations with regulators

Environmental factors:
    Regulatory climate
    Degree of social acceptance
	Interactions with other segments:
	    Market synergies
	    Operating synergies

Source: Adapted from George S. Day, *Analysis for Strategic Market Decisions* (St. Paul: West Publishing, 1986). pp. 198–99; and Derek F. Abell and John S. Hammond, *Strategic Market Planning Problems and Analytical Approaches* (Englewood Cliffs, N.J.: Prentice Hall, 1979), p. 214.

Factors underlying market attractiveness   As Exhibit 6–8 indicates, managers judge the attractiveness of a current or potential target market on the basis of four broad sets of variables. **Market factors** reflect the characteristics of the customers making up the market in question—the benefits they seek, their satisfaction with current product offerings, their power relative to suppliers—and factors that might shape the market's future volume potential, such as its overall size, growth rate, and the life cycle stage.

Economic and technological factors examine the capital and technology a firm needs to compete in the market, plus structural variables—such as entry and exit barriers—that help shape long-term competitiveness and profit potential. **Competitive factors** measure the number and strengths of existing competitors in the market and consider the possibility of future competitive changes through the appearance of substitute products. Finally, **environmental factors** reflect broad social or political constraints on the firm's ability to compete profitably in a market, such as governmental regulations or interest groups.

Each of the factors shown in the left column of Exhibit 6–8 can either increase or decrease the attractiveness of a market. Unfortunately, the relationship between a factor and market attractiveness is often complex and varies across industries and business units.

The first step in evaluating the relative attractiveness of current and potential market segments, then, is to identify the determinants of attractiveness that are appropriate for a given industry from the firm's perspective. One caveat is that the factors used to judge market attractiveness should be relevant to all of the markets considered as possible targets. Such comparability is essential if the aggregate attractiveness scores are to be a valid basis for rank ordering alternative markets.

Factors underlying competitive position/business strengths   The right side of Exhibit 6–8 displays factors managers might use to evaluate a business's current or potential competitive position within a given target market. Once again, these factors reflect the information discussed in earlier chapters dealing with the customer, industry, and competitor analysis.

The **market position factors** are most appropriate for evaluating markets that the business is already in because they reflect the strength of the firm's current share position and product offerings compared to existing competitors. **Economic and technological factors** can indicate either the business's current or potential competitive advantages or shortcomings in low-production costs (capacity use and process technology) or sustainable product differentiation (superior product technology or patent protection). The business's **capabilities** might reflect operational strengths or weaknesses relative to competitors— such as a more extensive distribution channel or more limited financial resources to support future growth. Finally, managers should consider the possible positive or negative **interactions across multiple target markets.** Such interactions or synergies result from sharing operational activities and resources across markets (say, the use of a common salesforce to cover two or more target markets). Or they can result from the carryover effects of customer perceptions from one market to another. For example, Honda felt that its reputation for quality and reliability in the small-car market would carry over and provide a competitive advantage when it decided to enter the residential lawnmower market.

Step 2: Weight each attractiveness and business strength factor

A numerical weight is assigned to each factor to indicate its relative importance. For example, the marketing managers of a large food company assigned the weights indicated in Exhibit 6–9. (Note that weights were assigned only to groups of factors although individual factors were taken into account in so doing.)

EXHIBIT 6–9

Examples of Weights and Ratings Accorded Market Attractiveness and Business Strength Factors by Large Packaged Food Company

Attractiveness			
Factor group	**Weight**	**Rating***	**Total**
Market	50	8	400
Economic technology	20	9	180
Competition	20	9	180
Environment	10	10	100
Total	100	36	860

Attractiveness rating $= \dfrac{860}{100} = 86$

Business strengths			
Factor group	**Weight**	**Rating***	**Total**
Market position	20	9	180
Economic/technology	20	8	160
Capabilities	50	9	450
Interaction with other segments	10	10	100
Total	100	36	890

Business strength rating $= \dfrac{890}{100} = 89$

*Rating scale $= 0 - 10$.

Steps 3–4: Rate each segment as to its market attractiveness and company strengths

These steps require that each market segment be rated as to its attractiveness and the company's strengths (using scales of 0 to 10). In the case of our large packaged food products company example (see Exhibit 6–9), the market received an attractiveness rating of 86 and a business strengths rating of 89. On the basis of these strong scores, management considered the segment to have high potential. Exhibit 6–10 on the following page shows a matrix of the two ratings, which indicates that management should strongly consider making the necessary investment to seek, or maintain, a strong (high-share) position.

Step 5: Project the future position of a market

Forecasting a market's future is more difficult than assessing its current state. Managers should first determine how the market's attractiveness is likely to change over the next three to five years. The starting point for this assessment is the product-market evolution analysis discussed in an earlier chapter, including consideration of possible shifts in customer needs and behavior, the entry or exit of competitors, and changes in their strategies. Managers must also address several broader issues, such as possible changes in product or process technology, shifts

EXHIBIT 6-10

Matrix Showing Position of a Given Segment Based on a Matching of Business Strengths and Market Attractiveness

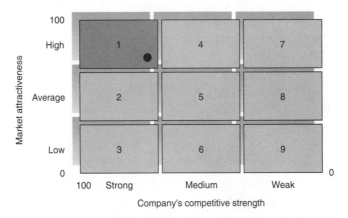

in the economic climate, the impact of social or political trends, and shifts in the bargaining power or vertical integration of customers.

Managers must next determine how the business's competitive position in the market is likely to change, assuming that it responds effectively to projected environmental changes but does not undertake any initiatives requiring a change in basic strategy. The expected changes in both market attractiveness and competitive position can then be plotted on the matrix in the form of a vector (arrow) that reflects the direction and magnitude of the expected changes.

Step 6: Evaluate implications for choosing target markets and allocating resources

Managers should consider a market to be a desirable target only if it is strongly positive on at least one of the two dimensions of market attractiveness and potential competitive position and at least moderately positive on the other. In Exhibit 6–11 this includes markets positioned in any of the three cells in the upper left corner of the matrix. However, a business may decide to enter a market that currently falls into one of the middle cells under these conditions: (1) managers believe that the market's attractiveness or their competitive strength is likely to improve over the next few years: (2) they see such markets as stepping-stones to entering larger, more attractive markets in the future; or (3) shared costs are present, thereby benefiting another entry.

The market attractiveness/business position matrix offers general guidance for strategic objectives and allocation of resources for segments currently targeted and suggests which new segments to enter. Exhibit 6–11 also summarizes generic guidelines for strategic objectives and resource allocations for markets in each of the matrix cells. The general thrust of these guidelines is that managers should concentrate resources in attractive markets where the

EXHIBIT 6–11

Implications of Alternative Positions within the Market Attractiveness/Business Position Matrix for Target Market Selections, StrategicObjectives, and Resource Allocation

	Competitive position		
	Strong	**Medium**	**Weak**
High	DESIRABLE POTENTIAL TARGET Protect position: • Invest to grow at maximum digestible rate • Concentrate on maintaining strength	DESIRABLE POTENTIAL TARGET Invest to build: • Challenge for leadership • Build selectively on strengths • Reinforce vulnerable areas	Build selectively: • Specialize around limited strengths • Seek ways to overcome weaknesses • Withdraw if indications of sustainable growth are lacking
Medium	DESIRABLE POTENTIAL TARGET Build selectively: • Emphasize profitability by increasing productivity • Build up ability to counter competition	Manage for earnings: • Protect existing strengths • Invest to improve position only in areas where risk is low	Limited expansion or harvest: • Look for ways to expand without high risk: otherwise, minimize investment and focus operations
Low	Protect and refocus: • Defend strengths • Seek ways to increase current earnings without speeding market's decline	Manage for earnings: • Protect position • Minimize investment	Divest: • Sell when possible to maximize cash value • Meantime, cut fixed costs and avoid further investment

Market attractiveness (vertical axis label)

SOURCE: Adapted from G. S. Day, *Analysis for Strategic Market Decisions* (St. Paul: West Publishing Co., 1986), p. 204; D. F. Abeil and J. S. Hammond, *Strategic Market Planning Problems and Analytical Approaches* (Englewood Cliffs, N.J.: Prentice Hall, 1979); and S. J. Robinson, R. E. Hitchens, and D. P. Wade, "The Directional Policy Matrix: Tool for Strategic Planning," *Long Range Planning* 11 (1978), pp. 8–15.

business is securely positioned, use them to improve a weak competitive position in attractive markets, and disengage from unattractive markets where the firm enjoys no competitive advantage.

TARGETING STRATEGIES

A number of strategies can help guide a manager's choice of target markets. Three of the more common of these are **mass-market, niche-market,** and **growth-market** strategies.

Mass-market strategy

A business can pursue a mass-market strategy in two ways. First, it can ignore any segment differences and design a single product and marketing program that will appeal to the largest number of consumers. The primary object of this strategy is to capture sufficient volume to gain economies of scale and a cost advantage. This strategy requires substantial resources, including production capacity, and good mass-marketing capabilities. Consequently, it is favored by larger business units or by those whose parent corporation provides substantial support. For example, when Honda first entered the American and European motorcycle markets, it targeted the high-volume segment consisting of buyers of low-displacement, low-priced cycles. Honda subsequently used the sales volume and scale economies it achieved in that mass-market segment to help it expand into smaller, more specialized segments of the market.

A second approach to the mass market is to design separate products and marketing programs for the differing segments. This is often called **differentiated marketing.** For example, Marriott did this with its various hotel chains. Although such a strategy can generate more sales than an undifferentiated strategy, it also increases costs in product design, manufacturing, inventory, and marketing, especially promotion.

Niche-market strategy

This strategy involves serving one or more segments that, while not the largest, consist of substantial numbers of customers seeking somewhat specialized benefits from a product or service. Such a strategy is designed to avoid direct competition with larger firms that are pursuing the bigger segments. For example, overall coffee consumption is down from three cups daily in 1962 to 1.75 cups in 1991, but gourmet coffee houses are booming—such as Gloria Jean's Coffee Bean and Starbucks.[26]

Growth-market strategy

Businesses pursuing a growth-market strategy target one or more fast-growth segments, even though they may not be very large currently. It is a strategy often favored by smaller competitors to avoid direct confrontations with larger firms while building volume and share for the future. However, such a strategy usually requires strong R & D and marketing capabilities to identify and develop products appealing to newly emerging user segments, plus the resources to finance rapid growth. The problem is that fast growth, if sustained, attracts large competitors. This happened to DEC when IBM entered the minicomputer business. The goal of the defender is to have developed an enduring competitive position via its products, service, distribution, and costs by the time competitors enter.

---

[26]Doris Jones Yang and Julia Flynn Siler, "Fewer Cups, But a Much Richer Brew," *Business Week,* November 18, 1991, p. 80.

SELECTING TARGET MARKETS IN THE INTERNATIONAL ARENA

Some companies go international to defend their home position against global competitors that are constantly looking for vulnerability. This forces the firm to target major developed countries (the United States and Japan as well as Western European countries). The reasoning here is that a global competitor can attack the home market by reducing price, the cost of which is subsidized by profits generated elsewhere in the world. If the defending company is solely a domestic player, it has to respond by cutting price on its entire volume, while the aggressor has to do so on only part of its total sales.

To prevent such attacks or minimize their impact, a firm must have the capacity to strike back in markets where the aggressor is vulnerable. For example, Caterpillar, through a joint venture with Mitsubishi Heavy Industries, has for the past 30 years made a substantial investment in Japan to deny their Japanese competitor, Komatsu, strength at home, thereby taking away its profit sanctuary. Had Cat not been successful in doing so, Komatsu would have been able to compete more aggressively with Cat not only in the United States but in other major world markets.[27]

Another reason why a firm may go overseas and in so doing target a specific country is to service customers who are also engaging in global expansion. In recent years Japanese automobile companies that have created U. S. manufacturing facilities have encouraged some of their parts suppliers to do the same. Firms also enter overseas markets to earn foreign exchange and, in some cases, are subsidized by their governments to do so.

The selection of one or more target countries may be dictated by the availability of an appropriate partner. For example, Kellogg has had a European presence since the 1920s and controls about half the market. General Mills, which is Kellogg's major U. S. competitor, has long wanted to enter the European market, but to do so on its own would have been an extremely expensive undertaking because of Kellogg's high market share. The solution was to enter in a joint venture (Cereal Partners Worldwide) with Nestlé, which has no cereals but does have a powerful distribution system. France, Spain, and Portugal constituted the initial target markets for General Mills's Honey Nut Cheerios and Golden Grahams.[28]

Other than these cases, the selection of overseas target markets follows essentially the same procedures as for domestic markets, although given the magnitude of economic, social, and political change, companies are paying considerably more attention to political risk.

Product strength versus geographic expansion[29]

For many companies the international targeting problem must consider **product strength** (share within country) and **geographic expansion.** At the corporate level the firm manages

---

[27]Douglas Lamont, *Winning Worldwide* (Burr Ridge, Ill.: Irwin Professional Publishing, 1991), pp. 59–69.

[28]Christopher Knowlton, "Europe Cooks up a Cereal Brawl," *Fortune,* June 3, 1991, p. 175.

[29]This section is based on Robert Gogel and Jean-Claude Larréché, "The Battlefield for 1992 Product Strength and Geographic Coverage," *European Management Journal* 2 (1989), pp. 132–140.

EXHIBIT 6-12

International Competitive Posture Matrix

Geographic coverage

		Low	High
Product strength	**High**	Barons	Kings
	Low	Commoners	Crusaders

a portfolio of products and geographical markets. Its main axis of product strength and geographic coverage (number and size of company target markets) must be managed in a balanced way. If the firm invests too much in attempting to gain product strength, it will miss some international opportunities; if it invests too much in geographic expansion, it may underinvest in products and weaken its competitive position.

The emphasis placed on one axis versus the other depends on the firm's current position relative to competition. To solve this allocation problem, firms can use an international competitive posture matrix with the two axes of product strength and geographic coverage to plot competitors who are categorized in four groups: kings, barons, crusaders, and commoners (see Exhibit 6–12).

Kings are companies with the strongest position given their wide geographic coverage and a strong product portfolio. If they selectively expand the latter, they can obtain important leverage because of their geographic coverage. *Barons* have a strong position in a limited number of countries and thus can expand in other countries or new product areas. They are attractive as a disposable acquisition.

Crusaders have geographic coverage but lack consistently strong product positions. They are highly vulnerable to competition. Their challenge is to consolidate their product position via internal development and/or acquisition—or even to disinvest in order to focus on a narrow product portfolio. *Commoners* have a weak position in both geographic coverage and product strength. Before expanding geographically, commoners must strengthen their product positions by divesting to build share of selected products or by developing niche strategies.

ETHICAL ISSUES IN MARKET TARGETING[30]

Over the years marketing managers have experienced a number of ethical problems relating to the selection of target markets. Problems can rise from targeting consumers who because of their *inclusion* in the targeted group may be influenced to make decisions thought by some

---

[30]The discussion in this section is based largely on N. Craig Smith and John A. Quelch, *Ethics in Marketing* (Burr Ridge, Ill.: Irwin, 1993), pp. 183–195.

to be not in their best interest.[31] In other cases *exclusion* issues are raised because the firm's marketing efforts did not include a particular group. These two types of issues are discussed below.

Inclusion issues

In an effort to simplify advertising messages, advertisers often resort to undesirable stereotypes. These include sex role, race, or age stereotypes. Thus, the portrayal of women as sex objects (bikini-clad models in calendars) and, in general, subordinate to males is thought by many to be dehumanizing and offensive. Reverse sexism, with men shown as sex objects and women as authority figures, has been on the increase to the dismay of some groups.

In recent years there has been an increase in the targeting of minority groups for the sale of such products as cigarettes and alcohol. In some cases a backlash against such targeting has prompted individual firms (and whole industries) to abandon or modify their targeting practices (for example, brewers have reduced their marketing programs that target students during spring break) and/or emphasize moderation (responsible drinking). But one can still question the ethics of using sports heroes as role models in the advertising of beer and products that may prove harmful. Indeed, the mass marketing of alcohol and tobacco products in general raises some serious ethical questions.

Exclusion issues

Exclusion issues are concerned not only with depriving certain groups of products and services but also that they may pay more for those they do receive. There is considerable evidence to support the latter claim. A recent survey in New York City found that food prices are highest in neighborhoods that can least afford it. Low-income shoppers paid 8.8 percent more for their groceries—$350 per year for a family of four. Further, inner-city stores were on average poorly stocked, had inferior foodstuffs, and offered poor service.[32]

Companies often have the problem of deciding whether to do business with certain groups they would rather not serve. For example, insurance companies want only low-risk policyholders, credit card companies only low-risk holders, and hospitals only patients with insurance.

SUMMARY

This chapter focused on two interrelated decisions that constitute the first steps toward the formulation of a strategic marketing program for a product-market entry—market segmentation and market targeting. A company must follow either a market aggregation or a market

---

[31]Some would argue that advertising $150 sneakers to inner-city teenagers also causes ethical considerations, as does the advertising of snack foods and soft drinks to children.

[32]Felix M. Freedman, "The Poor Pay More for Food in New York, Survey Finds," *The Wall Street Journal,* April 15, 1991.

segmentation strategy. Market aggregation strategy is appropriate when most customers have similar needs and desires. When customers are more diverse, however, a single standardized product and marketing program does not appeal to those who need or want something different. Segmentation has become increasingly popular because it reflects the realities faced by firms in most markets.

The process of segmentation involves describing the characteristics of customers and identifying the different needs or benefits sought by those customers. Descriptors are the variables used to explain the differences in product purchases across segments; there are four major categories—physical descriptors, general behavioral, product-related behavioral, and customer needs.

The more common descriptors used to segment consumer markets are demographics (such as age, sex, race, geographic area, and education), lifestyle, social class, product usage, product loyalty, and customer needs (benefits wanted). For industrial goods two segmentation stages are required. The first, *macrosegmentation,* divides the market according to the organizational characteristics of the customer, while *microsegmentation* groups customers by the characteristics of the individuals who influence the purchasing decision.

Product usage and geographic locations are examples of macrosegmentation descriptors, while purchase influence, loyalty, and area of expertise are microsegmentation descriptors. International segmentation is also a two-stage process, with the country selection being the first stage followed by segmentation within the country. To be effective and useful, the chosen segmentation scheme must meet four criteria: adequate size, measurability, accessibility, and differential response to marketing variables.

Market targeting uses a market attractiveness/business position matrix as an analytical framework to help managers decide which market segments to target and how to allocate resources and marketing efforts. In applying such a matrix, the manager must first identify a relevant set of variables underlying the attractiveness of alternative market segments. This typically involves selecting variables related to four broad sets of factors: market factors, economic and technological factors, competitive factors, and environmental factors. Similarly, the manager must select a relevant set of variables to judge the firm's relative competitive position within the market segment. These competitiveness variables typically include items related to market position factors, economic and technological factors, the business's capabilities, and interactions or synergies across multiple target markets.

After managers have weighted these factors according to their relative importance, they can rate the attractiveness of alternative market segments and the strength of the firm's competitive position within each of those segments. They can then test the validity of the combined ratings with a market attractiveness/business position matrix that shows the implications of alternative positions in the matrix. Because a firm or business unit has limited resources, however, it often identifies more attractive potential target markets than it is capable of pursuing. Consequently, a firm must develop a targeting strategy to guide managers' choices of alternative target markets in a manner consistent with corporate objectives, resources, and competitive strengths. The most common targeting strategies include mass-market, niche-market, and growth-market strategies.

Company objectives often influence the selection of target countries. These include the need to protect the firm from competitors who are constantly looking for vulnerability via the ability to retaliate. Another reason is to service customers who have gone overseas; the availability of a partner in a certain venture may be yet another factor influencing country targeting. For many companies, the international targeting problem must consider product strength within country and geographic expansion. For the most part the emphasis placed on one versus the other depends on the firm's current position relative to competition.

A number of ethical issues are associated with target marketing. These can be classified as relating to groups of consumers who are either included or excluded as target markets. *Inclusion issues* involve the use in advertising of stereotypes (women as sex objects) and the targeting of minority groups for the sale of such products as tobacco, liquor, and expensive sneakers. *Exclusion issues* are concerned not only with depriving certain groups of products and services: Certain groups may pay more for those they do receive.

Positioning Decisions

THE FORD EXPLORER VERSUS THE JEEP CHEROKEE[1]

For years Jeep dominated the sport utility vehicle market. Its four-door Cherokee, introduced in late 1983, was expected to sell 45,000 units annually. Because it became popular with many yuppies who used it as a family vehicle, annual sales by the late 1980s were about 220,000 units. During this period few competitors entered this market, and those that did were not well received. For example, General Motors entered two four-door models—the Chevrolet Blazer and the GMC Jimmy. Neither provided the space expected of a four-door because they were designed as two-door models and then modified to add two more doors.

The Ford Explorer, introduced in 1990 to replace the Bronco II, did what no other brand had been able to do: outsell the Jeep Cherokee. The main reason for this success was that Ford realized that the four-door sport utility vehicle was becoming socially acceptable and that a lot more women were buying or influencing the purchase of off-road vehicles. Ford was also convinced that the sales of such vehicles would increase dramatically in the years ahead.

Because of these factors, Ford invested substantially to design and produce a more spacious four-door vehicle that was considerably more comfortable, safe, luxurious, and easy to drive than its rivals. Compared with Cherokee, it had 8.5 more cubic feet of cargo space, more shoulder room (1.8 inches in the front and 2.6 inches in the

[1]Based on Lindsay Brooke, "Headaches at Ford," *Automotive Industries,* March 1992, pp. 38–41; Lindsay Brooke, "Make Way for ZJ," *Automotive Industries,* January 1992, pp. 41–42; James B. Treece and Mark Landler, "Beep, Beep! There Goes Ford's Explorer," *Business Week,* January 28, 1991, pp. 60–61; Jacqueline Mitchell, "Rivalry Accelerates for Sports Trucks, Dubbed the Family Sedans of the '90s," *The Wall Street Journal,* July 8, 1990, p. 31; Bob Plunkett, "Exploring Today's 4 X 4s," *Arkansas Gazette,* July 17, 1990, pp. G1, G5; Raymond Serafin, "'Heavy Traffic in Sport Utilities," *Advertising Age,* April 19, 1993, p. 12; James Healey, "Cadillac Considers Own Sport Utility," *The Wall Street Journal,* September 20, 1994; Raymond Serafin, "Chevy Fires Up Redesigned Chevy," *Advertising Age,* September 12, 1994; and Gall McCarthy, "'95 Cars and Trucks," *Parade Magazine,* October 1, 1994.

back), more headroom (1.6 inches in the front and 1.0 inches in the rear), and more leg room (1.3 inches in both front and rear).

In addition to space, the Explorer made driving a lot easier. To switch from two-wheel to four-wheel drive required only the press of a button, even during driving. This was not the case with the Jeep Cherokee, where drivers had to use a lever to make the change. The Explorer also had safety features not found in many off-road vehicles, such as head restraints and rear shoulder belts.

Ford has continued to invest substantial sums in the sport utility market. Its Ex-

plorer is still the sales leader even though Chrysler's major overhaul of its entire Jeep line enabled it to outsell Ford's sport utility line in 1993. Because of the anticipated future growth of such vehicles, greater competition is expected. General Motor's Chevrolet Division is expected to spend $60 million in 1994 advertising its re-designed Blazer. Honda has entered the market with a version of the Isuzu Rodeo. Jaguar and Cadillac are believed to be considering upscale entries in the next several years. And Mercedes-Benz is building a plant in the United States that will start turning out a luxury sport utility vehicle by 1997.

As the sport utility vehicle market demonstrates, the success of a product offering within a chosen target market depends on how well it is positioned within that market—that is, how well it is perceived to perform relative to competitive offerings *and* customers' needs in the target segment. Ford, by exploiting selected features of its 1990 Explorer model (roomier, easier to drive, and head restraints) in its advertising, was successful in getting women to perceive its new model as an about-town vehicle that was safe and comfortable while retaining its off-road abilities. **Positioning,** therefore, is the perceived fit between a particular product offering and the needs of the target market. The concept must be defined relative to two entities—competitive offerings and consumer needs.

Positioning is a critically important strategic concept that, while typically thought of in relation to the marketing of consumer goods, has equal value for industrial goods and services, requiring essentially the same procedure as for consumer goods.[2] Because services are characterized by their intangibility, perishability, consumer participation in their delivery, and the simultaneous nature of their production and consumption, they are—when compared to products—more difficult for consumers to understand, to compare with competing services, and to predict in terms of their performance.[3]

---

[2] For a discussion of the positioning of industrial goods, see Frederick E. Webster, Jr., *Industrial Marketing Strategy* (New York: John Wiley & Sons, 1991), pp. 102–3.

[3] For an interesting discussion of the positioning of services, see James H. Donnelly, Jr., Leonard L. Barry, and Thomas W. Thompson, *Marketing Financial Services* (Burr Ridge, Ill.: Irwin Professional Publishing, 1985), ch. 6. Also see Christopher H. Lovelock, *Services Marketing* (Englewood Cliffs, N.J.: Prentice Hall, 1991), ch. 4; and James L. Heskett, *Managing in the Service Economy* (Boston, Mass.: Harvard Business School Press, 1986), ch. 3.

A positioning statement helps the firm communicate its strategy to both the marketplace and its own organization as well as manage its relationship with consumers. For example, the Ford Explorer's advertising emphasized its comfort and safety—and encouraged drivers to exercise their curiosity, to explore new territory. To many families it was the best four-door, off-road driving machine suited for city life.

This chapter is concerned with answering the critical question, How can a business position its offering so that customers in the target market perceive it as providing the desired benefits, thereby giving it an advantage over current and potential competitors? The choice of a market position is a strategic decision with implications not only for how the firm's product or service should be designed but also for the detailing of the other elements of the associated marketing program.

In this chapter we first cover physical and perceptual positioning and then discuss the steps in the positioning process, including the criteria for identifying attractive positions in a given target market and the alternative positioning strategies a business might pursue.

PHYSICAL VERSUS PERCEPTUAL PRODUCT POSITIONING

One way to assess the current position of a product offering relative to competitors is on the basis of how the various offerings compare on some set of objective physical characteristics. For example, an article in *Automotive Industries* compared the 1993 Jeep Grand Cherokee and the 4-door Ford Explorer on such physical dimensions as length, width, weight, headroom, engines, and torque (see Exhibit 7–1). In many cases a physical product positioning analysis can provide useful information to a marketing manager, particularly in the early stages of identifying and designing new product offerings, as was probably the case with Ford's Explorer.

Despite being based primarily on technical rather than on market data, physical product positioning can be an essential step in undertaking a strategic marketing analysis. This is especially true with the competitive offerings of many industrial goods and services, which buyers typically evaluate on the basis of such characteristics. In addition, it contributes to a better marketing–R & D interface by determining key physical product characteristics; helps define the structure of competition by revealing the degree to which the various brands compete with one another; and may indicate the presence of meaningful product gaps (the lack of products having certain physical characteristics), which, in turn, may reveal opportunities for a new product entry.

Limitations of physical positioning

A simple comparison of only the physical dimensions of alternative offerings usually does *not* provide a complete picture of relative positions because positioning ultimately takes place in customers' minds. Even though a product's physical characteristics, package, brand name, price, and ancillary services can be designed to achieve a particular position in the market, customers may attach less importance to some of those characteristics, or perceive them differently, than the firm expects. Also, customers' attitudes toward a product are often based

EXHIBIT 7–1

1993 Jeep Grand Cherokee vs. Ford Explorer on Select Number of Physical Dimensions

	Jeep	Ford
Overall length (in.)	176.5	184.3
Overall width (in.)	69.7	70.2
Overall height (in.)	64.7	67.3
Wheelbase (in.)	105.9	111.9
Front/rear track (in.)	58.0/58.0	58.3/58.3
Ground clearance (in.)	8.2	6.3
Front/rear headroom (in.)	38.9/39.0	39.9/39.1
Front/rear shoulder room (in.)	58.2/57.6	57.1/57.1
Front/rear hip room (in.)	56.9/52.1	51.9/51.9
Cargo volume (ft^3), seat down	79.2	81.6
Base curb weight (lb.)	3628	4046
Engine type/displacement (L)	Ohv inline 6/4.0	Ohv V6/4.0
Maximum hp @ rpm	190 @ 4750	145 @ 3800 (160 @ 4400)
Maximum torque (lb-ft) @ rpm	225 @ 4000	220 @ 2400 (225 @ 2400) (with 4-speed automatic)

SOURCE: Lindsay Brooke, "Make Way for ZJ," *Automotive Industries,* January 1992, p. 41.

on social or psychological attributes not amenable to objective comparison, such as perceptions of the product's aesthetic appeal, sportiness, or status image (for example, when it was introduced, the Ford Explorer had a more modern look than the Jeep Cherokee). Consequently, *perceptual positioning analyses*—whether aimed at discovering opportunities for new product entries or at evaluating and adjusting the position of a current offering—are critically important. The remainder of this chapter is concerned with this type of positioning analysis.

Perceptual product positioning

Consumers know very little about the essential physical attributes of many products, especially those involving the household, and even if they did, they would not understand them well enough to use them as a basis for choosing between competitive offerings. (For the major differences between physical and perceptual product positioning analyses, see Exhibit 7–2.) Many consumers do not want to be bothered by information about a product's physical characteristics because they are not buying these physical properties but rather the benefits they provide. While the physical properties of a product definitely influence the benefits provided, a consumer can typically better evaluate a product on the basis of what it *does* than what it *is*. Thus, for example, a headache remedy is judged on how quickly it brings relief, a toothpaste on the freshness of breath provided, a beer on its taste, and a vehicle on how comfortably it rides.

EXHIBIT 7–2

Comparison of Physical and Perceptual Analyses

Physical positioning	Perceptual analyses
• Technical orientation	• Consumer orientation
• Physical characteristics	• Perceptual attributes
• Objective measures	• Perceptual measures
• Data readily available	• Need marketing research
• Physical brand properties	• Perceptual brand positions and positioning intensities
• Large number of dimensions	• Limited number of dimensions
• Represents impact of product specs and price	• Represents impact of products specs, price, and communication
• Direct R & D implications	• R & D implications need to be interpreted

The evaluation of many products is subjective because it is influenced by factors other than physical properties, including the way products are presented, past experiences with them, and the opinion of others. Thus, physically similar products may be perceived as being different because of different histories, names, and advertising campaigns. For example, some people pay considerably more for Bayer Aspirin than for an unadvertised private label even though they are essentially the same product.

Dimensions on which consumers perceive competitive offerings

Consumers perceive competitive offerings on various dimensions that can be classified as follows:

- *Simple physically based attributes.* These are directly related to a single physical dimension such as price, power, or size. While there is a direct correspondence between a physical dimension and a perceptual attribute, an analysis of the consumers' perception of products on these attributes may unveil some phenomena of interest to a marketing strategy. For instance, two cars with estimated gasoline mileage of 23.2 and 25.8 miles per gallon may be perceived as having similar gasoline consumption.

- *Complex physically based attributes.* Because of the presence of a large number of physical characteristics, consumers may use composite attributes to evaluate competitive offerings. The development of such summary indicators is usually subjective because of the relative importance attached to different cues. Examples of composite attributes are the efficiency of a computer system, roominess of a car, and a product or service being user friendly. For example, the *Harvard Business Review* has tried to be more reader friendly by putting an illustration on its cover and using a colorful two-page table of contents.[4]

- *Essentially abstract attributes.* Although these perceptual attributes are influenced by physical characteristics, they are not related to them in any direct way. Examples include bodiness of a beer, sexiness of a perfume, and prestige of a car. All of these attributes are highly subjective and difficult to relate to physical characteristics other than by experience.

While all perceptual attributes have a subjective component, its importance varies across consumers and product classes. Thus, it can be argued that consumers familiar with a given product class are apt to rely more on physical characteristics and less on perceptual attributes than consumers who are less familiar with that product class. It can also be argued that perceptual product positioning is essential for nondurable consumer goods and less important for consumer durables (such as sport utility vehicles) and many industrial goods.

Even though there is considerable truth in the previous statements, perceptual attributes must still be considered as a market strategy is formulated for most products. One reason is the similar physical characteristics of more and more products and services within product classes. This increases the importance of other, largely subjective dimensions; for example, consider how consumers might evaluate the quality of postpurchase service for an industrial product or the rugged appearance of an off-road vehicle.

THE POSITIONING PROCESS

Determining the perceived positions of a set of product offerings and evaluating strategies for positioning a new entry or repositioning an existing one involves the steps outlined in Exhibit 7–3. These steps are also applicable to any product or service in the international arena regardless of the country involved. This is not to suggest that the determinant product attributes and consumer perceptions of the various competitive offerings will remain constant across countries; rather, they are likely to vary with most products. In any event, after managers have selected a relevant set of competing offerings (Step 1), they must identify a set of critical or determinant product attributes (Step 2).

Step 3 involves collecting information from sample customers about their perceptions of the various offerings; and in Step 4 researchers analyze this information to determine the intensity of a product's current position in customers' minds (Does it occupy a predominant position?).

In Step 5 managers analyze the location in the **product space** of the product's position relative to those of competing products. They then ascertain the customers' most preferred combination of determinant attributes, which requires the collection of further data (Step 6). This allows an examination of the fit between the preferences of a given target segment of

---

[4]Julie Soloman, "Harvard Business Review Gets Sportier," *The Wall Street Journal,* September 18, 1990, p. B1.

EXHIBIT 7-3

Steps in the Positioning Process

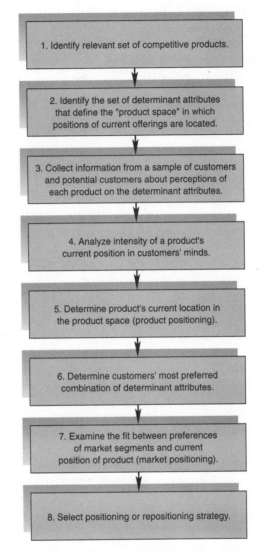

1. Identify relevant set of competitive products.

2. Identify the set of determinant attributes that define the "product space" in which positions of current offerings are located.

3. Collect information from a sample of customers and potential customers about perceptions of each product on the determinant attributes.

4. Analyze intensity of a product's current position in customers' minds.

5. Determine product's current location in the product space (product positioning).

6. Determine customers' most preferred combination of determinant attributes.

7. Examine the fit between preferences of market segments and current position of product (market positioning).

8. Select positioning or repositioning strategy.

customers and the current positions of competitive offerings (Step 7). And finally, in Step 8, managers examine the degree of fit between the positions of competitive products and the preferences of various market segments as a basis for choosing a successful strategy for positioning a new entry or for repositioning an existing product.

A discussion of each of these steps takes up the remainder of this chapter.

Step 1: Identify a relevant set of competitive products

This step is concerned with identifying a relevant set of products. A positioning analysis takes place at either the **product category** or the **brand level.** At the product category level the analysis examines customers' perceptions about types of products they might consider as substitutes to satisfy the same basic need. Suppose, for example, that a company is considering introducing a new instant breakfast drink. The new product would have to compete with other breakfast foods such as bacon, eggs, and breakfast cereals. To understand the new product's position in the market, a marketer could obtain customer perceptions of the new product concept relative to likely substitute products on various critical determinant attributes. Part A of Exhibit 7–4 shows a product positioning map constructed from such information. The two attributes defining the product space were price and convenience of preparation. The proposed new drink occupies a distinctive position because customers perceive it as a comparatively low-cost, convenient breakfast food.[5]

Once competitors introduce similar brands into the same product category, a marketer needs to find out how the brand is perceived compared to competitors. Thus, Part B of

EXHIBIT 7–4

Product Category and Brand Positioning

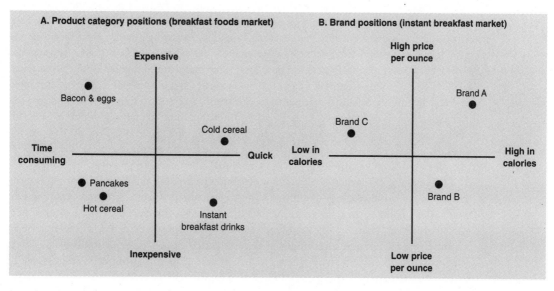

SOURCE: Adapted from P. S. Busch and M. J. Houston, *Marketing Strategic Foundations* (Homewood, Ill.: Richard D. Irwin, 1985), p. 430.

[5]For an interesting case study involving the difficulty of positioning Suzuki's Samurai (an upsizing of the company's mini-four-wheel-drive off-road vehicle) in the American market because of the positions occupied by substitute brands of both pickup trucks and sport utility vehicles, see John A. Quelch and Paul W. Farris, *Cases in Advertising and Promotion Management* (Burr Ridge, Ill.: Irwin, 1990), p. 257.

Exhibit 7–4 shows the results of a positioning analysis conducted at the brand level. It summarizes customer perceptions concerning three existing brands of instant breakfast drinks. Notice, however, that two different attributes define the product space in this analysis: relative price per ounce and calorie content. This brand-level analysis is very useful for helping marketers understand a brand's competitive strengths and weaknesses and for determining whether the brand should be repositioned to differentiate and strengthen its position. The danger in conducting only a brand-level positioning analysis, though, is that it can overlook threats from possible substitutes in other product categories.

Step 2: Identify determinant attributes

Positioning can be based on a product feature, a customer benefit, a use or application, or a surrogate. Features and benefits are often referred to collectively as *attributes* and are directly related to the product. Features are often used in physical product positioning, a subject discussed earlier. Examples of positioning based on benefits include Volvo, which has over the years emphasized safety and durability in its advertising; Sony's Handycam, marketed as being "convenient to pack and carry on a vacation"; and Norelco, promising a "close, comfortable shave."

Many products base their positioning efforts on use or application—especially during the mature stage of the product life cycle. Examples include Campbell's positioning many of its soups for use in other foods, sauces, and dips; Arm & Hammer baking soda, which has been successfully positioned as a food ingredient and an odor-destroying product in refrigerators; and Alka Seltzer, advertised as a cure for a hangover and as providing relief from colds. As was noted earlier, Ford positioned its Explorer as both an off-road vehicle and one for family city driving.

C. Merle Crawford reports that the use of surrogates as a positioning base (which implies desirable features or benefits) represents about a third of all positioning attempts and that this percentage is growing. A *surrogate* is a reason, other than one involving product features, for calling the company's product the best. Surrogates are popular because they do not provide "specific reasons *why* the product is better . . . the listener or viewer has to provide those."[6] A brief description and examples of each of Crawford's surrogates are presented in Exhibit 7–5.

Theoretically, consumers can use many attributes to evaluate products and brands, but the number actually influencing a consumer's choice is normally small. Consumers can consider only those attributes they are aware of, but the *importance* attached to those by consumers often varies. For instance, while the brands of soap or shampoo provided by a hotel may be an attribute that some consumers might use in evaluating hotels, most are unlikely to attach much importance to it when deciding which hotel chain to patronize. Further, even an important attribute may not greatly influence a consumer's preference if all the alternative brands are perceived to be about equal on that dimension. As another example, deposit safety is an important attribute to consider when choosing a bank, but most consumers perceive all banks to be about equally safe. Consequently, deposit safety is not a **determinant attribute:** It does not play a major role in helping customers to differentiate among the alternatives and determine which bank they prefer.

---

[6]C. Merle Crawford, *New Products Management* (Burr Ridge, Ill.: Irwin, 1991), p. 348.

EXHIBIT 7-5

Meaning of Various Surrogates and Examples of Each

Nonpareil: . . . because the product has no equal; it is the best (the Jaguar car).

Parentage: . . . because of where it comes from, who makes it, who sells it, who performs it, and so on. The three ways of parentage positioning are *brand* (Cadillac or Citizen printer), *company* (General Electric or McGraw-Hill), and *persons* (*Debt of Honor,* a new book by Tom Clancy).

Manufacture: . . . because of how the product was made. This includes *process* (Hunt's tomatoes are left longer on the vine), *ingredients* (Fruit of the Loom underwear of pure cotton), and *design* (Audi's engineering).

Target: . . . because the product was made especially for people or firms like you. Four types of targeting are *end use* (Vector tire designed especially for use on wet roads), *demographic* (Northwest Airlines, specially designed for the business traveler), *psychographic* (Michelob Light for "the people who want it all"), and *behavioral* (Hagar's Gallery line for men who work out a lot, "fit for the fit").

Rank: . . . because it is the best-selling product (Hertz and Blue Cross/Blue Shield).

Endorsement: . . . because people you respect say it is good. May be expert (the many doctors who recommend Preparation H) or a person to be emulated (Elizabeth Taylor perfume).

Experience: . . . because its long or frequent use attests to its desirable attributes. Modes are *other market* (Nuprin's extensive use in the prescription market), *bandwagon* (Stuart Hall's Executive line of business accessories are "the tools business professionals rely on"), and *time* (Bell's Yellow Pages).

Competitor: . . . because it is just or almost like another product that you know and like (IBM PC look-alikes Compaq and Packard Bell).

Predecessor: . . . because it is comparable (in some way) to an earlier product you liked (Hershey's new Solitaires addition to the Golden line).

Source: Adapted from C. Merle Crawford, *New Products Management* (Homewood, Ill.: Irwin, 1991), pp. 348–50.

Marketers therefore should use only determinant attributes to define the product space in a positioning analysis. The question is, How can a marketer find out which product dimensions are determinant attributes? The answer depends on the analytical technique the marketer uses. Choosing an appropriate statistical technique (the next step in the planning process) can help the marketer determine which of the important attributes are truly determinant in guiding customers' choices.

Step 3: Determine consumer's perceptions

Marketers can use several techniques to collect and analyze customers' perceptions about the competitive positioning of alternative products or brands. These include factor analysis, discriminant analysis, multiattribute compositional models, and multidimensional scaling. These analytical techniques and their advantages and disadvantages are described in the appendix to this chapter.[7]

----

[7] For a description of a perceptual mapping procedure that allows consumers to describe and rate the brands involved in their own terminology, see Jan-Benedict E.M. Steenkamp, Hans C. M. van Trijp, and Jos M. F. Ten Berge, "Perceptual Mapping Based on Idiosyncratic Sets of Attributes," *Journal of Marketing Research,* February 1994, p. 15.

Step 4: Analyze the intensity of a product's current position

The position of a brand may not exist in the minds of consumers or may vary in intensity. Often the awareness set for a product class is three or fewer brands even though the number of available brands may be greater than 20. Thus, many if not most brands have little or no position in the minds of many consumers. For example, in the last 10 or so years over 200 new soft drinks have been introduced, most of which were not noticed or remembered by consumers.

A brand that is not known by a consumer cannot, by definition, occupy a position in that consumer's mind. Thus, the first step in acquiring an intense position for a brand is to build brand awareness. In doing so, the brand needs to be strongly associated with several concepts relating to the purchase decision. An intense position is best obtained by developing a strong relationship between a brand and a limited number of attributes.

Aaker identifies 11 types of association as follows:[8]

1. Product attributes (Volvo and durability)

2. Intangibles (Bayer Aspirin and faster-acting)

3. Customer benefits (Grand Cherokee and a segment-leading towing capacity)

4. Relative price (Wal-Mart and low prices every day)

5. Use or application (AT&T for overseas phone calls)

6. User or customer (Gatorade and athletes)

7. Celebrity or person (Nike and Air Jordan)

8. Lifestyle or personality (the Pepsi generation with Michael Jackson)

9. Product class (baking soda as a dentifrice)

10. Competitors (Avis and Hertz)

11. Country or geographic area (French wines, Russian vodka, and Idaho potatoes)

Marketing opportunities to gain positioning intensity

In situations where one or a limited number of brands dominate a product class (or type) in the minds of consumers, the main opportunity for competitors lies in obtaining a profitable position within a market segment not dominated by a leading brand. Competing head-on against the leaders on the basis of attributes appropriated by larger competitors is not likely to be effective.

A better option is to concentrate on an attribute prized by members of a given market segment. Thus, Subaru positions its cars as being durable and practical, thereby providing high consumer satisfaction. Its advertising portrays "the Legacy and Loyale models as practical alternatives for individuals who don't follow the herd."[9]

---

[8]David A. Aaker, *Managing Brand Equity* (New York: The Free Press, 1991), pp. 109–79. BSN, Europe's third largest food company, recently opted to rename itself after its best-known brand (Danone) because its BSN name received a low name recognition rating among homemakers around the world. See "BSN Who?" *The Economist,* May 14, 1994, p. 70.

[9]Aaker, *Managing Brand Equity,* p. 87.

Constraints imposed by an intense position

Although marketers should seek an intense position for their brands, they must keep in mind that attaining such a position imposes some constraints on future strategies. If shifts in the market environment cause customers to reduce the importance they attach to a current determinant attribute, marketers may have difficulty repositioning a brand with an intensely perceived position on that attribute. This problem has plagued Sears for a number of years. Because of the prosperity and sophisticated tastes of the baby-boom generation, Sears has attempted to trade up many of its soft goods and fashion lines. But this has been difficult to accomplish because of the firm's strongly perceived position as a low-priced mass merchandiser.

The second threat concerns the dilution of an existing intense position. For example, British Leyland was formed through a series of mergers involving a number of British car manufacturers. For years the company did not have a clear identity because it was new and distributed a variety of brands, including Rover, Triumph, and Austin-Morris. Indeed, most Europeans had difficulty in spontaneously recalling any British car manufacturer after once-strong brand names such as Austin and Morris lost their identity and meaning.

Another danger associated with an intensely positioned brand is the temptation to overexploit that position by using the brand name on line extensions and new products. The danger here is that the new products may not fit the original positioning and the brand's strong image may become diluted. To avoid this, Sears uses separate brand names for its various product lines (such as Kenmore for its appliance line and Homart for its home-installation line).

Step 5: Analyze the product's current position

How does a marketer know if a brand occupies a strong position on a particular attribute? The only way to find out is to collect information through marketing research and analyze it using the techniques discussed in this chapter's appendix. An example of what can be done with such information can be found in Exhibit 7–6, which shows the results obtained from a study by Babson College that portrays how a sample of consumers positioned a number of women's clothing retailers in the Washington, D. C., area.[10] Respondents rated the various stores on the two determinant attributes of value and fashionability.

Some stores—such as Nordstrom and Kmart—occupy relatively distant positions from one another, indicating that consumers see them as being very different. Other stores occupy positions comparable to one another (for example, Neiman-Marcus and Saks) and thus are considered relatively alike. This means that the intensity of competition between these stores is likely to be considerably greater than for those that occupy widely divergent positions.[11]

The store positioning shown in Exhibit 7–6 also provides useful information about possible opportunities for launching a new store or repositioning an existing one. This can be

---

[10]Douglas Tigert and Stephen Arnold, "Nordstrom: How Good Are They?" *Babson College Retailing Research Reports,* September 1990.

[11]Michael Levy and Barton A. Weitz, *Retailing Management* (Burr Ridge, Ill.: Irwin, 1992), p. 205.

EXHIBIT 7–6

Perceptual Map of Women's Clothing Retailers in Washington, D.C.

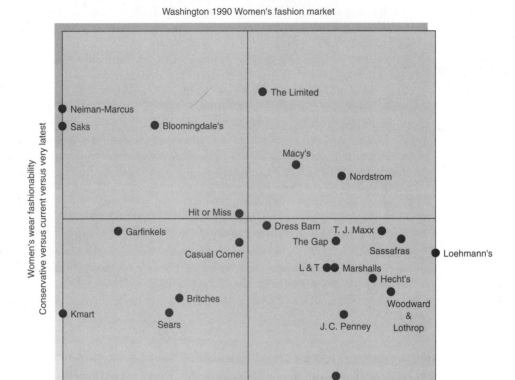

SOURCE: Adapted from Douglas Tigert and Stephen Arnold, "Nordstrom: How Good Are They?" *Babson College Retailing Research Reports,* September 1990, as shown in Michael Levy and Barton A. Weitz, *Retailing Management* (Burr Ridge, Ill.: Irwin, 1992), p. 205.

done by examining the positioning map for empty spaces (competitive gaps) where no exiting store is currently located. For example, there is such a gap in the upper right quadrant of the "value/fashionability" map in Exhibit 7–6. This gap may represent an opportunity for developing a new entry or repositioning an old one that is perceived to offer greater fashionability than Nordstrom at a lower price. Of course, such gaps may exist simply because a particular position is either (1) impossible for any brand to attain due to technical constraints or (2) undesirable because there are few prospective customers for a brand with that particular set of attributes.

Limitations of product positioning analysis

The analysis depicted in Exhibit 7–6 is usually referred to as *product positioning* because it indicates how alternative products or brands are positioned relative to one another in customers' minds. The problem with this analysis, though, is that it does not tell the marketer which positions are most appealing to customers.[12] Thus, there is no way to determine whether there is a market for a new brand or store that locates in an "open" position or whether customers in different market segments prefer brands with different attributes and positions. To solve such problems it is necessary to measure customers' preferences and locate them in the product space along with their perceptions of the positions of existing brands. This is called a *market positioning analysis.*

Step 6: Determine customers' most preferred combination of attributes

There are several ways analysts can measure customer preferences and include them in a positioning analysis. For instance, survey respondents can be asked to think of the ideal product or brand within a product category—a hypothetical brand possessing the perfect combination of attributes (from the customer's viewpoint). Respondents could then rate their ideal product and existing products on a number of attributes. An alternative approach is to ask respondents to not only judge the degree of similarity among pairs of existing brands but to also indicate their degree of preference for each. In either case the analyst, using the appropriate statistical techniques, can locate the respondents' ideal points relative to the positions of the various existing brands on the product space map.

Whichever approach is used, the results will look something like Exhibit 7–7, which shows a hypothetical cluster of ideal points for one segment of women's clothing consumers. As a group, this segment would seem to prefer Nordstrom over any other women's clothing retailer on the map. There are, however, several reasons why not all customers in this segment are likely to prefer Nordstrom. First, the ideal points of some customers are actually closer to Macy's than Nordstrom. Second, customers whose ideal point is equidistant between the two stores may be relatively indifferent in their choice of which store to patronize. And finally, customers sometimes may patronize stores somewhat further from their ideal—particularly when buying low-involvement, nondurable goods or services—to assess the qualities of new stores, to reassess older stores from time to time, or just for the sake of variety.

Step 7: Define market positioning and market segmentation

An important criterion for defining market segments is the difference in the benefits sought by different customers. Because differences between customers' ideal points reflect variations in the benefits they seek, a market positioning analysis can simultaneously identify distinct market segments and the perceived positions of different brands. When customer's ideal

---

[12]For existing brands, attractiveness can be inferred from current sales volumes and market shares. The position occupied by the share leader is obviously more appealing to a greater number of customers than the positions occupied by lesser brands.

EXHIBIT 7-7

Perceptual Map of Women's Clothing Retailers in Washington, D.C., Showing the Ideal Points of a Segment of Consumers

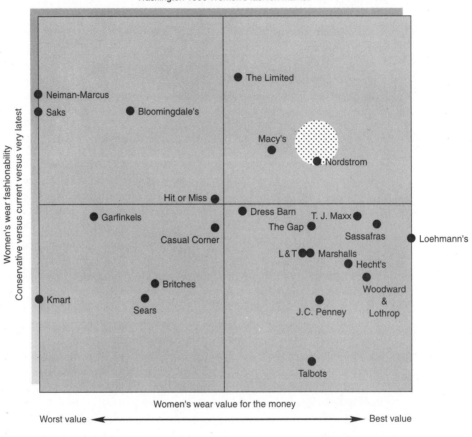

Washington 1990 Women's fashion market

SOURCE: Adapted from Douglas Tigert and Stephen Arnold, "Nordstrom: How Good Are They?" *Babson College Retailing Research Reports,* September 1990.

points cluster in two or more locations on the product space map, the analyst can consider each cluster a distinct market segment.[13] For analytical purposes, each cluster is represented by a circle that encloses most of the ideal points for that segment; the size of the circle reflects the relative proportion of customers within a particular segment.

---

[13] When using preference data to define market segments, however, the analyst should also collect information about customers' demographic characteristics, lifestyle, product usage, and other potential segmentation variables. This enables the analyst to develop a more complete picture of the differences among benefit segments. Such information can be useful for developing advertising appeals, selecting media, focusing personal selling efforts, and designing many other elements of a marketing program that can effectively appeal to a particular segment.

EXHIBIT 7–8

Perceptual Map of Women's Clothing Retailers in Washington, D.C., Showing Five Segments
Based on Ideal Points

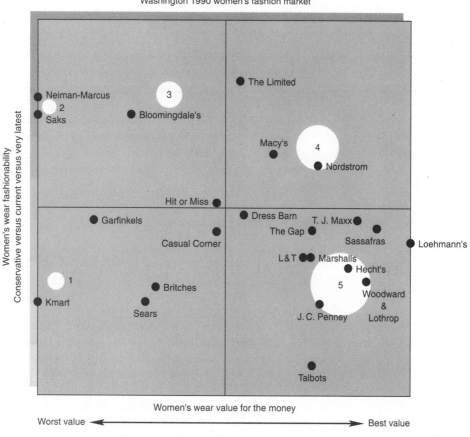

Washington 1990 women's fashion market

SOURCE: Adapted from Douglas Tigert and Stephen Arnold, "Nordstrom: How Good Are They?" *Babson College Retailing Research Reports,* September 1990.

Exhibit 7–8 groups the sample of Washington, D.C., respondents into five distinct segments on the basis of clusters of ideal points.[14] Segment 5 contains the largest proportion of customers; segment 1, the smallest.[15] By examining the preferences of customers in

_____

[14] The size of the individual circles in Exhibit 7–8 is fictitious and designed for illustrative purposes only.

[15] The map in Exhibit 7–8 shows five distinct preference segments but only one set of perceived product positions. The implication is that consumers in this sample were similar in the way they perceived existing brands but different in the product attributes they preferred. This is the most common situation; customers tend to vary more in the benefits they seek than in how they perceive available products or brands. Sometimes, however, various segments may perceive the positions of existing brands quite differently. They may even use different determinant attributes in assessing these positions. Under such circumstances, a marketer should construct a separate market positioning map for each segment.

different segments together with their perceptions of the positions of existing brands, analysts can learn much about (1) the competitive strength of different brands in different segments, (2) the intensity of the rivalry between brands in a given segment, and (3) the opportunities for gaining a differentiated position within a specific target segment.

Step 8: Select positioning strategies

The final decision about where to position a new brand or reposition an existing one should be based on both the market targeting analysis discussed in Chapter 6 and the results of a market positioning analysis. The position chosen should match the preferences of a particular market segment and should take into account the current positions of competing brands. It should also reflect the current and *future* attractiveness of the target market (its size, expected growth, and environmental constraints) and the relative strengths and weaknesses of competitors. Such information, together with an analysis of the costs required to acquire and maintain these positions, allows an assessment of the economic implications of different market positioning strategies.

Sales potential of market positions

The sales level of a brand is affected by many things, some of which are controlled by the firm (product, price, promotion, and distribution) and some that are not (competitive activities and the environment's evolution). All of these influence elements of the consumer's purchasing process, such as awareness, purchase intent, and search for the product. The **purchase intent share** represents the percentage of consumers who intend to buy a specific brand before actually searching for it. It is one of the most important indicators of the likely success of a given product and integrates all the factors that influence the perceived qualities of a product.

Analysts can estimate the purchase intent share a brand could acquire in a segment (assuming a certain positioning strategy) from the positions of existing brands and the preferences of consumers in the segments. In a perceptual map obtained via multidimensional scaling, the purchase intent is related to the inverse of the distance of the brand's position from the ideal point.

The estimation of the sales potential of two positions is illustrated in Exhibits 7–9 and 7–10 and is based upon the distance between a brand's position and the ideal points. Two segments are considered, with the size of the second being about half the size of the first. The overall market is currently dominated by three brands—E, H, and B, with brands E and B strongly positioned in segment 1 and H in segment 2. The firm owning brand B is considering the introduction of a new brand and, as a first step, evaluates the marketing potential of two positions, X and Y. They correspond to a reinforcement of the firm's position in segment 1 and a penetration of segment 2, respectively.

The estimates made in Exhibit 7–10 assume that the new brand—X or Y—will obtain adequate awareness and distribution. Brand X is expected to gain a 17.3 purchase intent share, of which about one-third would come from the cannibalization of brand B. The firm's total purchase intent share is expected to increase from 17.5 percent to 30.8 percent. Brand Y would cannibalize brand B less, but the expected purchase intent share of Y is only 10.9 percent because of the smaller size of segment 2 and the strong position of brand H in this

EXHIBIT 7–9

Perceptual Map of Sales Potential for Two Positions

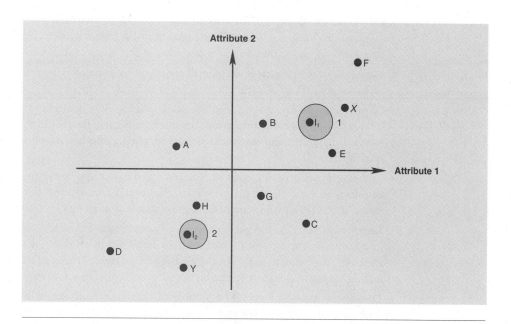

NOTE: Circles identify ideal points 1 and 2.

EXHIBIT 7–10

Illustration of Purchase Intent Shares before and after Introduction of New Product (in Percent)

		A		C		E	F			X or Y
						Existing				New brand
Current	Segment 1	3.9	24.0	6.4	1.3	38.1	12.2	9.6	4.4	—
	Segment 2	11.1	4.5	5.9	14.0	2.9	1.4	10.3	49.9	—
	Total	6.3	17.5	6.2	5.5	26.4	8.6	9.8	19.6	—
With X	Segment 1	2.9	18.0	4.8	1.0	28.6	9.2	7.2	3.3	25.0
	Segment 2	10.9	4.4	5.8	13.7	2.9	1.4	10.1	48.9	1.9
	Total	5.6	13.5	5.1	5.2	20.0	6.6	8.2	18.5	17.3
With Y	Segment 1	3.8	23.4	6.3	1.3	37.2	11.9	9.4	4.3	2.4
	Segment 2	8.0	3.3	4.2	10.1	2.1	1.0	7.4	36.0	27.8
	Total	5.2	16.7	5.6	4.2	25.5	8.3	8.7	14.9	10.9

segment. The expected increase in total purchase intent share would be greater for brand X than brand Y despite X's higher degree of cannibalization.

Evaluations of the sales potential of alternative positions should also consider the more pertinent market dynamics. These include:

- *Growth of market segments.* The current sales potential of a position close to the ideal point may be limited. If the segment's growth rate is higher than the market growth rate, however, the cumulative sales potential of this segment may be substantial.

- *Evolution of segments' ideal points.* If at all possible, brands should be positioned on the evolutionary path of a segment's ideal point to enjoy an increasing market share.

- *Changes in positioning intensity.* If an existing brand has a low positioning intensity and a favorable position in a segment, the firm marketing this brand should try to increase its positioning intensity, thereby increasing the brand's penetration and market share.

- *Evolution of existing brands' positions.* The shifts in the positions of existing brands may be difficult to predict, but their evolution can often be anticipated. For example, in recent years Chrysler has emphasized greater styling in its cars.

- *Emerging attributes.* The long-term sales potential of a brand will be affected not only by its position on the current determinant attributes but by its position on emerging attributes. For example, in the last decade the increasing importance of caloric content in food has had a significant impact on the sales potential of brands in the product class.

- *Development of new segments.* The number of consumers with similar needs distinct from the rest of the market may increase to the point where some firms consider these consumers a separate segment. The emergence of new segments will create new opportunities but may also weaken the sales potential of existing brands.

- *Introduction of new brands.* The introduction of new brands by competitors is often unpredictable. Analyzing a product space from a competitor's point of view gives an indication of moves that competitors might make.

Market positioning strategies

Formulating a market positioning strategy consists of selecting and defining a market position the firm plans to occupy in reaching its marketing objectives. This requires estimates of the economic potential of alternative positions, which are based largely on analysis of the sales potential of each position and the investments required to occupy the targeted position. The seven market position strategies described here are relevant to a large number of situations.

1. *Monosegment positioning.*   As the name suggests, monosegment positioning involves developing a product and marketing program tailored to the preference of a single market segment. Successful implementation of this strategy would give the brand an obvious advantage within the target segment but would not generate many sales from customers in other segments. This strategy is best used with mass marketing.

2. *Multisegment positioning.*   This consists of positioning a product so as to attract consumers from different segments. This attractive strategy provides higher economies of scale,

requires smaller investments, and avoids dispersion of managerial attention. It is particularly appropriate when individual segments are small, as is generally the case in the early stages of a product's life cycle.

3. *Standby positioning.*   It may not be in the best economic interest of a firm to switch from a multisegment positioning strategy to a monosegment strategy (assuming the use of several brands, each positioned to serve the needs of only one segment) even if it increases total market share. In such a case the firm may decide to implement a monosegment positioning strategy *only* when forced to do so. In order to minimize response time the firm prepares a standby plan specifying the products and their attributes as well as details of the marketing programs that would be used to position the new product.

4. *Imitative positioning.*   This is essentially the same as a head-on strategy where a new brand targets a position similar to that of an existing successful brand. It may be an appropriate strategy if the imitative firm has a distinctive advantage beyond positioning, such as better access to channels of distribution, a more effective salesforce, or substantially more money to spend on promotion including "price deals."

5. *Anticipatory positioning.*   A firm may position a new brand in anticipation of the evolution of a segment's needs. This is particularly appropriate when the new brand is not expected to have a fast acceptance, and market share will build as the needs of consumers become more and more aligned with the benefits being offered. At its best, this strategy enables a firm to preempt a market position that may have a substantial long-term potential. At its worst, it may cause the firm to face a difficult economic situation for an extended period if the needs of a segment do not evolve as expected.

6. *Adaptive positioning.*   This consists of periodically repositioning a brand to follow the evolution of the segment's needs.

7. *Defensive positioning.*   When a firm occupies a strong position in a market segment with a single brand, it is vulnerable to imitative positioning strategies. The firm may preempt competitive strategies by introducing an additional brand in a similar position for the same segment. This will reduce immediate profitability but may allow the firm to better protect itself against competitors in the long term. For example, Procter and Gamble has seven brands of laundry detergents, such as Tide and Bold, several of which occupy similar positions in consumers' minds.

SUMMARY

Positioning is concerned with how well the product performs relative to competitive offerings *and* the needs (benefits sought) of one or more targeted market segments. There are two types of positioning—one based on the physical product, the other on the market's perception of the product. The former depends primarily on technical versus market data but still represents an important step in the formulation and implementation of marketing strategy because it facilitates the interface between marketing and R & D, forces management to discriminate between selected physical characteristics, helps in identifying key competitors, and may reveal important product gaps.

Physical product positioning is flawed by its failure to explicitly consider the consumer. For many products, consumers know very little about the physical characteristics, and even if they did, they would not understand them well enough to use them as a basis for selecting one brand over another. Thus, consumers perceive competitive offerings using various dimensions, which can be classified as simple physically based attributes, complex physically based attributes, or essentially abstract attributes.

To determine which positioning strategy to adopt, a firm must proceed through the eight steps in the positioning process. These are (1) identify a relevant set of competitive products, (2) identify the set of determinant attributes that define the product space in which positions of current offerings are located, (3) collect data from a sample of customers and potential customers about perceptions of each product on the determinant attributes, (4) analyze the intensity of a product's current position in customers' minds, (5) determine the product's current location in the product space (product positioning), (6) determine customers' most preferred combination of determinant attributes, (7) examine the fit between preferences of market segments and the current position of the product (market positioning), and (8) select a positioning or repositioning strategy. The latter consists of common strategies such as those concerned with a monosegment, multiple segments, a standby position, an imitative position, an anticipatory position, an adaptive position, and a defensive position.

APPENDIX: STATISTICAL TECHNIQUES USED TO ANALYZE CONSUMERS' PERCEPTIONS ABOUT THE COMPETITIVE POSITIONS OF ALTERNATIVE PRODUCTS OR BRANDS[16]

Factor analysis

To employ factor analysis, the analyst must first identify the salient attributes consumers use to evaluate products in the category under study. The analyst then collects data from a sample of consumers concerning their ratings of each product or brand on all attributes. The factor analysis program next determines which attributes are related to the same underlying

---

[16]For a more technical discussion of how these techniques work, the data that must be collected as input for the different analyses, and their statistical strengths and weaknesses, see Harper W. Boyd, Jr., Ralph Westfall, and Stanley F. Stasch, *Marketing Research* (Burr Ridge, Ill.: Irwin, 1989), chs. 16 and 17. For extensive critical reviews of past marketing applications of these different approaches, see John R. Hauser and Frank S. Koppleman, "Alternative Perceptual Mapping Techniques: Relative Accuracy and Usefulness," *Journal of Marketing Research,* November 1979, pp. 495–506; and John W. Keon, "Product Positioning: TRINODAL Mapping of Brand Images, Ad Images, and Consumer Preference," *Journal of Marketing Research,* November 1983, pp. 380–92. Also see Paul E. Green, J. Douglas Carroll, and Stephen M. Goldberg, "A General Approach to Product Design Optimization via Conjoint Analysis," *Journal of Marketing,* Summer 1981, pp. 17–37; Michael R. Hagerty, "Improving the Predictive Power of Conjoint Analysis," *Journal of Marketing Research,* May 1985, pp. 168–84; Thomas W. Leigh, David M. McKay, and John O. Summers, "Reliability and Validity of Conjoint Analysis and Self-Explicated Weights," *Journal of Marketing Research,* November 1984, pp. 456–63; Paul E. Green, "Hybrid Models for Conjoint Analysis: An Expository Review," *Journal of Marketing Research,* May 1984, pp. 184–93; and Jan-Benedict E. M. Steenkamp, Hans C. M. van Trijp, and Jos M. F. Ten Berge, "Perceptual Mapping Based on Idiosyncratic Sets of Attributes," *Journal of Marketing Research,* February 1994, pp. 15–27.

construct ("load" on the same factor). The analyst uses those underlying constructs or factors as the dimensions for a product space map, and the program indicates where each product or brand is perceived to be located on each factor.

Discriminant analysis

Discriminant analysis requires the same input data as factor analysis. The discriminant analysis program then determines consumers' perceptual dimensions on the basis of which attributes best differentiate, or discriminate, among brands. Once again, those underlying dimensions can be used to construct a product space map; but they are usually not so easily interpretable as the factors identified through factor analysis. Also, as with factor analysis, the underlying dimensions may be more a function of the attributes used to collect consumer ratings than of the product characteristics that consumers actually consider to be most important.

Conjoint measurement

Conjoint measurement determines which combination of a limited number of attributes consumers most prefer. The technique is helpful for identifying appealing new product designs and important points that might be included in a product's advertising. Although it can provide some insights about consumer preferences, it cannot provide information about how consumers perceive the positioning of existing products in relation to product dimensions. In other words, it is not very useful for product positioning analysis because it does not show how similar two products are perceived to be on underlying determinant attributes.

Multidimensional scaling

Unlike the other techniques where the underlying dimensions identified depend on the attributes supplied by the researcher when collecting data, multidimensional scaling produces dimensions based on consumer judgments about the similarity of, or their preferences for, the actual brands. These underlying dimensions are thought to be the basic attractive dimensions that consumers actually use to evaluate alternative brands in the product class. Multidimensional scaling programs that use data on similarities construct geometrically spaced maps on which the brands perceived to be most similar are placed close together. Those that use consumer preferences produce joint space maps that show consumer ideal points and then position the most preferred brands close to those ideal points.

Unfortunately, the underlying dimensions of the maps produced by multidimensional scaling can be difficult to interpret. Also, the dimensions identified are only those that already exist for currently available brands. This makes the technique less useful for investigating new product concepts that might involve new characteristics. Finally, the technique is subject to statistical limitations when the number of alternative brands being investigated is small. As a rule of thumb, such techniques should only be applied when at least eight or more different products or brands are being examined.

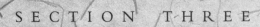

FORMULATING MARKETING STRATEGIES

Marketing Strategies for New Market Entries

THE HORMEL FOODS CORPORATION: FROM BACON TO SPAM TO TOP SHELF[1]

When asked to name the most innovative developers of new products and new markets, most people would think of high-tech firms like 3M, Apple, or Microsoft. Few would come up with a meat processor. Yet throughout its 100-year history, the Hormel Foods Corporation has been one of the most prolific and successful developers of new products in the food industry.

George Hormel began the firm in 1890 when he started making sausage to sell in his meat market in Austin, Minnesota. The firm's tradition of new product development began in 1895 with George's introduction of Hormel's Sugar-Cured Pig Back Bacon—a product that is now commonly known by the more appetizing name of Canadian bacon.

Hormel's long string of new product successes really got rolling after George's son Jay took over in the 1920s. The firm was a pioneer in canning meats and became the first U. S. producer of canned hams in 1927. Jay also introduced Dinty Moore stew and Hormel chili to the American palate. But probably his most famous (and most maligned) invention was Spam. Despite all the jokes associated with the product, it recently celebrated its 50th anniversary, holds a 75 percent share of the spiced ham market, produces annual sales of over $150 million, and—believe it or not—continues to grow.

[1]This example is based on material found in Jane Simon, "From Spam to Fish, Hormel Expands," *Compass Readings*, September 1990, pp. 26–32; and *The Hormel Foods Corporation 1993 Annual Report* (Austin, Minn.: Hormel Foods Corp., 1994).

Looking for the "point of difference"

In recent years Hormel has focused even more effort on developing unique new products for the consumer market. The firm's mission is "to be a leader in the food field with highly differentiated quality products that attain optimum share of market while meeting established objectives." Consistent with that mission, the company has moved away from the production of basic commoditylike meat products, such as bacon and ham. Several years ago, for instance, it closed its Austin slaughter house and leased the plant to Quality Pork Processors, Inc., which in turn buys the hogs, slaughters them, and sells the meat to Hormel. Thus Hormel avoids the cost of labor-intensive meat packing but still maintains some control over the quality of the meat the company buys.

Over the past decade Hormel has sought increased volume growth and profitability by developing high value-added products that fit newly emerging consumer preferences and lifestyles. As Richard Knowlton, the firm's recently retired CEO, puts it, "We have tried to transform the company into a food company with less and less dependence on red meat, . . . and we've tried to meet the need for foods that take less preparation time." The firm's basic strategy is to develop products that are differentiated from competitive offerings by designing in features that consumers want but that other companies do not offer. "We look at the market and ask what could be competitive?" says Knowlton. "What would be original? That's our main key in everything we do—to look for the point of difference, and if we can't bring forth a point of difference, then we don't go to the party."

Modifying existing products and entering new markets

In some cases Hormel achieved a point of difference by making only relatively minor modifications to some of its old familiar products. The company's Light & Lean wiener, a reduced-fat hot dog, is one example. Another is the firm's Frank 'N Stuff wieners. To differentiate the product from the 30 or so other brands of hot dogs on the market, Hormel designed, built, and patented a system capable of inserting a tunnel of chili or cheese inside every wiener.

In other instances Hormel's product introduction efforts have taken the company into product categories that are new to the company but relatively familiar to consumers. Several years ago, for instance, the firm acquired and expanded Chicken by George, a line of packaged chicken breasts marinated in various flavors, such as country mustard, that was developed by TV personality Phyllis George. The line represented Hormel's first entry into the already well-developed value-added, brand-name poultry market.

Developing innovative products

At the other extreme, some of Hormel's new product development efforts have been so innovative that they established a whole new product category in the grocery store: microwave prepared meals. The firm's first entry in this area was Top Shelf, a line of shelf-stable dinner entrees such as Italian-style lasagne and beef stroganoff with noodles. The products' taste equals that of high-quality frozen dinners, but Top Shelf doesn't require refrigeration and doesn't use preservatives. Unlike frozen food, which has a shorter shelf life, Top Shelf is guaranteed fresh for 18 months and can be microwaved in its container in about two minutes. Since Top Shelf was introduced in 1986, it has steadily gained consumer acceptance and has achieved sales of over $150 million. Hormel has further expanded the shelf-stable microwave meal category by introducing its Micro Cup and Kids Kitchen product lines as well as microwave versions of its best-selling Dinty Moore stew and Hormel chili.

A strategic repositioning

Hormel's aggressive product and market development efforts over the past decade have succeeded in repositioning the company and helping it attain substantial volume growth and profitability. In 1980 70 percent of the firm's sales were from commodity meat products, but now more than three-quarters of the firm's sales are generated by value-added prepared foods with wider profit margins and higher growth potential. As a result, the firm posted earnings increases every year over the past decade. Those earnings (before special accounting charges) reached a record $100 million on sales of $2.8 billion in 1993—a threefold increase from 10 years earlier.

SOME ISSUES CONCERNING NEW MARKET ENTRY STRATEGIES

What is a "new" product?

Hormel's approach to securing volume and profit growth illustrates several important points about new product and market development, each of which is explored later in this chapter. First, a firm's new market entries can involve products that differ in their degree of newness from the perspective of both the company and its customers. Top Shelf, for example, involved a shelf-stable food technology that was new to both the company and its customers. On the other hand, Hormel's foray into prepared poultry products with its Chicken by George line involved products that were new to the firm but not to its customers; other manufacturers already offered similar products. Finally, the development of Light & Lean wieners involved manufacturing technology, marketing, and distribution efforts that were ordinary for the company, but those efforts resulted in the first low-fat hot dogs on the market, a new product that appealed to many health-conscious consumers.

This chapter focuses on marketing objectives and programs appropriate for introducing and developing markets for offerings that are *new to the target customers*. We examine programs that firms who are **pioneers**, or first entrants, in a particular product-market might use. Of course, later entrants also face difficulties when developing and introducing their own versions of a product. But given that the challenge facing such **followers** is essentially to capture market share in the face of established competitors, we will postpone our discussion of marketing programs appropriate for later entrants until the next chapter, when we examine share-building strategies.

What are the objectives of new product-market development?

While Hormel pursues a variety of different approaches to new product-market development, all have a common objective of increasing the firm's future sales volume and profitability. However, different approaches can achieve a variety of secondary objectives as well. Developing new user segments for an existing product, for instance, can reduce the unit costs and increase the profitability of that product. Similarly, major product improvements or line extensions—such as Hormel's introduction of Frank 'N Stuff and Light & Lean wieners—can help protect a firm's market share in a product category in the face of increasing competition. This suggests that top management should establish explicit objectives for new market entries in a firm's various business units to provide useful guidelines for choosing appropriate development strategies. A later section of this chapter discusses some of the different objectives that new entries can achieve and the conditions under which various objectives are appropriate.

Should a firm be a pioneer or a follower?

Finally, the development of new market entries can be both expensive and risky. Hormel will not disclose the total development cost of its Top Shelf line, but no doubt it was enormous. The firm spent more than $1 million just for two pieces of specialized testing equipment to conduct research for product and package development, and a large team of R & D, production, and marketing people spent four years readying the line for introduction. And there was no guarantee that grocery stores would distribute or consumers would accept Top Shelf's unique new form.

This raises an intriguing strategic question: Is it better for a firm to be the pioneer in developing and introducing a new product—as Hormel was with Top Shelf—or to be a follower who watches other innovators bear the risks of product failure and marketing mistakes before joining the battle with its own entry? Before discussing alternative marketing programs pioneers might use to penetrate and develop new markets, we turn to this more basic strategic issue and examine the conditions in which pioneer and follower strategies each have the greatest probability of long-term success.

HOW NEW IS "NEW"?

A survey of the new product development practices of 700 U. S. corporations conducted by the consulting firm of Booz, Allen & Hamilton found that the products introduced by those firms over a five-year period were not all equally new. The study identified six categories of new products based on their degree of newness as perceived by both the company introducing them

EXHIBIT 8–1

Categories of New Products Defined According to Their Degree of Newness to the Company and Customers in the Target Market

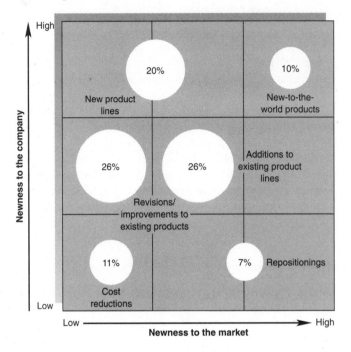

SOURCE: *New Products Management for the 1980s* (New York: Booz, Allen & Hamilton, 1982).

and the customers in the target market. These categories are discussed here and diagrammed in Exhibit 8–1, which also indicates the percentage of new entries falling in each category. Notice that only 10 percent of all new product introductions fell into the new-to-the-world category.[2]

- *New-to-the-world products* (10 percent)—True innovations that are new to the firm and create an entirely new market.

- *New product lines* (20 percent)—A product category that is new for the company introducing it but is not new to customers in the target market due to the existence of one or more competitive brands.

---

[2]*New Products Management for the 1980s* (New York: Booz, Allen & Hamilton, 1982). More recent studies, though focusing on smaller samples of new products, suggest that the relative proportions of new-to-the-world versus less innovative product introductions have not changed substantially over the past decade. For example, see Eric M. Olson, Orville C. Walker, Jr., and Robert W. Ruekert, "Organizing for Effective New Product Development: The Moderating Role of Product Innovativeness," *Journal of Marketing* 59, January 1995, pp. 48–62.

- *Additions to existing product lines* (26 percent)—New items that supplement a firm's established product line. These items may be moderately new to both the firm and the customers in its established product-markets. They may also serve to expand the market segments appealed to by the line.

- *Improvements in or revisions of existing products* (26 percent)—Items providing improved performance or greater perceived value brought out to replace existing products. These items may present moderately new marketing and production challenges to the firm, but unless they represent a technologically new generation of products, customers are likely to perceive them as similar to the products they replace.

- *Repositionings* (7 percent)—Existing products that are targeted at new applications and new market segments.

- *Cost reductions* (11 percent)—Product modifications providing similar performance at a lower cost.

A product's degree of newness to the company, its target customers, or both helps determine the amount of complexity and uncertainty involved in the engineering, operations, and marketing tasks necessary to make it a successful new entry. It also contributes to the amount of risk inherent in those tasks. Introducing a product that is new to both the firm and to target customers requires the greatest expenditure of effort and resources. It also involves the greatest amount of uncertainty and risk of failure due to the lack of information and experience with the technology and the target customers.

Products that are new to target customers but not to the firm (such as line extensions or modifications aimed at new customer segments or repositionings of existing products) are often not very innovative in design or manufacturing requirements, but they may present a great deal of marketing uncertainty. The marketing challenge here—as with new-to-the-world products—is to build **primary demand,** making target customers aware of the product and convincing them to adopt it. This is the marketing problem we investigate in this chapter.

Finally, products that are new to the company but not to the market (such as new product lines, line extensions, product modifications, and cost reductions) often present fewer challenges for R & D and product engineering. The company can study and learn from earlier designs or competitors' products. However, these products can present major challenges for process engineering, production scheduling, quality control, and inventory management. Once such a product is introduced into the market, the primary marketing objective becomes one of building **selective demand:** capturing market share and convincing customers that the new offering is better than existing competitive products. We discuss marketing programs a firm might use to accomplish these objectives in Chapter 9.

OBJECTIVES OF NEW PRODUCT AND MARKET DEVELOPMENT

The primary objective of most new product and market development efforts is to secure future volume and profit growth. This objective has become even more crucial in recent years due to rapidly advancing technology and more intense global competition. A steady flow of new products and the development of new markets, including those in foreign countries, are essential for the continued growth of most firms.

The Hormel case illustrates, however, that individual development projects may also accomplish a variety of other strategic objectives. When asked what strategic role was served by their most successful recent new entry, the respondents in the Booz, Allen & Hamilton survey mentioned eight different strategic objectives. Exhibit 8–2 lists these objectives and the percentage of respondents that mentioned each one. The exhibit also indicates which objectives focused on external concerns—such as defending market share—and which were driven by a desire to improve or build upon the firm's internal strengths. Most respondents indicated their new entry helped accomplish more than one objective.

Exhibit 8–3 shows that different types of new entries are appropriate for achieving different strategic objectives. For example, if the objective is to establish a foothold in or preempt a new market segment, the firm must introduce a product that is new to that market, although it may not be entirely new to the company. On the other hand, if the objective is to improve cash flow by adding another cash generator, simple line extensions or product modifications—particularly those that reduce unit costs—may do the trick.

EXHIBIT 8–2

Strategic Objectives Attained by Successful New Market Entries

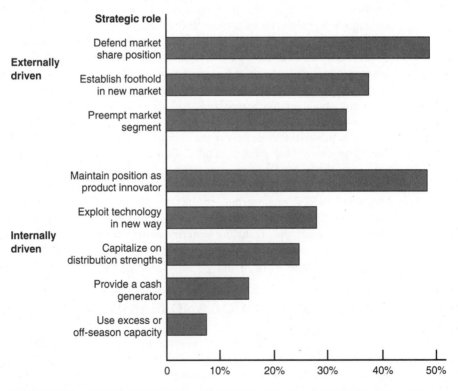

SOURCE: *New Products Management for the 1980s* (New York: Booz, Allen & Hamilton, 1982), p. 11.

EXHIBIT 8-3

Types of New Market Entries Appropriate for Different Strategic Objectives

Objective	New entry
Maintain position as a product innovator	New-to-the-world products; improvements or revisions to existing products
Defend a current market-share position	Improvements or revisions to existing products; additions to existing product line; cost reductions
Establish a foothold in a future new market; preempt a market segment	New-to-the-world products; additions to existing product line; repositionings
Exploit technology in a new way	New-to-the-world products; new product line; additions to or revisions of existing product line
Capitalize on distribution strengths	New-to-the-world products; new product line; additions to or revisions of existing product line
Provide a cash generator	Additions to or revisions of existing product line; repositionings; cost reductions
Use excess or off-season capacity	New-to-the-world product; new product line

The business's objectives for its new entries influence the kind of entry strategy it should pursue and the marketing and other functional programs needed to implement that strategy. For instance, if a business is pursuing a prospector strategy and its objectives are to maintain a position as a product innovator and establish footholds in a variety of new product-markets, it should attempt to be the pioneer in as many of those markets as possible. And as we saw in Chapter 3, successful implementation of such a strategy requires the business to be competent in and devote substantial resources to R & D, product engineering, marketing, and marketing research.

On the other hand, if the business is primarily concerned with defending an already strong market share position in its industry, it may prefer to be a follower. Usually entering new product-markets only after an innovator, a follower relies on superior quality, better customer service, or lower prices to offset the pioneer's early lead. Such a strategy usually requires fewer investments in R & D and product development, but marketing and sales still are critical in implementing it effectively. A more detailed comparison of these alternative new market entry strategies is the focus of the next section of this chapter.

MARKET ENTRY STRATEGIES: PIONEERS VERSUS FOLLOWERS

Even though IBM is viewed as one of the world's premier high-tech companies, it usually has not been a pioneer in the sense of being the first to enter new markets. For example, IBM did not enter the personal computer (PC) market until after several other firms, including Apple and Tandy, had already established substantial sales volumes. But as a follower, IBM developed an improved product design offering superior performance. It also had vast financial resources to support extensive advertising and promotional efforts, as well as an established reputation for reliability and customer service. Consequently, IBM was able to capture a commanding share of the PC market within a year of its entry.

Of course, in view of IBM's struggles during the 1990s one might ask whether the firm would have been better off pursuing a more innovative prospector strategy in at least some of its businesses. On the other hand, some of the more pioneering firms in the computer industry, such as Commodore and even Apple, have not always fared so well in the marketplace either. The important strategic question, then, is which of the two entry approaches—being the pioneer or a fast follower—*usually* makes the most sense? Or do both entry strategies have particular advantages under different sets of conditions?

Pioneer strategy

Although they take the greatest risks and probably experience more failures than their more conservative competitors, conventional wisdom holds that successful pioneers are handsomely rewarded. It is assumed that competitive advantages inherent in being the first to enter a new product-market can be sustained through the growth stage and into the maturity stage of the product life cycle, resulting in a strong share position and substantial returns.

Some of the potential sources of competitive advantage available to pioneers are briefly summarized in Exhibit 8–4 and discussed below.[3]

1. *First choice of market segments and positions.*   The pioneer has the opportunity to develop a product offering with attributes most important to the largest segment of customers, or to promote the importance of attributes that favor its brand. Thus, the pioneer's brand can become the standard of reference customers use to evaluate other brands. This can make it more difficult for followers with me-too products to convince existing customers that their new brands are superior to the older and more familiar pioneer. If the pioneer has successfully tied its offering to the choice criteria of the largest group of customers, it also becomes more difficult for followers to differentiate their offerings in ways that are attractive to the mass-market segment. They may have to target a smaller peripheral segment or niche instead.

2. *Ability to define the rules of the game.*   The pioneer's actions on such variables as product quality, price, distribution, warranties, postsale service, and promotional appeals and budgets set standards that subsequent competitors must meet or beat. If the pioneer sets those standards high enough, it can raise the costs of entry and perhaps preempt some potential competitors.

3. *Distribution advantages.*   The pioneer has the most options in designing a distribution channel to bring the new product to market. This is particularly important for industrial

---

[3]For a more extensive review of the potential competitive advantages of being a first-mover, and the controllable and uncontrollable forces that influence a firm's ability to capitalize on those potential advantages, see Roger A. Kerin, P. Rajan Varadarajan, and Robert A. Peterson, "First-Mover Advantage: A Synthesis, Conceptual Framework, and Research Propositions," *Journal of Marketing* 56, October 1992, pp. 33–52.

EXHIBIT 8-4

Potential Advantages of Pioneer and Follower Strategies

Pioneer	Follower
• Economies of scale and experience.	• Ability to take advantage of pioneer's positioning mistakes.
• High switching costs for early adopters.	
• Ability to define the rules of the game.	• Ability to take advantage of pioneer's product mistakes.
• Distribution advantage.	
• Influence on consumer choice criteria and attitudes.	• Ability to take advantage of pioneer's marketing mistakes.
• Possibility of preempting scarce resources.	• Ability to take advantage of pioneer's limited resources.
	• Ability to take advantage of the latest technology.

goods where, if the pioneer exercises its options well and with dispatch, it should end up with a network of the best distributors. This can exclude later entrants from some markets. Distributors are often reluctant to take on second or third brands. This is especially true when the product is technically complex and the distributor must carry large inventories of the product and spare parts and invest in specialized training and service.

For consumer packaged goods, it is more difficult to slow the entry of later competitors by preempting distribution alternatives. Nevertheless, the pioneer still has the advantage of attaining more shelf facings at the outset of the growth stage. By quickly expanding its product line following an initial success, the pioneer can appropriate still more shelf space, thereby making the challenge faced by followers even more difficult.

4. *Economies of scale and experience.* Being first means the pioneer can gain accumulated volume and experience and thereby lower per unit costs at a faster rate than followers. This advantage is particularly pronounced when the product is technically sophisticated and involves high development costs or when its life cycle is likely to be short with sales increasing rapidly during the introduction and early growth stages.

As we shall see later, the pioneer can deploy these cost advantages in a number of ways to protect its early lead against followers. One strategy is to lower price, which can discourage followers from entering the market because it raises the volume necessary for them to break even. Or the pioneer might invest its savings in additional marketing efforts to expand its penetration of the market, such as heavier advertising, a larger sales force, or continuing product improvements or line extensions.

5. *High switching costs for early adopters.* Customers who are early to adopt a pioneer's new product may be reluctant to change suppliers when competitive products appear. This is particularly true for industrial goods, where the costs of switching suppliers can be high. Compatible equipment and spare parts, investments in employee training, and the risks of lower product quality or customer service make it easier for the pioneer to retain its early customers over time.

In some cases, however, switching costs can work against the pioneer and in favor of followers. A pioneer may have trouble converting customers to a new technology if they must bear high switching costs to abandon their old way of doing things. Pioneers in the manufacture of ethanol, for instance, have had a difficult time convincing car owners to modify their engines to be able to use ethanol instead of gasoline. Once the pioneer has persuaded early adopters to change technologies, however, their costs of switching to a follower's brand within the new product category may be relatively low.

6. *Possibility of preempting scarce resources and suppliers.* The pioneer may be able to negotiate favorable deals with suppliers who are eager for new business or who do not appreciate the size of the opportunity for their raw materials or component parts. If later entrants subsequently find those materials and components in short supply, they may be constrained from expanding as fast as they might like or be forced to pay premium prices.

Not all pioneers capitalize on their potential advantages

The advantages just discussed can help pioneers gain and maintain a competitive edge in new markets. For instance, research has found that surviving pioneers hold a significantly larger average market share when their industries reach maturity than firms that were either fast followers or late entrants in the product category.[4]

On the other hand, some pioneers fail: They abandon the product category, go out of business, or get acquired before their industry matures. One recent study that averaged the performance of these failed pioneers together with that of the more successful survivors found that, overall, pioneers did not perform as well over the long haul as followers.[5]

Of course, volume and market share are not the only dimensions on which success can be measured. Unfortunately, there is little evidence concerning the effect of the timing of a firm's entry into a new market on its ultimate profitability in that market or the value generated for shareholders.[6]

In view of the mixed research evidence, then, it seems reasonable to conclude that while a pioneer may have some *potential* competitive advantages, not all pioneers are successful at capitalizing on them. Some fail during the introductory or shakeout stages of their industries' life cycles. And those that survive may lack the resources to keep up with rapid growth or the competencies needed to maintain their early lead in the face of onslaughts by strong followers.

---

[4]For example, see William T. Robinson, "Market Pioneering and Sustainable Market Share Advantages in Industrial Goods Manufacturing Industries," working paper, Purdue University, 1984; and Robert D. Buzzell and Bradley T. Gale, *The PIMS Principles: Linking Strategy to Performance* (New York: Free Press, 1987), p. 183.

[5]Peter N. Golder and Gerard J. Tellis, "Pioneer Advantage: Marketing Logic or Marketing Legend," *Journal of Marketing Research* 30, May 1993, pp. 158–70.

[6]Marvin B. Lieberman and David B. Montgomery, "First-Mover Advantages," *Strategic Management Journal* 9, 1988, pp. 41–59; and Michael J. Moore, William Boulding, and Ronald C. Goodstein, "Pioneering and Market Share: Is Entry Time Endogenous and Does It Matter?" *Journal of Marketing* 28, February 1991, pp. 97–104.

Follower strategy

In many cases a firm becomes a follower by default. It is simply beaten to a new product-market by a quicker competitor. But even when a company has the capability of being the first mover, the previous observations suggest there may be some advantages to letting other firms go first into a product-market. Let the pioneer shoulder the initial risks while the followers observe the pioneer's shortcomings and mistakes. Possible advantages of such a follower strategy are briefly summarized in Exhibit 8–4 and discussed here.

1. *Ability to take advantage of the pioneer's positioning mistakes.*   If the pioneer misjudges the preferences and purchase criteria of the mass-market segment or attempts to satisfy two or more segments at once, it is vulnerable to the introduction of more precisely positioned products by a follower. By tailoring its offerings to each distinct segment, the follower(s) can successfully encircle the pioneer.

2. *Ability to take advantage of the pioneer's product mistakes.*   If the pioneer's initial product has technical limitations or design flaws, the follower can benefit by overcoming these weaknesses. Even when the pioneering product is technically satisfactory, a follower may gain an advantage through product enhancements. For example, Compaq captured a substantial share of the commercial PC market by developing faster and more portable versions of IBM's original machine.

3. *Ability to take advantage of the pioneer's marketing mistakes.*   If the pioneer makes any marketing mistakes in introducing a new entry, it opens opportunities for later entrants. This observation is closely related to the first two points, yet goes beyond product positioning and design to the actual execution of the pioneer's marketing program. For example, the pioneer may fail to attain adequate distribution, spend too little on introductory advertising, or use ineffective promotional appeals to communicate the product's benefits. A follower can observe these mistakes, design a marketing program to overcome them, and successfully compete head-to-head with the pioneer.

4. *Ability to take advantage of the latest technology.*   In industries characterized by rapid technological advances, followers can possibly introduce products based on a superior, second-generation technology and thereby gain an advantage over the pioneer. And the pioneer may have difficulty reacting quickly to such advances if it is heavily committed to an earlier technology. Consumer popularity of the newer VHS format, for instance, gave followers in the videocassette recorder market an advantage over pioneer Sony, who was locked into the less popular Beta format.

5. *Ability to take advantage of the pioneer's limited resources.*   If the pioneer has limited resources for production facilities or marketing programs or fails to commit sufficient resources to its new entry, followers willing and able to outspend the pioneer experience few enduring constraints.

Determinants of success for pioneers and followers

Our discussion suggests that a pioneering firm stands the best chance for long-term success in market-share leadership and profitability when (1) the new product-market is insulated from the entry of competitors, at least for a while, by strong patent protection, proprietary technology (such as a unique production process), or substantial investment requirements; or (2) the firm has sufficient size, resources, and competencies to take full advantage of its pioneering position and preserve it in the face of later competitive entries. Indeed, some recent evidence suggests that not only do organizational competencies such as R & D and marketing skills affect a firm's success as a pioneer, they may also influence the company's decision about whether to be a pioneer in the first place. Firms that lack the competencies necessary to sustain a first-mover advantage may be more likely to wait for another company to take the lead and enter the market later.[7]

Polaroid Corporation is a pioneer that profited from the first kind of situation. Strong patent protection enabled the firm to grow from an entrepreneurial start-up to a $1.6 billion company with little direct competition. Kodak, the only firm that attempted to challenge Polaroid in the instant photography business, dropped out of the industry after losing a patent infringement suit in 1985. Consequently, Polaroid could grow and profit by introducing a steady but narrowly focused stream of product improvements and by supporting those products with only modest advertising and promotion. However, the firm's insulated market situation led it to focus largely on the instant photography business rather than expanding into other technologies or product-markets. As a result, the firm's primary concern now is that instant photography is declining as consumers shift their purchases to products based on newer technologies, such as video recorders.

McDonald's is an example of a pioneer that has succeeded by aggressively building on the foundations of its early advantage. Although the firm started small as a single hamburger restaurant, it used the franchise system of distribution to rapidly expand the number of McDonald's outlets with minimal cash investment. That expansion plus stringent quality and cost controls, relatively low prices made possible by experience curve effects, heavy advertising expenditures, and product line expansion aimed at specific market segments (such as Egg McMuffin for the breakfast crowd) have all enabled the firm to maintain a commanding share of the fast-food hamburger industry.

On the other hand, a follower will most likely succeed when there are few legal, technological, or financial barriers to inhibit entry and when it has sufficient resources or competencies to overwhelm the pioneer's early advantage. For example, given P&G's well-established brand name and superior advertising and promotional resources, the company was able to quickly take the market share lead away from pioneer Minnetonka, Inc., in the plaque-fighting toothpaste market with a reformulated version of Crest.

A study conducted across a broad range of industries in the PIMS database supports these observations.[8] The findings are briefly summarized in Exhibit 8–5. The author found that regardless of the industry involved, pioneers able to maintain their preeminent position well into the market's growth stage had supported their early entry with the following marketing strategy elements:

---

[7]Moore, Boulding, and Goodstein, "Pioneering and Market Share."

[8]Mary L. Coyle, "Competition in Developing Markets: The Impact of Order of Entry," unpublished doctoral dissertation, University of Toronto, 1986. Also see Kerin, Varadarajan, and Peterson, "First-Mover Advantage."

EXHIBIT 8–5

Marketing Strategy Elements Pursued by Successful Pioneers, Fast Followers, and Late Entrants

These marketers . . .	are characterized by one or more of these strategy elements:
Successful pioneers	• Large entry scale. • Broad product line. • High product quality. • Heavy promotional expenditures.

Successful fast followers	• Larger entry scale than the pioneer.
	• Leapfrogging the pioneer with superior:
	    product technology.
	    product quality.
	    customer service.

Successful late entrants	• Focus on peripheral target markets or niches.

- *Large entry scale.* Successful pioneers had sufficient capacity, or could expand quickly enough, to pursue a mass-market targeting strategy, usually on a national rather than a local or regional basis. Thus they could expand their volume quickly and achieve the benefits of experience curve effects before major competitors could confront them.

- *Broad product line.* Successful pioneers also quickly add line extensions or modifications to their initial product to tailor their offerings to specific market segments. This helps reduce their vulnerability to later entrants who might differentiate themselves by targeting one or more peripheral markets.

- *High product quality.* Successful pioneers offer a high-quality, well-designed product from the beginning, thus removing one potential differential advantage for later followers. Competent engineering, thorough product and market testing before commercialization, and good quality control during the production process are all important to the continued success of pioneers.

- *Heavy promotional expenditures.* Characterizing the marketing programs of pioneers who continue to be successful are relatively high advertising and promotional expenditures as a percentage of sales. Initially the promotion helps to stimulate awareness and primary demand for the new product category, build volume, and reduce unit costs. Later, this promotion focuses on building selective demand for the pioneer's brand and reinforcing loyalty as new competitors enter.

The same study found that the most successful fast followers tend to have the resources to enter the new market on a larger scale then the pioneer. Consequently, they can quickly reduce their unit costs and offer lower prices than incumbent competitors. Some fast followers achieve success, however, by leapfrogging earlier entrants by offering a product with more sophisticated technology, better quality, or superior service (like IBM in the PC market). As mentioned, followers in high-tech industries have the potential advantage of being able to use the second generation of technology to develop products technically superior to the pioneer's. As we shall see in the next chapter, however, the success of such a leapfrog strategy depends heavily on the speed and effectiveness of the follower's product development process.[9]

Finally, the study found that some late followers also achieve substantial profits by avoiding direct confrontation with established competitors and targeting peripheral markets. They offer products tailored to the needs of smaller market niches and support them with high levels of customer service.

A more detailed discussion of the marketing strategies appropriate for followers is presented in the next chapter. Followers typically enter a market after it has entered the growth stage of its life cycle, and they start with low market shares relative to the more established pioneer. Consequently, the next chapter's examination of strategies for low-share competitors in growth markets is relevant to both fast followers and late entrants. The remainder of this chapter concentrates only on the strategic marketing programs that pioneers in new product-markets might successfully pursue.

STRATEGIC MARKETING PROGRAMS FOR PIONEERS

The preceding discussion suggests that the ultimate success of a pioneering strategy depends on (1) the nature of the demand and potential competitive situation the pioneer encounters in the market and (2) the pioneer's ability to design and support an effective marketing program. The outcome of such a strategy also depends on how the pioneer defines *success* — in other words, the objectives it seeks to achieve. Thus, a pioneer might choose from one of three different types of marketing strategies geared to achieving different purposes in different market environments: mass-market penetration, niche penetration, or skimming and early withdrawal. Exhibit 8–6 summarizes the circumstances favoring the use of each strategy. Keep in mind, though, that while conditions may be suited to a given strategy, they do not guarantee its success. Much still depends on how effectively the strategy is implemented. Also, it is highly unlikely that all the listed conditions will exist simultaneously in any product-market.

Mass-market penetration

The ultimate objective of a **mass-market penetration** strategy is to capture and maintain a commanding share of the total market for the new product. Thus the critical marketing task is to get as many potential customers as possible to adopt the new product quickly to drive down unit costs and build a large contingent of loyal customers before competitors enter the market.

---

[9]Ralph E. Gomory, "From the 'Ladder of Science' to the Product Development Cycle," *Harvard Business Review*, November–December 1989, pp. 99–105.

EXHIBIT 8–6

Situations Favoring Alternative Marketing Strategies for New Product Pioneers

	Alternative marketing strategies		
	Mass-market penetration	**Niche penetration**	**Skimming; early withdrawal**
Market characteristics	• Large potential demand. • Relatively homogeneous customer needs. • Customers likely to adopt product relatively quickly; short diffusion process.	• Large potential demand. • Fragmented market; many different applications and benefit segments. • Customers likely to adopt product relatively quickly; short adoption process.	• Limited potential demand. • Customers likely to adopt product relatively slowly; long adoption process. • Early adopters willing to pay high price; demand is price inelastic.
Product characteristics	• Product technology patentable or difficult to copy. • Components or materials difficult to obtain; limited sources of supply. • Complex production process; substantial development and/or investment required.	• Product technology offers little patent protection; easily copied or adapted. • Components or materials easy to obtain; many sources of supply. • Relatively simple production process; little development or additional investment required.	• Product technology offers little patent protection; easily copied or adapted. • Components or materials easy to obtain; many sources of supply. • Relatively simple production process; little development or additional investment required.
Competitor characteristics	• Few potential competitors. • Most potential competitors have limited resources and competencies; few sources of differential advantage.	• Many potential competitors. • Some potential competitors have substantial resources and competencies; possible sources of differential advantage.	• Many potential competitors. • Some potential competitors have substantial resources and competencies; possible sources of differential advantage.
Firm characteristics	• Strong product engineering skills; able to quickly develop product modifications and line extensions for multiple market segments. • Strong marketing skills and resources; ability to identify and develop marketing programs for multiple segments; ability to shift from stimulation of primary demand to stimulation of selective demand as competitors enter. • Sufficient financial and organizational resources to build capacity in advance of growth in demand.	• Limited product engineering skills and resources. • Limited marketing skills and resources. • Insufficient financial or organizational resources to build capacity in advance of growing demand.	• Strong basic R & D and new product development skills; a prospector with good capability for continued new product innovation. • Good sales and promotional skills; able to quickly build primary demand in target market; perhaps has limited marketing resources for long-term market maintenance. • Limited financial or organizational resources to commit to building capacity in advance of growth in demand.

Mass-market penetration tends to be most successful when entry barriers inhibit or delay the entry of competitors, thus allowing the pioneer more time to build volume, lower unit costs, and gain loyal customers, or when the pioneer has resources or competencies that most potential competitors cannot match.

As Exhibit 8–6 suggests, barriers to entry can result from a number of factors, including patent protection for the pioneer's technology, limited supply of materials or components, substantial investment requirements, or the lack of resources required to enter the market on a major scale.

Successful implementation of a mass-market penetration strategy requires several different competencies, including product engineering and marketing skills and the financial and organizational resources necessary to expand capacity in advance of demand. In some cases, though, a smaller firm with limited resources can successfully employ a mass-market penetration strategy if the market has a protracted adoption process and slow initial growth. Slow growth can delay competitive entry because fewer competitors are attracted to a market with questionable future growth. This allows the pioneer more time to expand capacity. For example, while Medtronic introduced heart pacemakers in 1960, it took nearly a decade for cardiologists to embrace the new technology in large numbers. Consequently, even though Medtronic was a small entrepreneurial firm, it could keep pace with the slow rate of volume growth and expand its capacity and product line sufficiently to maintain a leading position in the pacemaker industry.[10]

Niche penetration

Even when a new product-market expands quickly, however, it may still be possible for a small firm with limited resources to be a successful pioneer. In such cases, though, the firm must define success in a more limited way. Instead of pursuing the objective of capturing and sustaining a leading share of the entire market, it may make more sense for such firms to focus their efforts on a single market segment. This **niche penetration** strategy can help the smaller pioneer gain the biggest bang for its limited bucks and avoid future direct confrontations with bigger competitors.

As Exhibit 8–6 suggests, a niche penetration strategy is most appropriate when the new market is expected to grow quickly and there are a number of different benefit or application segments to appeal to. It is particularly attractive when there are few barriers to the entry of major competitors and when the pioneer has only limited resources and competencies to defend any advantage it gains through early entry.

Stouffer provides an example of this strategy. As the first to introduce high-quality, relatively expensive frozen entrees, the firm focused solely on the upscale, working adult segment of the market. Stouffer threw all available resources into expanding the variety offered within the product line, consumer advertising, and trade promotion to obtain adequate shelf space; and the company concentrated all those efforts on the upscale singles segment. The firm has never attempted to expand into the higher-volume (but lower-

---

[10]David H. Gobeli and William Rudelius, "Managing Innovation: Lessons from the Cardiac-Pacing Industry," *Sloan Management Review*, Summer 1985, pp. 29–43.

margin) "quick, low-cost meals for the family" segment dominated by Swanson's and other low-priced brands.[11]

Some pioneers may intend to pursue a mass-market penetration strategy when introducing a new product or service but end up implementing a niche penetration strategy instead. This is particularly likely when the new market grows faster or is more fragmented than the pioneer expects. Facing such a situation, a pioneer with limited resources may decide to concentrate on holding its leading position in one or a few segments rather than spreading itself too thin developing unique line extensions and marketing programs for many different markets or going deep into debt to finance rapid expansion.

For example, Progressive—a property and casualty insurer that was one of America's fastest-growing companies during the late 1980s and early 1990s—prospered by developing insurance policies for high-risk drivers. It succeeded by developing an extensive database on the personalities, lifestyles, and driving habits of various high-risk groups. Then, by differentiating between, for instance, bartenders and rock musicians, the firm priced policies to match the underwriting risk. But Progressive ran into trouble after a plunge into trucking and transportation insurance. "We thought we were better than we really were," says CEO Peter H. Lewis. "We jumped into new markets and put on too much business too fast—our organization and support systems couldn't handle it." To get back on track the firm refocused its efforts on its original market niche and put its more aggressive expansion program on hold, at least for a while.[12]

Skimming and early withdrawal

Even when a firm has the resources and competencies necessary to sustain a leading position in a new product-market, it may choose not to. Competition is usually inevitable; and prices and margins tend to drop dramatically after followers enter the market. Therefore, some pioneers opt to pursue a **skimming** strategy while planning an early withdrawal from the market. This involves setting a high price and engaging in only limited introductory advertising and promotion to maximize per unit profits and recover the product's development costs as quickly as possible. At the same time the firm may work to develop new applications for its technology or the next generation of more advanced technology. Then when competitors enter the market and margins fall, the firm is ready to cannibalize its own product with one based on new technology or to move into new segments of the market.

The 3M Company is a master of the skimming strategy. According to one 3M manager, "We hit fast, price high (full economic value of the product to the user), and get the heck out when the me-too products pour in." The new markets pioneered by the company are often smaller ones of $20 million to $50 million; and the firm may dominate them for only about three years or so. By then it is ready to launch the next generation of new technology or to

---

[11] Kevin Higgins, "Meticulous Planning Pays Dividends at Stouffers," *Marketing News*, October 28, 1983, pp. 1, 20. For other recent examples, see "Hot Growth Companies," *Business Week*, May 23, 1994, pp. 92–96.

[12] William E. Sheeline, "Avoiding Growth's Perils," *Fortune*, August 13, 1990, pp. 55–58.

EXHIBIT 8-7

3M's Skimming Strategy in the Casting Tape Market

> 3M developed the first water-activated synthetic casting tape to set broken bones in 1980, but by 1982 eight other companies had brought out copycat products. 3M's R & D people retreated to their labs and developed and tested 140 new versions in a variety of fabrics. In 1983 the firm dropped the old product and introduced a technically superior version that was stronger and easier to use and commanded a premium price.

Source: Christopher Knowlton, "What America Makes Best," *Fortune*, March 28, 1988, p. 45.

move the old technology into new applications.[13] An example of 3M's approach is described in Exhibit 8–7.

Skimming and early withdrawal might be employed by either small or large firms. But it is critical that the company have good R & D and product development skills so it can produce a constant stream of new products or new applications to replace older ones as they attract heavy competition. Also, because a firm pursuing this kind of strategy plans to remain in a market only for a short term, it is most appropriate when there are few barriers to entry, the product is expected to diffuse rapidly, and the pioneer lacks the capacity or other resources necessary to defend a leading share position over the long haul.

Objectives of alternative pioneer strategies

Exhibit 8–8 outlines both the long-term and short-term strategic objectives on which pioneers should focus in pursuing mass-market, niche penetration, or skimming strategies. The ultimate long-term objective of a mass-market penetration strategy is to maximize ROI. But to accomplish this, the firm must seek in the intermediate term to gain and hold a leading share of the new product-market throughout its growth and perhaps to even preempt competitors from entering the market. Thus, the short-term objective should be to maximize the number of customers adopting the new product as quickly as possible.

The short-, intermediate-, and long-term objectives of a niche penetration strategy are largely the same as those of a mass-market penetration strategy. The one essential difference is that a firm pursuing a niche strategy tries to capture and maintain a leading share of a more narrowly focused market segment rather than diffusing its limited resources across the entire market.

Finally, since businesses pursuing a skimming strategy usually expect to leave the market eventually, they have no long-term objectives. Therefore, their intermediate-term objective is to maximize returns before competitors enter the market. When increasing competition begins to reduce profit margins, firms pursuing this strategy typically license the product to another firm, introduce a new generation of products, or move to other markets or product categories. Thus, the short-term objective should be to gain as much volume as possible

---

[13]George S. Day, *Analysis for Strategic Marketing Decisions* (St. Paul, Minn.: West Publishing, 1986), pp. 103–4.

EXHIBIT 8-8

Objectives of Strategic Marketing Programs for Pioneers

Strategic objectives	Alternative strategic marketing programs		
	Mass-market penetration	Niche penetration	Skimming; early withdrawal
Short-term objectives	• Maximize number of triers and adopters in total market; invest heavily to build future volume and share.	• Maximize number of triers and adopters in target segment; limited investment to build volume and share in chosen niche.	• Obtain as many adopters as possible with limited investment; maintain high margins to recoup product development and commercialization costs as soon as possible.
Intermediate-term objectives	• Attempt to preempt competition; maintain leading share position even if some sacrifice of margins is necessary in short term as new competitors enter.	• Maintain leading share position in target segment even if some sacrifice of short-term margins is necessary.	• Maximize ROI; withdraw from market when increasing competition puts downward pressure on margins.
Long-term objectives	• Maximize ROI	• Maximize ROI	• Withdraw

while simultaneously maintaining high margins to recoup development expenses and to generate profits quickly.

Marketing program components for a mass-market penetration strategy

As mentioned, the short-term objective of a mass-market penetration strategy is to maximize the number of customers adopting the firm's new product as quickly as possible. This requires a marketing program focused on (1) *aggressively building product awareness and motivation to buy* among a broad cross section of potential customers and (2) *making it as easy as possible for those customers to try the new product* on the assumption that they will try it, like it, develop loyalty, and make repeat purchases. Exhibit 8–9 outlines a number of marketing program activities in each of the four Ps that might help increase customers' awareness and willingness to buy or improve their ability to try the product. This is by no means an exhaustive list; nor do we mean to imply that a successful pioneer must necessarily engage in all of the listed activities. Marketing managers must develop programs combining activities that fit both the objectives of a mass-market penetration strategy and the specific market and potential competitive conditions the new product faces.

Increasing customers' awareness and willingness to buy

Obviously, heavy expenditures on advertising, introductory promotions such as sampling and couponing, and personal selling efforts can all increase awareness of a new product or service among potential customers. This is the critical first step in the adoption process for a new

EXHIBIT 8–9

Components of Strategic Marketing Programs for Pioneers

Strategic objectives and tasks	Alternative strategic marketing programs		
	Mass-market penetration	Niche penetration	Skimming; early withdrawal
Increase customers' awareness and willingness to buy	• Heavy advertising to generate awareness among customers in mass market; broad use of mass media. • Extensive salesforce efforts to win new adopters; possible use of incentives to encourage new product sales.	• Heavy advertising directed at target segment to generate awareness; use selective media relevant to target. • Extensive salesforce efforts focused on potential customers in target segment; possible use of incentives to encourage new product sales to target accounts.	• Limited advertising to generate awareness, particularly among least price-sensitive early adopters. • Extensive salesforce efforts, particularly focused on largest potential adopters; possible use of volume-based incentives to encourage new product sales.
	• Advertising and sales appeals stress generic benefits of new product type. • Extensive introductory sales promotions to induce trial (sampling, couponing, quantity discounts). • Move relatively quickly to expand offerings (line extensions, multiple package sizes) to appeal to multiple segments.	• Advertising and sales appeals stress generic benefits of new product type. • Extensive introductory sales promotions to induce trial, but focused on target segment. • Additional product development limited to improvements or modifications to increase appeal to target segment.	• Advertising and sales appeals stress generic benefits of new product type. • Limited use, if any, of introductory sales promotions; if used, they should be volume-based quantity discounts. • Little, if any, additional development within the product category.

entry. The relative importance of these promotional tools varies, however, depending on the nature of the product and the number of potential customers. For instance, personal selling efforts are often the most critical component of the promotional mix for highly technical industrial products with a limited potential customer base. Media advertising and sales promotion are usually more useful for building awareness and primary demand for a new consumer good among customers in the mass market. In either case, when designing a mass-market penetration marketing program, firms should broadly focus promotional efforts to expose and attract as many potential customers as possible before competitors show up.

Firms might also attempt to increase customers' willingness to buy their products by reducing the risk associated with buying something new. This can be done by letting

EXHIBIT 8–9 (*concluded*)

Strategic objectives and tasks	Alternative strategic marketing programs		
	Mass-market penetration	Niche penetration	Skimming; early withdrawal
Increase customers' ability to buy	• Offer free trial, liberal return, or extended warranty policies to reduce customers' perceived risk of adopting the new product.	• Offer free trial, liberal return, or extended warranty policies to reduce target customers' perceived risk of adopting the new product.	• Offer free trial, liberal return, or extended warranty policies to reduce target customers' perceived risk of adopting the new product.
	• Penetration pricing; or start with high price but bring out lower-priced versions in anticipation of competitive entries.	• Penetration pricing, or start with high price but bring out lower-priced versions in anticipation of competitive entries.	• Skimming pricing; attempt to maintain margins at level consistent with value of product to early adopters.
	• Extended credit terms to encourage initial purchases.	• Extended credit terms to encourage initial purchases.	• Extended credit terms to encourage initial purchases.
	• Heavy use of trade promotions aimed at gaining extensive distribution.	• Trade promotions aimed at gaining solid distribution among retailers or distributors pertinent for reaching target segment.	• Limited use of trade promotions; only as necessary to gain adequate distribution.
	• Offer engineering, installation, and training services to increase new product's compatibility with customers' current operations to reduce switching costs.	• Offer engineering, installation, and training services to increase new product's compatibility with customers' current operations to reduce switching costs.	• Offer limited engineering, installation, and services as necessary to overcome customers' objections.

customers try the product without obligation, as when car dealers allow potential customers to test-drive a new model, or by committing to liberal return or extended warranty policies for the product. When Lee Iacocca took over Chrysler, for instance, he decreed that all new car models should be introduced with the longest warranty in the industry to overcome the low-quality image of Chrysler products.

Finally, a firm committed to mass-market penetration might also broaden its product offerings to increase its appeal to as many market segments as possible. This helps reduce its vulnerability to later entrants who could focus on specific market niches. Firms can accomplish such market expansion by rapidly introducing line extensions, product modifications, and additional package sizes.

Increasing customers' ability to buy

For customers to adopt a new product and develop loyalty toward it, they must be aware of the item and be motivated to buy. But they must also have the wherewithal to purchase it. Thus, to capture as many customers in as short a time as possible, it usually makes sense for a firm pursuing mass-market penetration to keep prices low (penetration pricing) and perhaps offer liberal financing arrangements or easy credit terms during the introductory period.

Another factor that can inhibit customers' ability to buy is a lack of product availability within the distribution system. Thus, extensive personal selling and trade promotions aimed at gaining adequate distribution are usually a critical part of a mass-market penetration marketing program. Such efforts should take place before the start of promotional campaigns to ensure that the product is available as soon as customers are motivated to buy it.

A highly technical new product's incompatibility with other related products or systems currently used can also inhibit customers' purchases. It can result in high switching costs for a potential adopter. The pioneer might reduce those costs by designing the product to be as compatible as possible with related equipment. It might also offer engineering services to help make the new product more compatible with existing operations, provide free installation assistance, and conduct training programs for the customer's employees.

Additional considerations for pioneering global markets

Whether the product-market a pioneer is trying to penetrate is domestic or foreign, many of the marketing tasks appropriate for increasing potential customers' awareness, willingness, and ability to buy the new product or service are largely the same. Of course, some of the tactical aspects of the pioneer's strategic marketing program—such as specific product features, promotional appeals, or distribution channels—may have to be adjusted to fit different cultural, legal, or economic circumstances across national borders. In order for Bausch & Lomb to develop the Chinese market for contact lenses, for instance, it first had to develop an extensive training program for the country's opticians and build a network of retail outlets; these actions were not necessary in more developed markets.

Unless the firm already has an economic presence in a country via the manufacture or marketing of other products or services, however, a potential global pioneer faces at least one additional question: What mode of entry is most appropriate? As we shall see in Chapter 11, there are three basic mechanisms for entering a foreign market: exporting through agents (for example, using local manufacturers' representatives or distributors), contractual agreements such as licensing or franchise arrangements with local firms, and direct investment.

Exporting has the advantage of lowering the financial risk for the pioneer entering an unfamiliar foreign market. Unfortunately, such arrangements also afford the pioneer relatively little control over the marketing and distribution of its product or service, activities that are critical for winning customer awareness and loyalty in a new market. At the other extreme, investing in a wholly owned subsidiary typically makes little sense until it becomes clear that the pioneering product will win customer acceptance. Consequently, intermediate modes of entry, such as licensing or forming a joint venture with a local firm in the host country, tend to be the preferred means of developing global markets for new products. Joint ventures are particularly appropriate in this regard because they avoid quotas and import restrictions or taxes, and they allow the pioneer to share financial risks while gaining local marketing expertise.[14] Thus Bausch & Lomb established a joint venture with Beijing Optical as a basis for building contact lens factories in China and for gaining access to Chinese opticians.

Marketing program components for a niche penetration strategy

Because the objectives of a niche penetration strategy are similar to but more narrowly focused than those of a mass-market strategy, the marketing program elements are also likely to be similar under the two strategies. Obviously, however, the niche penetrator should keep its marketing efforts clearly focused on the target segment to gain as much impact as possible from its limited resources. This point is clearly evident in the outline of program components in Exhibit 8–9. For example, while a niche strategy calls for the same advertising, sales promotion, personal selling, and trade promotion activities as a mass-market program, the former should use more selective media, call schedules, and channel designs to precisely direct those activities toward the target segment.

Marketing program components for a skimming strategy

As Exhibit 8–9 suggests, one major difference between a skimming strategy and a mass-market strategy involves pricing policies. A relatively high price is appropriate for a skimming strategy to increase margins and revenues, even though some price-sensitive customers may be reluctant to adopt the product at that price.[15] This also suggests that introductory promotional programs might best focus on customer groups who are least sensitive to price and most likely to be early adopters of the new product. This can help hold down promotion costs and avoid wasting marketing efforts on less profitable market segments. Thus, in many consumer goods businesses, skimming strategies focus on relatively upscale customers because they are often more likely to be early adopters and less sensitive to price.

Another critical element of a skimming strategy is the nature of the firm's continuing product development efforts. A pioneer that plans to leave a market when competitors enter should not devote much effort to expanding its product line through line extensions or multiple package sizes. Instead, it should concentrate on the next generation of technology or on identifying new application segments—in other words, preparing its avenue of escape from the market.

Now that we have examined some strategies a pioneer might follow in entering a new market, we are left with two important strategic questions. The pioneer is by definition the early share leader in the new market; hence the first question is, What adjustments in strategy might be necessary for the pioneer to *maintain its leading share position* after competitors arrive

---

[14]Franklin R. Root, *Entry Strategy for International Markets* (Lexington, Mass.: D.C. Heath, 1987). Also see Jeremy Main, "Making Global Alliances Work," *Fortune*, December 17, 1990, pp. 121–26.

[15]This assumes that demand is relatively price inelastic. In markets where price elasticity is high, a skimming price strategy may lead to lower total revenues due to its dampening effect on total demand.

on the scene? The second is, What strategies might followers adopt to *take business away from the early leader and increase their relative share position* as the market grows? These two strategic issues are the focus of the next chapter.

SUMMARY

Not all new products are equally new. Only about 10 percent of the new product introductions made by U. S. companies involve new-to-the-world products. Many new entries, such as line extensions or modifications, are new to the customers in the target market but are relatively familiar to the company. Other new entries, like new product lines, extensions of an existing line, or cost reductions, may be quite new to the company but not to the target customers. The firm that introduces products new to the target market must build primary demand by making potential customers aware of the new product and stimulating their willingness and ability to buy.

The primary objective of most new market entries is to secure future volume and profit growth for the firm. However, individual market development efforts often accomplish a variety of secondary objectives as well: maintaining the firm's position as a product innovator, defending a current market-share position in an industry, establishing a foothold in a future new market, preempting a market segment, or exploiting technology in a new way. Top management must clearly specify the new market entry objectives for each SBU. If a prospector SBU's new entry objectives are to maintain a position as a product innovator and establish footholds in many new markets, for example, its most appropriate new entry strategy is to be the *pioneer*, or first entrant, in as many new product-markets as possible. But if the SBU is primarily concerned with defending a strong market-share position in its industry, it might adopt a *follower* strategy whereby it enters new product-markets later and relies on superior product quality, better customer service, or lower prices to offset the pioneer's early lead.

Both pioneer and follower new market entry strategies offer unique potential sources of competitive advantage. A pioneering strategy is most likely to lead to long-term share leadership and profitability when the new market is insulated from the entry of competitors by patent protection for the pioneer's product, proprietary technology, or other barriers or when the pioneer has sufficient marketing resources and competence to maintain its early lead in the face of competitive attacks. Pioneers are most likely to maintain their early market-share lead when they can enter the new market on a large scale, quickly add line extensions, offer and sustain high product quality, and support their product introduction with heavy promotional expenditures. Followers are most successful when they can enter the market on a larger scale and attain lower per unit costs than the pioneer or when they can leapfrog the pioneer by offering a superior product or better service.

Alternative strategic marketing programs that are appropriate for a pioneer include a *mass-market penetration* strategy, a *niche penetration* strategy, or a *skimming* strategy. A mass-market penetration strategy aims at getting as many potential customers as possible to try the new product and develop brand loyalty before competitors can enter. The pioneer must maximize customers' awareness of the new product and attempt to increase their willingness and ability to buy. Because the necessary actions require substantial resources, a mass-market strategy is most appropriate for larger businesses or when barriers slow competitive entry.

Pioneers with limited resources are better off adopting a niche penetration strategy. The marketing objectives and actions involved in a niche strategy are similar to those of mass-market penetration, but they focus on a smaller segment of customers where fewer resources are needed to defend the pioneer's early lead.

Finally, some technological leaders, particularly those pursuing a prospector business strategy, may prefer to enter many new markets, attain as much profit as possible before competitors enter, and then withdraw as competition increases and margins erode. A skimming strategy incorporating relatively high prices and low marketing expenditures is appropriate for such businesses.

Strategies for
Growth Markets

J & J'S VISTAKON: A CHALLENGER CAPTURES THE LEADING SHARE OF THE CONTACT LENS MARKET[1]

In Chapter 2 we saw how Bausch & Lomb, one of the pioneers in the development of soft contact lenses, has pursued growth by expanding its product line to include items for "every human organ above the neck" and by aggressively entering foreign markets. But in spite of the firm's overall success, it is no longer the share leader in the U. S. contact lens market. That position has been captured by an upstart challenger: Vistakon, a subsidiary of Johnson & Johnson.

In 1983 Vistakon was only a minor player in the contact lens business, generating $20 million in annual sales primarily from a specialty product designed for people with astigmatism. Then Vistakon's president got a tip from a salesperson working at another J & J subsidiary about a Copenhagen ophthalmologist who had

conceived a way of manufacturing inexpensive disposable contacts. Vistakon quickly bought the rights to the new technology, assembled a management team to oversee development, and invested heavily in a state-of-the-art facility in Florida capable of manufacturing lens at a cost of less than $2.50 a pair—one-tenth the cost of other soft contacts. At that price the lenses could be worn a week or two and thrown away, thus reducing the need for cleaning and maintenance.

By the summer of 1987 the new lenses, branded Acuvue, were ready for test-marketing. In less than a year they were rolled out across the United States with a high-visibility advertising campaign. However, Vistakon also needed to market the product to eye doctors and opticians, who feared they would lose money if disposable

[1]This example is based on information found in Brian O'Reilly, "J & J Is on a Roll," *Fortune*, December 26, 1994, pp. 178–92; and Michael Treacy and Fred Wiersema, "How Market Leaders Keep Their Edge," *Fortune*, February 6, 1995, pp. 88–98.

lens users didn't come back for checkups and new lenses. Consequently, the firm decided to sell its lenses only through eye specialists, not even by prescription in pharmacies, and in packs with just a few months' worth at a time. And when competitors challenged the safety of the lenses, Vistakon quickly responded by distributing data refuting the charges (via Federal Express) to 17,000 eye care professionals, thereby generating additional confidence and goodwill among its channel partners.

Because Vistakon and its parent, J & J, were willing to adopt an innovative new technology and to make substantial investments in manufacturing facilities and marketing programs, the firm was able to leapfrog over its more established rivals, including Bausch & Lomb. Caught off guard, the competition never caught up. Within three years the firm had captured 25 percent of the U. S. contact lens market. And by 1994 Acuvue sales had reached nearly half a billion dollars, and Vistakon had become the domestic market-share leader.

STRATEGIC ISSUES IN GROWTH MARKETS

Bausch & Lomb's experience in the domestic contact lens market, where increasingly intense competition has eroded its market-share position and its profitability, is common. As we discussed in Chapter 5, product-markets in the growth stage of their life cycles are usually characterized by the entry of many competitive followers. Both conventional wisdom and the various portfolio models suggest there are advantages in quickly entering and investing heavily to build share in growth markets. But a market is neither inherently attractive or unattractive simply because it promises rapid future growth. Managers must consider how the market and competitive situations are likely to evolve and whether their firms can exploit the rapid growth opportunities to establish a competitive advantage. The next section of this chapter examines both the opportunities and competitive risks often found in growing product-markets.

The primary objective of the early share leader, usually the market pioneer, in a growth market is **share maintenance**. From a marketing perspective the firm must accomplish two important tasks: (1) retain repeat or replacement business from its existing customers, and (2) continue to capture the major portion of sales to the growing number of new customers entering the market for the first time. The leader might use any of several marketing strategies to accomplish these objectives. It might try to build on its early scale and experience advantages to achieve low-cost production and reduce its prices. Alternatively, the leader might focus on rapid product improvements, expand its product line to appeal to newly emerging segments, and/or increase its marketing and sales efforts, as Bausch & Lomb has done in foreign markets. The third section of this chapter explores marketing strategies— both defensive and offensive—that leaders might use to maintain market share in the face of market growth and increasing competition.

A challenger's strategic objective in a growth market is usually to build its share by expanding its sales faster than the overall market growth rate. Firms do this by stealing existing customers away from the leader or other competitors, capturing a larger share of new customers than the market leader, or both. Once again, challengers might use a number of strategies to accomplish these objectives. These include developing a superior product technology, as Vistakon did with great success; differentiating through rapid product innovations, line extensions, or customer service; offering lower prices; or focusing on market niches where the leader is not well established. The fourth section details these and other **share-growth** strategies that market challengers use under different conditions.

The success of a firm's strategy during the growth stage is a critical determinant of its ability to reap profits, or even survive, as a product-market moves toward maturity. Unfortunately, the growth stage is often short; and increasingly rapid technological change and market fragmentation are causing it to become even shorter in many industries.[2] This shortening of the growth stage concerns many firms—particularly late entrants or those who fail to acquire a substantial market share—because as growth slows during the transition to maturity, there is often a shakeout of marginal competitors. Thus, when choosing marketing strategies for competing in a growing product-market, managers should keep one eye on building a competitive advantage that the business can sustain as growth slows and the market matures.

OPPORTUNITIES AND RISKS IN GROWTH MARKETS[3]

Why are followers attracted to rapidly growing markets? Conventional wisdom suggests such markets present attractive opportunities for future profits because

- It is easier to gain share when a market is growing.
- Share gains are worth more in a growth market than in a mature market.
- Price competition is likely to be less intense.
- Early participation in a growth market is necessary to make sure that the firm keeps pace with the technology.

While generally valid, each of these premises may be seriously misleading for a particular business in a specific situation. Many followers attracted to a market by its rapid growth rate are likely to be shaken out later when growth slows because either the preceding premises did not hold or they could not exploit growth advantages sufficiently to build a sustainable competitive position. By understanding the limitations of the assumptions about growth markets and the conditions under which they are most likely to hold, a manager can make better decisions about entering a market and the kind of marketing strategy likely to be most effective in doing so.

---

[2]Neil Gross, Peter Coy, and Otis Port, "The Technology Paradox," *Business Week*, March 6, 1995, pp. 76–84.

[3]For a more extensive discussion of the potential opportunities and pitfalls of rapidly growing markets, see David A. Aaker and George S. Day, "The Perils of High-Growth Markets," *Strategic Management Journal* 7 (1986), pp. 409–21; and Myron Magnet, "Let's Go for Growth," *Fortune*, March 7, 1994, pp. 60–72.

Gaining share is easier

The premise that it is easier for a business to increase its share in a growing market is based on two arguments. First, there may be many potential new users who have no established brand loyalties or supplier commitments and who may have different needs or preferences than earlier adopters. Thus there may be gaps or undeveloped segments in the market. It is easier, then, for a new competitor to attract those potential new users than to convert customers in a mature market. Second, established competitors are less likely to react aggressively to market-share erosion as long as their sales continue to grow at a satisfactory rate.

There is some truth to the first argument. It usually is easier for a new entrant to attract first-time users than to take business away from entrenched competitors. To take full advantage of the situation, however, the new entrant must be able to develop a product offering that new customers perceive as more attractive than other alternatives, and it must have the marketing resources and competence to effectively persuade them of that fact. This can be difficult, especially when the pioneer has had months or years to influence potential customer's decision criteria and preferences.[4]

The notion that established competitors are less likely to react to share losses so long as their revenues are growing at an acceptable rate is more tenuous. It overlooks the fact that those competitors may have higher expectations for increased revenues when the market itself is growing. Capital investments and annual operating budgets are usually tied to those sales expectations; therefore, competitors are likely to react aggressively when sales fall below expected levels whether or not their absolute volumes continue to grow. This is particularly true given that increased competition will likely erode the leader's relative market share even though its volume may continue to increase. As illustrated by the hypothetical example in Exhibit 9–1, the leader's market share might drop from a high of 100 percent at the beginning of the growth stage to 50 percent by the maturity stage, even though the firm's absolute volume shows steady growth.

Industry leaders often react forcefully when their sales growth falls below industry levels and their relative market share begins to decline. For example, IBM's objective for the PC market during the 1980s was to equal or exceed the growth rate for the overall market. Thus, when the entry of lower-priced IBM clones and Apple's new Macintosh knocked IBM's sales growth below the industry rate and reduced its relative market share in the middle of the decade, IBM took aggressive action—such as reducing prices and introducing the more technically advanced PS/2 line—even though the firm's absolute sales volume was still increasing.

Share gains are worth more

The premise that share gains are more valuable when the market is growing stems from the expectation that the earnings produced by each share point continue to expand as the market expands. The implicit assumption in this argument, of course, is that the business can hold its

---

[4] Gregory S. Carpenter and Kent Nakamoto, "Consumer Preference Formation and Pioneering Advantage," *Journal of Marketing Research*, August 1989, pp. 285–98.

EXHIBIT 9–1

Market Shares of the Leader and Followers over the Life Cycle of a Hypothetical Market

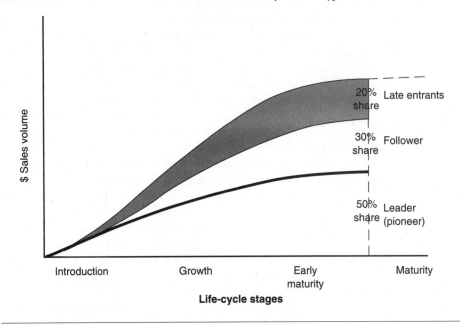

relative share as the market grows. The validity of such an assumption depends on a number of factors, including these:

- *Future changes in technology or other key success factors.* If the rules of the game change, the competencies a firm relied on to capture share may no longer be adequate to maintain that share. For instance, Sony was the pioneer and early share leader in the videocassette recorder industry with its Betamax technology. But Matsushita's longer-playing and lower-priced VHS format equipment ultimately proved much more popular with consumers, captured a commanding portion of the market, and dethroned Sony as industry leader.

- *Future competitive structure of the industry.* The number of firms that ultimately decide to compete for a share of the market may turn out to be larger than the early entrants anticipate, particularly if there are few barriers to entry. The sheer weight of numbers can make it difficult for any single competitor to maintain a substantial relative share of the total market.

- *Future fragmentation of the market.* As the market expands, it may fragment into numerous small segments, particularly if potential customers have relatively heterogeneous functional, distribution, or service needs. When such fragmentation occurs, the market in which a given competitor competes may shrink as segments splinter away.

In addition to these possible changes in future market conditions, a firm's ability to hold its early gains in market share also depends on how it obtained them. If a firm captures share through short-term promotions or price cuts that competitors can easily match and that may tarnish its image among customers, its gains may be short-lived.

Price competition is likely to be less intense

In many rapidly growing markets demand exceeds supply. The market exerts little pressure on prices initially; the excess demand may even support a price premium. Thus, early entry provides a good opportunity for a firm to recover its initial product development and commercialization investment relatively quickly. New customers may also be willing to pay a premium for technical service as they learn how to make full use of the new product. In contrast, as the market matures and customers gain more experience, the premium a firm can charge without losing market share slowly shrinks; it may eventually disappear entirely.[5]

However, this scenario does not hold true in every developing product-market. If there are few barriers to entry or if the adoption process is protracted and new customers enter the market slowly, demand may not exceed supply—at least not for very long. Also, the pioneer, or one of the earliest followers, might adopt a penetration strategy and set its initial prices relatively low to move quickly down the experience curve and discourage other potential competitors from entering the market.

Early entry is necessary to maintain technical expertise

In high-tech industries early involvement in new product categories may be critical for staying abreast of technology. The early experience gained in developing the first generation of products and in helping customers apply the new technology can put the firm in a strong position for developing the next generation of superior products. Later entrants, lacking such customer contact and production and R & D experience, are likely to be at a disadvantage.

There is substantial wisdom in these arguments. Sometimes, however, an early commitment to a specific technology can turn out to be a liability. This is particularly true when multiple unrelated technologies might serve a market or when a newly emerging technology might replace the current one. Once a firm is committed to one technology, adopting a new one can be difficult. Management is often reluctant to abandon a technology in which it has made substantial investments, and it might worry that a rapid shift to a new technology will upset present customers. As a result, early commitment to a technology has become increasingly problematic because of more rapid rates of technological change. This problem is dramatically illustrated by the experience of Medtronic, Inc., as described in Exhibit 9–2.

---

[5]Irwin Gross, "Insights from Pricing Research," *Pricing Practices and Strategies* (New York: The Conference Board, 1979). In some rapidly evolving high-tech markets price premiums can disappear *very* quickly, as pointed out in Neil Gross, Peter Coy, and Otis Port, "The Technology Paradox."

EXHIBIT 9-2

Medtronic's Commitment to an Old Technology Cost It Sales and Market Share

> The dangers inherent in being overly committed to an early technology are demonstrated by Medtronic, Inc., the pioneer in the cardiac pacemaker industry. Medtronic was reluctant to switch to a new lithium-based technology that enabled pacemakers to work much longer before being replaced. As a result, several Medtronic employees left the company and founded Cardiac Pacemakers Inc. to produce and market the new lithium-based product. They quickly captured nearly 20 percent of the total market. And Medtronic saw its share of the cardiac pacemaker market fall rapidly from nearly 70 percent to 40 percent.

SOURCE: Daniel H. Gobeli and William Rudelius, "Managing Innovation: Insights from the Cardiac-Pacing Industry." *Sloan Management Review*, Summer 1985, pp. 29–43.

GROWTH-MARKET STRATEGIES FOR MARKET LEADERS

For the share leader in a growing market, of course, the question of the relative advantages versus risks of market entry is moot. The leader is typically the pioneer, or at least one of the first entrants, who developed the product-market in the first place. Its strategic objective is to maintain its leading relative share in the face of increasing competition as the market expands. Share maintenance may not seem like a very aggressive objective because it implies the business is merely trying to stay even rather than forge ahead. But two important facts must be kept in mind. First, the dynamics of a growth market—including the increasing number of competitors, the fragmentation of market segments, and the threat of product innovation from within and outside the industry—make maintaining an early lead in relative market share very difficult. The continuing need for investment to finance growth, the likely negative cash flows that result, and the threat of governmental antitrust action can make it even more difficult. For example, 31 percent of the 877 market-share leaders in the PIMS database experienced losses in relative share, as shown in Exhibit 9–3. Note, too, that leaders are especially likely to suffer this fate when their market shares are very large.

Second, a firm can maintain its current share position in a growth market only if its sales volume continues to grow at a rate equal to that of the overall market, enabling the firm to stay even in *absolute* market share. It may, however, be able to maintain a *relative* share lead even if its volume growth is less than the industry's.

Marketing objectives for share leaders

Share maintenance for a market leader involves two important marketing objectives. First, the firm must *retain its current customers*, ensuring that those customers remain brand loyal when making repeat or replacement purchases. This is particularly critical for firms in consumer nondurable, service, and industrial materials and components industries, where a substantial portion of total sales volume consists of repeat purchases. Second, the firm must *stimulate selective demand among later adopters* to ensure that it captures a large share of the continuing growth in industry sales.

EXHIBIT 9-3

The Proportion of Market Leaders in the PIMS Database Who Lost Market Share, by Size of Their Initial Share

Leader's initial market share	Percent losing share
Under 20%	16%
20–29	24
30–39	34
40–49	41
Over 50	45
All leaders	31

SOURCE: Adapted with permission of The Free Press, an imprint of Simon & Schuster Inc. from *THE PIMS PRINCIPLES: Linking Strategy to Performance* by Robert D. Buzzell and Bradley T. Gale. Copyright © 1987 by The Free Press.

In some cases the market leader might pursue a third objective stimulating primary demand to help speed up overall market growth. This can be particularly important in product-markets where the adoption process is protracted because of the technical sophistication of the new product or high switching costs for potential customers.

The market leader is the logical one to stimulate market growth in such situations; it has the most to gain from increased volume, assuming, of course, that it can maintain its relative share of that volume. However, expanding total demand—by promoting new uses for the product or stimulating existing customers' usage and repeat purchase rates—is often more critical near the end of the growth and early in the maturity stages of a product's life cycle. Consequently, we discuss marketing actions appropriate to this objective in the next chapter.

Marketing actions and strategies to achieve share-maintenance objectives

A business might take a variety of marketing actions to maintain a leading share position in a growing market. Exhibit 9–4 outlines a lengthy, though by no means exhaustive, list of such actions and their specific marketing objectives. Because share maintenance involves multiple objectives, and different marketing actions may be needed to achieve each one, a strategic marketing program usually integrates a mix of the actions outlined in the exhibit.

Not all of the actions summarized in Exhibit 9–4 are consistent with one another. It would be unusual, for instance, for a business to invest heavily in new product improvements and promotion to enhance its product's high-quality image and simultaneously slash prices, unless it was trying to drive out weaker competitors in the short run with an eye on higher profits in the future. Thus, the activities outlined in Exhibit 9–4 cluster into five internally consistent strategies that a market leader might employ, singly or in combination, to maintain its leading share position: a **fortress** or **position defense strategy**, a **flanker strategy**, a **confrontation strategy**, a **market expansion** or **mobile strategy**, and a **contraction** or **strategic withdrawal strategy**. Exhibit 9–5 diagrams this set of strategies. It is consistent with what a number of military strategists and some marketing authorities have identified as

EXHIBIT 9–4

Marketing Actions to Achieve Share-Maintenance Objectives

Marketing objectives	Possible marketing actions
Retain current customers by:	
• Maintaining/improving satisfaction and loyalty	• Increase attention to quality control as output expands. • Continue product modification and improvement efforts to increase customer benefits and/or reduce costs. • Focus advertising on stimulation of selective demand; stress product's superior features and benefits; reminder advertising. • Increase salesforce's servicing of current accounts; consider formation of national or key account representatives for major customers; consider replacing independent manufacturers' reps with company salespeople. • Expand postsale service capabilities; develop or expand company's own service force, or develop training programs for distributors' and dealers' service people; expand parts inventory; consider development of customer service hotline.
• Encourage/simplify repeat purchase	• Expand production capacity in advance of increasing demand to avoid stockouts. • Improve inventory control and logistics systems to reduce delivery times. • Continue to build distribution channels; use periodic trade promotions to gain more extensive retail coverage and maintain shelf facings; strengthen relationships with strongest distributors/dealers. • Consider negotiating long-term requirements contracts with major customers. • Consider developing automatic reorder systems for major customers.
• Reduce attractiveness of switching	• Develop a second brand or product line with features or price more appealing to a specific segment of current customers (*flanker strategy*). • Develop multiple line extensions or brand offerings targeted to the needs of several user segments in the market (*market expansion, mobile strategy*). • Meet or beat lower prices or heavier promotional efforts by competitors — or try to preempt such efforts by potential competitors — when necessary to retain customers and when lower unit costs allow (*confrontation strategy*).
Stimulate selective demand among later adopters by:	
• Head-to-head positioning against competitive offerings or potential offerings	• Develop a second brand or product line with features or price more appealing to a specific segment of potential customers (*flanker strategy*). • Make product modifications or improvements to match or beat superior competitive offerings (*confrontation strategy*). • Meet or beat lower prices or heavier promotional efforts by competitors when necessary to retain customers and when lower unit costs allow (*confrontation strategy*). • When resources are limited relative to competitor's, consider withdrawing from smaller or slower-growing segments to focus product development and promotional efforts on higher-potential segments threatened by competitor (*contraction* or *strategic withdrawal strategy*).
• Differentiated positioning against competitive offerings or potential offerings	• Develop multiple line extensions or brand offerings targeted to the needs of various potential user applications or geographical segments within the market (*market expansion* or *mobile strategy*). • Build unique distribution channels to more effectively reach specific segments of potential customers (*market expansion* or *mobile strategy*). • Design multiple advertising and/or sales promotion campaigns targeted at specific segments of potential customers (*market expansion* or *mobile strategy*).

EXHIBIT 9–5

Strategic Choices for Share Leaders in Growth Markets

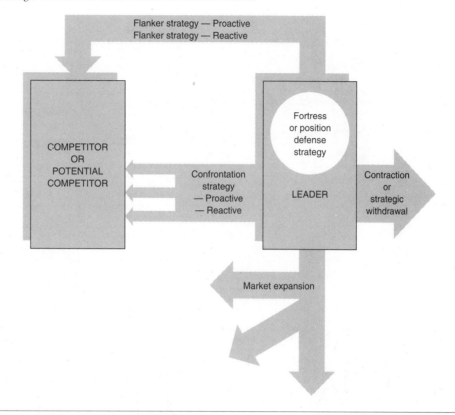

SOURCE: Adapted from P. Kotler and R. Singh, "Marketing Warfare in the 1980s," *Journal of Business Strategy*, Winter 1981, pp. 30–41.

common defensive strategies.[6] To think of them as strictly defensive, though, can be misleading. Companies can use some of these strategies offensively to preempt expected future actions by potential competitors. Or they can use them to capture an even larger share of future new customers.

Which, or what combination, of these five strategies is most appropriate for a particular product-market depends on (1) the market's size and its customers' characteristics; (2) the number and relative strengths of the competitors or potential competitors in that market; and (3) the leader's own resources and competencies. Exhibit 9–6 outlines the situations in which each strategy is most appropriate and the primary objectives for which they are best suited.

---

[6]For a detailed discussion of these strategies in a military context, see Carl von Clausewitz, *On War* (London: Routledge and Kegan Paul, 1980); and B. H. Liddell-Hart, *Strategy* (New York: Praeger, 1967). For a related discussion of the application of such strategies in a business setting, see Philip Kotler and Ravi Singh Achrol, "Marketing Warfare in the 1980s," *Journal of Business Strategy*, Winter 1981, pp. 30–41.

EXHIBIT 9–6

Marketing Objectives and Strategies for Share Leaders in Growth Markets

Situational variables	Share maintenance strategies				
	Fortress or position defense	Flanker	Confrontation	Market expansion	Contraction or strategic withdrawal
Primary objective	Increase satisfaction, loyalty, and repeat purchase among current customers by building on existing strengths; appeal to late adopters with same attributes and benefits offered to early adopters.	Protect against loss of specific segment of current customers by developing a second entry that covers a weakness in original offering; improve ability to attract new customers with specific needs or purchase criteria different from those of early adopters.	Protect against loss of share among current customers by meeting or beating a head-to-head competitive offering; improve ability to win new customers who might otherwise be attracted to competitor's offering.	Increase ability to attract new customers by developing new product offerings or line extensions aimed at a variety of new applications and user segments; improve ability to retain current customers as market fragments.	Increase ability to attract new customers in selected high-growth segments by focusing offerings and resources on those segments; withdraw from smaller or slower-growing segments to conserve resources.
Market characteristics	Relatively homogeneous market with respect to customer needs and purchase criteria; strong preference for leader's product amongst largest segment of customers.	Two or more major market segments with distinct needs or purchase criteria.	Relatively homogeneous market with respect to customers' needs and purchase criteria; little preference for, or loyalty toward, leader's product among largest segment of customers.	Relatively heterogeneous market with respect to customers' needs and purchase criteria; multiple product uses requiring different product or service attributes.	Relatively heterogeneous market with respect to customers' needs, purchase criteria, and growth potential; multiple product uses requiring different product or service attributes.

Fortress, or position defense, strategy

The most basic defensive strategy is to continually strengthen a strongly held current position—to build an impregnable fortress capable of repelling attacks by current or future competitors. This strategy is nearly always at least a part of a leader's share-maintenance efforts. By shoring up an already strong position, the firm can improve the satisfaction of

EXHIBIT 9–6 (*concluded*)

Situational variables	Share maintenance strategies				
	Fortress or position defense	Flanker	Confrontation	Market expansion	Contraction or strategic withdrawal
Competitors' characteristics	Current and potential competitors have relatively limited resources and competencies.	One or more current or potential competitors with sufficient resources and competencies to effectively implement a differentiation strategy.	One or more current or potential competitors with sufficient resources and competencies to effectively implement a head-to-head strategy.	Current and potential competitors have relatively limited resources and competencies, particularly with respect to R & D and marketing.	One or more current or potential competitors with sufficient resources and competencies to present a strong challenge in one or more growth segments.
Firm's characteristics	Current product offering enjoys high awareness and preference among major segment of current and potential customers; firm has marketing and R & D resources and competencies equal to or greater than any current or potential competitor.	Current product offering perceived as weak on at least one attribute by a major segment of current or potential customers; firm has sufficient R & D and marketing resources to introduce and support a second offering aimed at the disaffected segment.	Current product offering suffers low awareness, preference, and/or loyalty among major segment of current or potential customers; firm has R & D and marketing resources and competencies equal to or greater than any current or potential competitor.	No current offerings in one or more potential application segments; firm has marketing and R & D resources and competencies equal to or greater than any current or potential competitor.	Current product offering suffers low awareness, preference, and/or loyalty among current or potential customers in one or more major growth segments; firm's R & D and marketing resources and competencies are limited relative to those of one or more competitors.

current customers while increasing the attractiveness of its offering to new customers with needs and characteristics similar to those of earlier adopters.

Strengthening the firm's current position, then, makes particularly good sense when current and potential customers have relatively homogeneous needs and desires and the firm's offering already enjoys a high level of awareness and preference in the mass market. In some homogeneous markets, a well-implemented position defense strategy may be all that is needed for share maintenance.

Most of the marketing actions listed in Exhibit 9–4 as being relevant for retaining current customers might be incorporated into a position defense strategy. Anything the business can do to improve customer satisfaction and loyalty and encourage and simplify repeat purchasing should help the firm protect its current customer base and make its offering more attractive to new customers. Some of the specific actions appropriate for accomplishing these two objectives are discussed in more detail next.

Actions to improve customer satisfaction and loyalty

The rapid expansion of output necessary to keep up with a growth market can often lead to quality control problems for the market leader. As new plants, equipment, and personnel are quickly brought online, bugs can suddenly appear in the production process. Thus, the leader must pay particular attention to quality control during this phase. Most customers have only limited, if any, positive past experiences with the new brand to offset their disappointment when a purchase does not live up to expectations.

Perhaps the most obvious way a leader can strengthen its position is to continue to modify and improve its product. This can reduce the opportunities for competitors to differentiate their products by designing in features or performance levels the leader does not offer. The leader might also try to reduce unit costs to discourage low-price competition.

The leader should take steps to improve not only the physical product but customers' perceptions of it as well. As competitors enter or prepare to enter the market, the leader's advertising and sales promotion emphasis should shift from stimulating primary demand to building selective demand for the company's brand. This usually involves creating appeals that emphasize the brand's superior features and benefits. While the leader may continue sales promotion efforts aimed at stimulating trial among later adopters, some of those efforts might be shifted toward encouraging repeat purchases among existing customers. For instance, it might include cents-off coupons inside the package to give customers a price break on their next purchases of the brand.

For industrial goods, some salesforce efforts should shift from prospecting for new accounts to servicing existing customers. Firms that relied on independent manufacturers' representatives to introduce their new product might consider replacing them with company salespeople to increase the customer service orientation of their sales efforts. Firms whose own salespeople introduced the product might reorganize their salesforces into specialized groups focused on major industries or user segments. Or they might assign key account representatives, or cross-functional account teams, to service their largest customers.

Finally, a leader can strengthen its position as the market grows by giving increased attention to postsale service. Rapid growth in demand can not only outstrip a firm's ability to produce a high-quality product, it can also overload the firm's ability to service customers. Obviously, this can lead to a loss of existing customers as well as negative word-of-mouth that might inhibit the firm's ability to attract new users. Thus, the growth phase often requires increased investments to expand the firm's parts inventory and hire and train service personnel and dealers.

Actions to encourage and simplify repeat purchasing

One of the most critical actions a leader must take to ensure that customers continue buying its product is to maximize its availability. It must reduce stockouts on retail store shelves or shorten delivery times for industrial goods. To do this, the firm must invest in plant and equipment to expand capacity in advance of demand, and it must implement adequate inventory control and logistics systems to provide a steady flow of goods through the distribution system. The firm should also continue to build its distribution channels.

Some market leaders, particularly in industrial goods markets, can take more proactive steps to turn their major customers into captives and help guarantee future purchases. For example, a firm might negotiate requirements contracts or guaranteed price agreements with its customers to ensure future purchases, or it might tie them into a computerized reorder system or channel information system. For instance, Procter & Gamble has formed alliances with major super-market chains, such as Kroger, to develop a restocking system called continuous product replenishment. Sales information from Kroger's checkout scanners is sent directly to P & G's computers, which figure out automatically when to replenish each product and schedule deliveries direct to each store. This paperless exchange minimizes mistakes and billbacks, minimizes inventory, decreases out-of-stocks, and improves cash flow.[7]

Flanker strategy

One shortcoming of a fortress strategy is that a challenger might simply choose to bypass the leader's fortress and try to capture territory where the leader has not yet established a strong presence. This can represent a particular threat when the market is fragmented into major segments with different needs and preferences and the leader's current brand does not meet the needs of one or more of those segments. A competitor with sufficient resources and competencies can develop a differentiated product offering to appeal to the segment where the leader is weak and thereby capture a substantial share of the overall market.

To defend against an attack directed at a weakness in its current offering (its exposed flank), a leader might develop a second brand (a flanker or fighting brand) to compete directly against the challenger's offering. This might involve trading up, where the leader develops a high-quality brand offered at a higher price to appeal to the prestige segment of the market. Honda did this with the development of the Acura. The new brand not only penetrated the higher-priced segment of the market, it also helped Honda hold on to former Accord owners who were beginning to trade up to more expensive European brands as they got older and earned higher incomes.

More commonly, though, a flanker brand is a lower-quality product designed to appeal to a low-price segment to protect the leader's primary brand from direct price competition. Pillsbury's premium-quality Hungry Jack brand holds the major share of the refrigerated biscuit dough market; however, a substantial number of consumers prefer to pay less for a somewhat lower-quality biscuit. Rather than conceding that low-price segment to competitors or reducing Hungry Jack prices and margins in an attempt to attract price-sensitive consumers, Pillsbury introduced Ballard, a low-priced flanker brand.

A flanker strategy is always used in conjunction with a position defense strategy. The leader simultaneously strengthens its primary brand while introducing a flanker to compete

---

[7]Bill Saporito, "Behind the Tumult at P & G," *Fortune*, March 7, 1994, pp. 74–82. For other examples involving industrial goods, see Joseph B. Fuller, James O'Conor, and Richard Rawlinson, "Tailored Logistics: The Next Advantage," *Harvard Business Review,* May–June 1993, pp. 87–98.

in segments where the primary brand is vulnerable. This suggests that a flanker strategy is only appropriate when the firm has sufficient resources to develop and fully support two or more entries. After all, a flanker is of little value if it is so lightly supported that a competitor can easily wipe it out.

Finally, a flanker strategy can be either proactive or reactive. The leader might introduce a flanker in anticipation of a competitor's entry either to establish a strong position before the competitor arrives or to dissuade the competitor from entering. In some cases, however, the leader does not recognize the severity of the threat until a competitor has already begun to enjoy a measure of success. Pillsbury did not develop its Ballard brand, for instance, until after a number of low-priced regional private labels began capturing significant chunks of the market.

Confrontation strategy

Suppose a competitor chooses to attack the leader head-to-head and attempts to steal customers in the leader's main target market. If the leader has established a strong position and attained a high level of preference and loyalty among customers and the trade, it may be able to sit back and wait for the competitor to fail. In many cases, though, the leader's brand is not strong enough to withstand a frontal assault from a well-funded, competent competitor. Even mighty IBM, for instance, lost 20 market-share points in the commercial PC market during the mid-1980s to competitors like Compaq—whose machines cost about the same but offered features or performance levels that were better—and to the clones who offered IBM-compatible machines at much lower prices.

In such situations, the leader may have no choice but to confront the competitive threat directly. If the leader's competitive intelligence is good, it may decide to move proactively and change its marketing program before a suspected competitive challenge occurs. A confrontational strategy, though, is more commonly reactive. The leader usually decides to meet or beat the attractive features of a competitor's offering—by making product improvements, increasing promotional efforts, or lowering prices—only after the challenger's success has become obvious.

Simply meeting the improved features or lower price of a challenger, however, does nothing to reestablish a sustainable competitive advantage for the leader. And a confrontation based largely on lowering prices creates an additional problem of shrinking margins for all concerned.[8] Unless decreased prices generate substantial new industry volume and the leader's production costs fall with that increasing volume, the leader may be better off responding to price threats with increased promotion or product improvements while trying to maintain its profit margins. Evidence also suggests that in product-markets with high repeat purchase rates or a protracted diffusion process, the leader may be wise to adopt a penetration pricing policy in the first place. This would strengthen its share position and may preempt low-price competitors from entering.[9]

---

[8] Thomas T. Nagle, "Managing Price Competition," *Marketing Management* 2, Spring 1993, pp. 36–45.

[9] Robert J. Dolan and Abel P. Jewland, "Experience Curves and Dynamic Demand Models: Implications for Optimal Pricing Strategy," *Journal of Marketing*, Winter 1981, p. 52.

The leader can avoid the problems of a confrontation strategy by reestablishing the competitive advantage eroded by challengers' frontal attacks. But this typically requires additional investments in process improvements aimed at reducing unit costs, improvements in product quality or customer service, or even the development of the next generation of improved products to offer customers greater value for their dollars.

Market expansion or mobile strategy

A market expansion or mobile strategy is a more aggressive and proactive version of the flanker strategy. Here the leader defends its relative market share by establishing positions in a number of different market segments. This strategy's primary objective is to capture a large share of new customer groups who may prefer something different than the firm's initial offering, protecting the firm from future competitive threats from a number of different directions. Such a strategy is particularly appropriate in fragmented markets if the leader has the resources to undertake multiple product development and marketing efforts.

The most obvious way a leader can implement a market expansion strategy is to develop line extensions, new brands, or even alternative product forms utilizing similar technologies to appeal to multiple market segments. For instance, although Pillsbury holds a strong position in the refrigerated biscuit dough category, biscuit consumption is concentrated among older, more traditional consumers in the South. To expand its total market, gain increased experience curve effects, and protect its overall technological lead, Pillsbury developed a variety of other product forms that use the same refrigerated dough technology and production facilities but appeal to different customer segments. The expanded line includes crescent rolls, Danish rolls, and soft breadsticks.

A less expensive way to appeal to a variety of customer segments is to retain the basic product but vary other elements of the marketing program to make it relatively more attractive to specific users. Thus, a leader might create specialized salesforces to deal with the unique concerns of different user groups. Or it might offer different ancillary services to different types of customers or tailor sales promotion efforts to different segments. Thus performing arts groups often promote reduced ticket prices, transportation services, and other inducements to attract senior citizens and students to matinee performances.

Contraction or strategic withdrawal

In some highly fragmented markets, a leader may be unable to defend itself adequately in all segments. This is particularly likely when newly emerging competitors have more resources than the leader. The firm may then have to reduce or abandon its efforts in some segments to focus on areas where it enjoys the greatest relative advantages or that have the greatest potential for future growth. Even some very large firms may decide that certain segments are not profitable enough to continue pursuing. For example, IBM made an early attempt to capture the low end of the home hobbyist market for personal computers with the introduction of the PC Jr. But the firm eventually abandoned that effort to concentrate on the more lucrative commercial and education segments.

SHARE-GROWTH STRATEGIES FOR FOLLOWERS

Marketing objectives for followers

Not all late entrants to a growing product-market have illusions about eventually surpassing the leader and capturing a dominant market share. Some competitors, particularly those with limited resources and competencies, may simply seek to build a small but profitable business within a specialized segment of the larger market that earlier entrants have overlooked. As we have seen, this kind of niche strategy is one of the few entry options that small, late entrants can pursue with a reasonable degree of success. If a firm can successfully build a profitable business in a small segment while avoiding direct competition with larger competitors, it can often survive the shakeout period near the end of the growth stage and remain profitable throughout the maturity stage.

On the other hand, many followers—particularly larger firms entering a product-market shortly after the pioneer—have more grandiose objectives. They often seek to displace the leader or at least to become a powerful competitor within the total market. Thus, their major marketing objective is to attain *share growth*, and the size of the increased relative share such challengers seek is usually substantial. For instance, although it was a later entrant into the personal computer wars, Compaq competed aggressively to become the share leader in the U. S. commercial PC market—knocking off both Apple and IBM—and it has set its sights on becoming the share leader worldwide.[10]

Marketing actions and strategies to achieve share growth

A challenger with visions of taking over the leading share position in an industry has two basic strategic options, each involving somewhat different marketing objectives and actions. Where the share leader and perhaps some other early followers have already penetrated a large portion of the potential market, a challenger may have no choice but to *steal away some of the repeat purchase or replacement demand from the competitors' current customers.* As Exhibit 9–7 indicates, the challenger can attempt this through marketing activities that give it an advantage in a head-to-head confrontation with a target competitor. Or it can attempt to leapfrog over the leader by developing a new generation of products with enough benefits to induce customers to trade in their existing brand for a new one. Secondarily, such actions may also help the challenger attract a larger share of late adopters in the mass market.

If the market is relatively early in the growth phase and no previous entrant has captured a commanding share of potential customers, the challenger can focus on *attracting a larger share of potential new customers* who enter the market for the first time. This may also be a viable option when the overall market is heterogeneous and fragmented and the current share leader has established a strong position in only one or a few segments. In either case, the primary marketing activities for increasing share via this approach should aim at *differentiating* the

---

[10]Stephanie Losee, "How Compaq Keeps the Magic Going," *Fortune*, February 21, 1994, pp. 90–92.

EXHIBIT 9–7

Marketing Actions to Achieve Share-Growth Objectives

Marketing objectives	Possible marketing actions
Capture repeat/replacement purchases from current customers of the leader or other target competitor by:	
• Head-to-head positioning against competitor's offering in primary target market	• Develop products with features and/or performance levels superior to those of the target competitor.
	• Draw on superior product design, process engineering, and supplier relationships to achieve lower unit costs.
	• Set prices below target competitor's for comparable level of quality or performance, but only if low-cost position is achieved.
	• Outspend the target competitor on promotion aimed at stimulating selective demand:
	Comparative advertising appeals directed at gaining a more favorable positioning than the target competitor's brand enjoys among customers in the mass market.
	Sales promotions to encourage trial if offering's quality or performance is perceptively better than target competitor's, or induce brand switching.
	Build more extensive and/or better-trained salesforce than target competitor's.
	• Outspend the target competitor on trade promotion to attain more extensive retail coverage, better shelf space, and/or representation by the best distributors/dealers.
	• Outperform the target competitor on customer service:
	Develop superior production scheduling, inventory control, and logistics systems to minimize delivery times and stockouts.
	Develop superior postsales service capabilities; build a more extensive company service force, or provide better training programs for distributor/dealer service people than target competitor.
	• If resources are limited, engage in one or more of the preceding actions (such as an advertising blitz or sales or trade promotions) on a sporadic basis in selected territories (*guerrilla attack strategy*).

(continues)

challenger's offering from those of existing competitors by making it more appealing to new customers in untapped or underdeveloped segments of the market.

Once again, Exhibit 9–7's list of possible marketing actions for challengers is not exhaustive; and it contains actions that do not always fit well together. The activities that do fit tend to cluster into five internally consistent strategies that a challenger might use singly or in combination to secure growth in its relative market share. As Exhibit 9–8 indicates, these five share-growth strategies are *frontal attack, leapfrog strategy, flanking attack, encirclement,* and *guerrilla attack.* Many of these strategies are mirror images of the share-maintenance strategies discussed earlier.

EXHIBIT 9 – 7 *(concluded)*

Marketing objectives	Possible marketing actions
• Technological differentiation from target competitor's offering in its primary target market	• Develop a new generation of products based on different technology that offers superior performance or additional benefits desired by current and potential customers in the mass market (*leapfrog strategy*). • Build awareness, preference, and replacement demand through heavy introductory promotion: 　　Comparative advertising stressing product's superiority. 　　Sales promotions to stimulate trial or encourage switching. 　　Extensive, well-trained salesforce; heavy use of product demonstrations in sales presentations. • Build adequate distribution through trade promotions and dealer training programs.
Stimulate selective demand among later adopters by: • Head-to-head positioning against target competitor's offering in established market segments	• See preceding actions.
• Differentiated positioning focused on untapped or underdeveloped segments	• Develop a differentiated brand or product line with unique features or price that is more appealing to a major segment of potential customers whose needs are not met by existing offerings (*flanking strategy*). or • Develop multiple line extensions or brand offerings with features or prices targeted to the unique needs and preferences of several smaller potential applications or regional segments (*encirclement strategy*). • Design advertising, personal selling, and/or sales promotion campaigns that address specific interests and concerns of potential customers in one or multiple underdeveloped segments to stimulate selective demand. • Build unique distribution channels to more effectively reach potential customers in one or multiple underdeveloped segments. • Design service programs to reduce the perceived risks of trail and/or solve the unique problems faced by potential customers in one or multiple underdeveloped segments (for example, systems engineering, installation, operator training, or extended warranties).

Which, or what combination, of these five strategies is best for a particular challenger depends on market characteristics, the existing competitors' current positions and strengths, and the challenger's own resources and competencies. The situations in which each of the five strategies is likely to work best are briefly outlined in Exhibit 9–9 and discussed in greater depth in the following sections.

Deciding whom to attack

When more than one competitor is already established in the market, a challenger must decide which competitor, if any, to target. There are several options:

EXHIBIT 9–8

Strategic Choices for Challengers in Growth Markets

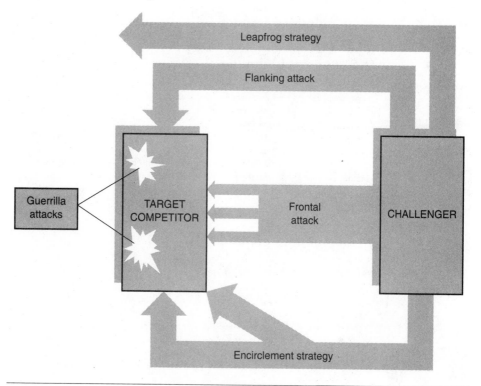

- *Attack the market-share leader within its primary target market.* As we shall see, this typically involves either a *frontal assault* or an attempt to *leapfrog* the leader through the development of superior technology or product design. It may seem logical to try to win customers away from the competitor with the most customers to lose, but this can be a dangerous strategy unless the challenger has superior resources and competencies that can be converted into a sustainable advantage. In some cases, however, a smaller challenger may be able to avoid disastrous retaliation by confronting the leader only occasionally in limited geographic territories through a series of *guerrilla attacks.*

- *Attack another follower who has an established position within a major market segment.* This also usually involves a *frontal assault,* but it may be easier for the challenger to gain a sustainable advantage if the target competitor is not as well established as the market leader in the minds and buying habits of customers.

EXHIBIT 9–9

Marketing Objectives and Strategies for Challengers in Growth-Market Situations

	Share-growth strategies				
Situational variables	**Frontal attack**	**Leapfrog**	**Flank attack**	**Encirclement**	**Guerrilla attack**
Primary objective	Capture substantial repeat/replacement purchases from target competitor's current customers; attract new customers among later adopters by offering lower price or more attractive features.	Induce current customers in mass market to replace their current brand with superior new offering; attract new customers by providing enhanced benefits.	Attract substantial share of new customers in one or more major segments where customer's needs are different from those of early adopters in the mass market.	Attract a substantial share of new customers in a variety of smaller, specialized segments where customers' needs or preferences differ from those of early adopters in the mass market.	Capture a modest share of repeat/replacement purchases in several market segments or territories; attract a share of new customers in a number of existing segments.
Market characteristics	Relatively homogeneous market with respect to customers' needs and purchase criteria; relatively little preference or loyalty for existing brands.	Relatively homogeneous market with respect to customers' needs and purchase criteria, but some needs or criteria not currently met by existing brands.	Two or more major segments with distinct needs and purchase criteria; needs of customers in at least one segment not currently met by existing brands.	Relatively heterogeneous market with a number of small, specialized segments; needs and preferences of customers in some segments not currently satisfied by competing brands.	Relatively heterogeneous market with a number of larger segments; needs and preferences of customers in most segments currently satisfied by competing brands.

- *Attack one or more smaller competitors who have only limited resources.* Because smaller competitors usually hold only a small share of the total market, this may seem like an inefficient way to attain substantial share increases. But by focusing on several small regional competitors one at a time, a challenger can sometimes achieve major gains without inviting retaliation from stronger firms. For example, by first challenging and ultimately acquiring a series of smaller regional manufacturers, Borden has managed to capture the leading share of the fragmented domestic pasta market.

- *Avoid direct attacks on any established competitor.* In fragmented markets in which the leader or other major competitors are not currently satisfying one or more segments, a challenger is often best advised to "hit 'em where they ain't." This usually involves either a *flanking* or an *encirclement* strategy, with the challenger developing differentiated

EXHIBIT 9-9 (*concluded*)

	Share-growth strategies				
Situational variables	Frontal attack	Leapfrog	Flank attack	Encirclement	Guerrilla attack
Competitors' characteristics	Target competitor has relatively limited resources and competencies, particularly in marketing and R & D; would probably be vulnerable to direct attack.	One or more current competitors have relatively strong resources and competencies in marketing, but relatively unsophisticated technology and limited R & D competencies.	Target competitor has relatively strong resources and competencies, particularly in marketing and R & D; would probably be able to withstand direct attack.	One or more competitors have relatively strong marketing. R & D resources and competencies, and/or lower costs; could probably withstand a direct attack.	A number of competitors have relatively strong marketing, R & D resources and competencies, and/or lower costs; could probably withstand a direct attack.
Firm characteristics	Firm has stronger resources and competencies in R & D and marketing and/or lower operating costs than target competitor.	Firm has proprietary technology superior to that of competitors; firm has necessary marketing and production resources to stimulate and meet primary demand for new generation of products.	Firms' resources and competencies are limited but sufficient to effectively penetrate and serve at least one major market segment.	Firm has marketing, R & D and production resources and competencies necessary to serve multiple smaller segments; firm has decentralized and adaptable management structure.	Firm has relatively limited marketing, R & D, and/or production resources and competencies; firm has decentralized and adaptable management structure.

product offerings targeted at one large or several smaller segments in which no competitor currently holds a strong position.

Deciding which competitor to attack necessitates a comparison of relative strengths and weaknesses, a critical first step in developing an effective share-growth strategy. It can also help limit the scope of the battlefield, a particularly important consideration for challengers with limited resources.

Frontal attack strategy

Where the market for a product category is relatively homogeneous, with few untapped segments and at least one well-established competitor, a follower wanting to capture an increased market share may have little choice but to tackle a major competitor head-on. Such an approach is most likely to succeed when most existing customers do not have strong brand preferences or loyalties and when the challenger's resources and competencies—particularly in marketing—are greater than the target competitor's. But even superior resources are no guarantee of success if the challenger's assault merely imitates the target competitor's offering.

To successfully implement a frontal attack, a challenger should seek one or more ways to achieve a sustainable advantage over the target competitor. As discussed earlier, such an advantage is usually based on attaining lower costs or a differentiated position in the market. If the challenger has a cost advantage, it can cut prices to lure away the target competitor's customers (as a number of the clone manufacturers did to IBM in the commercial PC market) or it can maintain a similar price but engage in more extensive promotion.

Challenging a leader solely on the basis of low price is a highway to disaster, however, unless the challenger really does have a sustainable cost advantage. Otherwise, the leader might simply match the lower prices until the challenger is driven from the market. The problem is that initially a challenger is often at a cost *disadvantage* due to the experience curve effects established competitors have accumulated. The challenger must have offsetting advantages like superior production technology, established relations with low-cost suppliers, the ability to share production facilities or marketing efforts across multiple SBUs, or other sources of synergy before a low-price assault makes sense.

A similar caveat applies to frontal assaults based solely on heftier promotional budgets. Unless the target competitor's resources are substantially more limited than the challenger's, it can retaliate against any attempt to win away customers through more extensive advertising or attractive sales and trade promotions.

One possible exception to this limitation of greater promotional effort is the use of a more extensive and better-trained salesforce to gain a competitive advantage. A knowledgeable salesperson's technical advice and problem-solving abilities can add additional value to a firm's product offering, particularly in newly developing high-tech industries.

In general, the best way for a challenger to effectively implement a frontal attack is to differentiate its product or associated services in ways that better meet the needs and preferences of many customers in the mass market. If the challenger can support those meaningful product differences with strong promotion or an attractive price, so much the better, but usually the unique features or services offered are the foundation for a sustainable advantage. Thus, Compaq has achieved some recent success in its battles with IBM and Apple in the PC market by developing a variety of product offerings that offer *both* superior features and lower prices than its bigger competitors. The firm makes extensive use of marketing research to stay in touch with changing customer needs, and it invests a relatively large percentage of revenues in R & D and in strategic alliances with suppliers to produce a continuing stream of product modifications and improvements.[11]

Variables that might limit the competitor's willingness or ability to retaliate can also improve the chances for successful frontal attack. For instance, a target competitor with a reputation for high product quality may be loath to cut prices in response to a lower-priced

---

[11]Losee, "How Compaq Keeps the Magic Going."

challenger for fear of cheapening its brand's image. And a competitor pursuing high ROI or cash flow objectives may be reluctant to increase its promotion or R & D expenditures in the short run to fend off an attack.[12]

Leapfrog Strategy

A challenger stands the best chance of attracting repeat or replacement purchases from a competitor's current customers when it can offer a product that is attractively differentiated from the competitor's offerings. The odds of success might be even greater if the challenger can offer a far superior product based on advanced technology or a more sophisticated design. This is the essence of a leapfrog strategy, which attempts to gain a significant advantage over the existing competition by introducing a new generation of products that significantly outperform or offer more desirable customer benefits than existing brands. For example, Vistakon's development of low-cost disposable lenses enabled it to capture a leading share of the U. S. contact lens market.

In addition, such a strategy often inhibits quick retaliation by established competitors. Firms that have achieved some success with one technology—or that have committed substantial resources to plant and equipment dedicated to a current product—may be reluctant to switch to a new one because of the large investments involved or a fear of disrupting current customers.

On the other hand, a leapfrog strategy is not viable for all challengers. To be successful, the challenger must have technology superior to that of established competitors as well as the product and process engineering capabilities to turn that technology into an appealing product. Also, the challenger must have the marketing resources to effectively promote its new offering and convince customers already committed to an earlier technology that the new product offers sufficient benefits to justify the costs of switching. Vistakon reduced such problems by limiting the distribution of its disposable lenses to eye care professionals and relying on them to prescribe the lenses for patients who might benefit from their unique advantages.

Unfortunately, a leapfrog strategy is harder to implement in durable goods industries where customers engage in replacement purchases less frequently. To speed up the replacement process in such markets, the challenger may have to offer substantial trade-in allowances or develop sales promotion or customer service programs aimed at reducing switching costs. For industrial goods, the offer of systems engineering services or product features that help potential customers integrate the new technology with their existing equipment and processes can encourage them to switch suppliers. Apple, for example, worked feverishly to develop an open operating system that would allow its Macintosh computers to run DOS-based software and thereby enable IBM customers to switch systems while preserving their earlier software investments.

---

[12]For a more extensive discussion of factors that can limit a leader's willingness or ability to retaliate against a direct attack, see Michael E. Porter, *Competitive Advantage* (New York: Free Press, 1985), ch. 15.

Flanking and encirclement strategies

The military historian B. H. Liddell-Hart, after analyzing battles ranging from the Greek Wars to World War I, determined that only 6 out of 280 victories were the result of a frontal attack.[13] He concluded that it is usually wiser to avoid attacking an established adversary's point of strength and to focus instead on an area of weakness in the adversary's defenses. This is the basic premise behind flanking and encirclement strategies. They both seek to avoid direct confrontations by focusing on market segments whose needs are not being satisfied by existing brands and where no current competitor has a strongly held position.

Flank attack

A flank attack is appropriate when the market can be broken into two or more large segments, when the leader and/or other major competitors hold a strong position in the primary segment, and when no existing brand fully satisfies the needs of customers in at least one other segment. A challenger may be able to capture a significant share of the total market by concentrating primarily on one large untapped segment. This usually involves developing product features or services tailored to the needs and preferences of the targeted customers, together with appropriate promotional and pricing policies to quickly build selective demand. Japanese auto companies, for instance, first penetrated the U. S. car market by focusing on the low-price segment, where domestic manufacturers' offerings were limited. Domestic car manufacturers were relatively unconcerned by this flanking action at first. They failed to retaliate very aggressively because the Japanese were pursuing a segment they considered to be rather small and unprofitable. History proved them wrong.

In some cases a successful flank attack need not involve unique product features. Instead, a challenger can sometimes meet the special needs of an untapped segment by providing specially designed customer services or distribution channels. One major reason for the success of L'eggs pantyhose, for instance, was that it was the first brand to be distributed through an extensive channel of convenience goods retailers, such as grocery and drug stores, instead of more fashionable department and clothing stores. The greater shopping convenience provided by this new distribution channel appealed strongly to the growing segment of working women.

Encirclement

An encirclement strategy involves targeting several smaller untapped or underdeveloped segments in the market simultaneously. The idea is to surround the leader's brand with a variety of offerings aimed at several peripheral segments. This strategy makes most sense when the market is fragmented into many different application segments or geographical regions with somewhat unique needs or tastes.

Once again, this strategy usually involves developing a varied line of products with features tailored to the needs of different segments. Thus, while Compaq has frontally

---

[13]Liddell-Hart, *Strategy*, p. 163.

assaulted IBM by offering similar products at lower prices, it has also launched an encirclement strategy aimed at developing and promoting different computer lines for distinct
segments in the fragmenting PC market. For instance, the firm introduced the Presario line,
with friendly features such as factory-installed software and a built-in telephone answering
machine, to appeal to technophobes and the lower-priced Prolinea line to attract more price-
sensitive customers. Also, the firm budgeted $12 million for advertising in 1994 to introduce
its new lines to their various target segments.[14]

Guerrilla attack

When well-established competitors already cover all major segments of the market and the
challenger's resources are relatively limited, flanking, encirclement, or all-out frontal attacks
may be impossible. In such cases, the challenger may be reduced to making a series of surprise
raids against its more established competitors. To avoid massive retaliation, the challenger
should use such guerrilla attacks sporadically, perhaps in limited geographic areas where the
target competitor is not particularly well entrenched.

A challenger can choose from a variety of means for carrying out guerrilla attacks. These
include sales promotion efforts—such as coupon drops and merchandising deals (send in
three box tops and receive a magic decoder ring)—local advertising blitzes, and even legal
action. Short-term price reductions through sales promotion campaigns are a particularly
favored guerrilla tactic in consumer goods markets. They can target specific customer groups
in limited geographic areas; they can be implemented quickly; and they are often difficult for
a larger competitor to respond to because that firm's higher share level means that a given
discount will cost it more in absolute dollars.[15]

In some cases the ultimate objective of a series of guerrilla attacks is not so much for the
challenger to build its own share as it is to prevent a powerful leader from further expanding
its share or engaging in aggressive actions that would be costly for the followers to respond to.
Lawsuits brought against the leader by several smaller competitors over a range of activities
can effectively slow down the leader's expansionist tendencies by diverting some of its
resources and attention.

Empirical evidence

Several empirical studies conducted with the PIMS database provide empirical support for
many of the managerial prescriptions discussed.[16] These studies compare businesses that
achieved high market shares during the growth stage of the product life cycle, or that
increased their market shares over time, with low-share businesses. As shown in Exhibit 9–10,

---

[14]Losee, "How Compaq Keeps the Magic Going."

[15]A. L. Stern, "New Marketing Game: Stealing Customers," *Dun's Business Month*, February 1985, pp. 48–50.

[16]Robert D. Buzzell and Frederik D. Wiersema, "Successful Share-Building Strategies," *Harvard Business Review*,
January–February 1981, pp. 135–43; Carl R. Anderson and Carl P. Zeithaml, "Stages in the Product Life Cycle,
Business Strategy, and Business Performance," *Academy of Management Journal*, March 1984, pp. 5–25; and Robert D.
Buzzell and Bradley T. Gale, *The PIMS Principles: Linking Strategy to Performance* (New York: Free Press, 1987), ch. 9.

EXHIBIT 9-10

Strategic Changes Made by Challengers That Gained versus Lost Market Share

Strategic changes	Share-gaining challengers	Share-losing challengers
Relative product quality scores	+1.8	−0.6
New products as a percentage of sales	+0.1	−0.5
Relative price	+0.3	+0.2
Marketing expenditures (adjusted for market growth)		
Salesforce	+9.0%	−8.0%
Advertising		
Consumer products	+13.0%	−9.0%
Industrial products	−1.0	−14.0
Promotion		
Consumer products	+13.0%	−5.0%
Industrial products	+7.0	−10.0

SOURCE: Adapted with permission of The Free Press, an imprint of Simon & Schuster Inc. from *THE PIMS PRINCIPLES: Linking Strategy to Performance* by Robert D. Buzzell and Bradley T. Gale. Copyright © 1987 by The Free Press.

the marketing programs and activities of businesses that successfully increased market share differed from their less successful counterparts in the following ways:

- Businesses that increased the quality of their products relative to those of competitors achieved greater share increases than businesses whose product quality remained constant or declined.

- Share-gaining businesses typically developed and added more new products, line extensions, or product modifications to their line than share-losing businesses.

- Share-gaining businesses tended to increase their marketing expenditures faster than the rate of market growth. Increases in both salesforce and sales promotion expenditures were effective for producing share gains in both consumer and industrial goods businesses. Increased advertising expenditures were effective for producing share gains primarily in consumer goods businesses.

- Surprisingly, there was little difference in the relative prices charged between firms that gained and those that lost market share.

These findings are consistent with many of our earlier observations. For instance, they underline the folly of launching a frontal attack solely on the basis of lower price. Unless the challenger has substantially lower unit costs or the leader is inhibited from cutting its own prices for some reason, the challenger's price cuts are likely to be retaliated against and will therefore generate few new customers. On the other hand, frontal, leapfrog, flanking, or encirclement attacks based on product improvements tailored to specific segments are more likely to succeed, particularly when the challenger supports those attacks with substantial promotional efforts.

Regardless of the strategies pursued by market leaders and challengers during a product-market's growth stage, the competitive situation often changes as the market matures and its growth rate slows. In the next chapter we examine the environmental changes that occur as a market matures and the marketing strategies that firms might use to adapt to those changes.

SUMMARY

Both conventional wisdom and the various portfolio models suggest that firms gain advantages by quickly entering, and investing heavily to build share in, growth markets. Among the premises on which the early, aggressive pursuit of growing markets is based are (1) it is easier to gain share when a market is growing, (2) share gains are worth more when total volume is expanding rather than stable, (3) price competition is likely to be less intense in growing markets because demand often exceeds supply, and (4) early experience gained in developing products and applications for a growth market can give a firm the technical expertise needed to keep up with advancing technology.

Although true in general, each of these premises is not always valid for every firm in every situation. Thus a market does not always represent an attractive opportunity for a business simply because it promises rapid future growth. Managers must consider how the market and competitive situations are likely to evolve and whether their firms can exploit the market's rapid growth to establish a sustainable competitive advantage.

The primary strategic objective of the early share leader, typically the market pioneer, in a growth market is *share maintenance*. From a marketing view, the firm must accomplish two important tasks: (1) retain repeat or replacement business from its existing customers and (2) continue to capture the major portion of sales to the growing number of new customers entering the market for the first time. Among the marketing strategies a firm might use either singly or in combination to maintain a leading share position are (1) a fortress or position defense strategy, (2) a flanker strategy, (3) a confrontation strategy, (4) a market expansion or mobile strategy, and (5) a contraction or strategic withdrawal strategy.

A challenger's strategic objective in a growth market is usually to *build its share* by expanding its sales faster than the overall market growth rate. It can accomplish this by stealing existing customers away from other competitors, capturing a larger share of new customers than the market leader, or both. Possible share-growth strategies include (1) a frontal attack, (2) a leapfrog strategy, (3) a flanking attack, (4) encirclement, and (5) guerrilla attacks.

Strategies for Mature and Declining Markets

JOHNSON CONTROLS: MAKING MONEY IN MATURE MARKETS[1]

Jim Keyes, CEO of Johnson Controls in Glendale, Wisconsin, appears to deserve your condolences. After all, his conglomerate's success and future survival depend heavily on four product categories that have experienced little or no growth in recent years. Johnson makes batteries for cars, seats for cars, heating and cooling systems for office buildings and schools, and plastic beverage bottles.

But Mr. Keyes isn't looking for sympathy. Instead, he has developed a successful three-pronged strategy for making money in such mature markets. His strategy involves (1) acquiring weaker competitors to gain share and remove excess capacity, (2) fattening profit margins by improving operating efficiencies, and (3) gaining additional revenue via the development of new technologies, product offerings, and services.

A strong balance sheet and a long-term perspective help Johnson build market share by acquiring competitors. In some cases the company has used such acquisitions to help expand its product offerings in one of its established target markets. For instance, the firm spent $167 million to buy Pan Am's World Services division, a facility management operation that does everything from mow the lawn to run the cafeteria. That acquisition, together with some new products and services developed internally, helped the firm grow from just a manufacturer of heating and cooling systems for new buildings into a full-service facilities operator. Johnson can now manage a client's entire building while offering highly customized heating and cooling systems and controls that save money. This combination of custom products and full service has not only increased Johnson's

---

[1]This example is based on material in Rick Tetzeli, "Mining Money in Mature Markets," *Fortune*, March 22, 1993, pp. 77–80.

revenues in the commercial real estate market, it has also generated higher operating profit margins.

In other businesses, Johnson has combined the economies of scale generated through savvy acquisitions with process reengineering to drive down operating costs. For example, the firm has captured a 40 percent share of the U. S. market for outsourced automotive seats—and has begun to win a commanding share of the European market as well—by supplying successful lines like the Jeep Grand Cherokee. Says Tom Donoughe, the Chrysler engineer in charge of the interior of the company's Neon compact car, "Johnson is able to completely integrate the design, development, and manufacture of the seats" and does it for less than the auto companies could.

Product development based on new technology is another way that Johnson has managed to increase sales to current customers as well as penetrate new market segments. Until recently, for instance, only glass bottles could safely handle certain fruit juices, including cranberry and apple, that are poured into containers when they are hot. But Johnson's R & D people are among the leaders in developing blow-molded plastic bottles that don't shrivel at high temperatures. Consequently, the firm is winning substantial business from new customers like Ocean Spray and Gatorade.

Despite the maturity of its markets, Johnson's three-pronged strategy is paying off. The firm strung together several years of record sales and profits during the early 1990s. In 1993, for instance, sales advanced 18 percent to more than $5.5 billion and profits rose 30 percent to $130 million.

STRATEGIC ISSUES IN MATURE AND DECLINING MARKETS

Many managers, particularly those in marketing, seem obsessed with growth. Their objectives tend to emphasize annual increases in sales volume, market share, or both. But the biggest challenge for many managers in developed nations in future years will be making money in markets that grow slowly, if at all. The majority of product-markets in those nations are in the mature or decline stages of their life cycles. And as accelerating rates of technological and social change continue to shorten such life cycles, today's innovations will move from growth to maturity—and ultimately to decline—ever faster.

But the situation is not always as depressing as it sounds, as Johnson Controls's recent performance confirms. In many cases managers can find opportunities to earn substantial profits and even increase volume in such markets.

Issues during the transition to market maturity

A period of competitive turbulence almost always accompanies the market transition from growth to maturity in an industry. This period often begins after approximately half the potential customers have adopted the product and the rate of sales growth starts to decline. As the growth rate slows, many competitors tend to overestimate future sales volume and consequently end up developing too much production capacity. Competition becomes more intense as firms battle to increase sales volume to cover their high fixed costs and maintain profitability.

Such transition periods are commonly accompanied by a **shakeout**, during which weaker businesses fail, withdraw from the industry, or are acquired by other firms—as has happened to some of Johnson Controls's competitors in the U. S. and European automotive seat and battery industries. The shakeout period is pivotal in influencing a brand's continued survival and the strength of its competitive position during the later maturity and decline stages of the life cycle. The next section of this chapter examines some common strategic traps that can threaten a firm's survival during an industry shakeout.

Issues in mature markets

Businesses that survive the shakeout face new challenges as market growth stagnates. As a market matures, total volume stabilizes; replacement purchases rather than first-time buyers account for the vast majority of that volume. A primary marketing objective of all competitors in mature markets, therefore, is simply to hold their existing customers—to sustain a meaningful competitive advantage that will help ensure the continued satisfaction and loyalty of those customers. Thus a product's financial success during the mature life cycle stage depends heavily on the firm's ability to achieve and sustain a lower delivered cost or some perceived product quality or customer service superiority.

Some firms tend to passively defend mature products while using the bulk of the revenues produced by those items to develop and aggressively market new products with more growth potential. This can be shortsighted, however. All segments of a market and all brands in an industry do not necessarily reach maturity at the same time. Aging brands like Jell-O, Johnson's baby shampoo, and Arm & Hammer baking soda experienced sales revivals in recent years because of creative marketing strategies. Thus a share leader in a mature industry might build upon a cost or product differentiation advantage and pursue a marketing strategy aimed at increasing volume by promoting new uses for an old product or by encouraging current customers to buy and use the product more often. A later section of this chapter examines basic business strategies necessary for survival in mature markets and marketing strategies a firm might use to extend a brand's sales and profits.

Issues in declining markets

Eventually, technological advances, changing customer demographics, tastes, or lifestyles, and development of substitutes result in declining demand for most product forms and brands. As a product starts to decline, managers face the critical question of whether to divest or liquidate the business. Unfortunately, firms sometimes support dying products too long at the expense of current profitability and the aggressive pursuit of future breadwinners.

An appropriate marketing strategy can, however, produce substantial sales and profits even in a declining market. If few exit barriers exist, an industry leader might attempt to increase market share via aggressive pricing or promotion policies aimed at driving out weaker competitors. Or it might try to consolidate the industry by acquiring weaker brands and

EXHIBIT 10–1

The Transition or Shakeout Stage of the Generalized Product Life Cycle

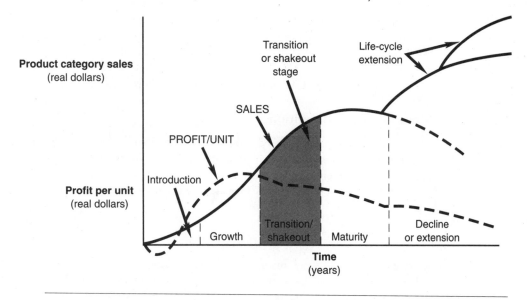

reducing overhead by eliminating excess capacity and duplicate marketing programs. Alternatively, a firm might decide to harvest a mature product by maximizing cash flow and profit over the product's remaining life. The last section of this chapter discusses specific marketing strategies for gaining the greatest possible returns from products approaching the end of their life cycle.

SHAKEOUT: THE TRANSITION FROM MARKET GROWTH TO MATURITY

Characteristics of the transition period

The transition from growth to maturity typically begins when the market is still growing but the rate of growth starts to decline, as shown in Exhibit 10–1. This declining growth either sparks or occurs simultaneously with other changes in the market and competitive environment. Such changes include the appearance of excess capacity, increased intensity of competition, increased difficulty of maintaining product differentiation, worsening distribution problems, and growing pressures on costs and profits. Weaker members of the industry often fail or are acquired by larger competitors during this shakeout stage.

Excess capacity

During a market's growth stage, manufacturers must usually invest heavily in new plants, equipment, and personnel to keep up with increasing demand. Some competitors fail to anticipate the transition from growth to maturity, however, and their expansion plans eventually overshoot market demand. Thus excess production capacity often develops at the end of the growth stage. This leads to an intense struggle for market share as firms seek increased volume to hold down unit costs and maintain profit margins.

More intense competition

The intensified battle for increased volume and market share at this stage often leads to price reductions and increased selling and promotional efforts. Firms modify products to appeal to more specialized user segments, make deals to produce for private labels, and take other actions that lower per unit revenues, increase R & D and marketing costs, and put pressure on profit margins.

Difficulty of maintaining differentiation

As an industry's technology matures, the better and more popular designs tend to become industry standards, and the physical differences among brands become less substantial. The popularity of the VHS format among video-cassette recorder customers, for example, eventually made it the industry standard, and Sony's alternative Beta format disappeared from the market. This decline in differentiation across brands often leads to a weakening of brand preference among consumers and makes it more difficult for even the market leaders to command premium prices for their products.[2] Such problems have been magnified in recent years as consumers have become more demanding and more willing to objectively evaluate alternatives rather than rely on past loyalty.[3]

Diminishing product differentiation can also increase costs as firms seek differentiation in other ways, such as through improved service. As the products and prices offered by competing suppliers become more similar, many purchasing agents become increasingly concerned with service and its impact on their firm's costs. For instance, they may demand a higher level of delivery reliability (as in just-in-time [JIT] deliveries) to help reduce their cost of capital tied up in inventory.

Distribution problems

During an industry's transition from growth to maturity, channel members often become more assertive in ways particularly detrimental to smaller-share competitors. As sales growth slows, for example, retailers may reduce the number of brands they carry to reduce inventory costs and space requirements. Much the same can happen at the wholesale/distributor level. Because any reduction in product availability has serious repercussions for a manufacturer,

---

[2]Neil Gross, Peter Coy, and Otis Port, "The Technology Paradox," *Business Week*, March 6, 1995, pp. 76–84.

[3]Rahul Jacob, "Beyond Quality and Value," *Fortune*, Special Issue, Fall–Winter 1993, pp. 8–11.

low-share firms often must offer additional trade incentives simply to hold their distribution coverage during this period.

Pressures on prices and profits

Prices typically decrease and margins get squeezed during shakeout, which increases the industry's instability and volatility. Given their higher per unit costs, smaller-share businesses often operate at a loss during transition. Some are ultimately forced to leave the industry. This is particularly likely with commodity-type products, when few unique market niches exist in which the firm can maintain a competitive advantage and when heavy investments in fixed assets are required and experience curve effects are high.

Firms that enter the transition period with high relative market shares are more likely to survive. Even these firms may experience a severe drop in profits, however. As the shakeout proceeds, the shares held by firms exiting the industry pass to the surviving firms, increasing their volumes and lowering per unit costs. This does not necessarily mean, though, that the leaders' market shares remain stable after shakeout. One study indicates that larger firms tend to lose share during market maturity because they fail to maintain their cost advantage.[4] We will discuss this danger in more detail later in this chapter.

Strategic traps during the transition period

A business's ability to survive the transition from market growth to maturity also depends to a great extent on whether it can avoid some common strategic traps.[5] Four such traps are summarized in Exhibit 10–2.

The most obvious trap is simply the *failure to recognize the events signaling the beginning of the shakeout period*. The best way to minimize the impact of slowing growth is to accurately forecast the slowdown in sales and hold the firm's production capacity to a sustainable level. For both industrial and consumer durable goods markets, models can forecast when replacement sales will begin to outweigh first-time purchases, a common signal that a market is beginning to mature.[6] But in consumer nondurable markets—particularly those where growth slows because of shifting consumer preferences or the emergence of substitute products—the start of the transition period can be nearly impossible to predict.

A second strategic trap is for a business to *get caught in the middle during the transition period without a clear strategic advantage*. A business may survive and prosper during the growth stage even though it has neither differentiated its offering from competitors nor attained the lowest-cost position in its industry. But during the transition period, such is not the case.

A third trap is the *failure to recognize the declining importance of product differentiation and the increasing importance of price or service*. Businesses that have built their success on technological

[4]Robert D. Buzzell, "Are There 'Natural' Market Structures?" *Journal of Marketing*, Winter 1981, pp. 42–51.

[5]For a more detailed discussion of these traps, see Michael E. Porter, *Competitive Strategy* (New York: Free Press, 1980), pp. 247–49.

[6]Fareena Sultan, John U. Farley, and Donald R. Lehmann, "A Meta-Analysis of Applications of Diffusion Models," *Journal of Marketing Research*, February 1990, pp. 70–77.

EXHIBIT 10-2

Common Strategic Traps Firms Can Fall into During the Shakeout Period

1. Failure to anticipate transition from growth to maturity.
   - Firms may make overly optimistic forecasts of future sales volume.
   - As a result, they expand too rapidly and production capacity overshoots demand as growth slows.
   - Their excess capacity leads to higher costs per unit.
   - Consequently, they must cut prices or increase promotion in an attempt to increase their volume.
2. No clear competitive advantage as growth slows.
   - Many firms can succeed without a strong competitive advantage during periods of rapid growth.
   - However, firms that do not have the lowest costs or a superior offering in terms of product quality or service can have difficulty sustaining their market share and volume as growth slows and competition intensifies.
3. Assumption that an early advantage will insulate the firm from price or service competition.
   - In many cases, technological differentials become smaller as more competitors enter and initiate product improvements as an industry approaches maturity.
   - If customers perceive that the quality of competing brands has become more equal, they are likely to attach greater importance to price or service differences.
   - Failure to detect such trends can cause an early leader to be complacent and slow to respond to competitive threats.
4. Sacrificing market share in favor of short-run profit.
   - A firm may cut marketing or R & D budgets or forgo other expenditures in order to maintain its historical level of profitability even though industry profits tend to fall during the transition period.
   - This can cause long-run erosion of market share and further increases in unit costs as the industry matures.

superiority or other forms of product differentiation often disdain aggressive pricing or marketing practices even though such differentiation typically erodes as markets mature.[7] As a result, such firms may delay meeting their more aggressive competitors head-on and end up losing market share.

Why should a firm not put off responding to the more aggressive pricing or marketing actions of its competitors? Because doing so may lead to a fourth trap—*giving up market share too easily in favor of short-run profit.* Many businesses try to maintain the profitability of the recent past as markets enter the transition period. They usually do this at the expense of market share or by forgoing marketing, R & D, and other investments crucial for maintaining future market position. While some smaller firms with limited resources may have no choice, this tendency can be seriously shortsighted, particularly if economies of scale are crucial for the business's continued success during market maturity.

---

[7]Ming Jer Chen and Ian C. MacMillan, "Nonresponse and Delayed Response to Competitive Moves: The Roles of Competitor Dependence and Action Irreversibility," *Academy of Management Journal* 35 (1992), pp. 539–70; and Hubert Gatignon, Eric Anderson, and Kristiaan Helsen, "Competitive Reactions to Market Entry: Explaining Interfirm Differences," *Journal of Marketing Research*, February 1989, pp. 44–55.

BUSINESS STRATEGIES FOR MATURE MARKETS

The maturity phase of an industry's life cycle is often depicted as one of stability characterized by few changes in the market shares of leading competitors and steady prices. The industry leaders, because of their low per unit costs and little need to make any further investments, enjoy high profits and positive cash flows. These cash flows are harvested and diverted to other SBUs or products in the firm's portfolio that promise greater future growth.

Unfortunately, this conventional scenario provides an overly simplistic description of the situation businesses face in most mature markets. For one thing, it is not always easy to tell when a market has reached maturity. Variations in brands, marketing programs, and customer groups can mean that different brands and market segments reach maturity at different times.

Further, as the maturity stage progresses, a variety of threats and opportunities can disrupt an industry's stability. Shifts in customer needs or preferences, product substitutes, increased raw material costs, changes in government regulations, or factors such as the entry of low-cost foreign producers or mergers and acquisitions can threaten individual competitors and even throw the entire industry into early decline. Consider, for example, the competitive position of Timex, a brand that dominated the low-price segment of the American watch market in the 1970s. First the appearance of imported digital watches and later a shift in consumer preferences toward more fashionable and prestigious brands buffeted the firm and eroded its market share.

On the positive side, such changes can also open new growth opportunities in mature industries. Product improvements (such as the development of high-fiber nutritional cereals), advances in process technology (for example, the creation of minimills for steel production), falling raw materials costs, increased prices for close substitutes, or environmental changes (such as the increased demand for storm windows in the energy crisis of the 1970s and early 80s) can all provide opportunities for a firm to dramatically increase its sales and profits. An entire industry can even experience a period of renewed growth.

Discontinuities during industry maturity suggest that it is dangerously shortsighted for a firm to simply milk its cash cows. Even industry followers can substantially improve volume, share, and profitability during industry maturity if they can adjust their marketing objectives and programs to fit the new opportunities that arise.[8] Thus success in mature markets requires two sets of strategic actions: (1) the development of a well-implemented business strategy to sustain a competitive advantage and (2) flexible and creative marketing programs geared to pursue growth or profit opportunities as conditions change in specific product-markets.

Strategies for maintaining competitive advantage

As discussed in Chapter 3, both *analyzer* and *defender strategies* may be appropriate for units with a leading, or at least a profitable, share of one or more major segments in a mature

---

[8]Cathy Anterasian and Lynn W. Phillips, "Discontinuities, Value Delivery, and the Share-Returns Association: A Reexamination of the 'Share-Causes-Profits' Controversy," Distributed working paper (Cambridge, Mass.: Marketing Science Institute, April 1988). Also see Robert Jacobson, "Distinguishing among Competing Theories of the Market Share Effect," *Journal of Marketing*, October 1988, pp. 68–80.

industry. Analyzers and defenders are both concerned with maintaining a strong share position in established product-markets. But analyzers also do some product and market development to avoid being leapfrogged by competitors with more advanced products or being left behind in new application segments. On the other hand, defenders may initiate some product improvements or line extensions to protect and strengthen their position in existing markets, but they spend relatively little on new product R & D. Thus, an analyzer strategy is most appropriate for developed industries that are still experiencing some technological change and may have opportunities for continued growth, such as the computer and commercial aircraft industries. The defender strategy works best in industries where the basic technology is not very complex or is unlikely to change dramatically in the short run, as in the food industry.

Both analyzers and defenders can attempt to sustain a competitive advantage in established product-markets through *differentiation* of their product offering (either on the basis of superior quality or service) or by maintaining a *low-cost* position. Evidence suggests the ability to maintain either a strongly differentiated or a low-cost position continues to be a critical determinant of success throughout both the transition and the maturity stages. One study examined the competitive strategies pursued by the two leading firms (in terms of return on investment) in eight mature industries characterized by slow growth and intense competition. In each industry the two leading firms offered either the lowest relative delivered cost or high relative product differentiation.[9] Similarly, more recent observations by Treacy and Wiersema found that market leaders tend to pursue one of three strategic disciplines. They either stress operational excellence—which typically translates into lower costs—or they differentiate themselves through product leadership or customer intimacy and superior service.[10] These three disciplines are summarized in Exhibit 10–3 together with some of the traits of businesses that are able to implement them effectively.

Generally, it is difficult for a single business to pursue both low-cost and differentiation strategies at the same time. For instance, businesses taking the low-cost approach typically compete primarily by offering the lowest prices in the industry. Such prices allow little room for the firm to make the investments or cover the costs inherent in maintaining superior product quality, performance, or service over time.

It is important to keep in mind, however, that pursuit of a low-cost strategy does not mean that a business can ignore the delivery of desirable benefits to the customer. Similarly, customers will not pay an unlimited price premium for superior quality or service, no matter how superior it is. In both consumer and commercial markets customers seek good *value* for their money—either a solid, no-frills product or service at an outstanding price, or an offering whose higher price is justified by the superior benefits it delivers on one or more dimensions.[11] Thus, even low-cost producers should continually seek ways to improve the quality and performance of their offerings within the financial constraints of their competitive strategy.

---

[9]William K. Hall, "Survival Strategies in a Hostile Environment," *Harvard Business Review*, September–October 1980, pp. 75–85.

[10]Michael Treacy and Fred Wiersema, *The Discipline of Market Leaders* (Reading, Mass.: Addison-Wesley, 1995).

[11]Rahul Jacob, "Beyond Quality and Value."

EXHIBIT 10-3

Three Strategic Disciplines of Market Leaders and the Traits of Businesses That Implement Them Effectively

Company traits	Disciplines		
	Operational excellence	**Product leadership**	**Customer intimacy**
Core business processes	Sharpen distribution systems and provide no-hassle service	Nurture ideas, translate them into products, and market them skillfully	Provide solutions and help customers run their businesses
Structure	Has strong, central authority and a finite level of empowerment	Acts in an ad hoc, organic, loosely knit, and ever-changing way	Pushes empowerment close to customer contact
Management systems	Maintain standard operating procedures	Reward individuals' innovative capacity and new product success	Measure the cost of providing service and of maintaining customer loyalty
Culture	Acts predictably and believes "one size fits all"	Experiments and thinks "out-of-the-box"	Is flexible and thinks "have it your way"

SOURCE: *THE DISCIPLINE OF MARKET LEADERS: CHOOSE YOUR CUSTOMERS, NARROW YOUR FOCUS, DOMINATE YOUR MARKET* (adapted from pp. 34–35, 37–38 and 41), © 1995 by Michael Treacy, Fred Wiersema and CSC Index, Inc. Reprinted by permission of Addison-Wesley Publishing Company, Inc.

And even differentiated defenders should continually work to improve efficiency without sacrificing product quality or performance. The critical strategic questions, then, are "How can a business continue to differentiate its offerings and justify a premium price as its market matures and becomes more competitive?" and "How can businesses—particularly those pursuing low-cost strategies—continue to reduce their costs and improve their efficiency as their markets mature?"

Methods of differentiation

At the most basic level, a business can attempt to differentiate its offering from competitors' by offering either superior product quality, superior service, or both. The problem is that *quality* and *service* may be defined in a variety of different ways by different customers.

Dimensions of product quality[12]

To maintain a competitive advantage in product quality, a firm must understand what *dimensions customers perceive to underlie differences across products* within a given category. One authority has identified eight such dimensions of product quality. These are summarized in Exhibit 10–4 and discussed here.

---

[12]The following discussion is based on material found in David A. Garvin, "What Does 'Product Quality' Really Mean?" *Sloan Management Review*, Fall 1984, pp. 25–43; and David A. Aaker, *Strategic Market Management*, 2nd ed. (New York: John Wiley & Sons, 1988), 11.

EXHIBIT 10-4

Dimensions of Product Quality

• Performance	How well does the washing machine wash clothes?
• Durability	How long will the lawn mower last?
• Conformance with specifications	What is the incidence of product defects?
• Features	Does an airline flight offer a movie and dinner?
• Reliability	Will each visit to a restaurant result in consistent quality? What percentage of the time will a product perform satisfactorily?
• Serviceability	Is the product easy to service? Is the service system efficient, competent, and convenient?
• Fit and finish	Does the product look and feel like a quality product?
• Brand name	Is this a name that customers associate with quality? What is the brand's image?

SOURCE: Adapted from "What Does 'Product Quality' Really Mean?" by David A. Garvin, *Sloan Management Review*, Fall 1984, pp. 25–43. Copyright © 1984 by the Sloan Management Review Association. All rights reserved. Used by permission of the publisher.

European manufacturers of prestige automobiles, such as Mercedes-Benz and Porsche, have emphasized the first dimension of product quality—**functional performance**. These automakers have designed cars that provide excellent performance on such attributes as handling, acceleration, and comfort. Volvo, on the other hand, has emphasized and aggressively promoted a different quality dimension—**durability** (and the related attribute of safety). A third quality dimension, **conformance to specifications**, or the absence of defects, has been a major focus of the Japanese automakers. Until recent years American carmakers relied heavily on broad product lines and a wide **variety of features**, both standard and optional, to offset their shortcomings on some of the other quality dimensions.

The **reliability** quality dimension can refer to the consistency of performance from purchase to purchase or to a product's uptime, the percentage of time that it can perform satisfactorily over its life. Tandem Computers has maintained a competitive advantage based on reliability by designing computers with several processors that work in tandem, so that if one fails, the only impact is the slowing of low-priority tasks. IBM cannot match Tandem's reliability because of its commitment to an operating system not easily adapted to the multiple-processor concept. Consequently, Tandem has maintained a strong position in market segments consisting of large-scale computer users—such as financial institutions and large retailers—for whom system downtime is particularly undesirable.

The quality dimension of **serviceability** refers to a customer's ability to obtain prompt and competent service when the product does break down. For example, Catepillar Tractor has long differentiated itself with a parts and service organization dedicated to providing "24-hour parts service anywhere in the world."

Many of these quality dimensions can be difficult for customers to evaluate, particularly for consumer products. As a result, consumers often generalize from quality dimensions that are more visual or qualitative. Thus, the **fit and finish** dimension can help convince consumers

EXHIBIT 10–5

Dimensions of Service Quality

• Tangibles	Appearance of physical facilities, equipment, personnel, and communications materials
• Reliability	Ability to perform the promised service dependably and accurately
• Responsiveness	Willingness to help customers and provide prompt service
• Assurance	Knowledge and courtesy of employees and their ability to convey trust and confidence
• Empathy	Caring, individualized attention the firm provides its customers

SOURCE: Reprinted with permission of The Free Press, an imprint of Simon & Schuster Inc. from *DELIVERING QUALITY SERVICE: Balancing Customer Perceptions and Expectations* by Valarie A. Zeithaml, A. Parasuraman, and Leonard L. Berry. Copyright © 1990 by The Free Press.

that a product is of high quality. They tend to perceive attractive and well-designed products as generally high in quality, as witnessed by the success of the Krups line of small appliances. Similarly, the **quality reputation of the brand name**, and the promotional activities that sustain that reputation, can strongly influence consumers' perceptions of a product's quality. Indeed, a brand's quality reputation together with psychological factors such as name recognition and loyalty substantially determine a brand's *equity*—the perceived value customers associate with a particular brand name and its logo or symbol.[13] To successfully pursue a differentiation strategy based on quality, then, a business must understand what dimensions or cues its potential customers use to judge quality, and it should pay particular attention to some of the less concrete but more visible and symbolic attributes of the product.

Dimensions of service quality

Customers also judge the quality of the service they receive on multiple dimensions. A number of such dimensions of perceived service quality have been identified by a series of studies conducted across diverse industries such as retail banking and appliance repair, and five of those dimensions are listed and briefly defined in Exhibit 10–5.[14]

The quality dimensions listed in Exhibit 10–5 apply specifically to service businesses, but most of them are also relevant for judging the service component of a product offering. This pertains to both the objective performance dimensions of the service delivery system—such as its **reliability** and **responsiveness**—as well as to elements of the performance of service personnel, such as their **empathy** and level of **assurance**.

The results of a number of surveys suggest that customers perceive all five dimensions of service quality to be very important regardless of the kind of service being evaluated. As

---

[13]For a more extensive discussion of brand equity, see David A. Aaker, *Brand Equity* (New York: The Free Press, 1991).

[14]Valarie A. Zeithaml, A. Parasuraman, and Leonard L. Berry, *Delivering Quality Service: Balancing Customer Perceptions and Expectations* (New York: The Free Press, 1990).

EXHIBIT 10–6

Perceived Importance of Service Quality Dimensions in Four Different Industries

	Mean importance rating on 10-point scale★	Percentage of respondents indicating dimension is most important
Credit card customers (*n* = 187)		
Tangibles	7.43	0.6
Reliability	9.45	48.6
Responsiveness	9.37	19.8
Assurance	9.25	17.5
Empathy	9.09	13.6
Repair and maintenance customers (*n* = 183)		
Tangibles	8.48	1.2
Reliability	9.64	57.2
Responsiveness	9.54	19.9
Assurance	9.62	12.0
Empathy	9.30	9.6
Long-distance telephone customers (*n* = 184)		
Tangibles	7.14	0.6
Reliability	9.67	60.6
Responsiveness	9.57	16.0
Assurance	9.29	12.6
Empathy	9.25	10.3
Bank customers (*n* = 177)		
Tangibles	8.56	1.1
Reliability	9.44	42.1
Responsiveness	9.34	18.0
Assurance	9.18	13.6
Empathy	9.30	25.1

★Scale ranges from 1 (not at all important) to 10 (extremely important).

Source: Reprinted with permission of The Free Press, an imprint of Simon & Schuster Inc. from *DELIVERING QUALITY SERVICE: Balancing Customer Perceptions and Expectations* by Valarie A. Zeithaml, A. Parasuraman, and Leonard L. Berry. Copyright © 1990 by The Free Press.

Exhibit 10–6 indicates, customers of four different kinds of services gave reliability, responsiveness, assurance, and empathy mean importance ratings of more than 9 on a 10-point rating scale. And though the mean ratings for tangibles were somewhat lower in comparison, they still fell toward the upper end of the scale, ranging from 7.14 to 8.56.

The same respondents were also asked which of the five dimensions they would choose as being the most critical in their assessment of service quality. Their responses—which are shown in Exhibit 10–6—suggest that reliability is the most important aspect of service quality to the greatest number of customers. The key to a differentiation strategy based on providing superior service, then, is to meet or exceed target customers' service quality expectations and to do it more consistently than competitors. The problem is that sometimes managers underestimate the level of those customer expectations, and sometimes those expectations can be unrealistically high. Therefore, a firm needs to clearly identify target customers' desires with respect to service quality and clearly define and communicate what level of service they intend to deliver. When this is done, customers have a more realistic idea of what to expect and are less likely to be disappointed with the service they receive.

Improving customer perceptions of service quality

The major factors that determine a customer's expectations and perceptions concerning service quality—and five gaps that can lead to dissatisfaction with service delivery—are outlined in Exhibit 10–7 and discussed next.

1. *Gap between the customer's expectations and the marketer's perceptions.*   Managers do not always have an accurate understanding of what customers want or how they will evaluate a firm's service efforts. The first step in providing good service, then, is to collect information—through customer surveys, evaluations of customer complaints, or other methods—to determine what service attributes customers consider important.

2. *Gap between management perceptions and service quality specifications.*   Even when management has a clear understanding of what customers want, that understanding might not get translated into effective operating standards. A firm's policies concerning customer service may be unclear, poorly communicated to employees, or haphazardly enforced. Unless a firm's employees know what the company's service policies are and believe that management is seriously committed to those standards, their performance is likely to fall short of desired levels.

3. *Gap between service quality specifications and service delivery.*   Lip service by management is not enough to produce high-quality service. High standards must be backed by the programs, resources, and rewards necessary to enable and encourage employees to deliver good service. Employees must be provided with the training, equipment, and time necessary to deliver good service. Their service performance must be measured and evaluated. And good performance must be rewarded by making it part of the criteria for pay raises or promotions, or by other more direct inducements, in order to motivate the additional effort good service requires.

4. *Gap between service delivery and external communications.*   Even good service performance may disappoint some customers if the firm's marketing communications cause them to have unrealistically high expectations. If the photographs in a vacation resort's advertising and brochures make the rooms look more spacious and luxurious than they really are, for instance, first-time customers are likely to be disappointed no matter how clean or well-tended those rooms are kept by the resort's staff.

5. *Gap between perceived service and expected service.*   This results when management fails to close one or more of the other four gaps. It is this difference between a customer's expectations and his or her actual experience with the firm that leads to dissatisfaction.

This discussion suggests a number of actions management can take to close the possible gaps and improve customer satisfaction with a company's service. An example of how such

EXHIBIT 10-7

Determinants of Perceived Service Quality

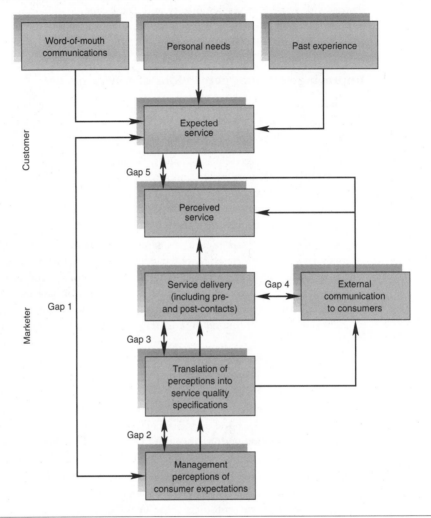

Source: Reprinted from A. Parasuraman, Valarie A. Zeithaml, and Leonard L. Berry, "A Conceptual Model of Service Quality and Its Implications for Future Research," *Journal of Marketing*, Fall 1985, p. 44. Published by the American Marketing Association.

actions can be translated into a successful service program that satisfies customers is provided by Hertz's #1 Club Gold program, which is described in Exhibit 10–8. Achieving and sustaining such high levels of service quality can present some difficult implementation problems, however, because it often involves the coordination of efforts of many different employees from different functional departments and organizational levels. Some of these coordination problems are examined later in Chapter 12.

EXHIBIT 10-8

Hertz's Program for Excellent Customer Service

No.1 has been trying harder, and as a result **Hertz** tops all five categories in the Zagat 1992 survey of car rental customers. Hertz's secret: the #1 Club Gold program. Pay $50 a year to become a member, and skip endless late-night lines at rental counters. Just call up to reserve your car, hop on the courtesy airport bus when you arrive at your destination, tell the driver your last name, and get dropped off in front of your auto. You'll know it's yours because your surname is in glowing lights above it. Since the bus driver radios ahead, Hertz starts your car up and turns on the a.c. or heat, depending on the temperature. Show the gate attendant your driver's license, and off you go. Says Boston Consulting Group VP Gary Curtis, who travels a lot: "This is the best thing that ever happened to rental cars."

Methods for maintaining a low-cost position

Moving down the experience curve is the most commonly discussed method for achieving and sustaining a low-cost position in an industry. But a firm does not necessarily need a large relative market share to implement a low-cost strategy. The small clone manufacturers in the PC industry, for instance, found other ways to hold their costs well below those of the industry leaders. Other means for obtaining a sustainable cost advantage include producing a no-frills product, creating an innovative product design, finding cheaper raw materials, automating production, developing low-cost distribution channels, and reducing overhead.[15]

A no-frills product

A direct approach to obtaining a low-cost position involves simply removing all frills and extras from the basic product or service. Thus Suzuki cars, warehouse furniture stores, legal services clinics, and grocery stores selling canned goods out of crates all offer lower costs and prices than their competitors. This lower production cost is often sustainable because

---

[15]For a more detailed discussion of these and other approaches for lowering costs, see Aaker, *Strategic Market Management*, Ch. 12.

established differentiated competitors find it difficult to stop offering features and services their customers have come to expect. However, those established firms may lower their own prices in the short run—even to the point of suffering losses—in an attempt to drive out a no-frills competitor that poses a serious threat. This was the response of the major airlines to inroads made by People Express. Thus a firm considering a no-frills strategy needs the resources to withstand a possible price war.

Innovative product design

A simplified product design and standardized component parts can also lead to cost advantages. In the office copier industry, for instance, Japanese firms overcame substantial entry barriers by designing extremely simple copiers with a fraction of the number of parts in the design used by market-leading Xerox.

Cheaper raw materials

A firm with the foresight to acquire or the creativity to find a way to use relatively cheap raw materials can also gain a sustainable cost advantage. For example, Fort Howard Paper achieved an advantage by being the only major papermaker to rely exclusively on recycled pulp. While the finished product was not so high in quality as paper from virgin wood, Fort Howard's lower cost gave it a competitive edge in the price-sensitive commercial market for toilet paper and other such products used in hotels, restaurants, and office buildings.

Innovative production processes

Although low-cost defender businesses typically spend little on *product R & D*, they often continue to devote substantial sums to *process R & D*. Innovations in the production process, including the development of automated or computer-controlled processes, can help them sustain cost advantages over competitors.

In some labor-intensive industries a business can achieve a cost advantage, at least in the short term, by gaining access to inexpensive labor. This is usually achieved by moving all or part of the production process to countries with low wage rates, such as Taiwan, Korea, or Mexico. Unfortunately, because such moves are relatively easy to emulate, this kind of cost advantage may not be sustainable.

Low-cost distribution

When distribution accounts for a relatively high proportion of a product's total delivered cost, a firm might gain a substantial advantage by developing lower-cost alternative channels. Typically, this involves eliminating, or shifting to the customer, some of the functions performed by traditional channels in return for a lower price. In the PC hardware and software industries, for example, mail-order discounters can offer lower prices because they have fewer fixed costs than the retail stores with which they compete. However, they also do not provide technical advice or postsale service to their customers.

Reductions in overhead

Successfully sustaining a low-cost strategy requires that the firm pare and control its major overhead costs as quickly as possible as its industry matures. Indeed, many U. S. companies learned this lesson the hard way during the 1980s when high costs of old plants, labor, and large inventories left them vulnerable to more efficient foreign competitors and to corporate raiders.

Business strategy and performance

Analyzer, and particularly defender, businesses are mostly concerned with protecting their existing positions in one or more mature market segments and maximizing profitability over the remaining life of those product-markets. Thus financial dimensions of performance, such as return on investment and cash flow, are usually of greater interest to such businesses than more growth-oriented dimensions like volume increases or new product success. Businesses can achieve such financial objectives by either successfully differentiating their offerings or by maintaining a low-cost position.

While the primary emphasis in many businesses during the early 1990s was on improving efficiency through downsizing and reengineering,[16] there is substantial evidence that firms with superior quality goods and services also obtain higher returns on investment than businesses with average or below-average quality offerings.[17] The lesson to be learned, then, is that the choice between a differentiation or a low-cost strategy is probably not the critical determinant of success in mature markets. What is critical is that a business *continually work to improve the value* of its offerings—either by improving product or service quality, reducing costs, or some combination—as a basis for maintaining its customer base as its markets mature and become increasingly competitive.

Measuring customer satisfaction

In order to gain the knowledge necessary to continually improve the value of their offerings to target customers, firms must understand how satisfied existing and potential customers are with their current offerings. This focus on customer satisfaction is become increasingly important as more firms question whether all attempts to improve the *absolute* quality of their products and services generate sufficient additional sales and profits to justify their cost. This growing concern with the economic "return on quality" has motivated firms to ask which dimensions of product or service quality are most important to customers, and which dimensions customers might be willing to sacrifice for lower prices. For instance, United Parcel Service recently discovered that many of its customers wanted more time to interact with the company's drivers in order to seek advice on their shipping problems, and they were willing to put up with slightly slower delivery times in return. Consequently, UPS now

---

[16]Ronald Henkoff, "Getting beyond Downsizing," *Fortune*, January 10, 1994, pp. 58–64.

[17]Robert Jacobson and David A. Aaker, "The Strategic Role of Product Quality," *Journal of Marketing*, October 1987, pp. 31–44.

EXHIBIT 10–9

Sources of Increased Profit from Loyal Customers

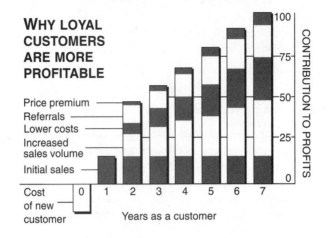

SOURCE: Rahul Jacob, "Why Some Customers Are More Equal Than Others," *Fortune*, September 19, 1994, p. 220.

allows its drivers an additional 30 minutes a day to spend at their discretion to strengthen ties with customers and perhaps bring in new sales.[18]

As the diagram in Exhibit 10–7 indicates, then, useful measures of customer satisfaction should examine both (1) customers' **expectations and preferences** concerning the various dimensions of product and service quality (such as product performance, features, reliability, on-time delivery, competence of service personnel, and so on) and (2) their **perceptions** concerning how well the firm is meeting those expectations. Any gaps where customer expectations exceed their recent experiences may indicate fruitful areas for the firm to work at improving customer value and satisfaction. Of course, such measurements must be made periodically to determine whether the actions taken have actually been effective.[19]

Improving customer retention

As Exhibit 10–9 indicates, maintaining the loyalty of existing customers is crucial for improving a business's profitability as markets mature. The exhibit shows that loyal customers become more profitable over time. The firm not only avoids the high costs associated with acquiring a new customer, but it typically benefits because loyal customers (1) tend to

---

[18]David Greising, "Quality: How to Make It Pay," *Business Week*, August 8, 1994, pp. 54–59.

[19]For a discussion of various approaches to measuring customer satisfaction, see J. Joseph Cronin and Steven A. Taylor, "Measuring Service Quality: A Reexamination and Extension," *Journal of Marketing*, July 1992, pp. 55–68; and Susan J. Devlin and H. K. Dong, "Service Quality from the Customers' Perspective," *Marketing Research* 6 (1994), pp. 5–13.

concentrate their purchases, thus leading to larger volumes and lower selling and distribution costs, (2) provide positive word-of-mouth and customer referrals, and (3) may be willing to pay premium prices for the value they receive.[20]

Periodic measurement of customer satisfaction is important, then, because a dissatisfied customer is unlikely to remain loyal to a company over time. Unfortunately, however, the corollary is not always true: Customers who describe themselves as satisfied are not necessarily loyal. Indeed, one author estimates that 60 to 80 percent of customer defectors in most businesses said they were "satisfied" or "very satisfied" on the last customer survey before their defection.[21] In the interim, perhaps, competitors improved their offerings, the customer's requirements changed, or other environmental factors shifted. The point is that businesses that measure customer satisfaction should be commended—but urged not to stop there. Satisfaction measures need to be supplemented with examinations of customer *behavior*, such as measures of the annual retention rate, frequency of purchases, and the percentage of a customer's total purchases captured by the firm.

Most important, defecting customers should be studied in detail to discover *why* the firm failed to provide sufficient value to retain their loyalty. Such failures often provide more valuable information than satisfaction measures because they stand out as a clear, understandable message telling the organization exactly where improvements are needed. The Micro-Scan division of Baxter Diagnostics, Inc., provides a good example of the intelligent use of such defector analysis. MicroScan makes instruments used by medical laboratories to identify microbes in patient cultures. In 1990 MicroScan was neck-and-neck with Vitek Systems, Inc., for market leadership, but its management knew they would have to do better to win the race. The firm analyzed its customer base, highlighting accounts that had been lost as well as those that remained active but showed a declining volume of testing. MicroScan interviewed all the lost customers and a large portion of the "decliners," probing deeply for the causes underlying their change in behavior. They found that such customers had concerns about the company's instrument features, reliability, and responsiveness to their problems.

In response, MicroScan's management shifted R & D priorities to address specific shortcomings its lost customers had identified, such as test accuracy and time-to-result. It also redesigned customer service protocols to ensure that immediate attention was given to equipment faults and delivery problems. As a result, MicroScan's sales began to improve and it established a clear market-share lead within two years.[22]

As MicroScan's experience shows, improving customer loyalty is crucial for maintaining market share and profitability as markets mature. As pointed out next, however, simply holding onto current customers may not be the only relevant objective in many mature markets.

---

[20]Frederick F. Reichheld, "Loyalty and the Renaissance of Marketing," *Marketing Management* 2 (1994), pp. 10–21. Also see Rahul Jacob, "Why Some Customers Are More Equal Than Others," *Fortune*, September 19, 1994, pp. 215–24.

[21]Reichheld, "Loyalty and the Renaissance of Marketing."

[22]Reichheld, "Loyalty and The Renaissance of Marketing."

MARKETING STRATEGIES FOR MATURE MARKETS

Strategies for maintaining current market share

Since markets can remain in the maturity stage for decades, milking or harvesting mature product-markets by maximizing short-run profits makes little sense. Pursuing such an objective typically involves substantial cuts in marketing and R & D expenses, which can lead to premature losses of volume and market share and lower profits in the longer term. The business should strive during the early years of market maturity to *maximize the flow of profits over the remaining life of the product-market*. Thus, the most critical marketing objective is to *maintain and protect the business's market share*. In a mature market where few new customers buy the product for the first time, the business must continue to win its share of repeat purchases from existing customers.

In Chapter 9 we discussed a number of marketing strategies that businesses might use to maintain their market share in growth markets. Many of those same strategies continue to be relevant for holding onto customers as markets mature, particularly for those firms that survived the shakeout period with a relatively strong share position. The most obvious strategy for such share leaders is simply to continue strengthening their position through a *fortress defense*. Recall that such a strategy involves two sets of marketing actions: those aimed at improving customer satisfaction and loyalty, and those intended to encourage and simplify repeat purchasing. Actions like those discussed earlier for improving the quality of a firm's offering and for reducing costs suggest ways to increase customer satisfaction and loyalty. Similarly, improvements to service quality—such as just-in-time delivery arrangements or computerized reordering systems—can help encourage repeat purchases.

Since markets often become more fragmented as they grow and mature, share leaders may also have to expand their product lines or add one or more *flanker* brands to protect their position against competitive inroads. Thus, Johnson Controls has strengthened its position in the commercial facilities management arena by expanding its array of services through a combination of acquisitions and continued internal development.

Small-share competitors can also earn substantial profits in a mature market. To do so, however, it is often wise for them to focus on strategies that avoid prolonged direct confrontations with larger share leaders. A *niche strategy* can be particularly effective when the target segment is too small to appeal to larger competitors or when the smaller firm can establish a strong differential advantage or brand preference in the segment. For instance, with only 36 hotels worldwide the Four Seasons chain is a small player in the lodging industry. But by focusing on the high end of the business travel market, the chain has grown and prospered. The chain's hotels differentiate themselves by offering a wide range of amenities—such as free overnight shoe shining—that are important to business travelers. Thus, while they charge relatively high prices, they are also seen as delivering good value and rank first in the *Business Travel News* survey of customer satisfaction.[23]

---

[23]Patricia Sellers, "Companies That Serve You Best," *Fortune*, May 31, 1993, p. 80.

Strategies for extending volume growth

Market maturity is defined by a flattening of the growth rate. In some instances growth slows for structural reasons, such as the emergence of substitute products or a shift in customer preferences. Marketers can do little to revitalize the market under such conditions. But in some cases a market only *appears* to be mature because of the limitations of current marketing programs, such as target segments that are too narrowly defined or limited product offerings. Here more innovative or aggressive marketing strategies might successfully extend the market's life cycle into a period of renewed growth. Thus, *stimulating additional volume growth* can be an important secondary objective under such circumstances, particularly for industry share leaders because they often can capture a relatively large share of any additional volume generated.

A firm might pursue several different marketing strategies either singly or in combination to squeeze additional volume from a mature market. These include an *increased penetration strategy*, an *extended use strategy*, and a *market expansion strategy*. Exhibit 10–10 summarizes the environmental situations where each of these strategies is most appropriate and the objectives each is best suited for accomplishing. Exhibit 10–11 outlines some specific marketing actions a firm might employ to implement each of the strategies, as discussed in more detail in the following paragraphs.

Increased penetration strategy

The total sales volume produced by a target segment of customers is a function of (1) the number of potential customers in the segment, (2) the product's penetration of that segment, that is, the proportion of potential customers who actually use the product, and (3) the average frequency with which customers consume the product and make another purchase. Where usage frequency is quite high among current customers but only a relatively small portion of all potential users actually buy the product, a firm might aim at increasing market penetration. This is an appropriate strategy for an industry's share leader because such firms can more likely gain and retain a substantial share of new customers than smaller firms with less well-known brands.

The secret to a successful increased penetration strategy lies in discovering why nonusers are uninterested in the product. Very often the product does not offer sufficient value from the potential customer's point of view to justify the effort or expense involved in buying and using it. One obvious solution to such a problem is to enhance the product's value to potential customers by adding features or benefits, usually via line extensions.

Another way to add value to a product is to develop and sell integrated systems that help improve the basic product's performance or ease of use. For instance, instead of simply selling control mechanisms for heating and cooling systems, Johnson Controls offers integrated facilities management programs designed to lower the total costs of operating a commercial building.

A firm may also enhance a product's value by offering services that improve its performance or ease of use for the potential customer. Since it is unlikely that people who do not know how to knit will ever buy yarn or knitting needles, for example, most yarn shops offer free knitting lessons.

EXHIBIT 10–10

Situational Determinants of Appropriate Marketing Objectives and Strategies for
Extending Growth in Mature Markets

Situational variables	Growth extension strategies		
	Increased penetration	**Extended use**	**Market expansion**
Primary objective	Increase the proportion of users by converting current nonusers in one or more major market segments.	Increase the amount of product used by the average customer by increasing frequency of use or developing new and more varied ways to use the product.	Expand the number of potential customers by targeting underdeveloped geographic areas or applications segments.
Market characteristics	Relatively low penetration in one or more segments (a low percentage of potential users have adopted the product); relatively homogeneous market with only a few large segments.	Relatively high penetration but low frequency of use in one or more major segments; product used in only limited ways or for special occasions; relatively homogeneous market with only a few large segments.	Relatively heterogeneous market with a variety of segments; some geographic areas, including foreign countries, with low penetration; some product applications underdeveloped.
Competitor characteristics	Competitors hold relatively small market shares; comparatively limited resources or competencies make it unlikely they will steal a significant portion of converted nonusers.	Competitors hold relatively small market shares; comparatively limited resources or competencies make it unlikely their brands will be purchased for newly developed uses.	Competitors hold relatively small market shares; have insufficient resources or competencies to preempt underdeveloped geographic areas or application segments.
Firm characteristics	A market share leader in the industry; has R & D and marketing competencies to produce product modifications or line extensions; has promotional resources to stimulate primary demand among current nonusers.	A market share leader in the industry; has marketing competencies and resources to develop and promote new uses.	A market share leader in the industry; has marketing and distribution competencies and resources to develop new global markets or application segments.

Product modifications or line extensions will not, however, attract nonusers unless the enhanced benefits are effectively promoted. For industrial goods, this may mean redirecting some sales efforts toward nonusers. The firm may offer additional incentives for new account sales or assign specific salespeople to call on targeted nonusers and convert them into new customers. For consumer goods, some combination of advertising to stimulate primary demand in the target segment and sales promotions to encourage trial, such as free samples or tie-in promotions with complementary products that nonusers currently buy, can be effective.

EXHIBIT 10–11

Possible Marketing Actions for Accomplishing Growth Extension Objectives

Marketing strategy and objectives	Possible marketing actions

Increased penetration Convert current nonusers in target segment into users.	• Enhance product's value by adding features, benefits, or services.
	 • Enhance product's value by including it in the design of integrated systems.
	 • Stimulate additional primary demand through promotional efforts stressing new features or benefits:
	   Advertising through selective media aimed at the target segment.
	   Sales promotions directed at stimulating trial among current nonusers (such as tie-ins with other products).
	   Some sales efforts redirected toward new account generation, perhaps by assigning some sales personnel as account development reps or by offering incentives for new account sales.
	 • Improve product's availability by developing innovative distribution systems.

Extended use Increase frequency of use among current users.	• Move storage of the product closer to the point of end use by offering additional package sizes or designs.
	 • Encourage larger-volume purchases (for nonperishable products):
	   Offer quantity discounts.
	   Offer consumer promotions to stimulate volume purchases or more frequent use (for example, multipack deals, frequent flier programs).
	 • Reminder advertising stressing basic product benefits for a variety of usage occasions.

Encourage a wider variety of uses among current users.	• Develop line extensions suitable for additional uses or applications. • Develop and promote new uses, applications, or recipes for the basic product.

(continues)

Finally, some potential customers may be having trouble finding the product due to limited distribution, or the product's benefits may simply be too modest to justify much purchasing effort. In such cases, expanding distribution or developing more convenient and accessible channels may help expand market penetration. For example, few travelers are so leery of flying that they would go through the effort of calling an insurance agent to buy an accident policy for a single flight. But the sales of such policies are greatly increased by making them conveniently available through vending machines in airport terminals.

Extended use strategy

Some years ago, the manager of General Foods' Cool Whip frozen dessert topping discovered through marketing research that nearly three-fourths of all households used the product, but the average consumer used it only four times per year and served it on only 7 percent of all toppable desserts. In situations of good market penetration but low

EXHIBIT 10–11 (*concluded*)

Marketing strategy and objectives	Possible marketing actions
	Include information about new applications/recipes on package. Develop extended use advertising campaign, particularly with print media. Communicate new application ideas through sales presentations to current customers.
	• Encourage new uses through sales promotions (such as tie-ins with complementary products).
Market expansion Develop differentiated positioning focused on untapped or underdeveloped segments.	• Develop a differentiated flanker brand or product line with unique features or price that is more appealing to a segment of potential customers whose needs are not met by existing offerings.
	or
	• Develop multiple line extensions or brand offerings with features or prices targeted to the unique needs and preferences of several smaller potential applications or regional segments.
	• Consider producing for private labels.
	• Design advertising, personal selling, and/or sales promotion campaigns that address specific interests and concerns of potential customers in one or multiple underdeveloped segments to stimulate selective demand.
	• Build unique distribution channels to more effectively reach potential customers in one or multiple underdeveloped segments.
	• Design service programs to reduce the perceived risks of trial and/or solve the unique problems faced by potential customers in one or multiple underdeveloped segments (for example, systems engineering, installation, operator trailing, extended warranties).
	• Enter global markets where product category is in an earlier stage of its life cycle.

frequency of use, an extended use strategy may effectively increase volume. This was particularly true in the Cool Whip case; the relatively large and homogeneous target market consisted for the most part of a single mass-market segment. Also, General Foods held nearly a two-thirds share of the frozen topping market, and it had the marketing resources and competencies to capture most of the additional volume that an extended use strategy might generate.

One effective approach for stimulating increased frequency of use is to move product inventories closer to the point of use. This approach works particularly well with low-involvement consumer goods. Marketers know that most consumers are unlikely to expend any additional time or effort to obtain such products when they are ready to use them. If there is no Cool Whip in the refrigerator when the consumer is preparing dessert, for instance, he or she is unlikely to run to the store immediately and will probably serve the dessert without topping.

One obvious way to move inventory closer to the point of consumption is to offer larger package sizes. The more customers buy at one time, the less likely they are to be out of stock when a usage opportunity arises. This approach can backfire, though, for a perishable product or one that consumers perceive to be an impulse indulgence. Thus many super-premium ice creams, such as Häagen-Dazs, are sold in small pint containers; most consumers want to avoid the temptation of having large quantities of such a high-calorie indulgence too readily available.

The design of a package can also help increase use frequency by making the product more convenient or easy to use. Examples include single-serving packages of Jell-O pudding to pack in lunches, packages of paper cups that include a convenient dispenser, and frozen-food packages that can go directly into a microwave oven.

Various sales promotion programs also help move inventories of a product closer to the point of use by encouraging larger volume purchases. Marketers commonly offer quantity discounts for this purpose in selling industrial goods. For consumer products, multi-item discounts or two-for-one deals serve the same purpose. Promotional programs also encourage greater frequency of use and increase customer loyalty in many service industries. Consider, for instance, the frequent flier programs offered by major airlines.

Sometimes the product's characteristics inhibit customers from using it more frequently. If marketers can change those characteristics, such as difficulty of preparation or high caloric content, a new line extension might encourage customers to use more of the product or to use it more often. Microwave waffles and low-calorie salad dressings are examples of such line extensions. For industrial goods, however, firms may have to develop new technology to overcome a product's limitations for some applications. Thus Johnson Controls is working to develop plastic containers that will not shrivel when filled with hot liquids as a means of expanding its potential market.

Finally, advertising can sometimes effectively increase use frequency by simply reminding customers to use the product more often. For instance, General Foods conducted a reminder campaign for Jell-O pudding that featured Bill Cosby asking, "When was the last time you served pudding, Mom?"

Another approach for extending use among current customers involves finding and promoting new functional uses for the product. Jell-O gelatin is a classic example, having generated substantial new sales volume over the years by promoting the use of Jell-O as an ingredient in salads, pie fillings, and other dishes.

Firms promote new ways to use a product through a variety of methods. For industrial products, firms send technical advisories about new applications to the salesforce to present to their customers during regular sales calls. For consumer products, new use suggestions or recipes may be included on the package or in an advertising campaign. Sales promotions, such as including cents-off coupons in ads featuring a new recipe, encourage customers to try a new application. To reduce costs, two or more manufacturers of complementary products sometimes cooperate in running such promotions. A recent ad promoting a simple Italian dinner, for instance, featured coupons for Kraft's Parmesan cheese, Pillsbury's Soft Bread-sticks, and Campbell's Prego spaghetti sauce.

In some cases slightly modified line extensions might encourage customers to use the product in different ways. Thus Kraft introduced a jalapeño-flavored Cheese-Whiz in a microwavable container and promoted the product as an easy-to-prepare topping for nachos.

Market expansion strategy

In a mature industry with a fragmented and heterogeneous market where some segments are less well developed than others, a market expansion strategy may generate substantial additional volume growth. Such a strategy aims at gaining new customers by targeting new or underdeveloped geographic markets (either regional or foreign) or new customer segments. Once again, share leaders tend to be best suited for implementing this strategy. But even smaller competitors can employ such a strategy successfully if they focus on relatively small or specialized market niches.

Pursuing market expansion by strengthening a firm's position in new or underdeveloped **domestic geographic markets** can lead to experience curve benefits and operating synergies. The firm can rely on largely the same expertise and technology, and perhaps even the same production and distribution facilities, it has already developed. Unfortunately, domestic geographic expansion is often not viable in a mature industry because the share leaders usually have attained national market coverage. Smaller regional competitors, on the other hand, might consider domestic geographic expansion a means for improving their volume and share position. However, such a move risks retaliation from the large national brands as well as from entrenched regional competitors in the prospective new territory.

To get around the retaliation problem, a regional producer might try to expand by acquiring small producers in other regions. This can be a viable option when (1) the low profitability of some regional producers enables the acquiring firm to buy their assets for less than the replacement cost of the capacity involved, and (2) synergies gained by combining regional operations and the infusion of resources from the acquiring firm can improve the effectiveness and profitability of the acquired producers. For example, Heileman Brewing Company grew from the 31st largest brewer of beer in the mid-1960s to the fourth largest by the mid-1980s through the acquisition of nearly 30 regional brands. Heileman took control of strong regional brands such as Old Style, Carling, and Rainier, but because it had no dominant national brand it avoided antitrust opposition to its acquisition program. After acquisition, Heileman maintained the identity of each brand, increased its advertising budget, and expanded its distribution by incorporating it into the firm's distribution system in other regions. As a result, Heileman achieved a strong earnings record for two decades.

In a different approach to domestic market expansion, the firm identifies and develops entirely **new customer** or **application segments**. Sometimes the firm can effectively reach new customer segments by simply expanding the distribution system without changing the product's characteristics or the other marketing mix elements. A sporting goods manufacturer that sells its products to consumers through retail stores, for instance, might expand into the commercial market consisting of schools and amateur and professional sports teams by establishing a direct salesforce. In most instances, though, developing new market segments requires modifying the product to make it more suitable for the application or to provide more of the benefits desired by customers in the new segment.

One final possibility for domestic market expansion is to produce **private-label brands** for large retailers such as Sears or Safeway. Firms whose own brands hold relatively weak positions and who have excess production capacity find this a particularly attractive option. Private labeling allows such firms to gain access to established customer segments without making substantial marketing expenditures, thus increasing the firm's volume and lowering its per unit costs. However, because private labels typically compete with low prices and their sponsors usually have strong bargaining power, producing private labels is often not a very profitable option unless a manufacturer already has a relatively low-cost position in the industry. It can also be a risky strategy, particularly for the smaller firm, because reliance on one or a few large private-label customers can result in drastic volume reductions and unit cost increases should those customers decide to switch suppliers.

Global market expansion—sequential strategies

For firms with leading positions in mature domestic markets, less developed markets in foreign countries often present the most viable opportunities for geographic expansion. As we shall see in the next chapter, firms can enter foreign markets in a variety of ways, from simply relying on import agents to developing joint ventures to establishing wholly owned subsidiaries—as Johnson Controls has done by acquiring an automotive seat manufacturer in Europe.

Regardless of which mode of entry a firm chooses, it can follow a number of different routes when pursuing global expansion.[24] By *route* we mean the sequence or order in which the firm enters global markets. Japanese companies provide illustrations of different global expansion paths. The most common expansion route involves moving from Japan to developing countries to developed countries. They used this path, for example, with automobiles (Toyota), consumer electronics (National), watches (Seiko), cameras (Minolta), and home appliances, steel, and petrochemicals. This routing reduced manufacturing costs and enabled them to gain marketing experience. In penetrating the U. S. market, the Japanese obtained further economies of scale and gained recognition for their products, which made penetration of European markets easier.

This sequential strategy succeeded: By the early 1970s, 60 percent of Japanese exports went to developed countries—more than half to the United States. Japanese motorcycles dominate Europe, as do its watches and cameras. Its cars have been able to gain a respectable share in most European countries.

A second type of *expansion path* has been used primarily for high-tech products such as computers and semiconductors. For the Japanese it consists of first securing their home market and then targeting developed countries. Japan largely ignored developing countries in this strategy because of their small demand for high-tech products. When demand increased to a point where developing countries became "interesting," Japanese producers quickly entered and established strong market positions using price cuts of up to 50 percent.

A home market–developed markets–developing markets sequence is also usually appropriate for discretionary goods such as soft drinks or candy. Note, for instance, the wide differences in consumption of Coca-Cola shown in Exhibit 10–12. As disposable incomes and discretionary expenditures grow in the markets of Asia and Africa, however, those markets will drive much of Coca-Cola's future growth.

---

[24]The following discussion of sequential strategies is based largely on material found in Somkid Jatusripitak, Liam Fahey, and Philip Kotler, "Strategic Global Marketing: Lessons from the Japanese," *Columbia Journal of World Business*, Spring 1985, pp. 47–53.

EXHIBIT 10–12

Global Differences in Coca-Cola Consumption

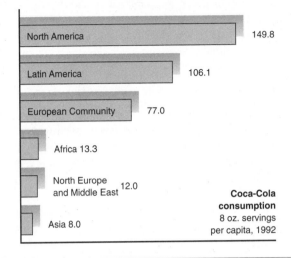

Source: Reprinted with permission from "The New Global Consumer," by Ricardo Sookdeo. *Fortune*. Special issue, Autumn–Winter 1993, p. 69. © 1993 Time Inc. All rights reserved.

STRATEGIES FOR DECLINING MARKETS

Most products eventually enter a decline phase in their life cycles. As sales decline, excess capacity once again develops. As the remaining competitors fight to hold volume in the face of falling sales, industry profits erode. Consequently, conventional wisdom suggests that firms should either divest declining products quickly or harvest them to maximize short-term profits. Not all markets decline in the same way or at the same speed, however; nor do all firms have the same competitive strengths and weaknesses within those markets. Therefore, as in most other situations, the relative attractiveness of the declining product-market and the business's competitive position within it should dictate the appropriate strategy.

Relative attractiveness of declining markets

Although U. S. high school enrollment declined by about 2 million students from its peak in 1976 through the end of the 1980s, Jostens, Inc.—the leading manufacturer of class rings and other school merchandise—achieved annual increases in revenues and profits every year during that period. One reason for the firm's success was that it saw the market decline coming and prepared for it by improving the efficiency of its operations and developing marketing programs that were effective at persuading a larger proportion of students to buy class rings.[25]

---

[25]Jaclyn Fierman, "How to Make Money in Mature Markets," *Fortune*, November 25, 1985, p. 47.

Josten's experience shows that some declining product-markets can offer attractive opportunities well into the future, at least for one or a few strong competitors. In other product-markets, particularly those where decline is the result of customers switching to a new technology (for example, more students buying personal computers instead of portable typewriters), the potential for continued profits during the decline stage is more bleak.

Three sets of factors help determine the strategic attractiveness of declining product-markets: *conditions of demand*, including the rate and certainty of future declines in volume; *exit barriers*, or the ease with which weaker competitors can leave the market; and factors affecting the *intensity of future competitive rivalry* within the market.[26] The impact of these variables on the attractiveness of declining market environments is summarized in Exhibit 10–13 and discussed next.

Conditions of demand

Demand in a product-market declines for a number of reasons. Technological advances produce substitute products (such as electronic calculators for slide rules), often with higher quality or lower cost. Demographic shifts lead to a shrinking target market (for example, baby foods). Customers' needs, tastes, or lifestyles change (consider the falling consumption of beef). Finally, the cost of inputs or complementary products rises and shrinks demand (as can be seen in the effects of rising gasoline prices on sales of recreational vehicles).

The cause of a decline in demand can affect both the rate and the predictability of that decline. A fall in sales due to a demographic shift, for instance, is likely to be gradual, whereas the switch to a technically superior substitute can be abrupt. Similarly, the fall in demand as customers switch to a better substitute is predictable, while a decline in sales due to a change in tastes is not.

As Exhibit 10–13 indicates, both the rate and certainty of sales decline are demand characteristics that affect a market's attractiveness. A slow and gradual decline allows an orderly withdrawal of weaker competitors. Overcapacity does not become excessive and lead to predatory competitive behavior, and the competitors who remain are more likely to make profits than in a quick or erratic decline. Also, when most industry managers believe market decline is predictable and certain, reduction of capacity is more likely to be orderly than when they feel substantial uncertainty about whether demand might level off or even become revitalized.

Of course, not all segments of a market decline at the same time or at the same rate. The number and size of enduring niches or pockets of demand and the customer purchase behavior within them also influence the continuing attractiveness of the market. When the demand pockets are large or numerous and the customers in those niches are brand loyal and relatively insensitive to price, competitors with large shares and differentiated products can continue to make substantial profits. For example, even though the market for cigars has been shrinking for years, there continues to be a sizable number of smokers who prefer premium-

[26]Katherine Rudie Harrigan and Michael E. Porter, "End-Game Strategies for Declining Industries," *Harvard Business Review,* July–August 1983, pp. 111–20. Also see Katherine Rudie Harrigan, *Strategies for Declining Businesses* (Lexington, Mass.: D.C. Heath, 1980).

EXHIBIT 10–13

Factors Affecting the Attractiveness of Declining Markets

	Environmental attractiveness	
	Hospitable	Inhospitable
Conditions of demand		
Speed of decline	Very slow	Rapid or erratic
Certainty of decline	100% certain predictable patterns	Great uncertainty, erratic patterns
Pockets of enduring demand	Several or major ones	No niches
Product differentiation	Brand loyalty	Commonditylike products
Price stability	Stable, price premiums attainable	Very unstable, pricing below costs
Exit barriers		
Reinvestment requirements	None	High, often mandatory and involving capital assets
Excess capacity	Little	Substantial
Asset age	Mostly old assets	Sizable new assets and old ones not retired
Resale markets for assets	Easy to convert or sell	No markets available, substantial costs to retire
Shared facilities	Few freestanding plants	Substantial and interconnected with important businesses
Vertical integration	Little	Substantial
Single-product competitors	None	Several large companies
Rivalry determinants		
Customer industries	Fragmented, weak	Strong bargaining power
Customer switching costs	High	Minimal
Diseconomies of scale	None	Substantial penalty
Dissimilar strategic groups	Few	Several in same target markets

SOURCE: Reprinted by permission of *Harvard Business Review.* An exhibit from "End-Game Strategies for Declining Industries," by Kathryn Rudie Harrigan, July–August 1983. Copyright © 1983 by the President and Fellows of Harvard College; all rights reserved.

quality cigars. Those firms with well-established positions at the premium end of the cigar industry have continued to earn above-average returns.

Exit barriers

The higher the exit barriers, the less hospitable a product-market will be during the decline phase of its life cycle. When weaker competitors find it hard to leave a product-market as demand falls, excess capacity develops and firms engage in aggressive pricing or promotional efforts to try to prop up their volume and hold down unit costs. Thus exit barriers lead to competitive volatility.

Once again, Exhibit 10–13 indicates that a variety of factors influence the ease with which businesses can exit an industry. One critical consideration involves the amount of highly specialized assets. Assets unique to a given business are difficult to divest because of their low liquidation value. The only potential buyers for such assets are other firms who would use them for a similar purpose, which is unlikely in a declining industry. Thus, the firm may have little choice but to remain in the business or to sell the assets for their scrap value. This option is particularly unattractive when the assets are relatively new and not fully depreciated.

Another major exit barrier occurs when the assets or resources of the declining business intertwine with the firm's other business units, either through shared facilities and programs or through vertical integration. Exit from the declining business might shut down shared production facilities, lower salesforce commissions, damage customer relations, and increase unit costs in the firm's other businesses to a point that damages their profitability.

Emotional factors can also act as exit barriers. Managers often feel reluctant to admit failure by divesting a business even though it no longer produces acceptable returns. This is especially true when the business played an important role in the firm's history and it houses a large number of senior managers.

Intensity of future competitive rivalry

Even when substantial pockets of continuing demand remain within a declining business, it may not be wise for a firm to pursue them in the face of future intense competitive rivalry. In addition to exit barriers, other factors also affect the ability of the remaining firms to avoid intense price competition and maintain reasonable margins: size and bargaining power of the customers who continue to buy the product; customers' ability to switch to substitute products or to alternative suppliers; and any potential diseconomies of scale involved in capturing an increased share of the remaining volume.

Divestment or liquidation

When the market environment in a declining industry is unattractive or a business has a relatively weak competitive position, the firm may recover more of its investment by selling the business in the early stages of decline rather than later. The earlier the business is sold, the more uncertain potential buyers are likely to be about the future direction of demand in the industry and thus the more likely that a willing buyer can be found. Thus, Raytheon sold its vacuum-tube business in the early 1960s even though transistors had just begun replacing tubes in radios and TV sets and there was still a strong replacement demand for tubes. By moving early, the firm achieved a much higher liquidation value than companies that tried to unload their tube-making facilities in the 1970s when the industry was clearly in its twilight years.[27]

Of course, the firm that divests early runs the risk that its forecast of the industry's future may be wrong. Also, quick divestment may not be possible if the firm faces high exit barriers, such as interdependencies across business units or customer expectations of continued

---

[27]Harrigan and Porter, "End-Game Strategies," p. 114.

product availability. By planning early for departure, however, the firm may be able to reduce some of those barriers before the liquidation is necessary.

Marketing strategies for remaining competitors

Conventional wisdom suggests that a business remaining in a declining product-market should pursue a harvesting strategy aimed at maximizing its cash flow in the short run. But such businesses also have other strategic options. They might attempt to maintain their position as the market declines, improve their position to become the profitable survivor, or focus efforts on one or more remaining demand pockets or market niches. Once again, the appropriateness of these strategies depends on factors affecting the attractiveness of the declining market and on the business's competitive strengths and weaknesses. Exhibit 10–14 summarizes the situational determinants of the appropriateness of each strategy. Some of the marketing actions a firm might take to implement them are discussed here and listed in Exhibit 10–15.

Harvesting strategy

The objective of a harvesting or milking strategy is to generate cash quickly by maximizing cash flow over a relatively short term. This typically involves avoiding any additional investment in the business, greatly reducing operating (including marketing) expenses, and perhaps raising prices. Since the firm usually expects to ultimately divest or abandon the business, some loss of sales and market share during the pursuit of this strategy is likely. The trick is to hold the business's volume and share declines to a relatively slow and steady rate. A precipitous and premature loss of share would limit the total amount of cash the business could generate during the market's decline.

A harvesting strategy is most appropriate for a firm holding a relatively strong competitive position in the market at the start of the decline and a cadre of current customers likely to continue buying the brand even after marketing support is reduced. Such a strategy also works best when the market's decline is inevitable but likely to occur at a relatively slow and steady rate and when rivalry among remaining competitors is not likely to be very intense. Such conditions help enable the business to maintain adequate price levels and profit margins as volume gradually falls.

Implementing a harvesting strategy means avoiding any additional long-term investments in plants, equipment, or R & D. It also necessitates substantial cuts in operating expenditures for marketing activities. This often means that the firm should greatly reduce the number of models or package sizes in its product line in order to reduce inventory and manufacturing costs.

The business should improve the efficiency of sales and distribution. For instance, an industrial goods manufacturer might service its smaller accounts through telemarketing rather than a field salesforce or assign its smaller customers to agent intermediaries. For consumer goods the business might move to more selective distribution by concentrating its efforts on the larger retail chains.

The firm would likely reduce advertising and promotion expenditures, usually to the minimum level necessary to retain adequate distribution. Finally, the business should attempt to maintain or perhaps even increase its price levels to increase margins.

EXHIBIT 10–14

Situational Determinants of Appropriate Marketing Objectives and Strategies for Declining Markets

Situational variables	Strategies for declining markets			
	Harvesting	Maintenance	Profitable survivor	Niche
Primary objective	Maximize short-term cash flow; maintain or increase margins even at the expense of a slow decline in market share.	Maintain share in short term as market declines, even if margins must be sacrificed.	Increase share of the declining market with an eye to future profits; encourage weaker competitors to exit.	Focus on strengthening position in one or a few relatively substantial segments with potential for future profits.
Market characteristics	Future market decline is certain but likely to occur at a slow and steady rate.	Market has experienced recent declines, but future direction and attractiveness are currently hard to predict.	Future market decline is certain but likely to occur at a slow and steady rate; substantial pockets of demand will continue to exist.	Overall market may decline quickly, but one or more segments will remain as demand pockets or decay slowly.
Competitor characteristics	Few strong competitors, low exit barriers; future rivalry not likely to be intense.	Few strong competitors, but intensity of future rivalry is hard to predict.	Few strong competitors; exit barriers are low or can be reduced by firm's intervention.	One or more stronger competitors in mass market, but not in the target segment.
Firm's characteristics	Has a leading share position; has a substantial proportion of loyal customers who are likely to continue buying brand even if marketing support is reduced.	Has a leading share of the market and a relatively strong competitive position.	Has a leading share of the market and a strong competitive position; has superior resources or competencies necessary to encourage competitors to exit or to acquire them.	Has a sustainable competitive advantage in target segment, but overall resources may be limited.

Maintenance strategy

In markets where future volume trends are highly uncertain, a business with a leading share position might consider pursuing a strategy aimed at maintaining its market share, at least until the market's future becomes more predictable. In such a maintenance strategy the business continues to pursue the same strategy that brought it success during the market's mature stage. This approach often results in reduced margins and profits in the short term, though, because firms usually must reduce prices or increase marketing expenditures to hold share in the face of declining industry volume. Thus a firm should consider share maintenance an interim strategy. Once it becomes clear that the market will continue to decline, the business should switch to a different strategy that will provide better cash flows and return on investment over the market's remaining life.

EXHIBIT 10–15

Possible Marketing Actions Appropriate for Different Strategies in Declining Markets

Marketing strategy and objectives	Possible marketing actions

Harvesting strategy
Maximize short-term cash flow: maintain or increase margins even at the expense of market share decline.
	• Eliminate R & D expenditures and capital investments related to the business.
	• Reduce marketing and sales budgets.
	    Greatly reduce or eliminate advertising and sales promotion expenditures, with the possible exception of periodic reminder advertising targeted at current customers.
	    Reduce trade promotions to minimum level necessary to prevent rapid loss of distribution coverage.
	    Focus salesforce efforts on attaining repeat purchases from current customers.
	• Seek ways to reduce production costs, even at the expense of slow erosion in product quality.
	• Raise price if necessary to maintain margins.

Maintenance strategy Maintain market share for the short term, even at the expense of margins.	• Continue product and process R & D expenditures in short term aimed at maintaining or improving product quality. • Continue maintenance levels of advertising and sales promotion targeted at current users. • Continue trade promotion at levels sufficient to avoid any reduction in distribution coverage. • Focus salesforce efforts on attaining repeat purchases from current users. • Lower prices if necessary to maintain share, even at the expense of reduced margins.
Profitable survivor strategy Increase share of the declining market; encourage weaker competitors to exit.	• Signal competitors that firm intends to remain in industry and pursue an increased share.

Profitable survivor strategy

An aggressive alternative for a business with a strong share position and a sustainable competitive advantage in a declining product-market is to invest enough to increase its share position and establish itself as the industry leader for the remainder of the market's decline. This kind of strategy makes the most sense when the firm expects a gradual decline in market demand or when substantial pockets of continuing demand are likely well into the future. It is also an attractive strategy when a firm's declining business is closely intertwined with other SBUs through shared facilities and programs or common customer segments.

A strong competitor can often improve its share position in a declining market at relatively low cost because other competitors may be harvesting their businesses or preparing to exit.

EXHIBIT 10–15 *(concluded)*

Marketing strategy and objectives	Possible marketing actions
	Maintain or increase advertising and sales promotion budgets.
	Maintain or increase distribution coverage through aggressive trade promotion.
	Focus some salesforce effort on winning away competitors' customers.
	Continue product and process R & D to seek product improvements or cost reductions.
	• Consider introducing line extensions to appeal to remaining demand segments.
	• Lower prices if necessary to increase share, even at the expense of short-term margins.
	• Consider agreements to produce replacement parts or private labels for smaller competitors considering getting out of production.
Niche strategy Strengthen share position in one or a few segments with potential for continued profit.	• Continue product and process R & D aimed at product improvements or modifications that will appeal to target segment(s).
	• Consider producing for private labels in order to maintain volume and hold down unit costs.
	• Focus advertising, sales promotion, and personal selling campaigns on customers in target segment(s); stress appeals of greatest importance to those customers.
	• Maintain distribution channels appropriate for reaching target segment; seek unique channel arrangements to more effectively reach customers in target segment(s).
	• Design service programs that address unique concerns/problems of customers in the target segment(s).

The key to the success of such a strategy is to encourage other competitors to leave the market early. Once the firm has achieved a strong and unchallenged position, it can switch to a harvesting strategy and reap substantial profits over the remaining life of the product-market.

A firm might encourage smaller competitors to abandon the industry by being visible and explicit about its commitment to become the leading survivor. It should aggressively seek increased market share, either by cutting prices or by increasing advertising and promotion expenditures. It might also introduce line extensions aimed at remaining pockets of demand to make it more difficult for smaller competitors to find profitable niches. Finally, the firm might act to reduce its competitors' exit barriers, making it easier for them to leave the industry. This could involve taking over competitors' long-term contracts, agreeing to supply spare parts, service their products in the field, or provide them with components or private-label products. For instance, large regional bakeries have encouraged grocery chains to abandon their own bakery operations by supplying them with private-label baked goods.

The ultimate way to remove competitors' exit barriers is to purchase their operations and either improve their efficiency or remove them from the industry to avoid excess capacity. With continued decline in industry sales a certainty, smaller competitors may be forced to sell their assets at a book value price low enough for the survivor to reap high returns on its investment, as Heileman Brewing Company did on its acquisitions of smaller regional brewers during the 1970s and 80s.

Niche strategy

Even when most segments of an industry are expected to decline rapidly, a niche strategy may still be viable if one or more substantial segments will either remain as stable pockets of demand or decay slowly. The business pursuing such a strategy should have a strong competitive position in the target segment or be able to build a sustainable competitive advantage relatively quickly to preempt competitors. This is one strategy that even smaller competitors can sometimes successfully pursue because they can focus the required assets and resources on a limited portion of the total market. The marketing actions a business might take to strengthen and preserve its position in a target niche are similar to those discussed earlier concerning niche strategies in mature markets.

SUMMARY

An industry's transition from growth to maturity begins when approximately half the potential customers have adopted the product and, while sales are still growing, the rate of growth begins to decline. As growth slows, some competitors are likely to find themselves with excess production capacity. Other changes in the competitive environment, including a reduction in the degree of differentiation across brands and increased difficulty in maintaining adequate distribution, occur at about the same time. As a result, competition becomes more intense with firms either cutting prices or increasing their marketing expenditures as they battle to increase volume, cover high fixed costs, and maintain profitability. This transition is usually accompanied by a shakeout as weaker competitors fail or leave the industry.

Success during the maturity stage of a product-market's life cycle requires two sets of strategic actions. First, managers should work to maintain and strengthen either the differentiation of the firm's offerings on quality and/or service dimensions or its position as a low-cost competitor within the industry. The second strategic consideration during the maturity stage is to develop meaningful marketing objectives and a marketing strategy appropriate for achieving them. Since maturity can last for many years, the most critical marketing objective is to maintain and protect the business's market share. For share leaders, some variation of the fortress defense, confrontation, or flanker strategies are often appropriate for achieving that objective. Smaller competitors, on the other hand, may have to rely on a niche strategy to hold their position.

Since different market segments may mature at different times and environmental conditions can change over the mature phase of a product's life, firms often find opportunities to extend the growth of seemingly mature product-markets. Thus an important secondary objective for firms in many mature markets is to stimulate additional volume growth. Among the marketing strategies firms might use to accomplish that objective are an increased penetration strategy, an extended use strategy, or a market expansion strategy focused on developing either new geographic territories (including global markets) or new application segments.

Conventional wisdom suggests that declining products should be either divested or harvested to maximize short-term profits. However, some declining product-markets remain attractive enough to justify more aggressive marketing strategies. The attractiveness of such markets is determined by three sets of factors: (1) conditions of demand, including the rate and certainty of future declines in volume; (2) exit barriers, or the ease with which weaker competitors can leave the market; and (3) factors affecting the intensity of future competitive rivalry. When a declining product-market is judged to offer continuing opportunities for profitable sales, managers might consider one of several strategic alternatives to divestment or harvesting. Those alternative strategies include a maintenance strategy, a profitable survivor strategy, and a niche strategy.

International Marketing Strategy

TAKING ADVANTAGE OF THE GLOBAL MARKETPLACE

Since 1986 U. S. exports have grown at an average annual rate of 9 percent (adjusted for inflation)—roughly four times as fast as Gross Domestic Product (GDP). In 1994 exports were estimated at $700 billion, or 10 percent of GDP, with much of this increase coming from U.S. exports to the developing countries where 77 percent of the world's population lives. More and more companies are recognizing that the developed countries, with their mature markets, have considerably less growth potential than the developing countries, which are expanding at 5 to 6 percent annually versus much lower rates elsewhere.[1]

General Electric is targeting China, India, Mexico, and Southeast Asia for its future growth and profits because it is convinced that prospects for strong growth in the U. S., Europe, and Japan are mar-

ginal. By the year 2000 sales to the developing countries could realistically account for more than 25 percent of GE's total sales. Overall, the company's overseas revenues represent 40 percent of total sales—up from 29 percent five years ago.[2]

Citicorp has experienced substantial growth in its consumer accounts and deposits in its Asia–Pacific region (16 nations not including Japan). In the last 10 years its number of accounts has increased from 600,000 to 3.7 million while deposits have grown from $2 billion to $12.5 billion. Earnings have increased at an annual rate of 40 percent with Hong Kong accounting for about 25 percent of the net income.[3]

But U. S. export success is not limited to the developing countries. Only a few years ago Whirlpool turned to overseas markets to generate increased sales and

[1]Rob Norton, "Strategies for the New Export Boom," *Fortune*, August 22, 1994, p. 124; and Bill Saporito, "Where the Global Action Is," *Fortune,*, Autumn–Winter 1993, p. 63.

[2]Tim Smart, Pete Engardio, and Geri Smith, "GE's Brave New World," *Business Week*, November 8, 1993, p. 64.

[3]Rahul Jacobs, "Capturing the Global Consumer," *Fortune*, November 13, 1993, p. 166.

profits. It did so by buying N. V. Philip's floundering European appliance division for $1 billion and then combining this firm with the U. S. company to form a single consumer-oriented organization with manufacturing facilities in 11 countries and sales offices in 120 locations. The results, measured in terms of sharehold value, show the company performing nearly twice as well as members of its peer group.[4] In another example, not too long ago McDonald's seemed destined to become a cash cow in a mature industry. But such has not been the case: Profits have tripled to over $1 billion over the past 10 years on revenues of $7.4 billion and systemwide sales of $23 billion. The gains have come largely from the company's overseas operations, consisting of nearly 5,000 outlets with annual sales of $3.34 billion. These units are also contributing innovative operating ideas, such as a prefab franchise unit that can be moved over a weekend (Dutch), an enhanced meat freezer (Sweden), and low-overhead satellite stores (Singapore).[5]

In addition to large companies, many small and medium-size companies are find-ing overseas markets an important source of growth and profits. For example, Petrofsky's, a St. Louis maker of frozen bagel dough, recently sold its domestic business to Quaker Oats to concentrate on foreign sales. The firm made this decision largely because of its success in Japan, where, based on marketing research, it reformulated its product (a bigger and softer bagel offered in a variety of flavors including cinnamon raisin). It also learned that selecting the right partner to help in entering a new market is critically important.[6]

What successful export companies have in common is a willingness to customize their products and services to meet local needs, no matter what the obstacles. In commenting on this subject, the CEO of Whirlpool sums up the subject well by noting that the only way to attain a company's objectives in the long term "is by focusing on the customer. Only prolonged intensive effort to understand and respond to genuine customer needs can lead to breakthrough products and services that earn long-term customer loyalty."[7]

As the previous discussion illustrates, the internationalization of competition has become one of the most important challenges facing many businesses today. Since the late 1970s, international trade has grown at an annual rate of nearly 7 percent and is expected to sustain an even higher rate during the remainder of the 1990s. This figure does not include the output of an increasing number of firms who produce their goods overseas

---

[4]Regina Fazio Maruca, "The Right Way to Go Global: An Interview with Whirlpool CEO David Whitwam," *Harvard Business Review*, March–April 1994, p. 135.

[5]Andrew E. Sarver, "McDonald's Conquers the World," *Fortune*, October 17, 1994, p. 103.

[6]Norton, "Strategies for the New Export Boom."

[7]Maruca, "The Right Way to Go Global," p. 137.

EXHIBIT 11-1

Growth in the Number of Transnational Corporations

For years large firms around the world talked about being "multinational," which led, for many, to a "globalization" strategy and discussion about the need to be a "borderless corporation." That many took these concepts seriously is demonstrated by the fact that there are some 37,000 transnational companies in the world, which account for about a third of all private sector assets and enjoy worldwide sales of $5.5 trillion (a bit less than America's annual GDP). Revenues from manufacturing by U. S. firms abroad are now twice their export earnings.

The strength of multinational firms emphasizes two modern business concepts. First, innovation is critical to success; and relying solely on a single culture (that of the home country) is dysfunctional. Second, technology makes the world smaller and more manageable. These developments have wide-ranging implications for corporate management, especially in terms of organizational systems and structures.

SOURCE: "The Discreet Charm of the Multicultural Multinational," *The Economist*, July 30, 1994, p. 57.

instead of exporting from their home country. Recent negotiations (the Uruguay round of GATT) resulted in the most sweeping tariff cuts in history. The agreement mandated $744 billion in tariff cuts that are estimated as potentially saving $500 billion a year by 2005.[8]

This dramatic change and the array of new international competitors have caused a basic change in the nature and scope of global competition. Exhibit 11–1 discusses the growth in the number of transnational corporations.

International trade has become increasingly important to American business; in 1993 the 100 largest U. S.-based multinationals had foreign sales of over $700 billion despite weakness in the major foreign markets (Japan, Europe, and Canada). A substantial number of America's leading companies had more than half their sales overseas—for example, Exxon (77.3 percent), IBM (59 percent), CitiCorp (64.5 percent), DuPont (51.4 percent), Procter & Gamble (52.1 percent), Coca-Cola (67 percent), Colgate-Palmolive (64.5 percent), and Gillette (67.5 percent). Growth areas included firms selling computers, communications equipment, consumer branded goods, and financial services.[9]

A major question facing large segments of American business—including many smaller firms—is, What is the best way to compete in this new world order? While the process involved is similar to that used for marketing domestic products, there are some important differences in the way the various steps in the process are made operational. These differences are discussed throughout this chapter. Exhibit 11–2 presents the issues firms need to address in developing and implementing an international strategy. This chapter is organized around a discussion of these issues.

---

[8]"Dancing around GATT," *The Economist*, November 26, 1994, p. 25.

[9]Brian Zajac, "Getting the Welcome Carpet," *Forbes*, July 18, 1994, p. 276.

EXHIBIT 11-2

Issues to Be Addressed in Developing and Implementing an International Marketing Strategy

- **International business environment — physical, legal, economic, political, cultural, and competitive**

  Issues: What is the relative attractiveness of each country? What opportunities are present? What threats exist? What are the major differences between each overseas market and the home market?

- **International marketing objectives — other than profitability**

  Issues: What does a company hope to achieve by going overseas other than increase its profitability? How important is it to protect *market leadership*? To benefit from *scale economies*? To *service* customers who have moved overseas?

- **Selecting export target markets**

  Issues: What candidate product(s) should be selected? What countries are most attractive and where does the firm have strong relative business advantages? Which countries should be targeted and in what order?

- **Alternative overall strategies**

  Issues: What are the characteristics of a global high-share strategy? A global niche strategy? A national high-share strategy? A national niche strategy? Under what conditions would each of these strategies be used?

- **Market entry strategies**

  Issues: What are the major ways by which a firm can enter a foreign country? Within each of these ways, what are the specific entry modes and under what set of conditions should each be used?

- **International marketing mix**

  Issues: To what extent can a firm standardize its marketing plan across countries? Under what conditions should it market the same product to all countries? How much should the other elements in the marketing mix be localized?

- **Exporting services**

  Issues: What kinds of services has the United States exported? What has happened to the value of these exports?

THE INTERNATIONAL BUSINESS ENVIRONMENT

Strong environmental differences between countries present international firms an array of opportunities and threats. To select and prioritize their target markets firms must analyze these different environments. An obvious factor is a country's **physical environment,** including its geographical location. Special conditions (extreme temperatures, high humidity) can affect the design of products as well as alter their demand. For example, concern over water pollution in certain countries has triggered a substantial increase in the sale of bottled water. In the United States, annual sales of bottled water have reached billions of dollars.

Countries differ in their demand for particular products and services not only because of their physical environments but also because of the political, legal, demographic, economic, cultural, competitive, and infrastructure environments. Each of these environmental dimensions is discussed briefly here.

- *Political/legal environment.* The main element in this component of the macro-environment is legislation, which defines the regulatory environment within which both local and foreign firms must operate. New regulations or deregulations may open or close markets, change their revenue potential, or destabilize industries. Countries have long enacted certain regulations to protect local industries, provide income, and inhibit the flow of foreign exchange. These include a variety of legal and quasilegal barriers such as tariffs, quotas, customs and administrative entry procedures, requirements and restrictions on the quality, packaging, and labeling of goods entering a country, procurement policies, export subsidies, local content laws, import restrictions, taxes, and price controls.

- *Demographic/economic environment.* Population and the general level of economic well-being are the demand drivers in a given country. But size is only one important measure; others include characteristics of people such as age and geographical groups (urban versus rural population, for example). These measures need to be analyzed for their basic trends.

Because of the importance of the economic environment, marketers must consider such measures as per capita income and GNP (gross national product), a country's real economic growth (GNP less inflation), exchange rates, and the distribution of income by age and geographical groups. Further, in order to realistically compare incomes between countries, it is necessary to adjust what a given sum of money will buy in each. Because many developing countries heavily subsidize a household's basic needs (such as those relating to food, shelter, and medical care), many low-income families are potential markets for TVs, major appliances, and the like. For example, in Mexico City homes with color TVs outnumber those with running water, while in Warsaw (average annual income $2,500) Christian Dior perfume, Valentino shoes, and French cheeses are sold in large quantities.[10]

- *Cultural environment.* This represents the values, beliefs, and norms (the general behavior) of individuals in a given society. Culture strongly affects not only the demand for a given product but also the way firms market their goods. This is particularly true with respect to how a product is positioned, the product's package design, and how a product is advertised.

- *Competitive and infrastructure environment.* Knowledge about the competitive environment (the structure of the relevant industry and the strengths and weaknesses of potential close rivals) of a particular country is important because substantial differences typically exist between countries. Companies must tailor their marketing programs to accommodate these different competitive conditions. For example, Nestlé was able to obtain a 60 percent market share for instant coffee in Japan, in good part because of weak domestic competition. This is in sharp contrast to the

---

[10]Bill Saporito, "Where the Global Action Is," *Fortune*, Autumn–Winter 1993, p. 62.

United States where Nestlé has two strong competitors (General Foods and P & G) and holds less than a 30 percent share.

Differences in the infrastructure environment of target countries may, to some extent, force companies to individualize marketing programs. Particularly important here are the local transport system, media (to be discussed later in this chapter), and channels of distribution. There are considerable differences among countries in the availability of certain channel intermediaries and the functions performed, how well they are performed, and at what cost. As a result, many companies use vastly different channels abroad than at home; for example, P & G uses mass merchandising in the United States and Europe but sells door-to-door in many developing countries.

INTERNATIONAL MARKETING OBJECTIVES

A company's profitability objectives for its foreign trade are essentially the same as for its domestic market. They include return on investment, return on assets managed, marginal contribution, cash flow, and market share. These economic objectives are typically specified for each foreign country and vary from country to country depending on the local environment, including the strength of local competitors.

Some companies have no alternative but to seek a strong international presence if they are to protect their leadership position at home from competitors who can attack by reducing prices, the cost of which is subsidized by profits generated elsewhere in the world. The domestic player can respond only by cutting price on its entire volume.[11]

Economic reasons

Companies also seek foreign sales to benefit from scale economies. This is particularly the case when such economies depend on volumes greater than those provided by the home market (for example, production of jet airliners). Indeed, a firm may have no alternative if it is to remain cost competitive and retain its position within its industry.

Other economic reasons may also prompt a company to export. One is a comparative advantage in factor cost or quality tied to the production of a given product. Thus the firm's location in countries possessing such advantages is critical to its world position. For example, the relatively low cost of quality labor in South Korea, Singapore, and Taiwan has given these countries an economic advantage over the United States in the production of certain goods (shipbuilding, textiles, consumer electronics, and certain automobile models). Other sources of global competitive advantage include logistical economies of scale (Japan's use of specialized

[11]Hirotaka Takeuchi and Michael E. Porter, "Three Roles of International Marketing in Global Strategy," in Michael E. Porter (ed.), *Competition in Global Industries* (Boston: Harvard Business School Press, 1986), p. 114; Gary Hamel and C. K. Prahalad, "Do You Really Have a Global Strategy?" *Harvard Business Review*, July–August 1985, pp. 139–48; also see Craig M. Watson, "Countercompetition Abroad to Protect Home Markets," *Harvard Business Review*, January–February 1982, p. 40.

oceangoing bulk carriers to transport raw materials) and R & D (pharmaceuticals, jet engines, and computers).[12]

Other reasons

Another reason firms go overseas is to service their customers who do so. Firms also go abroad to earn foreign exchange (they may be subsidized to do so), counter demographic trends in the home market, utilize excess facilities, and dispose of surplus products.

SELECTING TARGET MARKETS

Selection of overseas target markets follow essentially the same procedure as for domestic markets, discussed in Chapter 6. As would be expected, targeting overseas markets is more difficult because of a lack of readily available data, including that pertaining to political risk. The traditional approach to global market segmentation has viewed a country as a single segment, but increasingly firms are attempting to determine the existence of homogeneous groups (segments) of consumers (based on needs and wants) *across* countries.[13] Teenagers provide an example of such a segment because regardless of their nationality they have similar tastes and attitudes and "buy a common gallery of products—Reebok sport shoes, Proctor & Gamble Cover Girl make-up, Sega and Nintendo videogames, and PepsiCo's new Pepsi Max."[14]

The *market attractiveness/business position matrix* discussed in Chapter 6 provides a useful analytical framework for prioritizing potential target overseas markets. Management needs to identify factors to use in measuring the relative attractiveness of a given market as well as the firm's competitive position in that market. These ratings are also useful in helping to position the product in each of the markets selected as targets.

Despite the optimism concerning the opportunities provided by international trade, there is still plenty of risk involved that needs to be taken into account in the targeting process. Examples abound including North Korea, Russia's war in Chechnya, the Civil War in the former Yugoslavia, Iraq, Iran, and parts of Africa. Mexico's recent dramatic devaluation of its peso was caused by forces (social unrest, an uncertain economic policy, and large trade deficits) that "are present, to varying degrees, in Russia, Hungary, Poland, and Turkey, as well as China, Malaysia, and other fast-growing Southeast Asian economies."[15]

---

[12]Michael E. Porter, *Competitive Strategy* (New York: Free Press, 1980), ch. 13.

[13]Increasingly firms are targeting regions within countries—such as the West Coast of the United States. See Keniche Ohmae, "New World Order: The Rise of the Region-State," *The Wall Street Journal*, August 16, 1994, p. A10.

[14]Sharon Tully, "Teens—The Most Global Market of All," *Fortune*, May 16, 1994, p. 90.

[15]Michael R. Sesit, "Mexico's Economic Troubles a Reminder of Risks in Emerging Market Investments," *The Wall Street Journal*, December 28, 1994, p. C1.

GLOBAL VERSUS NATIONAL MARKETING STRATEGIES

Firms can use two kinds of marketing strategies to compete in the international arena—global and national. Global strategy is concerned with opportunities and threats on a world basis. Hence a firm adopting a global strategy must develop a set of competitive strengths that will enable it to compete successfully against other international firms. These strengths include (1) scale effects that reduce unit costs below those of national firms and are competitive with other international firms; (2) the ability to transfer ideas, experience, and know-how from one country to another; (3) global recognition of brand names and reputation for quality that makes it easier to introduce new products; (4) the ability to shift resources across countries to reduce risks; and (5) access to such place economies as low-cost labor and raw materials.

National strategies, in contrast, are based on a more localized presence—that is, on the firm's operations in a defined national environment. The firm's success lies in its national performance or its market share. National strategies are not undertaken solely by local companies because multinationals may permit their subsidiaries considerable freedom in formulating such a strategy. In other situations, a company's strategy may center primarily on the home market while viewing overseas operations as secondary.

Global market strategies

The success of a global strategy depends heavily on the extent to which the product—and to a lesser degree the marketing program—can be standardized across countries; this has brought about the use of the term **standardized strategy**.[16] Many see global strategy as the trend of the future because of the growing homogenization of needs across countries, which leads to substantial economies of scale, which, in turn, lead to lower prices.

The growing convergence of consumer needs and preferences is attributed to the influences of mass communications, especially TV. Regardless of their nationality, consumers in western Europe, Japan, and the United States increasingly are receiving the same kinds of information, want the same kinds of products, and desire the same lifestyles.[17]

The nature of the product or the extent to which it can be standardized is a primary factor in a firm's decision to adopt a global strategy. As would be expected, industrial goods lend themselves more to a global strategy than do consumer goods. This is especially the case with heavy machinery and such high-tech products as computers, airplanes, medical electronic equipment, and robotics. Durable consumer goods (such as TVs, VCRs, cameras, and automobiles) offer a better opportunity for standardization than do nondurables, which are more apt to be affected by the local culture. Food, clothing, and personal care items have

---

[16]Levitt and Ohmae are two of the more articulate advocates for such a strategy. See Theodore Levitt, "The Globalization of Marketing," *Harvard Business Review*, May–June 1983, p. 92; and Kenichi Ohmae, "The Global Logic of International Alliances," *Harvard Business Review*, March–April 1989, p. 143.

[17]Much the same can be said of the less developed countries with regard to certain segments—for example, teenagers and the more affluent upper classes.

traditionally not been considered good candidates for a standardization strategy. But even here, growing evidence shows that tastes are becoming more common across countries, as can be seen in the increasing popularity of coffee in Japan, frozen dinners in Europe, and expensive athletic footwear (Nike and Reebok) in most countries.

Leontiades notes that there are two types of global strategy: those involving high market share and those concerned with global niche.[18] Such firms as Sony, Honda, Ford, IBM, Electrolux, and SKF pursue a high-share strategy characterized by

- A drive for a strong international market share position.
- Products with a high degree of international standardization.
- A marketing program—especially with respect to price, product line, and advertising—geared to the mass market.
- Large expenditures on design and R & D relative to the industry norm.
- The use of regional production facilities or a rationalized global production network designed to reduce logistics costs.

These characteristics, both individually and collectively, make it difficult for firms using a national strategy to compete in the same industry. For example, the U. S. TV industry has been decimated by Japanese firms that have adopted a high-share global strategy. Because of the enormous resources required to implement a high-share global strategy, many firms opt for some kind of specialization, focusing on a global niche. Such strategies can take many forms including specialization by technology (genetic engineering), product (low-cost motorcars), market segment (designer apparel), and stage of production (components versus final assembly).

Global niche strategies are characterized by a product line that is relatively insensitive to price competition, avoids direct competition with global high-share competitors, uses alliances to reduce research costs and enter new markets, has a narrow product-market scope, and takes advantage of possible linkages with products offered by large competitors (for example, the sale of Jaguar cars by distributors selling such competitive makes as Cadillac and Mercedes-Benz).

Localization strategy

Localization strategy is based on the premise that products and programs must be adapted to the needs and wants of the consumers of individual countries because of environmental differences, especially cultural ones. Critics of global standardization strategy argue that because most marketing activities are situation-specific, marketing programs (even those involving standardized products), especially price and advertising, cannot be standardized. For example, Procter & Gamble adjusts both its products and marketing programs to country-specific markets whenever it is expedient to do so.

---

[18]James C. Leontiades, *Multinational Corporate Strategy* (Lexington, Mass.: D. C. Heath, 1985), ch. 5.

Localization often occurs because of **mandatory adaptation** (that is, the foreign market requires it). Examples include the use of the metric system (still not used in the United States), different electrical system voltages, and product regulations designed to protect the consumer (red dye and sweeteners in food, bumper strength) and the environment (automobile emission standards).[19] Mandatory adaptation is often difficult to cope with—especially when product specifications vary substantially across countries, as Ford found out in building Mondeo, its world car.

Some market conditions are not mandatory but need to be taken seriously. For example, the Japanese differ from their U. S. and European counterparts in their physical proportions. Because they have shorter limbs and relatively longer bodies, their hands and feet are narrower and shorter than those of Americans and Europeans. Thus, for example, electric shavers need to be designed to fit the size of Japanese hands and golf clubs need to have thinner grips and less weight. Industrial equipment such as tools and safety clothes are also affected.[20] **Discretionary product adaptations** occur primarily because of differences across countries relating to income, tastes, and level of educational and technical sophistication. For example, Singer sewing machines sold in Africa are simple and hand-powered, and Johnson & Johnson reformulated its baby lotion for Japan to make it white and less scented than its U. S. product because of Japanese sensitivity to certain colors and fragrances.[21]

National high-share versus national niche strategies

Companies adopting a national high-share strategy must achieve high volume and low relative costs to be successful. Even so, the firm remains vulnerable to companies following a similar strategy at the global level. To protect themselves, national companies must, whenever possible

- Exploit and do everything possible to maintain existing legal trade barriers, especially tariffs and quotas.
- Enhance their ability to respond to consumer preferences, especially regarding certain product features.
- Lobby aggressively for government purchasing arrangements that give preference to national companies.
- Provide a fast response to changes in local conditions, especially in the form of new or modified products.

National niche strategies are the same as global niche strategies except they apply at the national or local level. They seek to take advantage of some form of specialization in a narrow

---

[19] Vern Tepstra, *International Dimensions of Marketing* (Boston: PWS-Kent, 1988), pp. 85–90.

[20] Robert M. March, *The Honourable Consumer* (London: Pitman, 1990), pp. 36–37; and Michael R. Czinkota and Jon Waronoff, *Unlocking Japan's Markets* (Chicago: Probus, 1991), p. 174.

[21] *Ibid.*

market segment to defend against both national and global competitors. Typically, the target market is too small to be of interest to the global competitor and perhaps even to large national companies.

Using both global and national strategies

Many companies combine global and national strategies. Some firms use a global strategy in parts of the world while pursuing a national strategy elsewhere because some countries and some products are more receptive to global strategies than others. Global strategies are directed at

> those national product-markets that are large and have low barriers to foreign products and companies. They are also likely to comprise the center of world demand, particularly in the newer, more technologically intensive products. For example, Japan, the United States, and the member countries of the European community account for over 75 percent of total world demand for integrated circuits. Securing a position as a global competitor will require active participation in one, and very likely more than one, of these national markets.[22]

Companies adopting global strategies are not likely to target seriously countries with high barriers and small national product-markets. However, given the long-term trend in declining trade barriers coupled with economic growth, more companies will likely adopt global strategies.

Much the same reasoning for the use of a mix of global and national strategies applies to adopting a standardized or a localized marketing program. It does not have to be an either/or proposition—there can be degrees of standardization just as there can be degrees of localization. What is important is management's global orientation, which reflects itself in

> a marketing plan that strives for standardization whenever it is cost and culturally effective. This might mean a company's global marketing plan has standardized product but country-specific advertising or a standardized theme in all countries with country or cultural-specific appeals. In other words, where feasible in the marketing mix, efficiencies of standardization are sought. Whenever cultural uniqueness dictates the need for adaptation of the product, its image, and so on, it is accommodated.[23]

In the final analysis, if a firm's upper-level managers are not strongly oriented toward doing business on a global basis, a nationalized strategy is most apt to emerge. This is particularly the case when the headquarters/subsidiary relationship is loosely defined. The more a firm delegates decision making, the less likely it will adopt a global strategy. Such delegation is most apt to occur with decisions pertaining to price, advertising, and channels of distribution.

---

[22]Leontiades, *Multinational Corporate Strategy*, p. 57.

[23]Philip R. Cateora, *International Marketing* (Burr Ridge, Ill.: Irwin, 1990). ch. 4.

EXHIBIT 11–3
Classification of Major Entry Modes

Export entry modes
  Direct
  Indirect
Contractual entry modes
  Licensing   Coproduction
  Franchising   Counter trade
  Contract manufacturing   Buyback arrangement
  Turnkey construction contract
Investment entry modes
  Joint ventures
  Sole ownership

SOURCE: Adapted from Franklin R. Root, *Entry Strategies for International Markets* (Lexington, Mass.: D. C. Heath, 1987), p. 6.

MARKET ENTRY STRATEGIES

There are three major ways of entering a foreign country: via export, by transferring technology and the skills needed to produce and market the goods to an organization in a foreign country through a contractual agreement, and through direct investment (see Exhibit 11–3).[24]

Exporting is the simplest way to enter a foreign market because it involves the least commitment and risk. It can be direct or indirect. The former uses foreign-based distributors/agents or operating units (branches or subsidiaries set up in the foreign country). Indirect exporting relies on the expertise of domestic international intermediaries: **export merchants,** who buy the product and sell it overseas for their own account; **export agents,** who sell on a commission basis; and **cooperative organizations,** which export for several producers, especially those selling farm products.

Contractual entry modes are nonequity arrangements that involve the transfer of technology and/or skills to an entity in a foreign country. In **licensing** a firm offers the right to use its intangible assets (technology, know-how, patents, company name, trademarks) in exchange for royalties or some other form of payment. Licensing is less flexible and provides less control than exporting. Further, if the contract is terminated, the licensor may have developed a competitor. It is an appropriate strategy, however, when the market is unstable or difficult to penetrate.

Franchising grants the rights to use the company's name, trademarks, and technology. It is an especially attractive way to penetrate foreign markets at low cost and to exploit local

---

[24]This section has benefited from Franklin Root, *Entry Strategies for International Markets* (Lexington, Mass.: D. C. Heath, 1987), chs. 1–3 and 5.

knowledge and entrepreneurial spirit. Host countries are typically receptive to this type of entry because it involves local ownership. American companies have largely pioneered franchising—especially such fast-food companies as McDonald's, Pizza Hut, Burger King, and Kentucky Fried Chicken. In recent years foreign franchisors have entered the U. S.—largely from Canada, England, and Japan—in a variety of fields including food, shoe repair, leather furniture, and wall cleaning.[25]

Other contractual entry modes include **contract manufacturing,** which involves sourcing a product from a manufacturer located in a foreign country for sale there or elsewhere (auto parts, clothes, furniture). Contract manufacturing is most attractive when the local market is too small to warrant an investment, export is blocked, and a quality licensee is not available. A **turnkey construction contract** requires the contractor to have the project up and operating before releasing it to the owner. **Coproduction** involves a company's providing technical know-how and components in return for a share of the output, which it must sell. **Countertrade** transactions include barter (direct exchange of goods), compensation packages (cash and local goods), counterpurchase (delayed sale of bartered goods to enable the local buyer to sell the goods), and a **buyback arrangement** in which the products being sold are used to produce other goods.

Overseas direct investment can be implemented in two ways: by **joint venture** or **sole ownership.** The former involves a joint ownership arrangement to produce and/or market goods in a foreign country. Today such entry modes are commonplace because they avoid quotas and import taxes and satisfy government demands to produce locally. They also have the advantage of sharing investment costs and gaining local marketing expertise. For example, Motorola had difficulty penetrating the Japanese market until it formed an alliance with Toshiba to set up a joint chip-making venture. In addition, Motorola received considerable marketing help.[26]

A sole ownership investment entry strategy involves setting up or acquiring product facilities in a foreign country. Such an approach usually allows the parent organization to retain total control of the overseas operation and is particularly appropriate when the politics of the situation require a dedicated facility. Firms using this strategy extensively include General Motors, Procter & Gamble, General Foods, Hewlett-Packard, and General Electric. Despite the high risks associated with direct investment, its use is accelerating because companies have concluded that capturing and retaining customers demands a rapid, flexible response to the dynamics of the environment.

INTERNATIONAL MARKETING MIX

Here again the major question is, To what extent can firms standardize the elements of the marketing plan? Standardization is greatest for product features, packaging, and branding because of the substantial savings in manufacturing and marketing costs. Firms also use

---

[25]Jerry A. Tannenbaum, "Foreign Franchisers Entering U. S. in Greater Numbers," *The Wall Street Journal*, June 11, 1990, p. B2.

[26]"Asia Beckons," *The Economist*, May 30, 1992, p. 63.

EXHIBIT 11–4

ISO 9000 Certification

> Increasingly an ISO 9000 product quality assurance certification (an international seal of approval) is being viewed as necessary to gain access to the European Economic Community. ISO refers to the International Organization for Standardization and its activities pertaining to the registration and certification of a manufacturer's quality system. It is actually a series of standards a company (if it is to be certified) is required to meet regarding product design and development, production, installation and servicing systems, management practices, inspection methods, and numerous other operations. ISO certification does not guarantee that a manufacturer will produce a quality product — it certifies only the production processes used.

SOURCE: Adapted from Randy Tardy, "Certification Opens Doors to the World," *Arkansas Democrat-Gazette*, June 27, 1993, p. G1.

similar channels of distribution whenever possible to capitalize on the experience gained in serving a particular channel system.

Pricing tends to be localized because of differences in both manufacturing and marketing costs, taxes, and the prices of competitive products. Cultural and language differences frequently require firms to adapt advertising messages to local conditions. Media allocations vary substantially among countries because of vast differences in media availability and, in the case of print media, the quality of reproduction.

Product strategy

Regardless of whether a company adopts a standardized or a localized international marketing strategy for its products, it must make sure the products are of the highest quality. A variety of studies linking quality and market share position have alerted managers to quality's competitive potential. Recently the need for products sold internationally to be quality certified is being viewed as a prerequisite to gaining access to the European Economic Community (see Exhibit 11–4). Successful quality management programs stress the importance of looking at quality from the customer's point of view.

Producing a world product is not easy; it requires setting standards that reflect the conditions under which the product is used. The standards developed from use in the United States may not produce a product acceptable to the rest of the world; therefore marketing research is necessary. (For an example of the problems of adapting a product to the environments of target markets, see Exhibit 11–5.) A company has three basic product options based on the extent to which it modifies the product's physical dimensions:

1. *Market the same product to all countries (a "world" product).*   This strategy requires that the physical product sold in each country be the same except for labeling and the language used in the product manuals. It assumes customer needs are essentially the same across national boundaries or can be made the same; a quality product is offered at a relatively low price resulting from scale effects.

2. *Adapt the product to local conditions.*   This strategy keeps the physical product essentially the same. Only modifications that represent a small percentage of total costs are permitted,

EXHIBIT 11–5

The High Cost of Developing a World Car

Ford recently introduced its Mondeo, a midsize "world car" that cost some $6 billion to develop (sales may never reach the break-even point). Ford's primary problem in developing the Mondeo was the need to create uniform worldwide engineering standards for raw materials, design, procurement, and manufacture of individual parts. To force the necessary reconciliations, Ford flew hundreds of technicians across the Atlantic, which took lots of time and money, especially for late design changes. The Mondeo project ended up taking eight years versus the normal four.

SOURCE: Alex Taylor III, "Ford's $6 Billion Baby," *Fortune*, June 28, 1993, pp. 76–89.

such as changes in voltage, packaging, and color. Examples include computers, copiers, over-the-road construction equipment, cars, calculators, and motorcycles. P & G reformulated its Cheer detergent in Japan to accommodate differences in the way the Japanese wash clothes.

3. *Develop a country-specific product.*   In this situation the physical product is substantially altered (affects a significant part of total costs) across countries or groups of countries. Such a strategy is often used with packaged food and personal care items.

Pricing

Companies find it difficult to adopt a standardized pricing strategy across countries because of different transportation costs; fluctuating and different exchange rates; variation in competition, market demand, or strategic objectives (such as volume versus profits); different governmental tax policies or legal regulations; and other factors such as differences in channels of distribution and global buyers who demand equal price treatment regardless of location.

In some cases firms attempt to minimize such adjustments by adopting a global pricing policy similar to an FOB (free on board) origin policy in the domestic market. They charge the same price around the world and require each customer to absorb all freight and import duties. Such a policy has the obvious virtue of simplicity but fails to take into account variations in local demand or competitive conditions.

Other firms charge a transfer price to their various branches or subsidiaries but then give their country managers wide latitude to charge their customers whatever price they think is most appropriate. Although sensitive to variations in local conditions, this policy may lead to arbitrage involving the transshipment of goods across countries when price differences exceed the freight-and-duty costs separating markets.

For these reasons most firms follow an intermediate approach to global pricing.[27] First corporate management establishes an acceptable range of prices. Local managers are then

---

[27] Warren J. Keegan, *Global Marketing Management* (Englewood Cliffs, N.J.: Prentice Hall, 1989), ch. 13.

EXHIBIT 11-6

Global Countertrade

Countertrade, which occurs in international transactions where the potential customer lacks sufficient hard currency to pay for a purchase, can take a variety of forms:

- *Barter.* Barter involves the direct exchange of goods with no money and no third party involved. For instance, a German firm might agree to build a steel plant in Mexico in exchange for a given amount of Mexican oil.

- *Compensation deals.* Here the seller agrees to take some percentage of the payment in cash and the rest in goods, as when Boeing sells airplanes to Brazil for 70 percent cash and an agreed-upon number of tons of coffee.

- *Buyback arrangements.* Under such arrangements a seller offers a plant, equipment, or technical expertise to a customer and agrees to accept as partial payment products manufactured with the equipment or training supplied. For example, a U. S. chemical company built a plant for an Indian company in return for some cash and a volume of chemicals to be made in the plant.

- *Offsets.* The seller is compensated in cash but agrees to spend a substantial amount of that cash with the customer or its government over a stated period. For instance, Pepsi sells its cola syrup to Russia for rubles and agrees to buy Russian vodka at a given rate for sale in the United States.

Source: Adapted from Stephen S. Cohen and John Zysman, "Countertrade, Offsets, Barter, and Buybacks." *California Management Review* (Winter 1986), pp. 41–56.

given the flexibility to select the price within that range that is best suited to local demand and competitive conditions, though their decisions are often subject to review by top management. Thus a firm might permit a high price in a country where its product had a strong competitive position and high perceived value but settle for a lower penetration price in less established markets.

Countertrade

An additional pricing problem often arises when a firm sells to customers in developing economies that may lack sufficient hard currency to pay for their purchases. Such customers may offer items other than money as payment. While companies dislike such deals, it is often in their best interest to facilitate them via a set of activities known as **countertrade,** which can take a variety of forms (see Exhibit 11–6).

Channels

Two types of international channel alternatives are available to a domestic producer. The first is the use of domestic intermediaries who provide marketing services from their local base; the second is the use of foreign intermediaries. The more common of the former are **export merchants,** who carry a full line of manufactured goods; **export jobbers,** who handle mostly raw materials (but don't take physical control of them); and **trading companies,** which sell manufactured goods to developing countries and buy back raw material and unprocessed goods. All take title of the merchandise they sell. Domestic intermediaries also include agents such as **brokers, buying offices, selling groups,** and the **manufacturer's**

export agent. None of these take title to the merchandise they handle. Rather than dealing with domestic intermediaries a manufacturer may decide to deal with **foreign agents or wholesalers,** which shortens the channel and brings the manufacturer closer to the marketplace. A major problem is that foreign channel members are some distance away and therefore more difficult to control. Further, because many such channel intermediaries are prone to act independently of their suppliers, it is difficult to use them for market cultivation.

Wholesalers around the world, while performing similar functions, vary a great deal in size, margins, and service quality to both customers and suppliers. A broad generalization is that the less developed a country, the smaller the wholesaler and the more fragmented the wholesale channels. Recent years have seen a worldwide trend of vertical integration from the wholesale or retail level to the manufacturer, and the growth of national wholesalers has made it easier for manufacturers to distribute their products nationwide.

Retail structures in foreign countries

These vary tremendously across countries because of differences in cultural, economic, and political environments. A generalization is that the size of retail stores increases as per capita GNP increases (see Exhibit 11–7). Recently both European and Japanese retailing have followed a path similar to that pioneered by the United States with respect to larger store size,

EXHIBIT 11–7
Retailing in Selected Countries

	Per capita GNP*	Retail outlets (000)	Population per outlet
United States	$21,790	1,441	172
Austria	18,980	38	193
France	19,520	518	108
Germany	22,260	366	166
Hungary	2,780	77	136
Italy	16,860	871	65
Japan	25,890	1,629	75
Poland	1,690	250	191
Spain	11,000	907	43
Sweden	23,760	45	188
Turkey	1,640	369	151
United Kingdom	16,060	335	170

*GNP = gross national product in U. S. dollars.

SOURCE: The per capita GNP data came from *World Tables 1992*, published for the World Bank by the Johns Hopkins University Press. Baltimore, Md. Population data came from *World Population Prospects 1990* (New York: The United Nations, 1991). The number of retail outlets came from the Retailing and Retailing Distribution section of *Euro-Monitor*. London, 1993, and *International Marketing Data and Statistics*. London, 1991.

longer store hours, greater use of automation (use of checkout counters), more discounting (including the appearance of warehouse clubs), and direct marketing. Even so, the average store is still small by U. S. standards. Change will not come easily in Japan because about one in five workers is employed in distribution. The government, over the years, has enacted legislation making it hard for large retailers to displace mom-and-pop operators.[28] In Europe and the United States more and more retail chains are going international, some by opening stores (Toys-R-Us), some by licensing (Hart-Marx—clothing), and still others by joint venture (Ralph Lauren).[29]

Channel problems

Although the problems encountered by a manufacturer in establishing and maintaining a channel system overseas are similar to those experienced domestically, there are some important differences:

1. The kind of channel needed may not be available because of the country's low level of economic development (such as a lack of refrigeration) or the presence of only state-controlled intermediaries.

2. Existing distributors have already been appropriated by other manufacturers (particularly local ones) via various arrangements, including financial, and the exclusive use of private labels. This has often been the case in Japan.

4. Control is yet another problem. An international marketer will almost always use a variety of channel systems to penetrate and service its various markets, no two of which are identical. The problems of controlling this varied set of distribution systems are so numerous that many companies use a contractual entry mode (licensing or franchising) whenever possible to facilitate control.

5. It is hard to maintain interest in a manufacturer's product(s) because of the number of intermediaries involved (a situation often found in developing countries and where the brand name is relatively unknown). Consequently, a higher percentage of the advertising budget is spent communicating with the various channels than is typically the case in the United States.

Despite these problems, international wholesalers have not only increased in number, they have also become more adept at fulfilling their functions. Even so, the establishment and maintenance of an effective and efficient overseas distribution network remains one of the biggest challenges the international marketer faces.

---

[28]See "Can This Catalog Company Crack the Japanese Marketing Maze?" *Business Week*, March 19, 1990, p. 60; and Emily Thornton, "Revolution in Japanese Retailing," *Fortune*, February 7, 1994, p. 140.

[29]For further information, see Paula Dwyer, Karen Lowery Miller, Stewart Toy, and Patrick Oster, "Shop til You Drop Hits Europe," *Business Week*, November 29, 1993; "Europe's Discount Dogfights," *The Economist*, May 8, 1993, p. 69; and "Taking Aim," *The Economist*, April 24, 1993, p. 74.

EXHIBIT 11-8

How Different Kinds of Environments Affect Promotion across Countries

Type of environment	Examples of effect
Social	Languages, culture, religion, and lifestyles vary substantially across most countries. For example, because attitudes differ regarding cleanliness, Gillette promotes its razors, deodorants, and other men's grooming products differently in the developing countries than in the United States.
Economic	Because of substantial variations in standards of living across countries as well as the distribution of wealth within countries, demand for a particular product varies, as does the way a product is perceived. For example, cameras are considered a reasonably standard item in developed countries. Not so in the developing countries, however.
Political	Some countries prevent the importation of some U. S. products under any condition. Political control also determines what products can be advertised (pharmaceuticals, alcohol, airlines, and candy are forbidden in some Arabic countries); what media can be used (no TV advertising is permitted in Scandinavia); and what can be said about products (comparative advertising is not allowed in Germany).

Promotion

The issue of whether to adopt a standardized advertising strategy versus a local one has been much debated in recent years. The benefits of standardization derive primarily from scale effectiveness in production (including creative time) and the use of international media. Localization advocates argue that it is extremely difficult to standardize the nonproduct marketing mix components because prospective consumers live in very different social, economic, and political environments (see Exhibit 11–8).

The importance of local cultures is clearly evident in how consumers respond to the use of humor, sexual appeal, and the prevalence of symbols. For example, German consumers have a different feeling about humor than do those in the United States and England, while French and Italian consumers are more tolerant and respond more favorably than English consumers to sexual appeals. Japan is an example of a culture that benefits substantially from nonverbal cues. At the other extreme are Scandinavia and Germany.[30]

Adaptation

International advertisers should not have to choose between a standardization or a localization strategy; the objective should be to obtain a similar response—not run the identical ad across

---

[30]Dora L. Alden, Wayne D. Hoyer, and Chol Lee, "Identifying Global and Culture-Specific Dimensions of Humor in Advertising: A Multinational Approach," *Journal of Marketing*, April 1993, p. 44; and Rita Martenson, "International Advertising in Cross-Cultural Environments," *Journal of International Consumer Marketing*, 1 (1989), p. 7.

countries.[31] Advertisers are increasingly urged to "plan global, act locally."[32] In other words, start with standardization because of its advantages and adapt to local needs when it is advantageous to do so. It is often possible "to use the same brand concept, possibly even the same advertising concept and executional 'format' across borders—but the executions must be customized to fit local environments, to enable consumers to relate to and empathize with the advertising."[33] For example, Procter & Gamble's American ad of its all-in-one shampoo featured a woman slamming a locker door in a gym. This scene was considered too confrontational for Thailand, so a new, softer ad was developed that preserved the theme of convenience.[34]

International media

Global advertising has been helped by recent media developments. CNN now reaches nearly 80 million households in over 200 countries, and Viacom's MTV network estimates its audience at 210 million in 18 countries. Europe now has some 80 satellite-borne TV channels. Recent start-ups include a Middle East Broadcast Center, which uses an Arab-language satellite channel.[35]

International print media have also increased substantially. A growing number of publications have international editions, including *The Wall Street Journal, USA Today, Time, Business Week, Fortune,* the *Harvard Business Review, Cosmopolitan,* and *Elle.* While such publications offer large worldwide audiences, their coverage within any given country may be low and confined to upscale readers.[36]

While most media types are available throughout the world, print is the one most frequently used because all countries have local newspapers (some of which are national or regional in scope) and most have magazines that circulate nationally. The use of TV has until recently been inhibited by limited programming, government regulation limiting the use of advertising, and low rates of TV ownership. These conditions are improving rapidly, and the use of TV as a strong advertising medium in the near future in most countries seems assured.[37]

Personal selling

One of the more critical marketing decisions facing a firm expanding its sales efforts into other countries is how to organize their selling efforts across national boundaries. While

---

[31] Ashish Banerjee, "Global Campaigns Don't Work; Multinationals Do," *Advertising Age,* April 18, 1994, p. 23.

[32] Roger Blackwell, Riad Ajami, and Kristina Stephan, "Winning the Global Advertising Race: Planning Globally, Acting Locally," *Journal of International Consumer Marketing* 3, no. 2 (1991), p. 97.

[33] Banerjee, "Global Campaigns Don't Work," p. 23.

[34] "Advertising in Asia: Full of Western Promise," *The Economist,* November 4, 1992, p. 84.

[35] Ken Wells, "Global Ad Campaigns after Many Missteps Finally Pay Dividends," *The Wall Street Journal,* August 27, 1992, p. 1.

[36] George E. Belch and Michael A. Belch, *An Introduction to Advertising and Promotion* (Burr Ridge, Ill.: Irwin, 1993), pp. 764–67.

[37] For example, Belgium, Denmark, and Sweden have no commercial TV or radio. Germany permits TV commercials only between 6 and 8 P.M. and none on Sunday. The Netherlands and Switzerland permit no more than two TV commercials per week per product. See Cortland L. Bovee and William F. Arens, *Contemporary Advertising* (Burr Ridge, Ill.: Irwin, 1992), p. 695.

globalization obviously adds complexity to the problem, the basic questions to be answered are the same as those faced in domestic markets. First, should the firm use independent agents or hire its own salesforce in a foreign country? If the firm decides on the latter, a second question arises concerning whether the salesforce should be organized geographically, by product line, by type of customer, or in some other way.

A recent survey of 14 large multinational corporations examined their sales management practices across 135 subsidiaries located in 45 countries.[38] The results showed that about 25 percent used agents either alone or in cooperation with company salespeople (about one-third of all firms used manufacturers' representatives in the United States). Firms selling complex high-tech products like computers and pharmaceuticals were likely to employ their own salesforce. About half the sample of subsidiaries used geographic territories to organize their selling efforts within a given country. The rest used more specialized structures with different sales people assigned to specific products and/or customer types, especially when selling a broad line of complex products in highly developed countries.

EXPORTING SERVICES

Because of the characteristics of services (intangibility, perishability, amount of customer contact, and quality variability), many do not require the same physical export distribution channels as manufactured goods.[39] Some services are embodied in a good, thereby making them easier to export.[40] For example, America's pop culture can easily be exported in the form of novels, CDs, tapes, and TV programs.[41] Much the same can be said of some business services such as data processing, consulting services, and some banking services (those provided by automatic teller machines). Such services can use not only exporting but franchising, licensing, direct investment, and joint ventures.

Other services such as airline services, hotels, tourism, food, entertainment, and medical and legal services require that production and consumption occur simultaneously; thus these are not suitable for export. However, they can be internationalized via franchising, licensing, and direct investment. Increasingly, internationally minded service companies are facing a complex array of trade barriers ranging from exclusion to certification of selected professionals (such as lawyers) rendering services.

---

[38] John S. Hill and Richard R. Still, "Organizing the Overseas Sales Force: How Multinationals Do It," *Journal of Personal Selling and Sales Management*, Spring 1990, pp. 57–66.

[39] For a discussion of the extent to which consumers are involved in service marketing across countries, see Lee D. Dahringer, Charles D. Frame, Oliver Yaw, and Janet McCall-Kennedy, "Consumer Involvement in Services: An International Evaluation," *Journal of International Consumer Marketing* 3, no. 2 (1991), pp. 61–77.

[40] For a classification system based on degree of consumer involvement, see Sandra Vandermerine and Michael Chadwick, "The Internationalization of Services," *The Services Industries Journal*, January 1989, pp. 79–93.

[41] American music, basically rock and roll, collects a majority of its over $20 billion annual sales from overseas. Annual overseas sales of U.S. television programs to Europe are over $600 million. American entertainment software collectively has an annual trade surplus of over $8 billion. See John Huey, "America's Hottest Export: Pop Culture," *Fortune*, December 31, 1990, p. 50.

IMPLEMENTATION AND CONTROL

Both implementation and control as practiced by the global company are discussed as part of the next two chapters and hence are not covered here. With regard to implementation, emphasis is placed on organization design and decision making and how they change as the company becomes more involved with the global marketplace. The impact of culture on organization design and decision making is also discussed.

The subject of global marketing control is examined primarily from the point of view of the various factors affecting the nature and scope of the control system used. Also discussed are the trend toward centralization and how culture affects the kind of control system used.

SUMMARY

International marketing has become increasingly important to U.S. firms in recent years. International sales provide an important source of profits, but they are also critical for some firms' survival because of their impact on both scale effects and the ability to retaliate against competitive attacks without lowering profits drastically in the home market. International marketing follows many of the same principles as domestic marketing. There are, however, major differences between countries, and the development of strategy options and marketing programs build on these differences.

In considering which foreign markets to target, a firm must analyze each country's physical, legal, economic, political, cultural, competitive, and infrastructure environments. Legal barriers come in a variety of forms, including tariffs and embargoes. There are also a variety of indirect legal barriers. The other environments affect demand as well as targeting, product positioning, and the development of marketing programs. The latter depends heavily on the major marketing mix elements, all of which are strongly affected by the various environments.

Reasons for entering overseas markets include economies of scale that extend beyond the size of the home market, defending against a global competitor, and satisfying customers going international. Global trade strategies revolve for the most part around either localization or standardization. The extent to which a firm opts for one or the other strategy depends on the product involved. Products that enjoy strong experience effects and are not highly culture-bound are candidates for standardized marketing. Achieving a commanding world competitive position requires low-cost manufacturing and a well-integrated distribution system.

Market entry strategies include both direct and indirect exporting; contractual agreements, including licensing, franchising, and a variety of other types; and investment, which can occur via joint or sole venture. Companies can mix these to service different overseas markets.

As in the formulation of an international strategy, the major issue regarding the international marketing mix is the extent to which it can be standardized across countries. Standardization is greatest in product features, branding, and packaging because of manufacturing and marketing scale effects. Firms use similar channels whenever possible, but prices tend to be localized because of differences in cost and competition.

Advertising messages typically need to be adapted to local conditions, although it is often possible to use the same product concept across countries. In recent years global advertising has been helped by the internationalization of certain TV programs and print media. Organizing a sales effort across countries is a difficult operation, but the basic questions to be answered are the same as those faced domestically.

Because of their characteristics, services do not usually require the same physical distribution system as manufactured goods. Some can be exported in the form of a product; others can use franchising, licensing, direct investment, and joint ventures. Internationally minded service companies are facing an increasing array of complex trade barriers.

IMPLEMENTATION AND CONTROL

Implementing Business and Marketing Strategies

HEWLETT-PACKARD: ON A ROLL[1]

Only a few years ago Hewlett-Packard was in the doldrums and seemed headed for trouble. Now it is one of America's most successful and admired computer companies—number two in sales (IBM is number one) with annual revenues of $21.4 billion, net profit $1.3 billion, and return on equity of 14.7 percent. A primary reason for this turnaround is that management runs the company as a conglomerate of little ventures, each responsible for its own success. In so doing they have changed H-P's focus from technology to people.

One reason for this magnitude of change is that new or revamped products within the past two years have accounted for 70 percent of H-P's sales versus some 30 percent a decade ago. To accomplish this outpouring of new and successful products, H-P relied on teams. The PC division, for example, was reorganized into small teams (8–10 people), each focused

on a market segment, and parallel teams were used to develop each component of a new computer simultaneously, resulting in a two-thirds cut in the time to develop a new product.

H-P also uses teams in its sales programs. Each team builds an information database on the leading prospects in each industry (including their data processing budget) and develops an account sales strategy. A team member, designated as the development manager responsible for building a close relationship with the account's key decision makers, decides which prospects to invite to H-P's offices for a daylong presentation on how H-P's capabilities can solve their problems. A senior vice president who is the CEO's deputy spends 40 to 50 percent of his time listening to customers.

These changes have made H-P into a highly flexible technology company driven by its customers. Despite its huge size, it

[1]"The metamorphosis of Hewlett-Packard," *The Economist*, June 19, 1993, p. 67; Thayer C. Taylor, "Hewlett-Packard: Computers & Office Equipment," *Sales & Marketing Management*, January 1993, p. 59; Alan Deutschman, "How H-P Continues to Grow and Grow," *Fortune*, May 2, 1994, p. 90; and Kevin Manley, "Giant Goes from Stodgy to Nimble," *USA Today*, May 18, 1994, p. B1.

has many more parts "than an Erector set. Pull one piece off, bolt a couple others together, and—voila! The company can quickly change and attack any emerging market."[2] In this sense "it's more like a biological system than a company."[3]

ISSUES IN THE IMPLEMENTATION OF BUSINESS AND MARKETING STRATEGIES

The recent changes at Hewlett-Packard illustrate that a business's success is determined by two aspects of strategic fit. First, its competitive and marketing strategy must fit the needs and constraints of the external environment. Second, the business must be able to effectively implement that strategy via its internal structure, policies, procedures, and resources. When it cannot effectively implement its chosen strategy—even if the strategy is appropriate for the circumstances it faces—trouble will ensue. Worse, management may conclude the strategy was not appropriate, switch to a less desirable one, and ultimately depress the business's performance even further. On one hand, excellent execution may offset the negative effects of a poorly conceived strategy. But on the other hand, good implementation of the wrong strategy can speed the business along the road to failure.

In this chapter we discuss the subject of organizational fit—the fit between a business's strategies and the organizational structures, policies, processes, and plans necessary to implement those strategies. Four major sets of internal variables affect a business's ability to implement particular strategies:

- The fit between the marketing strategies pursued in individual product-markets and the firm's higher-level corporate and business strategies.
- Administrative relationships between the SBU and corporate headquarters.
- The SBU's organization structure and coordination mechanisms, including such variables as the technical competence of the various functional departments within the SBU, the manner in which resources are allocated across functions, and the mechanisms used to coordinate and resolve conflicts among the departments.
- The contents of a marketing action plan for each product-market entry.

These four sets of variables serve as the framework for organizing the remainder of this chapter. Before beginning our discussion, we should note that the dynamics of global markets coupled with strong competition make for opportunities that demand a fast response. This in turn requires highly adaptive organizations—like that at H-P—that can quickly analyze the marketplace, formulate a response strategy, and develop an appropriate plan of action. Thus in recent years high-level executives have tried to find ways to simplify their organizational structures and procedures. The pressure to do so has led many CEOs to conclude that organizations of the future will be dramatically different from those of today.

---

[2]Manley, "Giant Goes from Stodgy to Nimble," p. B1.
[3]Manley, p. B2.

EXHIBIT 12-1

The Fit between Business Strategies, the Environment, and SBU Objectives

Situational variables and objectives	Business strategies			
	Prospector	Analyzer	Differentiated defender	Low-cost defender
Industry environment	Industry in the introductory or growth stage of its life cycle; relatively few competitors; technology still evolving.	Industry in growth or early maturity stage of its life cycle; substantial competition; technological advances or new product applications still possible.	Industry in maturity or decline stage of its life cycle; substantial competition; technology is mature, but new applications may still be possible.	Industry in maturity or decline stage of its life cycle; substantial competition; technology is mature, but new applications may still be possible.
Appropriate SBU objectives	High increases in sales volume and market share; relatively large proportion of volume from new products and markets; relatively low ROI and cash flow.	Moderate increases in volume and share; some volume from new products and markets; moderate levels of ROI and cash flow.	Low increases in sales volume and market share; relatively little volume from new products, but some volume may be gained from new customers or markets; high ROI and cash flow.	Low increases in sales volume and market share; relatively little volume from new products or markets; moderate to high ROI and cash flow.

These restructuring efforts include a reduction in the number of organizational levels; use of joint ventures and strategic alliances; attempts to develop innovative, entrepreneurial managers; use of self-managing teams; emphasizing the notion of "pay for performance"; and greater leeway to "run your own business" at the SBU level.[4]

RELATIONSHIPS BETWEEN BUSINESS AND MARKETING STRATEGIES

As discussed in an earlier chapter, generic business-level strategies define how an SBU intends to compete in its industry. Exhibit 12–1 reviews the kinds of industry environments and the SBU objectives most appropriate for the pursuit of prospector, analyzer, differentiated defender, and low-cost defender strategies. An SBU may comprise a number of

---

[4]Thomas A. Stewart, "The Search for the Organization of Tomorrow," *Fortune*, May 18, 1992, p. 93.

product-markets, each facing different demand and competitive situations. Even so, an SBU's strategy does set a general direction for the types of markets to target, the way to compete in those markets, and the objectives to pursue. Also, an SBU strategy should reflect the general market and competitive conditions it faces within its industry. Therefore, a well-conceived competitive strategy should provide a foundation for and strongly influence an SBU's general policies concerning such marketing program elements as relative product quality, service levels, price, and promotional intensity.

Exhibit 12–2 summarizes some of the more basic relationships among business-level competitive strategies, marketing policies, and strategic marketing programs (these were discussed in earlier chapters). From this summary we can conclude that the SBU's strategy constrains the kinds of marketing policies appropriate for that SBU. Those same policies also limit the range of marketing strategies appropriate for the individual product-market entries within the SBU. Thus effective implementation of a particular business strategy involves implementing a specific set of marketing policies and strategies followed by the appropriate organizational structure, policies, and processes.

ADMINISTRATIVE RELATIONSHIPS AND STRATEGY IMPLEMENTATION

In organizations consisting of multiple divisions or SBUs, the administrative relationships between the unit and corporate headquarters influence the ability of the SBU's managers, including its marketing personnel, to implement specific competitive and marketing strategies successfully. This section will discuss three aspects of the corporate–business unit relationship that can affect the SBU's success in implementing a particular competitive strategy:

1. The degree of autonomy provided each business unit manager.

2. The degree to which the business unit shares functional programs and facilities with other units.

3. The manner in which the corporation evaluates and rewards the performance of its SBU managers.

Exhibit 12–3 summarizes how these variables relate to the successful implementation of different business strategies. Note that analyzer strategies are not included in our discussion because they incorporate some elements of both prospector and defender strategies; the administrative arrangements appropriate for implementing an analyzer strategy typically fall somewhere between those best suited for the other two types. To simplify the following discussion we focus only on the polar types—prospector, differentiated defender, and low-cost defender strategies.

Business-unit autonomy

Prospector business units likely perform better on the critical dimensions of new product success and increased volume and market share when organizational decision making is

EXHIBIT 12-2

The Fit between Business Strategies and Marketing Programs

Appropriate marketing policies and strategies	Business strategies			
	Prospector	Analyzer	Differentiated defender	Low-cost defender
Product and service policies	Broad, technically sophisticated product lines; moderate to high quality and levels of service, especially sales engineering services.	Moderately broad and technically sophisticated product lines; service levels and quality indeterminate.	Relatively narrow but high quality and technically sophisticated product lines; high quality and levels of service.	Narrow, less technically sophisticated product lines; relatively low levels of quality and service.
Price policy	Relatively high prices.	Relatively high prices.	Relatively high prices.	Relatively low to competitive prices.
Distribution policies	Little forward vertical integration; relatively high trade promotion expenses as a percentage of sales.	Degree of forward vertical integration indeterminate; moderate to high trade promotion expenses as a percentage of sales.	Relatively high degree of forward vertical integration; low trade promotion expenses as a percentage of sales.	Degree of forward vertical integration indeterminate; low trade promotion expenses as a percentage of sales.
Promotion policies	High advertising, sales promotion, and salesforce expenditures as a percentage of sales.	Moderate advertising and sales promotion expenditures as a percentage of sales; salesforce expenditures indeterminate.	Relatively low advertising and sales promotion expenditures as a percentage of sales; high salesforce expenditures as a percentage of sales.	Low advertising, sales promotion, and salesforce expenditures as a percentage of sales.
Common marketing strategies	Mass-market penetration; niche penetration; skimming and early withdrawal; market expansion; encirclement.	Flanker strategy; market expansion; leapfrog strategy; encirclement.	Fortress defense; confrontation; flanker strategy; increased penetration; extended use; market expansion; profitable survivor strategy; maintenance strategy; niche strategy.	Fortress defense; confrontation; profitable survivor strategy; maintenance strategy; niche strategy; harvesting strategy.

EXHIBIT 12-3

Administrative Factors Related to the Successful Implementation of Business Strategies

	Types of business strategy		
Administrative factor	Prospector	Differentiated defender	Low-cost defender
SBU autonomy	Relatively high level.	Moderate level.	Relatively low level.
Shared programs and synergy	Relatively little synergy — few shared programs.	Little synergy in areas central to differentiation — shared programs elsewhere.	High level of synergy and shared programs.
Evaluation and reward systems	High incentives based on sales and share growth.	High incentives based on profits or ROI.	High incentives based on profits or ROI.

relatively decentralized and the SBU's managers have substantial autonomy to make their own decisions. There are several reasons for this. First, more decentralized decision making allows the managers closest to the market to make more major decisions on their own. Greater autonomy also enables the SBU's managers to be more flexible and adaptable. It frees them from the restrictions of standard procedures imposed from above, allows them to make decisions with fewer consultations and participants, and disperses power. All of these conditions help produce quicker and more innovative responses to environmental opportunities—something H-P has been able to accomplish with considerable success.

On the other hand, low-cost defender SBUs perform better on ROI and cash flow by giving their managers relatively little autonomy. For a low-cost strategy to succeed, managers must relentlessly pursue cost economies and productivity improvements. Such efficiencies are more likely to be attained when decision making and control are relatively centralized.

The relationship between autonomy and the ROI performance of differentiated defenders is more difficult to predict. On the one hand, such businesses defend existing positions in established markets and their primary objective is ROI rather than volume growth. Thus the increased efficiency and tighter control associated with relatively low autonomy should lead to better performance. On the other hand, such businesses can maintain profitability only if they continue to differentiate themselves by offering superior products and services. As customers' wants change and new competitive threats emerge, the greater flexibility and market focus associated with greater autonomy may allow these businesses to more successfully maintain their differentiated positions and higher levels of ROI over time. These arguments suggest that the relationship between autonomy and performance for differentiated defenders may be mediated by the level of stability in their environments and by the proportion of offensive or proactive marketing strategies they employ. Units operating in relatively unstable environments and pursuing more proactive marketing programs (such as extended use or market expansion strategies) likely perform better when they have relatively greater autonomy.

Shared programs and facilities

Firms face a trade-off when designing strategic business units. An SBU should be large enough to afford critical resources and to operate on an efficient scale, but it should not be so large that its market scope is too broad or that it is inflexible and therefore cannot respond to its unique market opportunities. Some firms attempt to avoid this trade-off between efficiency and adaptability by designing relatively small, narrowly focused business units but then having two or more units share functional programs or facilities, such as common manufacturing plants, R & D programs, or a single salesforce.

Sharing resources poses a particular problem for prospector business units.[5] Suppose, for instance, a business wants to introduce a new product but shares a manufacturing plant and salesforce with other SBUs. The business would have to negotiate a production schedule for the new product, and it may not be able to produce adequate quantities as quickly as needed if other units sharing the plant are trying to maintain sufficient volumes of their own products. It may also be difficult to train salespeople on the new product or to motivate them to reduce the time spent on established products in order to push the new item. When Frito-Lay introduced Grandma's soft cookies, for instance, they relied on their 10,000 salty-snack route salespeople to attain supermarket shelf space for the new line. But because those salespeople were paid a commission based on their total sales revenue, they were reluctant to take time away from their profitable salty-snack lines to sell the new cookies. The resulting lack of strong sales support contributed to Grandma's failure to capture a sustainable share of the packaged cookie market.

One exception to this generalization, though, may be sharing sales and distribution programs across consumer packaged goods SBUs. In such cases a prospector's new product may have an easier time obtaining retailer support and shelf space if it is represented by salespeople who also sell established brands to the same retail outlets. For prospectors producing consumer durable or industrial goods, however, functional independence generally facilitates good performance, as has certainly been the case with H-P.

On the other hand, the increased efficiencies gained through sharing functional programs and facilities often boost the ROI performance of low-cost defender SBUs. Also, the inflexibility inherent in sharing is usually not a big problem for such businesses because their markets and technologies tend to be mature and relatively stable. Thus Heinz, the cost leader in a number of food categories, uses a single salesforce to represent a wide variety of products from different business units during calls on supermarkets.

The impact of shared programs on the performance of differentiated defenders is more difficult to predict because they must often modify their products and marketing programs in response to changing market conditions to maintain their competitive advantage over time. Thus greater functional independence in areas directly related to the SBU's differential

---

[5]Robert W. Ruekert and Orville C. Walker, Jr., "The Sharing of Marketing Resources across Strategic Business Units: The Effect of Strategy on Performance," in *Review of Marketing 1990* (Chicago: American Marketing Association, 1990).

advantage—such as R & D, sales, and marketing—tends to be positively associated with the long-run ROI performance of such businesses. But greater sharing of facilities and programs in less crucial functional areas, such as manufacturing or distribution, may also help improve efficiency and short-term ROI levels.

Evaluation and reward systems

SBU managers are often motivated to achieve their planned objectives by bonuses or other financial incentives tied to their unit's performance. Since these managers often remain in one position for only three to five years, such evaluation and reward systems encourage them to concentrate on short-term returns and adopt policies that may discourage innovation, the acceptance of risk, and the aggressive pursuit of growth for future returns.[6]

Reliance on evaluation and reward systems geared to short-term financial performance poses no major problems in SBUs pursuing defender strategies where most markets are stable and mature and where ROI and cash flows are the most important performance objectives. Such incentive systems are likely to be counterproductive, though, when an SBU pursues a prospector strategy requiring some level of risk taking and innovativeness in the short term to achieve long-term success. In such businesses evaluation and reward systems based on an increase in sales volume or market share or on the percentage of volume generated by new products (say, products introduced within the last five years) are more likely to motivate managers to engage in aggressive and innovative action. Because many firms incorporate both prospector and defender SBUs, they need to base their evaluation and reward systems on some combination of volume and profitability.

In recent years an increasing number of U.S. firms have adopted some form of a pay-for-performance compensation scheme. Some do it for individuals who meet specific goals, others on the basis of performance of small groups, and still others on the performance of the SBU or the company as a whole. But most companies admit that such programs are difficult to implement. Increasingly, individual performance is hard to define and even more difficult to measure.[7]

Many high-level U.S. executives receive some kind of a long-term performance incentive tied to stock price performance, options, direct stock awards, and so on. Such is not the case in Japan and continental Europe. U.S. executives are paid much more than their counterparts abroad. The CEO of a very large Japanese firm earns 17 times what the average Japanese worker does. In France and Germany this ratio is 24, while in the United States it is 109. One reason why managers in different countries are rewarded differently is that the nature and scope of their jobs differ—especially in Japan where greater reliance is placed on consensus

---

[6]Bernard J. Jaworski, "Toward a Theory of Marketing Control: Environmental Context, Control Types, and Consequences," *Journal of Marketing*, July 1988, pp. 23–39.

[7]Amanda Bennett, "Paying Workers to Meet Goals Spreads but Judging Performance Proves Tough," *The Wall Street Journal*, September 10, 1991, p. B1.

and bottom-up planning. Also, long-term growth is often considered more important than return to stockholders.[8]

ORGANIZATIONAL STRUCTURE, PROCESSES, AND STRATEGY IMPLEMENTATION

Different strategies emphasize different ways to gain a competitive advantage. Thus a given functional area may be key to the success of one type of strategy but less critical for others. For instance, competence in new product R & D is critical for the success of a prospector business (for example, H-P) but less so for a low-cost defender.

Successful implementation of a given strategy, then, is more likely when the business has the **functional competencies** demanded by its strategy and supports them with substantial **resources** relative to competitors, is organized suitably for its technical, market, and competitive environment, and has developed appropriate **mechanisms** for coordinating efforts and resolving conflicts across functional departments. Exhibit 12–4 summarizes the relationships between these organizational structure and process variables and the performance of different generic business strategies.

Functional competencies and resource allocation

Competence in marketing, sales, product R & D, and engineering are critical to the success of prospector businesses because those functions play pivotal roles in new product and market development and thus must be supported with budgets set at a larger percentage of sales than their competitors. Because marketing, sales, and R & D managers are closest to the changes occurring in a business's market, competitive, and technological environments, they should be given considerable authority in making strategic decisions. This argues that bottom-up strategic planning systems are particularly well suited to prospector businesses operating in unstable environments. Success here is positively affected by the extent to which customer orientation is an integral part of the unit's corporate culture.[9]

In low-cost defender businesses, on the other hand, the functional areas most directly related to operating efficiency—such as financial management and control, production, process R & D, and distribution or logistics—play the most crucial roles in enabling the SBU to attain good ROI performance. Because differentiated defenders need to attain high returns on their established products, functional areas related to efficiency are also critical for their

---

[8]Paul Milgram and John Roberts, "Pay, Perks, and Parachutes," *Stanford Business School Magazine*, June 1992, p. 18.

[9]For a discussion of the relation between customer orientation and corporate culture and the latter's impact on the firm's performance, see Rohit Despandé, John Farley, and Frederick Webster, Jr., "Corporate Culture, Customer Orientation, and Innovativeness in Japanese Firms: A Quadrad Analysis" (Cambridge, Mass.: Marketing Science Institute, Working Paper 92-100, January 1992). It is important to note, however, that strong cultures can lead to insularity and thus be an obstacle to change, as witness the troubles at IBM and General Motors. Only when the culture emphasizes strong support for those serving the customer is customer orientation apt to be a positive force over time. See "The Caring Company," *The Economist*, June 6, 1992, p. 79.

EXHIBIT 12-4

Organizational and Interfunctional Factors Related to the Successful Implementation
of Business Strategies

Organizational factor	Type of business strategy		
	Prospector	Differentiated defender	Low-cost defender
Functional competencies of the SBU	SBU will perform best on critical volume and share growth dimensions when its functional strengths include marketing, sales, product R & D, and engineering.	SBU will perform best on critical ROI dimension when its functional strengths include sales, financial management and control, and those functions related to its differential advantage (such as marketing, product R & D).	SBU will perform best on critical ROI and cash flow dimensions when its functional strengths include process engineering, production, distribution, and financial management and control.
Resource allocation across functions	SBU will perform best on volume and share growth dimensions when percentage of sales spent on marketing, sales, and product R & D are high and when gross fixed assets per employee and percentage of capacity utilization are low relative to competitors.	SBU will perform best on the ROI dimension when percentage of sales spent on the salesforce, gross fixed assets per employee, percentage of capacity utilization, and percentage of sales devoted to other functions related to the SBU's differential advantage are high relative to competitors.	SBU will perform best on ROI and cash flow dimensions when marketing, sales, and product R & D expenses are low but process R & D, fixed assets per employee, and percentage of capacity utilization are high relative to competitors.
Decision-making influence and participation	SBU will perform best on volume and share growth dimensions when managers from marketing, sales, product R & D, and engineering have substantial influence on unit's business and marketing strategy decisions.	SBU will perform best on ROI dimension when financial managers, controller, and managers of functions related to unit's differential advantage have substantial influence on business and marketing strategy decisions.	SBU will perform best on ROI and cash flow when controller, financial, and production managers have substantial influence on business and marketing strategy decisions.

(continues)

success. Similarly, such units also seek to improve efficiency by investing in process R & D, making needed capital investments, and maintaining a high level of capacity utilization. But because they must also maintain their differential advantage over time, functional departments related to the source of that advantage—the salesforce and product R & D for SBUs with a technical product advantage, or marketing and distribution for SBUs with a customer service advantage—are also critical for the unit's continued success.

EXHIBIT 12–4 (*concluded*)

Organizational factor	Type of business strategy		
	Prospector	**Differentiated defender**	**Low-cost defender**
SBU's organization structure	SBU will perform best on volume and share growth dimensions when structure has low levels of formalization and centralization but high level of specialization.	SBU will perform best on ROI dimension when structure has moderate levels of formalization, centralization, and specialization.	SBU will perform best on ROI and cash flow dimensions when structure has high levels of formalization and centralization but low level of specialization.
Functional coordination and conflict resolution	SBU will experience high levels of interfunctional conflict; SBU will perform best on volume and share growth dimensions when participative resolution mechanisms are used (for example, product teams).	SBU will experience moderate levels of interfunctional conflict; SBU will perform best on ROI dimension when resolution is participative for issues related to differential advantage but hierarchical for others (for example, product managers, product improvement teams, and so on).	SBU will experience low levels of interfunctional conflict; SBU will perform best on ROI and cash flow dimensions when conflict resolution mechanisms are hierarchical (such as functional organization).

SOURCE: Adapted from Orville C. Walker, Jr., and Robert W. Ruekert "Marketing's Role in the Implementation of Business Strategies," *Journal of Marketing*, July 1987, p. 31.

Additional considerations for service organizations

Given that service organizations pursue the same kinds of business-level competitive strategies as goods producers, they must meet the same functional and resource requirements to implement those strategies effectively. However, service organizations—and manufacturers that provide high levels of customer service as part of their product offering—often need some additional functional competencies because of the unique problems involved in delivering quality service.

This is particularly true for services involving high customer contact. Because the sale, production, and delivery of such services occur almost simultaneously, close coordination between operations, sales, and marketing is crucial. Also, because many different employees may be involved in producing and delivering the service—as when thousands of different cooks prepare Big Macs at McDonald's outlets around the world—production planning and standardization are needed to reduce variations in quality from one transaction to the next. Similarly, detailed policies and procedures for dealing with customers are necessary to reduce variability in customer treatment across employees. All of this suggests that personnel management—particularly the activities of employee selection, training, motivation, and evaluation—is an important adjunct to the production and marketing efforts of high-contact service organizations.

Competence in personnel management is more crucial for service businesses pursuing prospector strategies—and perhaps also for defenders and analyzers who differentiate their offerings on the basis of good service—than for those focused primarily on efficiency and low cost. In prospector service organizations employees often play a critical role in identifying potential new service offerings and in introducing them to potential customers. Consequently, the effective implementation of such a strategy requires employees with superior communication and social skills and necessitates frequent employee retraining and performance feedback. For instance, banks pursuing a prospector strategy not only have more branches and engage in more market scanning, advertising, and new service development than those with other types of competitive strategies, but they also devote more effort to screening potential employees and providing training and support after they are hired.[10]

Organizational structures

Three structural variables—formalization, centralization, and specialization—are important in shaping both an SBU's and its marketing department's performance within the context of a given competitive strategy. **Formalization** is the degree to which formal rules and standard policies and procedures govern decisions and working relationships. **Centralization** refers to the location of decision authority and control within an organization's hierarchy. In highly centralized SBUs or marketing departments, only one or a few top managers hold most decision-making authority. In more decentralized units, middle- and lower-level managers have more autonomy and participate in a wider range of decisions. Finally, **specialization** refers to the division of tasks and activities across positions within the organizational unit. A highly specialized marketing department, for instance, has a large number of specialists, such as market researchers, advertising managers, and sales promotion managers, who perform a narrowly defined set of activities.

High levels of formalization and centralization together with low levels of specialization likely promote relatively efficient performance within an SBU or its marketing department.[11] Formal rules and procedures help routinize activities and hold down risks and administrative costs. The relatively small number of specialists also helps make such units more cost efficient. Such highly structured businesses should perform well on ROI and cash flow dimensions, making them particularly appropriate for SBUs pursuing low-cost defender strategies.

But highly structured business units and marketing departments are unlikely to be very innovative or quick to adapt to changing environmental circumstances. Adaptiveness and innovativeness are enhanced when (1) decision-making authority is decentralized, (2) managerial discretion and informal coordination mechanisms replace rigid rules and policies,

[10]David O. McKee, P. Rajan Varadarajan, and William M. Pride, "Strategic Adaptability and Firm Performance: A Market-Contingent Perspective," *Journal of Marketing*, July 1989, p. 18. For an interesting discussion of recent developments in the implementation of strategies for service organizations, see James L. Heskett, W. Earl Sasser, Jr., and Christopher W. L. Hart, *Implementing Strategy: Service Breakthroughs: Changing the Rules of the Game* (Cambridge, Mass.: The Mac Group, n.d.).

[11]Robert W. Ruekert, Orville C. Walker, Jr., and Kenneth J. Roering, "The Organization of Marketing Activities: A Contingency Theory of Structure and Performance," *Journal of Marketing*, Winter 1985, pp. 13–25.

and (3) more specialists are present. Thus prospector business units and their marketing departments likely perform better when they are decentralized, have little formalization, and are highly specialized (as is the case with H-P).

Differentiated defenders perform best when their organization structures incorporate moderate levels of formalization, centralization, and specialization. Those departments most directly related to the source of a differentiated defender's competitive advantage (sales, marketing, and R & D), however, should be less highly structured than those more crucial for the efficiency of the unit's operations (production and logistics).

Interfunctional coordination and conflict resolution mechanisms

Levels of interfunctional conflict

Because of their emphasis on new product and market development, prospector businesses often have considerable complexity and uncertainty in their operations. Thus situations are likely to develop that result in substantial interfunctional conflict, particularly among such departments as marketing, sales, R & D, and production.[12] On the other hand, low-cost defenders commonly operate in more narrowly defined domains and in more mature, stable environments. Thus low-cost defender businesses are apt to have less interfunctional conflict across departments than businesses pursuing other strategies.

Conflict resolution mechanisms

Regardless of its competitive strategy, every business has some degree of conflict among its functional departments. How can these be resolved? While there are many variations, conflict resolution mechanisms fit into two broad categories. The first is a hierarchical approach whereby top managers impose a solution, either by adhering to formal rules and operating procedures or by judging on a case-by-case basis. The second is a participative approach, in which the parties themselves are expected to work out a mutually acceptable solution.[13] New product development teams are examples of the participative approach in practice.

Hierarchical resolution mechanisms are efficient because they reduce the amount of time and effort necessary to reach a decision, and they help ensure consistency in the relations across functional departments over time. Such efficiency and routinization are particularly helpful for low-cost defender businesses.

Participative approaches are less efficient because the parties involved typically require more time to work out their differences. But they often lead to a fuller understanding of, and more innovative solutions to, problems that cut across functional departments. They are

---

[12]Robert W. Ruekert and Orville C. Walker, Jr., "Interactions between Marketing and R & D Departments in Implementing Different Business Strategies," *Strategic Management Journal* 8 (1987), pp. 233–38.

[13]John McCann and Jay R. Galbraith, "Interdepartmental Relations," *Handbook of Organizational Design*, vol 2, ed. Paul C. Nystrom and William Starbuck (New York: Oxford University Press, 1981), pp. 60–84.

particularly appropriate for uncertain, nonroutine situations that call for innovative, adaptive actions—situations most commonly faced by prospector businesses.[14]

Once again, because differentiated defenders (and analyzers) need both efficiency and adaptiveness to maintain their differential advantage and profitability, some combination of resolution mechanisms is appropriate. Moderate use of participative methods can resolve conflicts among those areas directly involved in preserving the SBU's differential advantage. A greater reliance on rules, standard procedures, or top-management fiat can deal with disputes in other operational areas.

Alternative organizational designs

Several common organizational designs incorporate differences in both the structural variables (formalization, centralization, and specialization) and in the mechanisms for resolving interfunctional conflicts, as discussed. These include (1) functional, (2) product management, (3) market management, and (4) various types of matrix organizational designs.

Functional organizations

The functional form of organization is the simplest and most bureaucratic design. At the SBU level managers of each functional department, such as production or marketing, report to the general manager. Within the marketing department managers of specific marketing activity areas, such as sales, advertising, or marketing research, report to the marketing vice president or director. At each level the top manager coordinates the activities of all the functional areas reporting to him or her, often with heavy reliance on standard rules and operating procedures. Thus this is the most centralized and formalized organizational form and relies primarily on hierarchical mechanisms for resolving conflicts across functional areas. Also, because top managers perform their coordination activities across all product-markets in the SBU, there is little specialization by product or customer type.

These characteristics make the functional form simple, efficient, and particularly suitable for companies operating in stable and slow-growth industries where the environments are predictable. Thus the form is appropriate for low-cost defender SBUs attempting to maximize their efficiency and profitability in mature or declining industries. For example, Ingersol-Rand, a low-cost manufacturer of low-tech air compressors and air-driven tools such as jackhammers, uses a functional structure.

Product management organization

When an SBU has many product-market entries, the simple functional form of organization is inadequate. A single manager finds it difficult to stay abreast of functional activities across a variety of different product-markets or to coordinate them efficiently. One common means of dealing with this problem is to adopt a product management organization structure.

---

[14]McCann and Galbraith, "Interdepartmental Relations."

EXHIBIT 12–5

A Marketing Department with a Product Management Organization

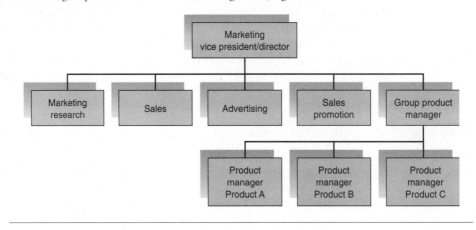

As Exhibit 12–5 illustrates, this form adds an additional layer of managers to the marketing department, usually called product managers, brand managers, or marketing managers, each of whom has the responsibility to plan and manage the marketing programs and to coordinate the activities of other functional departments for a specific product or product line.

A product management structure decentralizes decision making while increasing the amount of product specialization within the SBU. If the product managers are given substantial autonomy to develop their own marketing plans and programs, this structure can also decrease the formalization within the business. Finally, although the product managers are responsible for obtaining cooperation from other functional areas both within and outside the marketing department, they have no formal authority over these areas. They must rely on persuasion and compromise—in other words, more participative methods—to overcome conflicts and objections when coordinating functional activities. These factors make the product management form of organization less bureaucratic than the functional structure. It is more appropriate, then, for businesses pursuing differentiated defender and analyzer strategies, particularly when they operate in industries with complex and relatively unstable market and competitive environments.

Businesses that enact flanker, mobile, market penetration, or expansion marketing strategies as their industries mature often end up with a number of different brands in the same product category. In some cases the firm aims the different brands at different market segments, but the brands may also be direct competitors. To coordinate marketing strategies and allocate resources across some related brands, a product management organization typically includes one or more "group" or "category" marketing managers on the level immediately above the product managers. Category management also provides an opportunity for the involvement of more experienced managers in brand management, particularly in coordinating pricing and other marketing efforts.[15]

Product management organizations have a number of advantages, including the ability to identify and react more quickly to the threats and opportunities individual product-market entries face; improved coordination of functional activities within and across product-markets; and increased attention to smaller product-market entries that might be neglected in a functional organization. Consequently, about 85 percent of all consumer goods manufacturers use some form of product management organization.

Despite its advantages, a product manager organization has shortcomings. The major one is the difficulty of obtaining the cooperation necessary to develop and implement effective programs for a particular product given that a product manager has little direct authority. Also, the environment facing product managers is changing drastically. They increasingly encounter the facts that more and more consumers are buying on the basis of price (not brand name); that competition is becoming globalized and markets more open; that technological change creates new products and cost savings; and that the power of distributors has increased at the expense of manufacturers due in no small part to the distributors' ability to control information about the marketplace. These environmental trends have led to an increase in the sales of private-label brands and more aggressive bargaining by distributors.[16] As a result of these trends and the inherent weakness of the product manager type of organization, many companies have undertaken two types of modifications—market management and matrix organization—which are discussed next.

Market management organizations

In some industries an SBU may market a single product to a large number of different markets where customers have very different requirements and preferences. Pepsi Cola, for example, is sold through restaurants, fast-food outlets, and supermarkets. The syrup needed to make Pepsi is sold directly to institutions such as Kentucky Fried Chicken and Taco Bell. But marketing Pepsi to consumers for home consumption involves the use of franchised bottlers who process and package the product and distribute it to supermarkets. The intermediaries and marketing activities involved in selling to the two markets are so different that it makes sense to have a separate market manager in charge of each.

Recently some SBUs have adopted a combination of product and regional market management organizational structures. A product manager has overall responsibility for planning and implementing a national marketing program for the product, but several market managers are also given some authority and an independent budget to work with salespeople and develop promotion programs geared to a particular user segment or geographic market.

---

[15] Michael J. Zenor, "The Profit Benefits of Category Management," *Journal of Marketing Research*, May 1994, p. 202.

[16] Allen D. Shocker, Rajendra K. Srivastava, and Robert W. Ruekert, "Challenges and Opportunities Facing Brand Management," *Journal of Marketing Research*, May 1994, p. 149. Also see Donald H. Lehman and Russell S. Winer, *Product Management* (Burr Ridge, Ill.: Richard D. Irwin, 1994), ch. 16.

Frito-Lay Installs Regional Managers

Frito-Lay set up a regional organization (six zones) in 1986 to implement local and regional trade and consumer promotions. In June 1989 the company, a division of PepsiCo and the nation's leading marketer of salty-snack foods, created four business areas that replaced the six zones. Each business area is headed by a vice president/general manager. This move puts more senior management in the field and consolidates responsibility for sales, promotion, advertising, and possibly even production within each area. Each vice president reports to the Frito-Lay senior vice president/marketing and sales at headquarters. This type of organization is motivated by the desire to get closer to the trade and consumers to respond quickly and decisively to regional competition.

SOURCE: Jennifer Lawrence, "Frito Reorganizes," *Advertising Age*, June 26, 1989, p. 4.

This kind of decentralization or regionalization has become popular with consumer goods companies in their efforts to increase geographic segmentation and cope with the growing power of regional retail chains (see Exhibit 12–6).

Matrix organizations

A business facing an extremely complex and uncertain environment may find a matrix organization appropriate, as is the case with Hewlett-Packard. The matrix form is the least bureaucratic or centralized and the most specialized type of organization. It brings together two or more different types of specialists within a participative coordination structure. One example gaining increased popularity is the product team, which consists of representatives from a number of functional areas assembled for each product or product line. As a group, the team must agree on a business plan for the product and ensure the necessary resources and cooperation from each functional area. This kind of participative decision making can be very inefficient; it requires a good deal of time and effort for the team to reach mutually acceptable decisions and gain approval from all the affected functional areas. But once reached, those decisions are more likely to reflect the expertise of a variety of functional specialists, to be innovative, and to be quickly and effectively implemented. Thus the matrix form of organization particularly suits prospector businesses and the management of new product development projects within analyzer or differentiated defender businesses (see Exhibit 12–7).

Recent organizational design developments

As mentioned earlier, the ever-increasing dynamics of the marketplace have forced companies to respond more quickly to their opportunities and threats. This, in turn, has affected the firm's organizational structure. While we are only just beginning to gain insights into organizational structures of the future, certain aspects seem reasonably clear. We briefly discuss the more important of these.

Organizations will emphasize the **managing of business processes** in contrast to functional areas. Every business has about six basic processes, such as, for example, new

EXHIBIT 12–7

Using Teams to Get the Job Done

> Pillsbury (the American subsidiary of Britain's Grand Metropolitan Group) has replaced its traditional marketing department with multiple discipline teams centered around a product group (such as pizza snacks). Each involves managers from marketing, sales, R & D, and production. Lever Brothers has restructured in a similar fashion. It has reorganized its marketing and sales departments into a series of business groups and set up a separate customer development team responsible for retailer relations across all the various SBU brands.

SOURCE: "Death of the Brand Manager," *The Economist*, April 9, 1994, p. 67.

product development and materials flow. The former would be staffed by individuals from marketing, R & D, manufacturing, and finance. The latter would contain people with expertise in purchasing, manufacturing, order delivery, and billing.[17]

The managing of processes will make the organization essentially horizontal—flat (few layers) and lean versus a vertical or hierarchical model. Thus executive positions will no longer be defined in terms of managing a group of functionally oriented people; instead, executives will be concerned with a process. For example, a senior vice president in charge of "getting the product to the customer" would be responsible for sales, shipping, billing, and so on. There is considerable evidence that focusing on a given process can lead to substantial improvements. For example, Hallmark (sales in 1991 of $2.9 billion) produces 40,000 new cards a year using some 700 writers, artists, and designers. This "world's largest creative staff" was taking two years to develop a new card. Analyzing the process has cut the new product development cycle in half.

Process management is quite different from the management of a function because, first, it uses external objectives—for example, customer satisfaction versus simple revenues. Second, people with different skills are grouped to undertake a complete piece of work; their work is done simultaneously, not in sequence. Third, information flows directly to where it is used. Thus, if you have an upstream problem, you deal with the people involved directly rather than via your boss.[18]

Next, the use of **self-managing teams,** while not new, is increasing. Regardless of the form of worker self-management, all are based on the concept of *empowerment*—the theory that those doing the work should have the means to do what it takes to please the customer. In turn, this requires that performance objectives and evaluation of activities be linked to customer satisfaction. Successful teams can dramatically improve productivity. For example, Boeing used empowered teams to reduce the number of hang-ups by half on its new 777 jet.[19] But many teams fail because management is not serious about their empowerment, team members are poorly selected, and the team is launched in isolation with little training or support.

---

[17]Thomas A. Stewart, "The Search for the Organization of Tomorrow," *Fortune*, May 18, 1992, p. 93.

[18]See Brian Dumaine, "The Bureaucracy Busters," *Fortune*, June 17, 1991, p. 36.

[19]Brian Dumaine, "The Trouble with Teams," *Fortune*, September 5, 1994, p. 86.

In the future teams will form the basis for collaborative networks linking thousands of people together. Such networks enable businesses to form and dissolve relations quickly and to bring to bear on an opportunity or a threat the needed resources regardless of who owns them.[20] For example, AT & T used Japan's Marubeni Trading Company as a means to link with Matsushita Electric Industrial Company to jump-start the manufacture of its Safari Notebook Computer (designed by Henry Dreyfuss Associates).[21] Ford and Mazda have a successful 13-year marriage that has weathered many storms. Ford contributes expertise in international marketing and finance, Mazda in product development and manufacturing.[22]

But not all such joint ventures are successful, as witness in the automotive industry General Motor's despair with Isuzu's continuous red ink, the disappointment of Mitsubishi with its Chrysler relationship, and the poor results from the Fiat–Nissan alliance.[23] Partnering is at its best a difficult and demanding undertaking requiring considerable managerial skills as well as a great deal of trust." A major difficulty—especially for those involving companies from different parts of the world—is that "they cannot be controlled by formal systems, but require a dense web of interpersonal connections and internal infrastructures that enhance learning."[24] American companies are poor at handling such situations. Asian companies are best, with the Europeans being someplace in between.[25]

Organizational design and the international company

An organization's complexity increases, often quite dramatically, as it "goes international" and especially so as overseas sales increase as a percentage of total sales. The issue is essentially one of deciding what organizational design is best for developing and implementing worldwide strategies while simultaneously maintaining flexibility with regard to individual markets. Three types of international organizational structures are discussed here.[26]

Little or no formal organization

Early on in a firm's international involvement, the structure ranges between the domestic organization handling international transactions to a separate export department. The latter may be tied to the marketing department or may be a freestanding functional department in its own right.

---

[20]Samuel E. Blucker, "The Virtual Organization," *The Futurist*, March–April 1994, p. 9; Edward A. Gargan, "Virtual Companies Thrive, Let Others Do the Work," *Arkansas Democrat-Gazette*, July 25, 1994, p. 60; and Alan Deutschman, "The Managing Wisdom of High-Tech Superstars," *Fortune*, October 17, 1994, p. 197.

[21]John A. Byrne, Richard Brandt, and Otis Port, "The Virtual Corporation," *Business Week*, February 8, 1993, p. 98.

[22]Karen L. Miller and James B. Treece. "The Partners," *Business Week*, February 10, 1992, p. 102.

[23]Miller and Treece, "The Partners."

[24]Rosabeth Moss Kanter, "Collaborative Advantage: The Art of Alliance," *Harvard Business Review*, July–August 1994, p. 97.

[25]Kanter, "Collaborative Advantage."

[26]The discussion that follows draws heavily from Michael R. Czinkota, Pietra Rivali, and Idkka A. Ronkausen, *International Business* (New York: The Dryden Press, 1992), pp. 536–545.

An international division

In an effort to avoid having international customers discriminated against in comparison with domestic customers, an international division is often established to house all international activities, most of which relate to marketing. Manufacturing, engineering, finance, and R & D typically remain in their previous form to take advantage of scale effects. This type of organization serves best with a limited number of products that lack cultural sensitivity—for example, basic commodity types such as chemicals, metals, and industrial machinery.

Japanese firms have emphasized low-cost manufacturing coupled with quality assurance as the essence of their international competitive strategy. Both of these require strong centralized control and thus the use of an export-based organizational structure. In recent years, Japanese firms have become more interested in global structures based on products or areas.[27]

Global structures

There are a variety of global structural types, of which the simplest replicates the firm's basic functional departments. Thus a global company using the functional type of organization would have vice presidents (worldwide) for such areas as manufacturing, marketing, and finance—all reporting to the president.

By far the most common global structure is one based on products, which translates into giving SBUs worldwide control over their product lines. The main advantages of this type of structure are the economies derived from centralizing manufacturing activities and the ability to respond quickly to product-related problems originating in overseas markets. Marketing is localized at the country or regional level.

The area structure is another popular global organizational type and is especially appropriate when there is considerable variance across markets regarding product acceptance and marketing activities. Firms typically organize on a regional basis (North America, Latin America, Far East, Middle East, and Africa) using a central staff that coordinates worldwide planning and control activities.

Some companies use a hybrid organization that typically is some combination of the functional, product, or area types of structure. The global matrix is one such attempt. It has individual business managers reporting to both area and functional groups, or area managers reporting to business and functional groups, thereby enabling the company to balance the need for centralized efficiency and responsiveness to local needs. But the dual reporting sets up conflicts and slows the management process to such an extent that many companies, including Dow and CitiCorp, have returned to more traditional organizational designs.[28]

---

[27]Christopher A. Bartlett and Sumantra Ghoshal, *Transnational Management* (Burr Ridge, Ill.: Irwin, 1992), p. 520.

[28]Bartlett and Ghoshal, *Transnational Management.*

Decision making and organizational structure

Organization structures can be centralized or decentralized in terms of decision making. In the case of the latter, controls are relatively simple and relations between subsidiaries and headquarters are mainly financial. The logic here is that local management is closest to the market and can respond quickly to change. But multinationals faced with strong global competition require more centralization, which calls for headquarters to provide the overall strategy that subsidiaries (country units) implement within a range agreed upon with headquarters.[29]

Culture plays an important role in organizational design and decision making. For example, Americans believe that an organization with few hierarchical levels can be successful, while many European and Asian managers disagree. Also, most American managers believe that the primary role of a manager is to help subordinates solve problems and not simply answer questions, while most French managers disagree strongly with this view because they see managers as "experts" who must answer questions as a way of maintaining their credibility.[30]

MARKETING ACTION PLANS

Preparing written plans is a key step in ensuring the effective execution of a strategy because it spells out what actions are to be taken, when, and by whom. Each department, and perhaps its subunits (such as sales and marketing research within the marketing department), prepares an annual plan detailing its intended role in carrying out the business's strategy. The concern here, however, is with the annual marketing plan for a specific product-market entry.

As you might expect, marketing plans across companies vary a good deal in content and organization. In general, however, most annual marketing plans follow a format similar to that summarized in Exhibit 12–8. Although most plans offer an executive summary to facilitate a quick management review, the first substantive section is usually a brief analysis of the current situation. Next the key issues the brand will face during the planning period—including potential threats, competitive weaknesses, and possible opportunities for additional growth or profitability—are outlined.

The following section sets forth the specific objectives for the coming year, which should include both the financial objectives for the brand and its marketing objectives such as sales volume and market-share goals. Because there may be a number of different ways to accomplish these objectives, the plan must specify the overall marketing strategy the firm will pursue. That strategy is then broken down into more specific action plans for the coming period. These action plans are the most important part of the whole document for ensuring proper execution. They detail the specific activities the firm will undertake to implement the brand's marketing strategy, who is responsible for each action, when it will be undertaken, and how much is to be spent on each activity.

---

[29]Czinkota et al., *International Business*, p. 545.

[30]Nancy J. Adler, *International Dimensions of Organizational Behavior* (Boston: PWS Kent, 1991), ch. 2.

EXHIBIT 12–8

Contents of an Annual Marketing Plan

Section	Content
I. Executive summary	Presents for quick management review a short overview of the issues, objectives, strategy, and actions incorporated in the plan and their expected outcomes.
II. Current situation	Summarizes relevant background information on the market, competition, past performance of the product, and the various elements of its marketing program (such as distribution and promotion), as well as trends in the macroenvironment.
III. Key issues	Identifies the main opportunities and threats to the product that the plan must deal with in the coming year and the relative strengths and weaknesses of the product and business unit that must be taken into account in facing those issues.
IV. Objectives	Specifies the goals to be accomplished in terms of sales volume, market share, and profit.
V. Marketing strategy	Summarizes the overall strategic approach that will be used to meet the plan's objectives.
VI. Action plans	This is the most critical section of the annual plan for helping to ensure effective implementation and coordination of activities across functional departments. It specifies • What specific actions are to be taken. • Who is responsible for each action. • When the action will be engaged in. • How much will be budgeted for each action.
VII. Projected profit-and-loss statement	Presents the expected financial payoff from the plan.
VIII. Controls	Discusses how the plan's progress will be monitored; may present contingency plans to be used if performance falls below expectations or the situation changes.

Based on the brand's performance objectives and the expenses involved, a budget is developed that is essentially a projected profit-and-loss statement that top management reviews for approval or modification. The final section of the plan specifies how the brand's progress will be monitored and controlled over the course of the year.

For the interested reader, the kinds of information that might be included in each section of the annual marketing plan are discussed in more detail in the appendix following this chapter. That discussion is illustrated with the contents of a recent annual marketing plan for a Pillsbury refrigerated dough product.

SUMMARY

For a business to be successful it must not only have competitive and marketing strategies that fit the demands of the external market and competitive environment, it must also implement those strategies effectively. The business's internal structure, resources, policies, procedures, and plans must fit the demands of its strategies. This chapter examined four aspects of organizational fit that are critical for effective implementation: (1) the compatibility of strategies at different levels within the business, (2) the administrative relationships between the SBU and corporate headquarters, (3) the organization structure of the SBU and its interfunctional coordination mechanisms, and (4) annual marketing plans that detail the specific actions necessary to execute strategy in each of the SBU's product-markets.

Both the broad marketing policies guiding the development of marketing plans for individual product-markets and the specific marketing strategies pursued within those product-markets should be consistent with the SBU's overall competitive strategy. Thus higher-level strategies and policy decisions often place some constraints on a manager's freedom of action in designing a marketing program for an individual product-market entry.

Administrative relationships between an SBU and its corporate headquarters can influence its ability to implement different business and marketing strategies. Prospector businesses perform best when their managers have substantial autonomy to make independent decisions, when SBUs share few functional programs or facilities, and when evaluation and reward systems are primarily based on growth dimensions of performance such as increases in sales volume or market share. On the other hand, low-cost defender businesses perform best when their managers are relatively tightly controlled, when SBUs substantially share functional programs and facilities, and when evaluation and reward systems focus primarily on financial dimensions of performance.

The SBU's organizational structure and the processes it uses to coordinate functional activities and resolve conflicts across departments also influence its ability to implement different strategies. Prospector businesses perform best when their structures feature low centralization and formalization, high specialization, and participative methods of interfunctional coordination and conflict resolution. Consequently, matrix forms of organizational design, such as interfunctional product teams or product and market management structures, are particularly well suited to such businesses. At the other extreme, low-cost defenders perform best when their structures provide high centralization and formalization, relatively little specialization, and hierarchical methods of coordination. Highly structured and bureaucratic organizational designs, such as those organized along functional lines, are most appropriate for businesses pursuing low-cost defender strategies.

While the product management form of organization is most commonly used, especially in consumer products businesses, it is especially appropriate for businesses pursuing differentiated defender and analyzer strategies. The environment facing product managers is changing because consumers are buying more on price, competition is becoming globalized, private labels are increasing in numbers and quality, and the power of distributors is becoming greater because of their control over critical market data. Organization design will increasingly have to accommodate the management of processes versus functions and the use of empowered self-management teams.

Finally, a detailed annual marketing plan for each product-market entry within the business unit facilitates strategy implementation. Such plans should contain (1) an executive summary, (2) a discussion of the current market and competitive situation and the product's past performance, (3) a summary of the key issues facing the product, (4) the objectives for the coming year, (5) the overall marketing strategy, (6) action plans detailing the specific activities involved in carrying out the strategy, (7) a projected profit-and-loss statement, and (8) a summary of how the business will monitor and control the plan's performance. A detailed set of action plans is particularly crucial for effective implementation because it describes exactly what is to be done, by whom, when, and how much is to be spent on each activity.

APPENDIX THE CONTENTS OF THE ANNUAL MARKETING PLAN

To illustrate the kinds of information that might be included in each section of the annual marketing plan for a product-market entry, Appendix Exhibit 12A–1 summarizes a recent plan for a Pillsbury refrigerated bread dough, one of the smaller product lines within the firm's differentiated defender prepared dough products business unit.[31]

EXHIBIT 12A–1

Summary of an Annual Marketing Plan for a Refrigerated Bread Dough Product

I. Analysis of current situation
   A. Market situation
   - The total U.S. market for dinner breadstuffs is enormous, amounting to about 10.5 billion servings per year.
   - Specialty breads, such as whole grain breads, are growing in popularity, largely at the expense of traditional white breads.
   - Pillsbury's share of the total dinner breadstuffs market, accounted for by several brands, including Crescent rolls as well as refrigerated bread dough, is small, amounting to only about 2% of the total dollar volume.
   - Since its introduction several years ago, refrigerated bread dough (RBD) has been able to achieve only low levels of penetration (only about 15% of all households have used the product) and use frequency (nearly two-thirds of the product's volume comes from light users who buy only one or two cans per year).
   - RBD consumption is concentrated in the northern states and during the fall and winter months (about 75 percent of volume is achieved from September through February).
   - Marketing research results suggest consumers believe RBD is relatively expensive in terms of price/value compared to alternative forms of dinner breadstuffs.
   B. Competitive situation
   - RBD's share of the total dinner breadstuffs category is likely to remain low because of the wide variety of competing choices available to consumers.
   - The largest proportion of volume within the category is captured by ready-to-eat breads and rolls produced by supermarket chains and regional bakeries and distributed through retail grocery stores.
   - RBD's major competition within the refrigerated dough category comes from other Pillsbury products, such as Crescent rolls and Soft Breadsticks.
   - There are currently no other national competitors in the refrigerated bread dough category, but Merico, a small regional producer, was recently acquired by a major national food manufacturer. Evidence suggests Merico may be preparing to introduce a competing product line into national distribution at a price about 10 percent lower than Pillsbury's.

(continues)

---

[31] While this example is based on material contained in an actual marketing plan for a Pillsbury product, the name of the brand and some of the specific numbers included in this example have been changed to protect proprietary information.

EXHIBIT 12A-1 (*continued*)

C. Macroenvironmental situation
  • Changes in American eating habits may pose future problems for dinner breadstuffs in general and for RBD in particular:
      More meals are being eaten away from home, and this trend is likely to continue.
      People are eating fewer starchy foods.
      While total volume of dinner breadstuffs did not fall during the 1980s, neither did it keep pace with population growth.
  • Increasing numbers of women working outside the home, and the resulting desire for convenience, may reduce consumers' willingness to wait 30 minutes while RBD bakes, even though the dough is already prepared.
  • Because RBD does not use yeast as a leavening agent, Food and Drug Administration regulations prohibit the company from referring to it as "bread" in advertising or package copy even though the finished product looks, smells, and tastes like bread.

D. Past product performance
  • While sales volume in units increased only slightly last year, dollar volume increased by 24% due to a price increase.
  • The improvement to gross margin was even greater than the price increase due to an improvement in manufacturing costs.
  • The improvement in gross margin, however, was insufficient to produce a positive net margin due to high advertising and sales promotion expenditures aimed at stimulating primary demand and increasing market penetration of RBD.
  • Consequently, while RBD has shown improvement, it is still unable to make a positive contribution to overhead and profit.

II. Key issues
  A. Threats
    • Lack of growth in the dinner breadstuffs category suggests the market is mature and may decline in the future.
    • The large variety of alternatives available to consumers suggests it may be impossible for RBD to substantially increase its share of the total market.
    • Potential entry of a new, lower-priced competitor poses a threat to RBD's existing share and may result in lower margins if RBD responds by reducing its price.
  B. Opportunities
    • The largest percentage of RBD volume accounted for by light users suggests an opportunity of increasing volume among current users by stimulating frequency of use.
    • Trends toward increased consumption of specialty breads suggests possible line extensions, such as whole wheat or other whole grain flavors.
  C. Strengths
    • RBD has a strong distribution base, with shelf facings in nearly 90 percent of available retail outlets.
    • RBD sales have proved responsive to sales promotion efforts (such as cents-off coupons), primarily by increasing purchases among existing users.
    • The fact that most consumers who try RBD make repeat purchases indicates a high level of customer satisfaction.
  D. Weaknesses
    • RBD sales have proved unresponsive to advertising. Attempts to stimulate primary demand have not been able to increase market penetration.
    • Consumer concerns about RBD's price/value place limits on ability to take future price increases.

EXHIBIT 12A–1 (*concluded*)

III. Objectives

    A. Financial objectives

       • Achieve a positive contribution to overhead and profit of $4 million in current year.

       • Reach the target level of an average of 20% return on investment over the next five years.

    B. Marketing objectives

       • Maintain market share and net sales revenues at previous year's levels.

       • Maintain current levels of retail distribution coverage.

       • Reduce marketing expenditures sufficiently to achieve profit contribution objective.

       • Identify viable opportunities for future volume and profit expansion.

IV. Marketing strategy

    • Pursue a maintenance strategy aimed at holding or slightly increasing RBD volume and market share primarily by stimulating increased frequency of use among current users.

    • Reduce advertising aimed at stimulation of primary demand/penetration and reduce manufacturing costs in order to achieve profit contribution objective.

    • Initiate development and test marketing of possible line extensions to identify opportunities for future volume expansion.

V. Marketing action plans

    • Improve the perceived price/value of RBD by maintaining current suggested retail price at least through the peak selling season (February). Review the competitive situation and the brand's profit performance in March to assess the desirability of a price increase at that time.

    • Work with production to identify and implement cost savings opportunities that will reduce manufacturing costs by 5% without compromising product quality.

    • Maintain retail distribution coverage with two trade promotion discount offers totaling $855,000; one offered in October–November to support peak season inventories, and another offered in February–March to maintain inventories as volume slows.

    • Reduce advertising to a maintenance level of 1,100 gross rating points during the peak sales period of September to March. Focus copy on maintaining awareness among current users.

    • Encourage greater frequency of use among current users through three sales promotion events, with a total budget of $748,000 that will stimulate immediate purchase:

        One free-standing insert (FSI) coupon for 15 cents off next purchase to appear in newspapers on September 19.

        One tear-off offer (buy three, get one free) placed in retailers' shelving during November.

        A refund with proof-of-purchase offer placed in women's service books during March.

13 Controlling Marketing Strategies and Programs

CONTROLS PAY OFF AT WAL-MART[1]

Wal-Mart, a discount general merchandise retailer, is America's largest, most profitable, and most admired retailer. Founded only some 30 years ago, Wal-Mart had sales in excess of $67 billion in 1994 with a net income of over $2 billion for a 26.6 percent return on stockholders' equity. Over the past decade it has continuously ranked as one of the best companies in America in creating value for its stockholders.[2]

At the end of April 1994 the company operated 1,960 Wal-Mart stores, 77 supercenters, 122 Canadian Wal-Mart Stores, and 427 Sam's Clubs, which target small businesses and low-risk households.

Sam's Clubs operate on gross margins of 9 to 10 percent and stock only about 3,500 items versus over 50,000 for an average Wal-Mart store. Management has aggressive plans for new stores and club growth during fiscal year 1995: 110 Wal-Mart stores and 20 Sam's Clubs. Wal-Mart's recently formed International Division announced that at the end of fiscal 1994 it operated (in cooperation with CIFRA) 21 stores in Mexico and planned to open some 35 more in fiscal 1995. Stores will also be opened in Brazil, Argentina, and Hong Kong. The company will further consolidate its position in Canada with the stores it acquired from Woolco.

[1]Based on "Briefly . . . ," *USA Today*, April 10, 1991, p. 28; Sam Walton, *Sam Walton: Made in America* (New York: Doubleday, 1992), pp. 85–86, 118, 212–27; David Smith, "One Step Ahead," *Arkansas, Inc.*, Arkansas Gazette, September 30, 1991, pp. 7–9; Bill Saporito, "What Sam Walton Taught America," *Fortune*, May 4, 1992, p. 104; Wal-Mart's *1993 Annual Report*; Wal-Mart's First Quarter 1994 Report; Bill Saporito, "And the Winner Is Still . . . Wal-Mart," *Fortune*, May 2, 1994, p. 62; and D. R. Stewart, "Wal-Mart Charts Growth in '95," *Arkansas Democrat-Gazette*, September 1994, p. B1.

[2]In 1993 *Fortune* ranked Wal-Mart as America's best company in terms of market value added (MVA) or wealth creation. See Laura Walbert, "America's Best Wealth Creators," *Fortune*, December 27, 1993, p. 65.

A primary reason for Wal-Mart's success is its management control system, which emphasizes cost containment. In 1994 it was able to reduce its operating, selling, and general administrative costs to 15.3 percent of sales versus 15.8 percent three years ago. This is substantially below that of its closest competitor, Kmart, and partly explains the company's excellent profitability record.[3]

Today the company can convert information into action almost immediately. This has required a $700 million investment in its computer and satellite systems, which collectively generate the largest civilian database of its kind in the world. In addition to automated replenishment, the system can tell management the up-to-date sales of any item by region, district, and store. By looking at the computer screens in the satellite room, a manager can see such data as the day's sales adding up as they happen, the number of stolen bank cards retrieved that day, whether the seven-second credit card approval system is working properly, and the number of customer transactions completed that day.

Wal-Mart's philosophy has always been that its executives should spend at least half of their time in the field visiting with associates (employees) and customers. Sam Walton felt that the communication between his executives and store managers and their hourly associates played a major role in Wal-Mart's success. So every weekday company executives (often including David Glass, President and CEO) fly via corporate aircraft to at least 100 stores in the various regions. There they talk with store managers, associates, and customers.

At the end of the week they return to Bentonville to share their findings with headquarters personnel and prepare for a series of merchandise meetings attended by the regional vice presidents, the chairman, the president, and 100 or more other employees. These are no-holds-barred sessions concerned with moving merchandise. For example, in one meeting a regional vice president suggested that Wal-Mart was missing a great business opportunity in street hockey gear (part of the roller blade craze). Others agreed, and within just a few minutes appropriate action had been taken including the development of an eight-foot-long display section.[4] This and similar decisions will be communicated to all store managers by the following morning at the latest through Wal-Mart's computer-driven communication system.

By merging state-of-the-art computer communication technology with hands-on management, Wal-Mart has developed its distribution system to a point where stores should never be out of stock. Doing this better than its rivals has resulted in substantially more sales per square foot than competitors and hence a faster stock turn. This means less borrowing to carry less inventory and therefore lower interest payments—several hundred million dollars less than its nearest competitor. And lost sales due to stock-outs are minimized.

---

[3]For a discussion of Kmart's new centralized replenishment system, see "Remote Control," *The Economist*, May 29, 1993, p. 90.

[4]Bill Saporito, "A Week Aboard the Wal-Mart Express," *Fortune*, August 24, 1992, p. 77.

As the Wal–Mart example demonstrates, a well-functioning control and reappraisal system is critical to the success of a business. Such a system must be well integrated with the other steps in the marketing management process: setting objectives, formulating strategies, and implementing a plan of action. A control and reappraisal system monitors the extent to which a firm is achieving its objectives. If it is not, the firm determines whether the reason lies in the environment, the strategies employed, the action plans, the way the plans are implemented, or some combination thereof. Thus control and reappraisal are diagnostic, serving to start anew the marketing management process.

Control processes differ at each organization level. Corporate management is concerned with how well its various SBUs are performing relative to the opportunities and threats each faces and the resources given them.[5] Control here would be strategic in nature. At the SBU level concern is primarily with the unit's own strategy, especially as it pertains to its individual segments and product-market entries. We will concentrate mainly on this latter organizational level because it constitutes the bulk of any control system.

In this chapter we first discuss the control process and then examine strategic controls. Next we discuss controls pertaining to individual product-market entries, particularly their competitive position, their adherence to plan (including budget and share determinants), and the efficiency with which marketing manages its resources. The chapter ends with a discussion of global marketing control, marketing audits, and marketing decision support systems.

THE CONTROL PROCESS

Regardless of the organization level involved, the control process is essentially the same. It consists of setting performance standards, specifying and obtaining feedback data, evaluating that data, and taking corrective action (see Exhibit 13–1). Although the staff organization is largely responsible for generating the control data, the line organization administers the control process. Certainly this is the case with Wal–Mart, as can be seen in the involvement of regional vice presidents, district managers, store managers, and department heads in obtaining and processing control data as well as taking corrective action.

Setting standards of performance

Performance standards derive largely from the objectives and strategies set forth at the SBU and individual product-market entry level. These generate a series of performance expectations for profitability (return on equity or return on assets managed), market share, and sales. At the product-market level standards of performance also include sales and market-share determinants such as percentage of effective distribution, relative shelf facings, awareness, consumers' attitude change toward a given product attribute, customer satisfaction, and the

---

[5]For the story of a General Electric SBU that went out of control, see Terrence P. Paré, "Jack Welch's Nightmare on Wall Street," *Fortune*, September 5, 1994, p. 40.

EXHIBIT 13-1

The Control Process

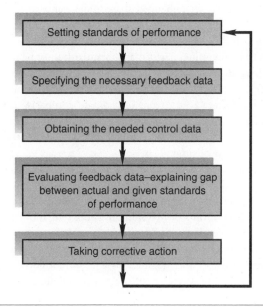

extent of price parity. And finally, budget line items having to do with expenses such as the salesforce (salary payments) and advertising (cost of a specific campaign) serve as cost controls and standards of performance. Without a reasonable set of performance standards, managers cannot know what results are being obtained, the extent to which they are satisfactory, or why they are or are not satisfactory.[6]

Recent years have witnessed a shift from using primarily financial-based performance measures to treating them as simply part of a broader array of measurements. This change is due primarily to shifts in the marketplace and new technology. In the case of the former, consumers are demanding increased variety in both products and services, and firms have responded affirmatively as a way of gaining a competitive advantage. For example, only a few years ago there were only two types of home telephones—wall and desk. Today there are dozens of models including designer phones, portable phones, kids' phones, fax phones, car phones, and even waterproof phones. Changes like this require firms to shift from mass production to batch-of-one customization at no extra cost. Such economies of flexibility can be attained only through changes in organization structure and in the management control system that emphasize measures better reflecting how

---

[6]See Gerald H. B. Ross, "Revolution in Management Control," *Management Accounting*, November 1990, p. 23. Also see Robert Eccles, "The Performance Measurement Manifesto," *Harvard Business Review*, January–February, 1991, p. 131.

managers in decentralized organizations think about what decisions drive the firm's success with respect to individual product-market entities.

If a firm has set enhanced shareholder value as its ultimate objective, then it needs to change from the traditional ROI concept to one using a valuation model that focuses on the future cash flow trend, discounted at an appropriate discount rate and adjusted for risk.

To be of any value, performance standards must be measurable and must be tied to specific time periods. Generally speaking, control systems at the product-market level operate on a monthly, quarterly, and annual basis, with the monthly and quarterly data accumulated to present a current picture and to facilitate comparison with prior years. In recent years the trend has been for control systems to operate over shorter periods (weekly and even daily) and for control data to be more readily available. Strategic control tends to operate over longer periods of time.

Of particular importance is whether the business unit as a whole and its individual product-market entries have set forth milestone achievement measures. For example, in a three-year strategy plan, a given SBU might have 12-month milestones such as annual sales of $100 million, profits of $10 million, and a return on assets managed of 14.5 percent. At the product-market entry level, milestones include such measures as product sales by segments, marginal contributions, and operating margins. At the marketing functional area level, examples of milestone measures for a consumer good are level of awareness, trial, and repeat purchases among members of the target audience, as well as percentage of stores stocking (weighted by sales).

In recent years major U. S. companies such as AT & T, DuPont, Ford, GM, IBM, and Motorola have used a new performance type of measure: benchmarking. This means that the firm's performance in a given area is compared against the performance of other companies. Thus Wal-Mart regularly compares itself with its competitors on merchandise assortment, service quality, and stockouts. The comparison does not, however, have to be with companies in the same industry. For example, Xerox benchmarked its order filling/shipping performance against L. L. Bean (a mail-order retailer catering to the outdoor set), which has a well-deserved reputation for fulfilling orders both quickly and accurately. A visit to Bean's warehouse revealed that they could "pick and pack" items three times as fast as Xerox.[7]

Profitability analysis

Regardless of the organizational level, control involves some form of profitability analysis. In brief, **profitability analysis** requires that analysts determine the costs associated with specific marketing activities to find out the profitability of different market segments, products, customer accounts, and distribution channels (intermediaries). More and more, management is attempting to obtain profitability measures for individual products by market segments.

Profitability is probably the single most important measure of performance, but it has limitations. First, many objectives can best be measured in nonfinancial terms (for example,

---

[7]Jeremy Mann, "How to Steal the Best Ideas Around," *Fortune*, October 19, 1992, p. 102.

maintaining market share). Also, profit is a short-term measure and can be manipulated by taking actions (such as reducing R & D expenses) that may prove dysfunctional in the longer term. Finally, profits can be affected by factors over which management has no control (such as the weather).

Analysts can use **direct** or **full costing** in determining the profitability of a product or market segment. Direct costing uses contribution accounting. Those favoring this approach argue that there is really no accurate way to assign indirect costs such as those involved with occupancy, general management, and the management of a multiproduct salesforce. Because indirect costs are mostly fixed, a product or a market may contribute to profits even if it shows a loss. Contribution analysis is helpful in determining what is gained or lost by adding or dropping a product or a customer—or by shifting resources from one product or segment to another.

In full costing analysts assign both direct (variable) and indirect costs to the unit of analysis. Indirect costs are increasing in proportion to many firms' total costs because multiproduct manufacturing centers are concerned with products of varying sales volumes distributed via multiple channels. Not surprisingly, companies are turning from traditional accounting methods, which identify costs largely on the basis of expense categories, to activity-based costing (ABC), which links costs to activities that, in turn, are linked to a cost object (products/services, customer types, segments, distribution channels). ABC supporters contend that this system improves the accuracy of product costing, trims waste and inefficiency, and provides for a better allocation of resources.[8]

Customer satisfaction

So far we have been discussing performance measures in essentially financial terms. But financial terms are insufficient because they fail to recognize the importance of customer satisfaction, which, as we have noted earlier, is an important driving force of the firm's market share and profitability.[9] As products and services become more alike in an already highly competitive marketplace, the ability to satisfy the customer across a variety of activities (of which the product is only one) will become an even greater success determinant. Thus measures relating to customer preferences and satisfaction are essential as an early warning of impending problems and opportunities.

A multiproduct firm will need customer satisfaction measures for each of its different products even if they are sold to the same customer. This is especially true if the choice criteria vary substantially between products—and even more so for expectations regarding service (such as delivery, repairs, and availability of spare parts). Also, we should note that a firm needs to develop its own satisfaction measures with its various intermediaries (channel members) and major suppliers (advertising agencies).

---

[8]Robert C. Culpepper and Thomas H. Oxner, "Activity Based Costing—A Tutorial Overview," paper presented at the Arkansas AIDCS Conference, October 1993; Robin Cooper and Robert S. Kaplan, "Activity-Based Systems: Measuring the Costs of Resource Usage," *Accounting Horizons*, September 1992, p. 1; and Alan J. Stratton, "Using ABC to Support Continuous Improvement," *Management Accounting*, September 1992, p. 46.

[9]For advice on how to hang onto customers and the financial benefits of doing so, see Patricia Sellers, "Keeping the Buyers You Already Have," *Fortune*, Autumn–Winter 1993, p. 50. Also see Robert Settle, *Retain Existing Customers through Relationships* (Burr Ridge, Ill.: Business One Irwin, 1992).

Finding out whether customers are satisfied with your product or service is no small undertaking. All too often satisfaction is defined much too narrowly, especially if only an overall measure is used. Some companies go to great length to hear what buyers think and feel about their product; for example, Honda factory workers recently called some 47,000 Accord owners to get ideas on how to improve their product.[10]

Developing a meaningful measure of customer satisfaction requires merging two kinds of measures. The first has to do with understanding and measurement of the criteria used by customers to evaluate the quality of the firm's relationship with them. Knowing the product/ service attributes that constitute the customer's choice criteria as well as the relative importance of each should facilitate this task.[11] The second type of measurement is concerned with how well the firm is meeting the customer's expectations on an individual attribute as well as an overall basis. Thus if the choice criteria of a cruise line's target market included such attributes as food, exercise facilities, and entertainment, then a performance measure would be developed for each. By weighting these by their relative importance, an overall performance measure can be obtained.

It is difficult to develop quantitative **expectation measures** for some attributes and their dimensions. Sometimes the customer can be asked to rate the firm's performance on a given attribute as less than, equal to, or better than the competition. Or the customer might be asked to respond using, for example, a 10-point scale where under 5 is unsatisfactory (below expectations), 5–8 is satisfactory (equal to expectations), and 9–10 is considered more than satisfactory (above expectations). Some expectations cannot be met for economic reasons— for example, 100 percent order fulfillment (no back orders). In such cases the company should study the process by which the customer(s) derived their expectations. Is the salesperson making unreasonable promises? Is the customer knowledgeable about the causes for stockouts over which the company has no control? Is the customer aware of what substitutes are available for some stockouts? Is it possible the customer is using the unreasonable expectations as a way of bargaining for certain concessions? **Performance measures** indicate how well the company has met the customer's expectation on a given attribute (as well as its dimensions). Of course, overall performance measures are meaningless unless they are compared to the appropriate expectation measure. The results can be negative when performance is less than expected, satisfactory when it is at least as good as expected, and positive when performance is better than expected.[12]

Performance measures come in a variety of forms. The two most common are absolute measures (delivery time/number of stockouts) and scaled measures as discussed earlier in

---

[10] See Darrell Edwards, Daniel A. Gorrell, J. Susan Johnson, and Sharon Shellrolf, "Typical Definition of Satisfaction Is Too Limited," *Marketing News*, January 3, 1994, p. 6. Also see Terence P. Paré, "How to Find Out What They Want," *Fortune*, Autumn-Winter 1993, p. 39.

[11] For a detailed discussion of how to conduct a customer service satisfaction audit, see Christopher H. Lovelock, *Services Marketing* (Englewood Cliffs, N.J.: Prentice Hall, 1991), pp. 269–72.

[12] For a discussion of customer satisfaction as a function of prepurchase expectation and postpurchase perceptions, see J. Paul Peter and Jerry C. Olson, *Consumer Behavior and Marketing Strategy* (Burr Ridge, Ill.: Irwin, 1993), pp. 578–82.

connection with expectation measures. Some companies use simple yes–no questions such as "Was our delivery satisfactory?" or "Was our salesperson courteous?" despite the obvious limitations of such feedback.

Even if a company has factual data about its performance on a given variable, it still needs customers' ratings because, in the final analysis, it is the customer's perception that matters. Where the perceived performance rating is less than the factual performance or considered unreasonable, the firm should make every effort to change the customer's perception of the situation.

Specifying and obtaining feedback data

Once a company has established its performance standards, its next step is to develop a system that provides usable and timely feedback on actual performance. In most cases someone must gather and process considerable data to obtain the performance measures, especially at the product-market level. Analysts obtain feedback data from a variety of sources, including company accounting records and syndicated marketing information services such as A. C. Nielsen. Using marketing research to obtain needed information is both expensive and time-consuming, but there may be no alternative (see Exhibit 13–2).

Evaluating feedback data

Typically managers use a variety of information to determine what the company's performance should have been under the actual market conditions that existed when the plan was executed. In some cases this information can be obtained in measured form; examples include a shift in personal disposable income (available from government sources), a change in the demand for a given product type (obtained in the process of measuring market share), the impact of a new brand on market share (reported by a commercial source), or a change in price by a major competitor. Often, however, the explanation rests on inferences drawn from generalized data, as would be the case in attributing poor sales performance to an improvement in a competitor's salesforce.

Taking corrective action

The last step in the control process concerns prescribing the action needed to correct the situation. At Wal-Mart this is partly accomplished at congresses held every Friday and Saturday in which managers decide how to solve selected problems. Successful corrective action depends on how well managers carry out the evaluation step. When linkages between inputs and outputs are clear, managers can presume a causal relationship and specify appropriate action. For example, assume that an advertising schedule specified how often to air a given TV message with the objective of changing attitudes about a given product attribute. If the attitude change did not occur, remedial action would start with an evaluation of the firm's advertising effort, particularly the advertising message and how frequently it was

EXHIBIT 13–2

Wal-Mart Uses Marketing Research to Maintain Price Image

Wal-Mart makes every effort to keep its regular everyday prices lower than competitors' on a set of critical products. These "image items" are thought to be the basis of a customer's perception of how expensive a store is. Every few weeks Wal-Mart undertakes research to determine the prices charged by its major competitors for these same items. The company then makes sure that Wal-Mart has the lowest price. Even management staff—including Sam Walton when he was alive—have been known to do comparison shopping.

run. In their work as consultants, Gouillart and Sturdivant have found that time spent with customers by senior executives is indispensable in understanding how a company's customers think and feel about the service they are receiving.[13]

But in most cases it is difficult to identify the cause of the problem. Almost always an interactive effect exists among the input variables as well as with the environment. There is also the problem of delayed responses and carryover effects. For example, advertisers can rarely separate the effects of the message, media, frequency of exposure, and competitive responses in an attempt to determine advertising effects. Even if a company could determine the cause of a problem, it faces the difficulty of prescribing the appropriate action to take. Most control systems are "based on the assumption that corrective action is known should significant variations arise. Unfortunately, marketing is not at a stage where performance deviations can be corrected with certainty."[14]

Sometimes the situation is so serious (shipping time lags competition by 30 percent) that radical change is needed. To more and more business managers this means "reengineering" or "starting all over"—rethinking and redesigning the relevant business processes "to achieve dramatic improvements in critical contemporary measures of performance such as cost, quality, service, and speed."[15] A business process uses a variety of activities to create an output that is of value to a customer. For example, the order-filling process exists only to deliver the goods to a customer in good condition and in the time promised.

Sometimes the outcome is greater or better than management had planned, such as when sales and market share exceed the schedule. In these cases marketers still need an evaluation to find out why such a variance occurred. Perhaps a more favorable environment evolved because demand was greater than expected and a major competitor failed to take advantage of it. Or perhaps the advertising message was more effective than expected. These different

---

[13]Frances J. Gouillart and Frederick D. Sturdivant, "Spend a Day in the Life of Your Customers," *Harvard Business Review*, January–February 1994, p. 117.

[14]Bernard J. Jaworski, "Toward a Theory of Marketing Control: Environmental Context, Control Types, and Consequences," *Journal of Marketing*, July 1988, p. 24.

[15]"The Promise of Reengineering," *Fortune*, May 3, 1993, p. 94. This article is based on excerpts from Michael Hammer and James Champy, *Reengineering the Corporation: A Manifesto for Business Revolution* (New York: Harper Collins, 1993).

explanations would call for different marketing responses to keep what had been obtained and to exploit the favorable situation.

STRATEGIC CONTROL

Strategic control is concerned with monitoring and evaluating a firm's SBU-level strategies. Such a system is difficult to implement because there is usually a substantial amount of time between strategy formulation and when a strategy takes hold and results are evident. Since both the external and internal environment are constantly evolving, strategic control must provide some way of changing the firm's thrust if new information about the environment and/or the firm's performance so dictates. Inevitably, much of this intermediate assessment is based on information about the marketplace and the results obtained from the firm's marketing plan.

Identifying key variables

To implement strategic control a company must identify the key variables to monitor, which are the major assumptions (planning premises) made in formulating the strategy. The key variables to monitor are of two types: those concerned with external forces and those concerned with the effects of certain actions taken by the firm to implement the strategy. Examples of the former includes changes in the external environment, such as changes in long-term demand, the advent of new technology, a change in governmental legislation, and actions by a competitor. Examples of the latter type for a consumer goods company include the firm's advertising efforts to change attitudes and in-store merchandising activities designed to improve product availability.

Deciding exactly which variables to monitor is a company-specific decision; in general, it should focus on the variables most likely to impact the company's future position within its industry group.

Tracking and monitoring

The next step is to specify what information or measures are needed on the key variable to determine whether the implementation of the strategic plan is on schedule—and if not, why. The firm can use the control plan as an early-warning system as well as a diagnostic tool. If, for example, the firm has made certain assumptions about the rate at which market demand will increase, it should monitor industry sales regularly. If it has made assumptions about advertising and its effect on attitudes, it would likely use measures of awareness, trial, and repeat buying. In any event, the firm must closely examine relevancy, accuracy, and cost of obtaining the needed measures.

Strategy reassessment

Strategy can be reassessed at periodic intervals—for example, quarterly or annually—at which time the firm evaluates its performance to date along with major changes in the external environment. The control system can alert management of a significant change in its external and/or its internal environment if triggers are set to signal the need to reassess the viability of the firm's strategy. This requires a specification of both the level at which an alert will be called and the combination of events that must occur before the firm reacts. For example, total sales of 10 percent less than expected for a single month might not trigger a response, but a 25 percent drop probably would. Or a firm may decide the triggering would occur only after three successive months in which a difference of 10 percent occurred.

PRODUCT-MARKET ENTRY CONTROL

These control systems are designed to ensure that the company achieves the sales, profits, and other objectives set forth in its annual product-market entry action plans. In the aggregate, these plans represent the SBU's short-term planning efforts, which specify how resources will be allocated across products and markets. These entry plans include a line-item budget and detail the actions required of each organizational unit both inside and outside the marketing department to attain certain financial and competitive position objectives. In this section we discuss budget analysis, sales/share determinants, and sales analysis.

Budget analysis

Because budgets project revenues and expenses for a given time period, they are a vital part of the firm's planning and control activities. They provide the basis for a continuous evaluation and comparison of what was planned with what actually happened. In this sense budgeted revenues and profits serve as objectives against which to measure performance in sales and profits as well as actual costs.

Budget analysis requires that managers continuously monitor marketing expenses to make certain that the company does not overspend in its effort to reach its objectives. They also evaluate the magnitude and pattern of deviations from the target ratios. Before taking corrective action, managers may need to disaggregate the data to help isolate the problem. For example, if total commissions as a percentage of sales are out of line, analysts need to specify them for each sales territory and product to help determine exactly where the problem lies.

Sales/share determinants

Sales and market share have a number of primary determinants. For a consumer product these include effective distribution, relative price, attitude maintenance or change toward one or more salient product characteristics relative to competition, and shelf facings. These, in turn, are a function of secondary determinants such as number and frequency of sales calls, trade deals, and the effectiveness of the advertising message with a given reach and frequency schedule. Analyzing the share determinants should provide insights into presumed linkages between the firm's inputs and outputs, such as number and frequency of sales calls and effective distribution. This, in turn, leads to a better understanding of the firm's marketing efficiency. Is the salesforce making as many calls per day as expected—and the right number of calls on target accounts to obtain a certain level of distribution?

Marketing research is usually required to ascertain the extent to which determinants are being attained. For example, consistently having as low a price on the same product as competitors is an important determinant of sales. As in the case of Wal-Mart, interviewers would need to shop the targeted stores to obtain the desired price data.

Sales analysis

Sales analysis involves breaking down aggregate sales data in such categories as products, end-user customers, channel intermediaries, sales territories, and order size. The objective of sales analysis is to find areas of strengths and weakness—for example, products producing the greatest and least volume, customers accounting for the most revenue, and salespeople and territories performing the best and the worst.

Sales analysis recognizes that aggregate sales and cost data often mask the real situation. By discerning the meaning of that aggregate data, sales analysis helps management evaluate and control marketing efforts, formulate objectives and strategies, and administer such nonmarketing activities as production planning, inventory management, and facilities planning.

An important decision in designing the firm's sales analysis system concerns which units of analysis to use. Most companies assemble data in the following groupings:

- Geographical areas—regions, counties, and sales territories.
- Product, package size, and grade.
- Customer—by type and size.
- Channel intermediary—such as type and/or size of retailer.
- Method of sale—mail, phone, channel, or direct.
- Size of order—less than $10, $10–25, and so on.

These breakdowns are not mutually exclusive. Most firms perform sales analysis hierarchically: for example, by county within a sales territory within a sales region. Further, they usually combine product and account breakdowns with geographical ones—say, the purchase of product X by large accounts located in sales territory Y, which is part of region A. Only by conducting sales analysis using a combination of breakdowns can analysts be sure that they have made every attempt to locate the opportunities and problems facing their firms.

Sales analysis by territory

The first step in a sales territory analysis is to decide which geographical control unit to use. The county is the typical choice because it can be combined into larger units such as sales territories and also represents the smallest geographical unit for which many data items are available, such as population, employment, income, and retail sales. Analysts can compare actual sales (derived from company invoices) by county against a standard such as a sales quota that takes into account such factors as market potential and last year's sales adjusted for inflation. They can single out territories that fall below standard for special attention. Is

EXHIBIT 13–3

Sales Analysis Based on Selected Sales Territories

Sales territory	Salesperson	(1) Company sales 1993	(2) Sales quota 1993	(3) Overage, Underage	(4) Percentage of potential performance
1	Barlow	$552,630	$585,206	−$32,576	94%
2	Burrows	470,912	452,800	+18,112	104
3	White	763,215	981,441	−218,226	77
4	Finch	287,184	297,000	−9,816	96
5	Brown	380,747	464,432	−83,685	82
6	Roberts	494,120	531,311	−37,191	93
7	Macini	316,592	329,783	−13,191	96

competition unusually strong? Has less selling effort been expended there? Is the salesforce weak? Studies dealing with such questions as these help a company improve its weak areas and exploit its stronger ones.

Exhibit 13–3 illustrates a sales territory analysis. It shows that only one territory out of seven exceeded its 1993 quota or standard of performance, and this was for only $18,112. The other six territories accounted for a total of $394,685 under quota. Territory 3 alone accounted for 55 percent of the total loss. The sales and the size of the quota in this territory suggest the need for further breakdowns, especially by accounts and products. Such breakdowns may reveal that the firm needs to allocate more selling resources to this territory. In any event, the company needs to improve its sales primarily in territories 3 and 5. If it can reach its potential in these two territories, overall sales would increase by $301,911, assuming that the quotas set are valid.

Without a standard against which to compare results, the conclusions would be much different. Thus, if only company sales were considered (column 1, Exhibit 13–3), White would be the best salesperson and Finch the worst. But using sales quotas as a performance standard, White was not the best but the worst salesperson with a rating of 77.

Sales analysis by product

Over time, a company's product line tends to become overcrowded and less profitable unless management takes strong and continuous action to eliminate items that are no longer profitable. By eliminating weak products and concentrating on strong ones, a company can increase its profits substantially. Before deciding which products to abandon, management must study such variables as market-share trends, contribution margins, scale effects, and the extent to which a product is complementary with other items in the line.[16] A product sales

---

[16]Activity-based accounting is particularly helpful in helping managers determine product profitability because it allocates costs to products more accurately than traditional methods by breaking down overhead costs more precisely.

analysis is particularly helpful when combined with account size and sales territory data. Using such an analysis, managers can often pinpoint substantial opportunities and develop specific tactics to take advantage of them.

Sales analysis by order size

Sales analysis by order size may identify which dollar-size orders are not profitable. For example, if some customers frequently place small orders that require salesforce attention and need to be processed, picked, and shipped, a problem of some importance likely exists. Analysis by order size locates products, sales territories, and customer types and sizes where small orders prevail. Such an analysis may lead to setting a minimum order size, charging extra for small orders, training sales representatives to develop larger orders, or dropping some accounts.

Sales analysis by customer

Analysts use procedures similar to those described earlier to analyze sales by customers. Such analyses typically show that a relatively small percentage of customers accounts for a large percentage of sales. For example, a needlework products distributor found that 13 percent of its accounts represented 67 percent of its total sales. Frequently, a study of sales calls shows that the salesforce spends as much time with the small accounts as with the larger ones. Shifting some of this effort to the larger accounts may well increase sales.

GLOBAL MARKETING CONTROL

Maintaining control over global marketing activities is more difficult than with domestic marketing primarily because the company operates in a number of countries, each presenting a unique set of opportunities and threats. This makes it difficult to simultaneously monitor a variety of environments and prescribe corrective action for individual countries. Differences in language and customs, accentuated by distance, further compound the control problem.

The extent of control exercised over an overseas subsidiary is largely a function of its size; differences in the environment, including its stability; and the extent to which the company employs a standardized rather than a localized strategy. The larger a company's international operation, the greater the likelihood that staff personnel specializing in control activities will be on site, making the control system more elaborate and precise. Small overseas operations tend to involve fewer specialists and a less intensive control system.

Another factor affecting the control system is the extent to which environmental differences exist. Ordinarily, the greater the differences between the home country and the foreign subsidiary, the more decision-making authority is delegated. Large multinationals compensate for these differences by clustering countries with similar environments into regions that have sufficient revenues to permit the use of a headquarters staff. When considerable environmental instability is present, it is difficult to employ a formal control system; the tendency is to delegate to local management the authority to make certain kinds of decisions without review and approval by the home office.

EXHIBIT 13–4

No Substitute for the Personal Touch in Global Management

> Many global managers, not unlike Wal-Mart's regional managers who spend part of most weeks in the field, have found that "faxes and electronic mail can't substitute for the personal touch that phone calls and visits provide." The manager for Asia and Latin America for Glaxo (a large British pharmaceutical company) in a recent year spent 43 days in London, 63 in Singapore, and 123 in other countries. He believes that the 20 managers who report to him are on a more intimate discussion basis with him because of his frequent visits. Also, they can better and more quickly appraise their opportunities and threats and decide what action to take.

SOURCE: Lour des Lee Valeriano, "Executives Find They're Always on Call as Computer Fax Supersede Time Zones," *The Wall Street Journal*, August 8, 1991, p. B1.

Parent country culture has also been found to affect the type and kind of control system employed. Thus, for example, Japanese firms typically rate high on uncertainty avoidance. As a consequence, they tend to rely on centralized decision making to a greater extent than U. S. and European firms. In addition, the cultural distance between the nations of the parent company and its subsidiaries has an impact on control mechanisms: The greater the cultural similarity between the parent and its subsidiary, the less the need to impose highly structured controls.[17]

A third major factor affecting the international control system is the extent to which a standardized strategy is used. The more standardized the strategy, especially with respect to the product, the greater the degree of control exercised over many activities, including purchasing raw materials and determining components, manufacturing, and quality specifications. Ordinarily, control over marketing activities is less stringent than with manufacturing. Also affecting control are the success of the subsidiary (the greater the success, the less the home office interference); the physical distance separating the home office and the subsidiary (the greater the distance, the less frequently the subsidiary will be visited). Rapidly improving voice and data communication systems throughout the world have greatly improved the effectiveness of global managers, but many managers still feel strongly that the personal touch is still important (see Exhibit 13–4).

In recent years more companies are centralizing authority in their home office instead of empowering local managers to make important decisions. A major reason for this trend is that customer needs are less dominated by geography and therefore can be satisfied by a standardized product. Global specialists located in the home office are being called upon to manage business categories around the world.[18]

---

[17]Philip M. Rosensweig and Jitendra V. Singh, "Organizational Environments and the Multinational Enterprise," *The Academy of Management Review*, April 1991, p. 340.

[18]Richard L. Hudson and Joana S. Lublin, "Power at Multinationals Shifts to Home Office," *The Wall Street Journal*, September 9, 1994, p. B1.

THE MARKETING AUDIT

Marketing audits are growing in popularity, especially for firms with a variety of SBUs that differ in their market orientation. They are both a control and a planning activity, involving a comprehensive review of the firm's total marketing efforts cutting across all products and business units. Thus they are broader in scope and cover longer time horizons than sales and profitability analyses.

An audit at the individual SBU level covers both the SBU's objectives and strategy and its plan of action for each product-market entry. It assesses each SBU's current overall competitive position as well as that of its individual product-market entries. A marketing audit requires an analysis of each marketing-mix element and how well it is being implemented in support of each entry. The audit must take into account the environmental changes that can affect the SBU's strategy and product-market action programs.[19]

The main areas covered in a marketing audit include the SBU's marketing environment, objectives and strategy, planning and control systems, organization, productivity, and individual marketing activities such as sales and advertising. These areas are shown in Exhibit 13–5 with examples of the kinds of questions that need to be answered.

Recently many firms are undertaking two relatively new types of audits involving ethics and product managers as follows:

- The company's **ethical audit** evaluates the extent to which the company engages in ethical and socially responsible marketing. Clearly this audit goes well beyond monitoring to make sure that the firm is well within the law in its market behavior. If the company has a written code of ethics, then the main purpose of this audit is to make certain that it is disseminated, understood, and practiced.

- The **product manager audit**—especially in consumer goods companies—seeks to determine whether product managers are channeling their efforts in the best ways possible. Product managers are queried on what they do versus what they ought to be doing. They are also asked to rate the extent to which various support units are helpful.[20]

MARKETING DECISION SUPPORT SYSTEMS (MDSSs)[21]

The final section of this chapter deals with the use of computer technology (both hardware and software) to make control possible as a more or less continuous activity using a marketing decision support system (MDSS). Such a system is "a coordinated collection

---

[19]Eric N. Berkowitz, Roger A. Kerin, Steven W. Hartley, and William Rudelius, *Marketing* (Burr Ridge, Ill.: Irwin, 1992), pp. 593–97.

[20]John A. Quelch, Paul W. Farris, and James M. Oliver, "The Product Manager Audit," *Harvard Business Review*, March–April 1987, p. 30. Based on their research, the authors conclude that product managers spend too much time on routine matters such as those relating to promotion execution and too little on product design and development.

[21]For a discussion of the concept of information as an asset, see Rashi Glazer, "Marketing in an Information-Intensive Environment: Strategic Implications of Knowledge as an Asset," *Journal of Marketing*, October 1991, p. 1.

EXHIBIT 13-5

Major Areas Covered in Marketing Audit and Questions Concerning Each for a Consumer Goods Company

Audit area	Examples of questions to be answered
Marketing environment	What opportunities and/or threats derive from the firm's present and future environment; that is, what technological, political, and social trends are significant? How will these trends affect the firm's target markets, competitors, and channel intermediaries? Which opportunities/threats emerge from within the firm?
Objectives and strategy	How logical are the company's objectives given the more significant opportunities/threats and its relative resources? How valid is the firm's strategy given the anticipated environment, including the actions of competitors?
Planning and control system	Does the firm have adequate and timely information about consumers' satisfaction with its products? With the actions of competitors? With the services of intermediaries?
Organization	Does the organization structure fit the evolving needs of the marketplace? Can it handle the planning needed at the individual product/brand level?
Marketing productivity	How profitable is each of the firm's products/brands? How effective is each of its major marketing activities?
Marketing functions	How well does the product line meet the line's objectives? How well do the products/brands meet the needs of the target markets? Does pricing reflect cross elasticities, experience effects, and relative costs? Is the product readily available? What is the level of retail stockouts? What percentage of large stores carries the firm's in-store displays? Is the salesforce large enough? Is the firm spending enough on advertising?

of data, systems, tools, and techniques with supporting software and hardware by which an organization gathers and interprets relevant information from business and the environment and turns it into a basis for marketing action.[22]

An MDSS permits the user to manipulate data to conduct any analysis desired, from simply adding a set of numbers to a sophisticated statistical analysis. MDSSs use dialogue systems that permit managers to explore the data banks using models to generate reports for their specific needs. Managers can query the computer and, based on the answer, ask another question. This can be done at a workstation rather than via a computer printout. For example, a marketing manager who notes that sales are down in a given region can ask the computer whether sales for the product type are down; whether the company's brand is losing share and, if so, to which competitors; or whether the decline is confined to a specific type of retailer. Marketing offers considerable opportunities for the use of a MDSS because of the lack of structure in many decision-making situations.

---

[22]John D. C. Little, "Decision Support Systems for Marketing Managers," *Journal of Marketing*, Summer 1979, p. 11.

EXHIBIT 13–6

Glaxo's Multimillion-Dollar Marketing Decision Support System

> Glaxo, Inc., is a pharmaceutical maker located in Research Triangle Park, North Carolina. The company spends about $2 million annually on its sales and marketing decision support system, including money spent on hardware, software, and operating personnel. According to Donald Rao, Glaxo's manager of market analysis and decision support, the company's return on investment has been substantial since the system was developed in 1987.
>
> Mr. Rao bases his claim on a consultant's study of the system, which showed that Glaxo had realized significant cost savings and productivity gains since its product managers started using the system. For example, with more detailed data available on physicians in Glaxo's sales territories, product managers were able to allocate product samples (which involve large expenditures) more accurately. Since the system also provided easier and faster access to data, the product managers were able to save valuable time in searching for information.

SOURCE: Tom Eisenhart, "Where's the Payoff?" *Business Marketing*, June 1990, p. 46. Copyright © 1990 by Crain Communications, Inc. All rights reserved. Reprinted with permission.

MDSSs are highly flexible and action-oriented. They enable managers to follow their instincts in solving a problem and to do so online. (For an example of a marketing decision support system, see Exhibit 13–6.) Serving the needs of different managers, they are interactive systems designed to facilitate decision making. They do so by providing access to relevant data and statistical models that increase the nature and scope of the manager's analysis.

Software programs are increasingly available to help managers better plan and control their activities, including segmenting markets, planning sales calls, determining media budgets, and setting prices. Such software is especially important in repetitive situations where management is interested in what would happen if the decision variables were changed—for example, decreasing the time of delivery.

Future of MDSSs

The systems just described have been used primarily by large companies, especially those engaged in retailing (Wal-Mart), banking, brokerage, airlines, and pharmaceuticals. However, many firms are using a relatively simple system with a database consisting of sales transactions tied to certain classification data concerned with buyers' characteristics, time periods, sales representatives, channels, and so on.

There is every reason to believe that an increasing number of companies will adopt more sophisticated MDSSs during the next decade. First, companies are increasingly asking their managers to make bigger, more complex decisions more quickly because of increased environmental change. Thus MDSSs will become critically needed resources—especially to enable marketers to correlate large quantities of external data with sales and company decision areas such as price and promotion. For managers who make decisions at the global level, an MDSS that facilitates group decision making is a necessity. These systems enable a group of users in different locations to access and work with the same data simultaneously.

Furthermore, interactive personal computer hardware—with more storage ability, more workstations, and user-friendly software—will make MDSSs faster, less expensive, and more convenient. And new software packages will be better able to determine the kinds of responses that can be obtained by varying inputs.[23]

SUMMARY

Marketing control and reappraisal is the final step in the marketing strategy process. It is necessary if the company is to operate profitably; and yet many companies have poor control procedures. Much of the problem is a failure to set measurable objectives; when coupled with a weak plan of action, this failure makes it almost impossible to set up an effective control system. Different control processes correspond to the organizational levels involved. Regardless of level, the control process sets standards of performance, specifies and obtains feedback data, evaluates it, and takes corrective action.

Control typically involves some form of profitability analysis. In these analyses managers determine the costs associated with specific marketing activities to find out the profitability of such units of analysis as different market segments, products, customer accounts, and channel intermediaries. In performing such investigations, analysts have the option of using direct or full costing to determine the unit's profitability. In full costing they assign both direct and indirect costs. Direct costing uses contribution accounting and is favored by those who argue that there is no really accurate way to assign indirect costs.

It is imperative that measures pertaining to customer satisfaction be obtained. Developing such measures requires that company performance be linked to customer expectations. Because customer satisfaction involves a number of variables, determining how well the company has performed is not an easy task.

Strategic control is concerned with the opportunities and threats pertaining to each SBU and their product-market entries and with the strategies adopted to exploit them. A strategic control system provides data to help answer questions about changes in the environment, strategies of major competitors, and the maturity of the industry. From these answers marketers can identify new opportunities and threats and determine whether the current strategy is still viable.

Product-market entry control is concerned with the product's competitive position, its sales/share determinants, and sales analyses. The first has to do with such key parameters as market share, market size, and market growth. It is important to determine whether any deviation from plan is caused by errors in forecasting or errors in management. Control systems are primarily concerned with the extent to which the plan is adhered to, especially the budget.

Sales analysis involves disaggregating sales data into breakdowns having to do with products, end-user customers, channel intermediaries, sales territories, and order size and comparing the results with a standard. The objective of such analyses is to find strengths and weaknesses in products, territories, and customers accounting for the bulk of revenues.

---

[23]Tom Eisenhart, "Where's the Pay-off?" *Business Marketing*, June 1990, p. 46.

The marketing audit is the mechanism by which corporate management evaluates the company's total market effort. It looks at an SBU's objectives, strategy, plan of action, and personnel and provides an assessment of each SBU's present competitive position and insights into its marketing strengths and weaknesses.

Control over a firm's international operations is a difficult undertaking largely because of the number of different environments present. The extent of control exercised over overseas units depends on the units' size, whether a standardized or a localized marketing strategy is used, and the extent of environmental differences, coupled with the magnitude of risk present.

Marketing decision support systems provide managers with flexible, responsive tools that help them solve problems faster and better. The outlook for greater use of these systems over the next decade is considered excellent because managers are being asked to make bigger, faster, and more complex decisions and because more powerful personal computers and better software are becoming available.

Gamar Plc.[1] Global Allocation of Marketing Resources

In October 1994 Sylvie Retchi was reviewing initial drafts of the 1995 marketing plans proposed by Gamar Plc.'s international team of product managers. Gamar was a well-known British consumer goods company with headquarters south of Oxford. It was listed on the London Stock Exchange (LSE) and operated in 43 countries, with brands in 14 product categories. Sylvie had joined Gamar as vice president for international marketing six months earlier, and it was the first time that she was involved in the preparation of the annual marketing plans of Gamar's country affiliates. She was not impressed by the inputs she received from their marketing departments. While they demonstrated knowledge of local conditions, they lacked strategic vision. The documents dwelt on promotion and advertising schedules in great detail, but where allocation of resources was concerned they were often content with extrapolating from past practice. Sylvie wanted to interfere as little as possible with local management on marketing execution. But she was convinced that substantial improvements were possible with more explicit guidelines on the international allocation of marketing funds and on the degree of local adaptation of marketing activities.

SYLVIE RETCHI'S CHALLENGE

Gamar's international operations were organized in terms of a matrix with two dimensions: countries and product categories. Because of the firm's historical development, the geographic dimension had traditionally dominated. The formulation of product marketing plans had been left to a large extent to local management. Only in recent years had the product dimension been emphasized. The appointment of Sylvie, who was recruited from a large

---

[1]This case was developed by Jean-Claude Larréché, Alfred H. Hemeken Professor of Marketing at INSEAD. It is based on actual business situations and is intended to illustrate key issues in the international allocation and local adaptation of marketing resources. Gamar Plc. is a fictitious firm. The Gamar simulation was designed by Jean-Claude Larréché and developed at Strat* X under the direction of Rémi Triolet. Copyright © 1994 INSEAD/STRAT* X.

Swiss multinational well known for its global brand management, marked a new stage in the strengthening of the international marketing function.

Every year an annual marketing budget was set for each brand in each country. In the past these budgets were determined through a bottom-up process: Local brand managers made initial proposals that were aggregated first at the country level, then at the international level. Adjustments were negotiated at each stage until a final, global agreement was reached. This led to domination by geographic function, the lack of a global product perspective, and fragmentation along country lines of the budget for a given product category. Sylvie also suspected that this "balkanization" of global brand plans resulted in overspending on well-established mature brands and underspending on brands with a higher growth potential.

Sylvie had managed to convince Gamar's top management that international headquarters should play a greater role in determining the annual brand marketing budgets—this she saw as her greatest victory since joining the firm. She had argued persuasively that stronger top-down guidelines were necessary to avoid local suboptimization. As the month of October drew to an end, she had to draw up these directives to enable brand managers to finalize their plans for 1995. In establishing these guidelines her main concern would be the long-term objective of maximizing shareholder value, ultimately measured by the share price on the LSE. In the planning process, however, the long-term valuation of the firm could be estimated only on the basis of the net present value of the future stream of cash flows. Sylvie identified the three key drivers of future cash flow generation as global market share, global revenue growth, and profitability. While attentive to the long-term objective of shareholder value, she knew that she also had to ensure satisfactory short-term profitability.

THE GAMAR SIMULATION

Soon after taking up her position Sylvie had commissioned the development of a simulation model from a firm specializing in such undertakings. The software was to simulate alternative international marketing strategies, especially in terms of the two key issues she had identified: allocation of resources and degree of local adaptation. The development of the new simulation had been completed a few weeks earlier, and technical tests had been carried out. The parameters used in the simulation, determined through cooperation between the international marketing staff, local marketing managers, and consultants from the software firm, were based on a combination of industry data, routine market surveys, ad hoc research studies, and managerial judgment. The parameterization of the simulation provided a very satisfactory fit with historical data.

A number of assumptions and simplifications were made in designing the GAMAR simulation. The model concentrated on strategic marketing issues in international product management. Therefore it did not explicitly incorporate financial, manufacturing, or human aspects of international business. All financial data were expressed in a single currency, the U. S. dollar ($)—the currency most commonly used in the industry to aggregate international data. Exchange rates between local currencies and the U. S. dollar were assumed to remain constant over the course of the simulation. Products were assumed to be available in all countries at the same cost. Sourcing, capital investments, inventories, working capital, and other cash flow dimensions were not represented in the simulation. The unit variable cost of a product was assumed to include all relevant costs except marketing expenditures, which were considered separately.

Gamar's country and product portfolio had also been simplified for the purpose of the simulation. Early on, Sylvie had decided to limit the scope of the analysis to the firm's three main product categories and five countries, which together accounted for most of Gamar's activities. The formulation of an effective international marketing strategy at this level was already a formidable challenge.

The simulation required decisions to be made on management priorities, consumer marketing expenditures, trade marketing expenditures, product specifications, and price. For five countries and three product categories, this represented a total of 69 decisions. The model could be run to simulate the way the market and the competition reacted to a specific set of decisions. It projected the impact of these decisions on a number of financial outcomes including revenues and share prices as well as measures concerned with consumer satisfaction, marketing effectiveness, and market forecasts, which were obtained from marketing research studies. Decisions and results covered a 12-month period, and the simulation could be run for 10 successive periods representing a 10-year time horizon.

Exhibit 1 contains the output of the simulation for period 0, which covered 1994. The year was well under way, and Gamar's management was confident that the numbers would be achieved. The authorized global marketing budget for the following period, 1995, or period 1 of the simulation, was set at $45 million, and total consumer and trade marketing expenditures in all countries for all product categories could not exceed that amount. Later on, the global marketing budget authorized for any one period would depend on the contribution achieved in the previous period. Improved financial results would generally lead to a higher authorization to spend, but the budget would always be above a $45 million floor while never exceeding a ceiling of $150 million.

The purpose of the simulation was to help formulate and test specific international marketing strategies for Gamar's key countries and product categories. Sylvie was particularly interested in developing a 10-year global marketing strategy that would maximize long-term shareholder value, as measured by Gamar's share price on December 31, 2004.

ALLOCATION OF MARKETING RESOURCES

Allocating marketing resources among products and countries was the most crucial aspect of international marketing strategy. The basic investment unit was a given product category in a given country. At Gamar this was called an OMU (operating market unit), which typically was the responsibility of a local product category manager. The simulation included 15 such OMUs, reflecting the firm's presence in three product categories in five countries.

Three main types of marketing resources were available to support Gamar's position in a given market: management time, consumer marketing expenditures, and trade marketing expenditures. Management time consisted of managerial resources invested at all levels, from associate product managers up to the vice president for international marketing, including various marketing line and staff positions. In the simulation this dimension was called

EXHIBIT 1

Situation at the End of Period 0

Period 0	Gamar Company Report—Firm Sample	Test 1

Global Scorecard

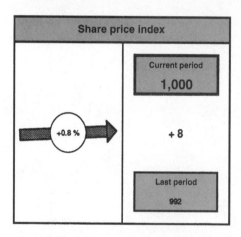

Share price index

	Current period
	1,000
+0.8 %	+ 8
	Last period
	992

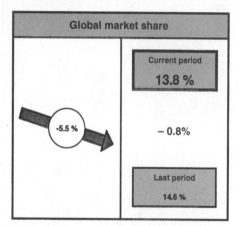

Global market share

	Current period
	13.8 %
-5.5 %	− 0.8%
	Last period
	14.6 %

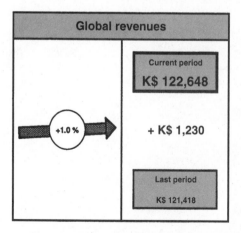

Global revenues

	Current period
	K$ 122,648
+1.0 %	+ K$ 1,230
	Last period
	K$ 121,418

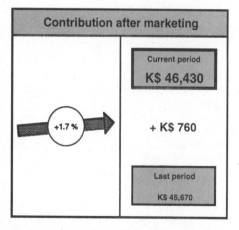

Contribution after marketing

	Current period
	K$ 46,430
+1.7 %	+ K$ 760
	Last period
	K$ 45,670

Marketing budget authorized next period	K$ 45,000

EXHIBIT 1 (*continued*)

Period 0   *Gamar Company Report — Firm Sample*   *Test 1*

Finance Section

Income statement — Ovadols

Item	Unit	Total	Starland	Ringland	Moonland	Sunland	Crossland
Volume sold	U	176,613	48,133	26,902	20,906	45,533	35,140
Price	$	321.1	309.0	301.0	319.0	332.0	340.0
Revenues	K$	56,704	14,873	8,097	6,669	15,117	11,947
Unit variable cost	$	127.0	127.0	127.0	127.0	127.0	127.0
Total variable cost	K$	−22,430	−6,113	−3,417	−2,655	−5,783	−4,463
Contribution before marketing	K$	34,274	8,760	4,681	4,014	9,334	7,485
Consumer marketing	K$	−8,300	−2,600	−1,000	−1,300	−1,800	−1,600
Trade marketing	K$	−4,600	−1,400	−600	−700	−1,000	−900
Contribution after marketing	K$	21,374	4,760	3,081	2,014	6,534	4,985

Income statement — Squazols

Item	Unit	Total	Starland	Ringland	Moonland	Sunland	Crossland
Volume sold	U	337,266	97,369	54,392	45,387	79,687	60,432
Price	$	130.8	124.0	115.2	132.0	138.0	145.2
Revenues	K$	44,102	12,074	6,266	5,991	10,997	8,775
Unit variable cost	$	41.8	41.8	41.8	41.8	41.8	41.8
Total variable cost	K$	−14,098	−4,070	−2,274	−1,897	−3,331	−2,526
Contribution before marketing	K$	30,004	8,004	3,992	4,094	7,666	6,249
Consumer marketing	K$	−7,000	−2,000	−1,000	−1,200	−1,600	−1,200
Trade marketing	K$	−4,200	−1,200	−600	−700	−1,000	−700
Contribution after marketing	K$	18,804	4,804	2,392	2,194	5,066	4,349

Income statement — Trigols

Item	Unit	Total	Starland	Ringland	Moonland	Sunland	Crossland
Volume sold	U	108,482	29,259	19,826	14,835	24,062	20,501
Price	$	201.3	190.8	181.8	205.2	211.8	220.2
Revenues	K$	21,842	5,583	3,604	3,044	5,096	4,514
Unit variable cost	$	67.2	67.2	67.2	67.2	67.2	67.2
Total variable cost	K$	−7,290	−1,966	−1,332	−997	−1,617	−1,376
Contribution before marketing	K$	14,552	3,616	2,272	2,047	3,479	3,137
Consumer marketing	K$	−5,600	−1,600	−800	−900	−1,200	−1,100
Trade marketing	K$	−2,700	−800	−400	−400	−600	−500
Contribution after marketing	K$	6,252	1,216	1,072	747	1,679	1,537

EXHIBIT 1 (*continued*)

Period 0   *Gamar Company Report — Firm Sample*   *Test 1*

Survey Section

Consumer satisfaction with product specifications

Product category	Satisfaction index (0–100)					
	Average	Starland	Ringland	Moonland	Sunland	Crossland
Ovadols	89	90	88	91	89	89
Squazols	83	86	79	84	81	87
Trigols	79	82	81	78	80	76
Overall average	84	86	83	84	84	84

Consumer satisfaction with price

Product category	Satisfaction index (0–100)					
	Average	Starland	Ringland	Moonland	Sunland	Crossland
Ovadols	41	38	47	39	40	41
Squazols	45	43	60	42	41	39
Trigols	38	37	45	40	34	34
Overall average	41	39	51	40	39	38

Effectiveness of consumer marketing

Product category	Effectiveness index (0–100)					
	Average	Starland	Ringland	Moonland	Sunland	Crossland
Ovadols	70	65	87	57	84	58
Squazols	61	55	75	55	70	52
Trigols	37	31	45	33	44	32
Overall average	56	50	69	48	66	47

Effectiveness of trade marketing

Product category	Effectiveness index (0–100)					
	Average	Starland	Ringland	Moonland	Sunland	Crossland
Ovadols	43	42	36	44	39	56
Squazols	62	62	46	61	58	82
Trigols	45	49	38	42	44	54
Overall average	50	51	40	49	47	64

(*continues*)

EXHIBIT 1 *(continued)*

Period 0   *Gamar Company Report — Firm Sample*   *Test 1*

Product Section

International product category report — Ovadols

Country name	Market size		Market share		Average price ($)	Market growth %U	Market size KU	Market growth %U
	KU	K$	%U	%$				
							Forecast for period 1	
Starland	393	121,288	12.3	12.3	309.0	6.0	431	9.9
Ringland	158	47,627	17.0	17.0	301.0	16.2	182	15.3
Moonland	197	62,739	10.6	10.6	319.0	8.1	221	12.6
Sunland	284	94,449	16.0	16.0	332.0	11.1	310	9.0
Crossland	244	82,813	14.4	14.4	340.0	9.1	265	8.9
Total	1,275	408,916	13.8	13.9	320.6	9.3	1,410	10.6

Results for period 0

International product category report — Squazols

Country name	Market size		Market share		Average price ($)	Market growth %U	Market size KU	Market growth %U
	KU	K$	%U	%$				
Starland	511	63,377	19.1	19.1	124.0	15.5	613	20.0
Ringland	251	28,914	21.7	21.7	115.2	26.5	320	27.7
Moonland	303	40,008	15.0	15.0	132.0	17.7	346	14.2
Sunland	409	56,482	19.5	19.5	138.0	21.0	504	23.1
Crossland	306	44,372	19.8	19.8	145.2	18.8	366	19.7
Total	1,780	233,153	18.9	18.9	131.0	19.3	2,150	20.8

Results for period 0 — *Forecast for period 1*

International product category report — Trigols

Country name	Market size		Market share		Average price ($)	Market growth %U	Market size KU	Market growth %U
	KU	K$	%U	%$				
Starland	424	80,829	6.9	6.9	190.8	10.3	480	13.3
Ringland	213	38,642	9.3	9.3	181.8	20.8	266	25.2
Moonland	238	48,832	6.2	6.2	205.2	12.4	258	8.5
Sunland	296	62,705	8.1	8.1	211.8	15.5	331	11.8
Crossland	271	59,745	7.6	7.6	220.2	13.4	315	16.2
Total	1,442	290,752	7.5	7.5	201.7	13.8	1,650	14.5

Results for period 0 — *Forecast for period 1*

EXHIBIT 1 (*concluded*)

Period 0   *Gamar Company Report — Firm Sample*   *Test 1*

Decision Section

Overview — Ovadols

Country name	Management priority in MM	Marketing expenditures in KS		Price in $
		Consumer	Trade	
Starland	24	2,600	1,400	309.00
Ringland	24	1,000	600	301.00
Moonland	24	1,300	700	319.00
Sunland	24	1,800	1,000	332.00
Crossland	24	1,600	900	340.00
Total	120	8,300	4,600	320.20

Overview — Squazols

Country name	Management priority in MM	Marketing expenditures in KS		Price in $
		Consumer	Trade	
Starland	24	2,000	1,200	124.00
Ringland	24	1,000	600	115.20
Moonland	24	1,200	700	132.00
Sunland	24	1,600	1,000	138.00
Crossland	24	1,200	700	145.20
Total	120	7,000	4,200	130.88

Overview — Trigols

Country name	Management priority in MM	Marketing expenditures in KS		Price in $
		Consumer	Trade	
Starland	24	1,600	800	190.80
Ringland	24	800	400	181.80
Moonland	24	900	400	205.20
Sunland	24	1,200	600	211.80
Crossland	24	1,100	500	220.20
Total	120	5,600	2,700	201.96

Global overview

Product category	Allocation of resources				Local adaptation			
	Managt. priority (MM)	Consumer marketing (K$)	Trade marketing (K$)	Average price ($)	Product specs. (0–100)	Consumer marketing (0–100)	Trade marketing (0–100)	Price variation (%)
Ovadols	120	8,300	4,600	320.20	90	60	90	12.2
Squazols	120	7,000	4,200	130.88	15	40	30	22.9
Trigols	120	5,600	2,700	201.96	40	20	30	19.0
Total	360	20,900	11,500	217.68	48	40	50	16.4

"Management Priority" and was represented by a pool of 360 man-months. Allocating more of this resource to an OMU meant that it would receive more management attention. This additional brainpower was expected to improve the quality—and hence the effectiveness—of marketing activities.

Consumer marketing expenditures financed activities directly aimed at the final consumer. Generally, the largest proportion was absorbed by media advertising. Trade marketing expenditures supported activities directed at channel intermediaries, especially mass retailers. They included a wide variety of elements such as personal selling, cooperative advertising, purchase of shelf space, promotional discounts, and in-store displays.

Consumer marketing played a role at each level of the hierarchy of effects: awareness, interest, trial, and repeat buying. Its impact generally was seen as being greater in the early steps of this hierarchy, while product quality, price, and distribution tended to have more influence on repeat purchases. Consumer marketing was also believed to play a more important role in the early stages of a product's life cycle than at maturity. Meanwhile trade marketing was aimed at making the product available to consumers in conditions more favorable than those enjoyed by competing goods. In Gamar's case an important concern was to achieve wide distribution so that consumers could conveniently find the products. Wide distribution was particularly difficult to achieve for new products and for mature products with a weak market share, both of which typically required higher levels of trade marketing. These general rules could guide the allocation of consumer and trade marketing expenditures but were not to be used as definite laws of marketing. Many other elements could influence the effectiveness of marketing activities. In the final analysis, allocation decisions had to be made on the reality of a given market and on a specific competitive situation, based on experience, market research, or experimentation.

Investing higher levels of marketing resources in an OMU would generally increase sales and market share. But the decision to invest a given resource for a given OMU had to take into account a number of considerations, such as the objectives of this OMU in the firm's overall portfolio, for instance in terms of growth versus profitability; the sensitivity of sales and market share to the type of investment considered; the effectiveness of the instrument considered, relative to alternatives; and the appropriateness of investing in this particular OMU instead of others. In addition, the impact on sales of an increase or decrease in a specific resource was rarely fully realized in the same time period; most marketing instruments had lagged effects. Finally, the direct, positive impact of an investment on sales did not automatically imply a positive impact on short-term contribution, long-term profitability, or shareholder value. These issues illustrated the complexity of the resource allocation challenge in marketing and the type of questions that could be tested in the GAMAR simulation.

THE GAMAR PRODUCT/COUNTRY PORTFOLIO

The major product categories in Gamar's portfolio were Ovadols, Squazols, and Trigols. All three were frequently purchased consumer goods distributed mainly through mass retailers. Each came in a variety of forms and packages, representing a significant number of SKUs (stock keeping units). However, to avoid too much complexity, decisions in the simulation referred only to the aggregate category level.

EXHIBIT 2

Expected Average Annual Market Growth Rates 1994–2004

Country	Product category		
	Ovadols	Squazols	Trigols
Starland	1.5%	9.0%	6.7%
Ringland	10.1	17.3	13.9
Moonland	5.8	12.7	9.2
Sunland	8.4	15.7	11.8
Crossland	6.8	13.7	11.1
Global	6.2	13.5	10.3

Ovadols, Gamar's initial core business, had become a mature category with little international growth, although the firm kept an attractive market-share position in that category. Trigols, Gamar's second oldest product line, enjoyed moderate global growth, but Gamar had a weak market share in most countries. Squazols, the newest category, had the best growth rate, and Gamar had become a global leader in the promising Squazol market.

The five countries included in Gamar's simulation—Starland, Ringland, Moonland, Sunland, and Crossland—were all industrialized nations but nevertheless presented somewhat different conditions for marketing Ovadols, Squazols, and Trigols. The largest country, Starland, was about twice as large as the smallest, Ringland, in terms of both population and gross national product. Ringland offered the best growth opportunities in 1994.

The international product category report on page 3 of the company report has essential data on the size, growth, and market share of the three product categories in the five countries. The situation in late 1994 is presented in Exhibit 1, and expected longer-term market growth rates for the various countries and product categories from 1994 to 2004 are shown in Exhibit 2. The numbers were speculative because many external factors were involved and the firm's own actions could either foster or hinder the development of markets, nevertheless they provided a good basis for planning purposes.

The decision form in Exhibit 3 gives an overview of the decisions to be made for the three product categories and the five countries. The first three columns correspond to the allocation of management time (management priority) and marketing funds (consumer marketing and trade marketing).

STANDARDIZATION VERSUS LOCAL ADAPTATION

Aside from the allocation of marketing resources, another important issue facing Gamar was the extent to which marketing strategy should be standardized. Traditionally, local subsidiaries had enjoyed a large degree of autonomy, a legacy of the days when communications were slow and difficult. Because of the influence of a number of factors, including the development of international communications and increasing cost pressures, support for standardization had

EXHIBIT 3

The Gamar Decision Form

Ovadols	Management priority (man-months)	Consumer marketing (K$)	Trade marketing (K$)	Price ($)	Local adaptation (0 = none, 100 = total)
Starland					Product specs.
Ringland					Consumer marketing
Moonland					Trade marketing
Sunland					
Crossland					

Squazols	Management priority (man-months)	Consumer marketing (K$)	Trade marketing (K$)	Price ($)	Local adaptation (0 = none, 100 = total)
Starland					Product specs.
Ringland					Consumer marketing
Moonland					Trade marketing
Sunland					
Crossland					

Trigols	Management priority (man-months)	Consumer marketing (K$)	Trade marketing (K$)	Price ($)	Local adaptation (0 = none, 100 = total)
Starland					Product specs.
Ringland					Consumer marketing
Moonland					Trade marketing
Sunland					
Crossland					

grown. Its proponents emphasized that global standardization had important cost benefits, that it resulted in a substantial simplification of management processes, and that it decreased response time to changes in the marketplace. Meanwhile the defenders of local adaptation claimed that it was economically preferable to fit the firm's marketing offering to the specific conditions of each country.

In the GAMAR simulation, four elements could be adapted or standardized: product specifications, consumer marketing, trade marketing, and price. (The decision form in Exhibit 3 gives an overview of these decisions by product categories and countries.) Adapting product specifications involved making product and packaging changes in each country. While such moves could make the product more attractive for local consumers, they pushed variable costs higher. Adapting consumer or trade marketing programs could involve, for instance, developing specific advertising copy, promotional schemes, merchandising tools, or services to the trade. Because the total marketing budget was fixed, the cost of such adaptations reduced the funds available to effectively support the product. In the GAMAR simulation, the degree of local adaptation for product specifications, consumer marketing, and trade marketing could be set on a scale from 0 (total standardization) to 100 (total local adaptation). In the case of total standardization, the marketing element considered was identical in all countries. In the case of maximum local adaptation, country management was free to make all modifications it deemed necessary. A value between these two extremes reflected an intermediate solution; in that case it was assumed that the adaptations with the highest returns were always considered and adopted first.

Sylvie's international marketing department could either set a standard price for a given product in all countries or allow different prices reflecting different local conditions. However, there was a high risk of parallel trading when the same product was available at significantly different prices in different countries: Wholesalers could then buy vast quantities in the low-price location and export them to a high-price country, where they would compete with the manufacturer's local subsidiary. For this reason Sylvie believed that price differentials between countries greater than 30 percent were not appropriate; this strategic constraint was implemented in the simulation. Antidumping regulations also forbade selling below the base unit variable cost, which was $100 for Ovadols, $40 for Squazols, and $60 for Trigols.

THE INTERNATIONAL MARKET SURVEY

Gamar regularly collected market information for each product category in each country using a standard format that made comparisons possible, whether longitudinal (over time) or cross-sectional (over products and countries). This information was incorporated in Gamar's international market survey, which consisted of four studies linked to indices on scales of 0 to 100. The first two studies investigated levels of consumer satisfaction toward product specifications and price. A 100 rating reflected perfect satisfaction and a rating of 0 total dissatisfaction. A greater level of local product adaptation generally increased consumer satisfaction with the product. Similarly, a lower price usually boosted satisfaction with price. However, it was not clear whether the benefits of these actions outweighed their cost.

The other two studies tracked the effectiveness of consumer and trade marketing. In the case of consumer marketing, a single index integrated dimensions as diverse as awareness, interest, perception on key dimensions, and trial rate. The variables pooled for the trade marketing index mostly related to professional buyers' perceptions of product quality, supplier service, and distributor's product profitability. A rating of 100 reflected the highest possible effectiveness; 0 denoted complete ineffectiveness. An increase in consumer or trade marketing spending generally was expected to result in a higher effectiveness index for the relevant marketing tool.

The GAMAR simulation estimated the consumer satisfaction and effectiveness ratings resulting from a set of marketing decisions. These ratings are shown on page 4 of the company report; their values at the end of Period 0 are shown in Exhibit 1.

FINANCIAL INFORMATION

The financial performance of product categories and of the subsidiaries' marketing departments was evaluated on the basis of their contribution before marketing minus consumer and trade marketing expenditures. Contribution before marketing was found by subtracting total variable costs from revenues. Financial statements for each product category are presented in page 2 of the company report, and values at the end of Period 0 are shown in Exhibit 1. At the top of these statements, "volume sold" indicates the quantity sold in a given period (in KU, or thousand units). This was the ultimate tangible measure of the market's response to the firm's actions. Price, consumer marketing, and trade marketing referred directly to management's decisions. Unit variable cost was specific to a given product. In line with Gamar's international sourcing and accounting policies, a product's unit variable cost was the same in all countries. The impact of volume on variable costs was negligible given the type of products and the quantities manufactured by Gamar, as long as production remained standard. The unit variable cost of a product could thus be considered constant, except if the degree of local product adaptation changed, because greater adaptation of a product's specifications increased its unit variable cost.

Page 1 of the company report (Exhibit 1) showed Gamar's global scorecard using four key indicators. The first was the share price index, which measured shareholder value. Set arbitrarily at 1,000 at the end of Period 0, it was influenced by a number of factors such as revenues, profitability, and trends. The index reflected past results but also, more appropriately, anticipated future performance based on past results. The other indicators—global market share, global revenues, and contribution after marketing—referred to Gamar's combined operations, aggregating all its product categories and countries of operation. The four indicators provided a concise overview of Gamar's health at a given time. Based on this, corporate management authorized the level of marketing expenditures for the following period. This authorized marketing budget was indicated at the bottom of the global scorecard.

THE NEED TO IMPROVE CURRENT PRACTICE

As a point of reference, Sylvie used the GAMAR simulation to project a status quo scenario (assuming no change in the firm's global marketing strategy) over 10 twelve-month periods from 1994 until 2004. (Key results are presented in Exhibit 4.) Sylvie was unhappy with the results. She hoped that the simulation would enable her to investigate better scenarios and to

EXHIBIT 4
Evolution of Key Results under the Status Quo Scenario

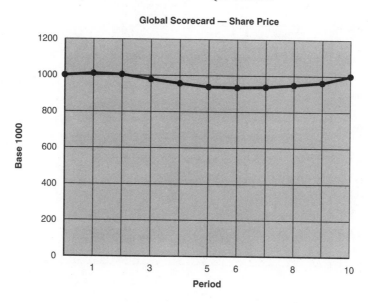

Global Scorecard — Share Price

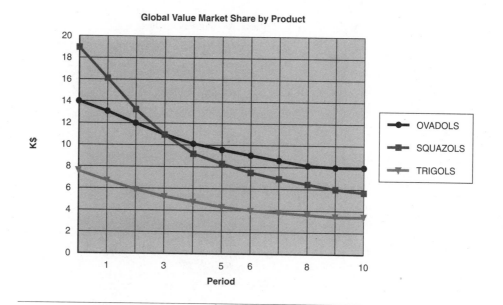

Global Value Market Share by Product

EXHIBIT 4 (*continued*)

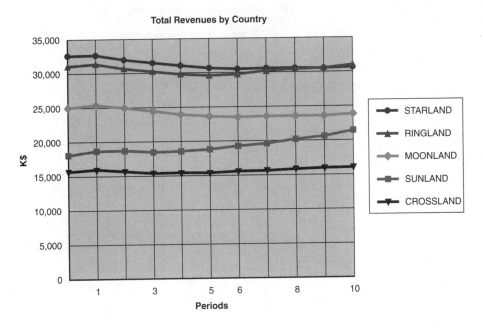

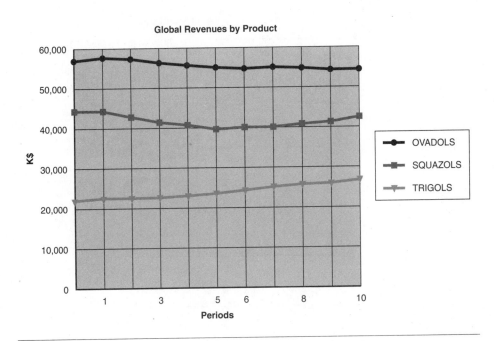

EXHIBIT 4 (*concluded*)

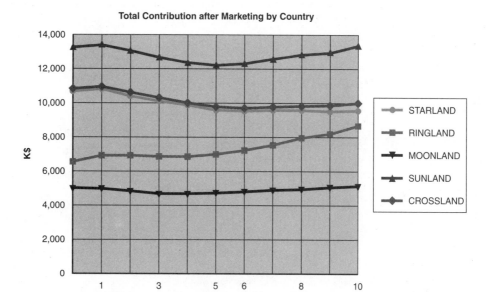

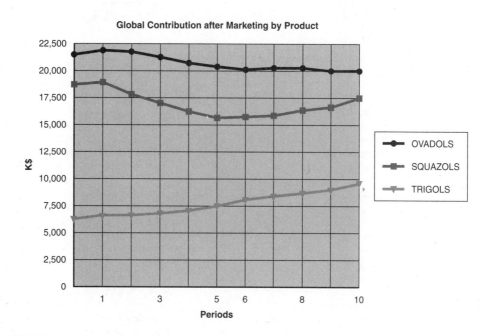

convince local managers of the need for more integrated and more effective international marketing strategies. In fact, she would start doing so immediately, she thought. She took a deep breath, pulled out of a drawer the summary software instructions (Exhibits 5 and 6), and turned her armchair toward the PC on her side table.

EXHIBIT 5

Instructions for Using the GAMAR Software

1. **Installing the GAMAR software on your PC.** The GAMAR software requires a PC operating under the MS Windows 3.1 environment. To install the software on your PC, follow the simple instructions on the GAMAR diskette.

2. **Understanding the format of a GAMAR screen.** Each GAMAR screen is composed of four main elements (see Exhibit 6 for an illustration). The first three contain command buttons that can be activated by clicking on them with the mouse when they appear in black. When a button appears as a gray shadow, this means that it is not accessible at this point in time. The four elements are:
   - The *Master Menu*, located at the top left corner, is composed of three buttons corresponding to the main components of the software: Decisions (to enter your decisions for a given period), Results (to obtain the results of a given simulation run), and Simulation (to run the simulation, create new firms, and compare different tests).
   - The *Submenus*, located in the left column, contain the options available for each of the three major components of the software and change as you click on different items in the Master Menu.
   - The *Top Line* allows you to specify key parameters (Period number, Test number, Country, Category) and gives you permanent access to common options (Help, Information, Print, and Exit). You will find the *Help* facility particularly useful at the beginning until you become familiar with the software.
   - The *Screen Center* can contain, in the Decisions and Results modes, a table of numbers, a graph, or both simultaneously. The graphs show the evolution of key variables from Period 0 to the present. When only the table or the graph is present, click on the *Unzoom* button to obtain both simultaneously. To have a larger representation of the table or graph, click on the corresponding *Zoom* button.

3. **Starting the GAMAR software.** Access the software by double-clicking on the GAMAR icon appearing in the Windows program manager. The first screen then appears showing the GAMAR map. The first task is to create a firm by clicking on the corresponding button in the left menu and then specifying a name up to eight characters long. Your results will be saved automatically under this name. You can create several firms with different names. You can always access data files of firms previously created by clicking the *Select Firm* button in the left menu.

4. **Displaying results.** Results can be obtained by clicking on the corresponding button in the top left corner. When a firm is created, the results correspond to Period 0 and are identical to those in Exhibit 1. They normally correspond to the last simulation run, but you can access the results of previous periods and tests by changing these parameters in the top line of the screen. You can access different parts of the company report through the menu in the left column or by turning the pages by clicking the *forward* and *backward* arrows in the top line.

5. **Entering decisions.** You can access the decision entry component of the software by clicking on the *Decisions* button in the top left corner. The menu in the left column allows you to directly access each type of decision. The *Country* and *Category* buttons in the top line specify the unit concerned by the decisions. Each table provides you with a reminder of the decisions for the previous period. After you have entered a decision, the corresponding percentage change is displayed in the right column. The two lower buttons in the left menu allow you to check for possible errors and

EXHIBIT 5 (*concluded*)

warnings and to display an overview of the decisions. Once you have run the simulation for a given period, you can change your decisions. You are allowed a maximum of 10 such tests for each period. When you are satisfied with your results, or if you have reached the limit of 10 tests, you should enter your decisions for the next period.

6. **Running the simulation.** Clicking on the *Simulation* button in the top left corner gives access to the simulation interface module. The menu for this section includes the creation and selection of firms as described in the Starting paragraph above, a display of the firm's status, and the best scores achieved in the tests of the current period. To run the simulation, click on the upper button in the menu. The simulation will be run based on your decisions and you will readily have access to the results. If constraints such as budgets or price limits are violated, the simulation will not run and you will be asked to make the appropriate corrections.

EXHIBIT 6

Sample GAMAR Screen

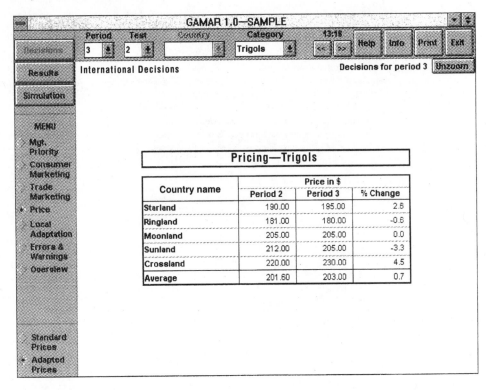

Name Index

Subject Index